LONG, OBSTINATE, AND

# BLOODY

THE BATTLE OF GUILFORD COURTHOUSE

LAWRENCE E. BABITS

THE UNIVERSITY OF NORTH CAROLINA PRESS CHAPEL HILL

# LONG, OBSTINATE, AND
# BLOODY

AND JOSHUA B. HOWARD

© 2009

THE
UNIVERSITY
OF NORTH
CAROLINA
PRESS

Designed by Courtney Leigh Baker
Set in Minion by Tseng Information Systems, Inc.
Manufactured in the United States of America

The paper in this book meets the guidelines for
permanence and durability of the Committee on
Production Guidelines for Book Longevity of the
Council on Library Resources.

The University of North Carolina Press has been a
member of the Green Press Initiative since 2003.

Library of Congress Cataloging-in-Publication Data
Babits, Lawrence Edward.
Long, obstinate, and bloody : the Battle of
Guilford Courthouse / Lawrence E. Babits and
Joshua B. Howard.
      p. cm.
Includes bibliographical references and index.
ISBN 978-0-8078-3266-0 (cloth : alk. paper)
      1. Guilford Courthouse, Battle of, N.C., 1781.
      I. Howard, Joshua B.  II. Title.
E241.G9B33  2009
975.6'62—DC22
2008037219

13 12 11 10 09   5 4 3 2 1

To the memory of those
who fought and died
at Guilford Courthouse
15 March 1781

AND

Don Higginbotham
scholar of the Revolutionary War
He wrote about the leaders
but never forgot the men in ranks

# CONTENTS

# ILLUSTRATIONS AND MAPS

MAPS

Guilford Courthouse was the largest Revolutionary War battle in North Carolina. Although Lt. Gen. Charles, Second Earl Cornwallis succeeded tactically
on 15 March 1781, his army was crippled. Forced to withdraw to Wilmington
for reinforcements and resupply, Cornwallis made the fateful decision to stop
chasing Nathanael Greene across the Carolinas, instead deciding to march
into Virginia and destroy what he perceived as his opponent's supply base.
Guilford, therefore, was one step, admittedly a very big step, in the British
army's path to Yorktown.

Incredible as it seems, given its importance, there has been no in-depth
scholarly monograph on the battle. Sad to say, this is true of most southern
campaign engagements, although the situation is being rectified. Scholarly
works on the southern campaign have devoted chapters to the battle, including John Buchanan's *The Road to Guilford Courthouse*, M. F. Treacy's
*Prelude to Yorktown*, and John S. Pancake's *The Destructive War*. Two small
works have been produced on the subject, John Hairr's *Guilford Courthouse*
and Thomas Baker's *Another Such Victory*. Baker's account, perhaps the most

readily available resource for the last twenty-five years or more, aside from taking our potential title, only whets the appetite for those wanting to know what really happened.

Whereas the other works have largely echoed traditional Whig and British accounts of the battle without actually analyzing their contents, Baker's booklet raised questions about what actually happened with the North Carolina militia on the first line. Did they all really panic and run away? The same questions come up about the second line, where some Virginians apparently fought very well while others took flight. The third line is better understood, but such details as the sequence of attacks and Cornwallis's ordering his artillery to fire into a melee of British and American soldiers were obviously only singular events in the climactic struggle to decide the battle's outcome. Finally, there is the problem of what happened on the southern flank, where the 1st Battalion of Guards and Hessians of the Von Bose Regiment fought Virginia Continentals, riflemen, and dragoons. Our work attempts to resolve these details once and for all.

We see this book as a successor to *A Devil of a Whipping*. However, Guilford Courthouse was fought on a larger scale than Cowpens. Where Cowpens might be seen as a company-oriented engagement, Guilford Courthouse was clearly fought at the battalion level of organization. Moreover, the difficulties faced by the combatants at Guilford create similar problems for historians. Unlike some other Revolutionary War battles, the ground fought over on 15 March 1781 was obscured by both landform and ground cover. Whereas Gen. Daniel Morgan and many other participants could see most of the Cowpens battlefield, neither Nathanael Greene, Charles Cornwallis, nor anyone else could see very much of the fighting around Guilford Courthouse, and that has contributed to some obscurity in the historical record. Consequently, it has been important not only to identify precisely *where* an observer was located but *when* he saw what he reported. Guilford Courthouse was a very fluid battle, and the same zones were fought over more than one time in many cases.

In determining what actually happened on 15 March, we have followed the steps utilized in *A Devil of a Whipping*. We treated participant accounts, whether written soon after the battle or as pension depositions, as artifacts. We sought internal consistency and agreement between the accounts of other combatants. In some cases, subsequent details confirmed the first account and then expanded our understanding by providing other material.

The status of the observer was also considered important. A general would not only be able to see more because he sat on horseback, at least some of the time, but also because he knew something of how the fighting was supposed to occur. A senior officer, major or above, would also be more likely to write down his initial account very soon after the battle, usually as a report of his unit's activity. A person with field-grade rank would have also likely been on horseback and would have moved over the field much more than someone ranked captain or below. Enlisted personnel, by contrast, were more likely to record their impressions long after the battle, as they were required to present confirmatory details of their services to claim a pension. Since the most utilized pension laws were not passed until 1818 and 1832, a veteran's account would be affected by elapsed time. Elapsed time itself affects the memory of events, but recollections are also influenced by the generation of a common memory of what happened, in this case a "Whig version" of historical events that might or might not reflect the reality of 15 March 1781.

Similarly, most participants' accounts concentrated on their "stand" at Guilford. The few who attempted broader overviews provided good details, but they were often very confusing as to timing, units involved, and precise location on the field. The most lucid account was given by the Hessian commander, Major Du Buy, and it is limited to what his regiment did. Even then it is confusing. Otho Holland Williams reported that the volume of gunfire was the worst he ever heard, and he had seen considerable fighting with even larger forces in the northern theater. In the dense woods around Guilford Courthouse, the confusion was simply magnified.

Therefore, the evaluation of accounts involved looking for commonalties and, more important, sequencing: that is, confirmation that if Unit A did something, another unit (on either side) had to have done something first and/or reacted to what Unit A did. Fortunately, after placing units on the landscape and organizing their activities in chronological fashion, this has been possible in a great many cases. In situations where this sort of confirmation was not possible, repetitive reporting of the same, or similar, events by men who served in the same units tends to confirm these accounts.

Finally, if a veteran reported that he was wounded or a brother was killed, or he provided a chain of command confirmed by others, thus indicating knowledge of the facts on the ground, his account had more credibility than a veteran who garbled chronology, commanders, and details. This is not to say that an account that was garbled, perhaps because the veteran was elderly when he gave it, lacked credibility, but rather that other accounts were rated higher. A few veterans who were definitely at Guilford, such as Virginians

Nathaniel Cocke and Peter Perkins, even had their pension applications rejected for various reasons.

As with Cowpens, there were spurious historical "events" attributed to Guilford that were obvious fabrications, such as the idea that Cornwallis fired his guns into the melee on the third line despite the remonstrations of Brig. Gen. Charles O'Hara. We have run many of these stories to ground and sorted them out. Sometimes the fabrication was simply an attempt to add detail, as in the stories told about Peter Francisco; others seem to be deliberate falsehoods. In all cases we could identify, something of the truth has emerged from tracing the tale through time and comparing what others had to say about the same incident.

As with archaeological artifacts, it is the patterns that emerge that make telling the battle's story possible. At some points of the battle, where only suppositions can be made from the documents, archaeological evidence provides confirmation. Such is the case in the route of the British 33rd Regiment of Foot on the northern flank and the second line fighting along the Great Salisbury Road.

In this text, we have attempted to bring the letters, memoirs, diaries, pension accounts, oral histories, and archaeological artifacts together to illuminate the battlefield. We make no claim that we have gotten all the facts right, or for that matter, that we have gotten all the facts. After 225 years, that would be impossible because in their own day not even the participants could relate much beyond their immediate experience, and any questions we might have of them cannot be asked so long after the battle. As we collected the data, we found new questions that required answers. Some we could lay to rest, others are waiting additional research. *Long, Obstinate, and Bloody* is a baseline from which we, and others, can build to a better understanding of what happened to the men who fought their way through the woods west of Guilford Courthouse on 15 March 1781.

# ACKNOWLEDGMENTS

The impetus for studying the battle of Guilford Courthouse came to each of us in quite diverse ways. For Lawrence Babits, the first reference to Guilford Courthouse came from George A. Ferguson Jr., commander of Bravo Company, 1st Battalion, 21st Infantry (Gimlets), United States Army. As a young specialist 4th class, Babits put a Stonewall Brigade crest on his door. Ferguson asked about its significance and then commented that he lived just up the road from Guilford Courthouse. In some ways, it has taken over forty years to conclude what we started that afternoon in the B/1/21 orderly room.

For Joshua Howard, visiting Guilford as a child remains one of his earliest memories. Nearly thirty years ago, as his parents pushed him in a stroller across the battlefield grounds, neither they nor he had any idea that the world would come full circle as it has. Guilford Courthouse is truly where he "cut his teeth" in history, so it is only proper that he has attempted to return the favor and give something back.

Completing this work was a labor of love by many beyond the two authors. We have arbitrarily divided our thanks into categories that related to areas of expertise, but our associates cross these artificial boundaries on many occasions. The sources we were exposed to reflect the expertise of true researchers who have wrung out incredible details of a particular regiment or type of soldier. Without their assistance, many details of the Guilford engagement would not have been included. This book is a tribute to their generous sharing of information.

For the British regiments, help came from several people. Linnea Bass opened her files on the Guards to us and spent hours answering our questions. For the Guards' movements at Guilford Courthouse, we also relied on Jay Callaham. His portrayal of a Guardsman and the hours he has spent on the battlefield proved useful. Dr. Gregory J. W. Urwin, of Temple University, provided a lot of help with the British 23rd Regiment of Foot, but more important, his "Redcoat Images" emails gave us an understanding of the uniforms and often included key information about the portrait's subject. He has probably done more for our overall understanding of British uniforms than any book published. His "staff" of commentators provided other information, but it was Greg who disseminated it. Don Hagist helped us immensely with the British 33rd Regiment of Foot and even provided a muster roll. In his case, we were able to cross-pollinate because we had copies of original material he had only seen in printed form. Our analysis of the British infantryman at Guilford owes a great deal to him. Peter Albertson shared everything he had on the 71st Regiment of Foot and then lent us microfilms so we could see for ourselves. The information he provided illuminated our understanding of Fraser's Highlanders.

Don Londahl-Smidt was our Hessian expert. He repeatedly came up with new materials that added to our understanding of what happened on 15 March 1781 and generously made available materials that were in press so that we would get things right. Todd Braisted helped us with the Provincial troops, the units formed by American loyalists who served with the British forces. His website is the single best source on British Provincials. Finally, whenever we had an officer question not already answered by the previous folk, we would turn to John Houlding. John's database stops about 1792, leaving us holding the proverbial bag on many participants and their later service, but the data he provided on Guilford's British warriors before that date are truly extraordinary.

For the Americans, we again relied on a network of regimentally oriented people. For the Delawares, Mitchell Hunt of Greensboro and Chuck Fithian of the Delaware State Museum shared information with us. Like Chuck, many "old" 1st Maryland Regiment reenactors provided hard facts and food for thought about the Maryland Line. While there are so many we can't possibly name them all, a representative sampling would have to include Denis Reen, Fred Gaede, Les Jenson, Dean Nelson, Tommy Murray, and Ross Kimmel. The other 1st Maryland officers, the Musick, and members of the 2nd ("Swamp") Platoon know who they are and that they helped too. One, Lt. Col. Steve St. Clair, is still on active duty and was last heard from "on command" in Afghanistan. We were really at a loss when it came to some combat maneuverings because Ernest "Pete" Peterkin was not available to provide guidance. Having passed on to the other side, he is likely now sitting at the foot of the Baron Von Steuben discussing the nuances of the musket's manual exercise. In the "new" 1st Maryland, Anne Henninger provided guidance, but mostly she was a gadfly, pressing us to get it right and develop more sources before we went to press.

For pension records, there is no better researcher and transcriber than Will Graves. He continually provided us with key updates from his pension application files research. His willingness to share made it possible to verify many original sources. In this work, you'll see the "rule of three" applied a great deal, because we cross-checked original sources against each other for internal consistency. Our task would have been a lot harder if Will had not provided us with his expertise and willingness to share data.

Two key resources were available for the Virginia Continentals: David McKissick and Todd Post. Dave copied numerous personal accounts and pension data files from the Draper Collection microfilm. Much of Dave's material actually dealt with the South Carolinians, but some covered southwestern Virginia. This information filled in gaps. Todd had a wealth of information on the 2nd Virginia and helped us understand the evolution of the Virginia Continental Line. In North Carolina, Tommy Murray, Mickey Black, and Luther Sowers shared thoughts on the battle. Tommy also provided information about the capability of eighteenth-century rifles.

At Guilford Courthouse National Military Park, we benefited from our association with Don Long, the late Tom Baker, John Durham, Steve Ware, and Nancy Stewart. We walked over the battlefield with them on many occasions, most recently when clarifying the southern flanks fighting. They also provided us with anecdotal evidence about clandestine relic hunting that supported some documentary conclusions. Without their more than 110 years of combined experience on the plateau that saw most of the fighting, we would have been hard-pressed to accurately place battle episodes where they occurred.

At the National Park Service, Southeastern Archaeological Center, Bennie Keel opened up information sources for us. Most important, he unleashed Virginia Hovak, who ran down the gray literature and got it to us in very quick order. She is the complete, and exceptionally diligent, multitasker. Her assessment of what was available and what was likely to be useful saved a lot of time. Although we do not agree with his conclusions, John Cornelison is a good field technician who collected important battle-related detritus and related it to the landscape. Archaeology is revealed truth that must be explained, given the knowledge available. We had a great deal of documentary material to clarify the artifacts John recovered.

Many thanks go to Edward J. Coss, professor of military history, United States Army General and Staff College, for his careful reading of the manuscript. Coss's dissertation, "All for the King's Shilling," an examination of the courage, strength, and endurance of the British "ranker" in the Peninsular Campaign of the Napoleonic Wars, provided a constant source of comparison to the enlisted redcoats of the southern campaign. His work, like ours, attempts to rescue truth from the clutches of long-held nationalist myth and misunderstanding.

The staff of the Research Branch, North Carolina Office of Archives and History, namely Michael Hill, Ansley Herring Wegner, Mark A. Moore, and Vivian McDuffie, all provided support and understanding throughout this venture. Without Mark Moore's extraordinary mapmaking skills, this book would be only a shadow of its current self. With the possible exception of the maps by Haldane and Stedman (both of whom were actually present on 15 March 1781) Mark's works are perhaps the most accurate visual representations available of what happened that day.

At East Carolina University, we benefited from our association with several colleagues. Friend and former student Matt Brenckle tracked down a great many sources before he moved on to studying maritime clothing and life aboard the USS *Constitution*. Carl Swanson of the Department of History, East Carolina University, although not directly involved in the production of this work, deserves thanks and praise for his role as a friend and mentor. Two current students, Tyler Morra and Megan Latta, spent hours with the Otho Holland Williams and Mordecai Gist orderly books. Identification of the officers and men in these two documents provided hard evidence for who was in which Maryland unit at Guilford Courthouse.

A special note of thanks is due Matt Spring, the author of a book on the British Revolutionary War soldier. We were fortunate to read this work in manuscript form and discovered a kindred spirit with incredible insight into the British infantryman. His analysis of British infantry tactics was particularly important for understanding the British battalions and how they fought against the North Carolina and Virginia militias. Thanks to him and his publisher, University of Oklahoma Press, we were allowed to cite his work long before it came into print. Similarly, Mark Urban provided the precise quotes from Lieutenant Calvert's unpublished work that he had earlier referred to in his *Fusiliers*.

We would also be remiss without thanking our families. Nancy and John Babits deserve a round of thanks for giving Larry time to run back and forth to Greensboro, shoot muskets, and wear wool clothing. This book could not have been done without their support. Norwood and Sherry Howard, as well as Michael Rowland, deserve thanks for their support and care and for pushing Josh in that stroller so many years ago. For them, as well as our dear friends and companions who patiently listened to us constantly banter on about Guilford and the Revolution over the years, we can offer only our many heartfelt thanks in return.

Although we have tried to include everyone, we know some who earned our appreciation may have been overlooked. This was not deliberate. To everyone who contributed in any way, we thank you. Any errors are, of course, our own.

*Spirit up the people,*

*to annoy the enemy*

*in that quarter.*

—MAJ. GEN.

NATHANAEL GREENE

*to* BRIG. GEN.

DANIEL MORGAN,

*16 December 1780*

INTRODUCTION **THE STRATEGIC SITUATION**

The battle of Guilford Courthouse was not preordained. Instead it resulted from strategies that had been initially put in play during the first stages of the American War of Independence. At the beginning of the conflict, long-standing political and economic differences between the Piedmont and the Tidewater marred relationships and divided the Carolinas. In both North and South Carolina, Whigs gained quick control, establishing new governments in 1775–76. Exiled loyalists nevertheless promised the British a massive out-pouring of support to coincide with the arrival of regular British troops in the South. The British believed that once their armies arrived, the loyalists in hiding would rise up and reestablish royal government. Those loyalists who rose, however, were defeated in minor skirmishes at Great Bridge, Virginia, and Moore's Creek Bridge, North Carolina, and when the British actually did arrive, at Charleston, South Carolina, in June 1776, they were defeated as well. With these victories, the Whigs considered the southern colonies secure after 1776. They were wrong.

Two years later the British returned. A surprise attack on Savannah in late December 1778 carried the town in less than an hour. Within two months,

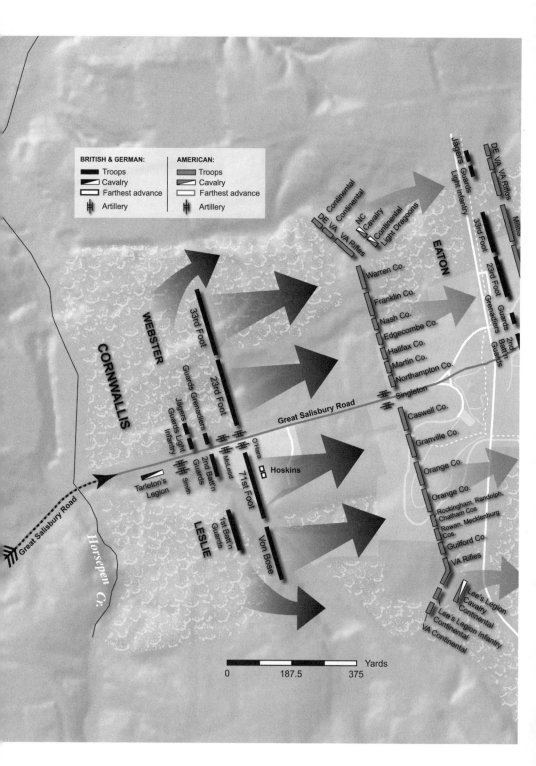

BRITISH & GERMAN:
- ■ Troops
- ◣ Cavalry
- ▭ Farthest advance
- ⚏ Artillery

AMERICAN:
- ▬ Troops
- ◣ Cavalry
- ▭ Farthest advance
- ⚏ Artillery

CORNWALLIS

WEBSTER

33rd Foot

23rd Foot

Guards Grenadiers
Jägers
Guards Light
Infantry

Tarleton's Legion

Smith

2nd Batt'n Guards

McLeod

O'Hara

71st Foot

Hoskins

1st Batt'n Guards

LESLIE

Von Bose

Great Salisbury Road

Horsepen Cr.

Continental
DE    Continental
VA    NC
      VA Rifles    Cavalry
                   Continental
                   Light Dragoons

Warren Co.

Franklin Co.

Nash Co.

Edgecombe Co.

Halifax Co.

Martin Co.

Northampton Co.

Singleton

Caswell Co.

Granville Co.

Orange Co.

Orange Co.

Rockingham, Randolph, Chatham Cos.
Rowan, Mecklenburg Cos.

Guilford Co.

VA Rifles

Lee's Legion Cavalry
Continental
Lee's Legion Infantry
Continental
VA Continental

EATON

Jägers    Guards
          Light Infantry

DE    VA Rifles
VA
Militia

33rd Foot

23rd Foot

Guards
Grenadiers    2nd
Guards        Batt'n
              Guards

Yards
0        187.5        375

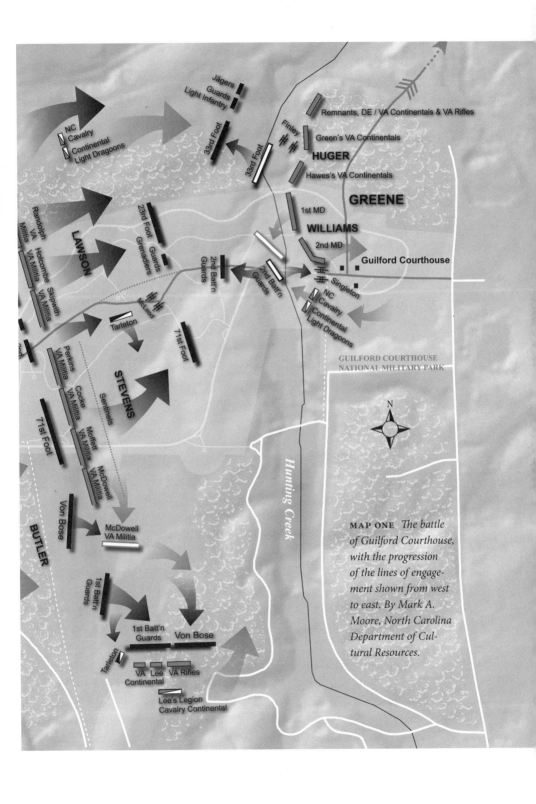

Jägers
Guards
Light Infantry

33rd Foot

33rd Foot

NC Cavalry
Continental Light Dragoons

Remnants, DE / VA Continentals & VA Rifles

Finley

Green's VA Continentals

HUGER

Hawes's VA Continentals

GREENE

23rd Foot  Guards Grenadiers

Randolph VA Militia

Holcombe VA Militia

Skipwith VA Militia

LAWSON

1st MD

WILLIAMS

2nd MD

2nd Batt'n Guards

2nd Batt'n Guards

Guilford Courthouse

Singleton

NC Cavalry
Continental Light Dragoons

McLeod

Tarleton

71st Foot

Perkins VA Militia

STEVENS

Cocke VA Militia

Sentinels

GUILFORD COURTHOUSE
NATIONAL MILITARY PARK

Moffett VA Militia

71st Foot

McDowell VA Militia

N

Von Bose

McDowell VA Militia

BUTLER

*Hunting Creek*

1st Batt'n Guards

MAP ONE  *The battle
of Guilford Courthouse,
with the progression
of the lines of engage-
ment shown from west
to east. By Mark A.
Moore, North Carolina
Department of Cul-
tural Resources.*

1st Batt'n Guards  Von Bose

Tarleton

VA  Lee  VA Rifles
Continental

Lee's Legion
Cavalry Continental

all of Georgia was under Royal control except remote frontier areas, with British garrison posts extending from Augusta to Savannah and down the coast. South Carolina and North Carolina Whigs reacted by attacking British outposts along the Savannah River but were defeated in a series of bloody engagements such as Briar Creek and driven north. When the British crossed the Savannah River and threatened Charleston, the Tidewater aristocracy, thinking more of themselves and their wealth than liberty, proposed neutrality. The British initially ignored the planters' offer but were forced away by arriving Continental forces that attacked their evacuation point at Stono Ferry.[1]

Over the summer of 1779, British hopes arose again as things began to unravel for the Whigs and their new state governments. A combined Franco-American force thoroughly bungled a counterattack on Savannah in October after the French officers rushed a siege into an all-out assault, fearful that by prolonging siege operations they would risk their accompanying fleet to the ravages of the hurricane season. The result was a disastrous American defeat with horrendous casualties that played directly into British hands when attempting to recruit locals into the ranks of the Continentals.

By 1780, the British strategy was predicated on two or three key features. First, the war in the north was stalemated because neither side could destroy the other's army and because occupying cities did not seem to improve the situation much. The northern campaigning should have taught the British that, if they moved away from naval logistical support, they could be in for serious difficulties, as had happened to Burgoyne's campaign that ended at Saratoga. The second fact underlying the British stratagem was that South Carolina was the richest colony in North America — and some attempt should be made to retain it. Finally, the British continued to believe, although less and less enthusiastically, that the key to conquering the South lay in the mass enlistment of loyalists.

The British leadership was well aware of the key element in any Tory uprising: the British army. If an army was not present, Tories would not turn out. Prophetically, when they issued authorization to raise militia units, they ordered that officers should not allow their units to take the field until they could protect themselves. In a letter to South Carolina Tory Richard Pearis, loyalist official James Simpson instructed him on recruiting militiamen:

> You are authorized to give them the Strongest Assurances of Effectual Countenance, Protection and Support. . . . [Have them] collect as much

ammunition and Provisions as the[y] can procure that they may not be distress'd for want of those Articles until they join the Royal Army. As soon as they are assembled in Sufficient numbers . . . Seize and Secure Such of the People as have been most Subservient. . . . [Tell them] their Junction with the King[']s Troops as soon as possible is of the first consequence . . . [and to] bring with them all [the horses] they can collect and also any Provisions. . . . It will be prudent not to attempt any doubtful Offensive operations that can be avoided until they meet the King[']s Troops. . . . [They should] destroy all Stores and Provisions belonging to the Rebels . . . [and] destroy all Posts or places of Strength erected by the Rebels. . . . It will be proper not to make the purposes of your Errand generally known amongst the common people until you have disclosed it to Such persons whose consequence and Influence amongst them will probably induce their Example to be followed. . . . Much will depend on the Secrecy with which you conduct yourself until the time Shall arrive when the people are to assemble, and that Vigour & dispatch after they are Assembled will be necessary to crush any Attempts of the Rebels to withstand them.[2]

Simpson's letter, authorized by British general Sir Henry Clinton, indicates that Pearis was to seize food and property as well as take precautions to be secretive until the army could support the loyalists. Everywhere the British put regular troops, locals turned out, forming militia and provincial regiments. Sometimes the Tories rose before the army was there to support them, with disastrous results, such as at Ramsour's Mill. In a letter written in the summer of 1781, British major James Craig at Wilmington, North Carolina, confirmed the importance of supporting Tories with regular forces: "This country is in a glorious situation for cutting one another's throats. I am very sincere in my efforts to prevent it, which however have not in every instance been effectual. The tories are the most numerous, and was I to give the word a fine scene would begin. However I think it cruelty without a certainty of being ready to support them. If I had that I should soon begin."[3]

The Americans also recognized the importance of providing main force support to their local partisans, as shown on 16 April 1779, when William Moultrie wrote Governor Rutledge of South Carolina that the people in western Georgia "should remain quiet at home until we should be able to cross the river and give them protection."[4]

After the British withdrew into their seacoast enclaves and repulsed the attack on Savannah, it seemed possible that the exiles had been right; the South was ripe for the plucking, and Georgia loyalists did turn out. The British therefore planned a larger effort in the South. In December, a British fleet of more than one hundred vessels sailed from New York. Despite storms that ravaged the vessels, the fleet gathered off Tybee Island, Georgia, at the mouth of the Savannah River, on 1 February 1780. After a brief respite, the British landed in South Carolina on Simmons (now Seabrook) Island the night of 11 February. By 2 April they commenced siege operations against Charleston. After a siege lasting five weeks, most of the rebellious forces in the South were prisoners of war or on parole, taken when Charleston surrendered on 12 May 1780. Seventeen days later, Lt. Col. Banastre Tarleton and his British Legion annihilated the lone surviving regular Whig unit in South Carolina, a detachment of Virginia Continentals, at Waxhaws.[5]

As the ports at Savannah, Charleston, and Georgetown all became British occupied, the war moved into the countryside. Most important, once Charleston fell, the focus of the British efforts was not on establishing peace but rather on forcing an engagement with American Continentals in traditional fashion. Clinton, far too optimistically, stated, "I am clear in opinion that the Carolinas have been conquered in Charleston." In the next two months, the British still had a chance to secure Georgia and South Carolina. Safe behind an arch of garrison posts stretching from Savannah to Augusta, then north to Ninety Six and Camden, then east to Georgetown, the loyalists, backed by the British army, could have established Royal government throughout the state. They failed to do so largely because the politicians misunderstood the situation and the regulars were spread too thin to control the Tories. Understandably, after three years of oppression, the Tories wanted to get even. Both General Clinton and Lt. Gen. Charles Cornwallis understood that the people had to be satisfied with the British role. At the highest command levels, things were seen in broad terms, best expressed by Clinton: "The good will of the inhabitants is absolutely requisite to retain a country after we have conquered it. I fear it will be some time before we can recover the confidence of those in Carolina, as their past sufferings will of course make them cautious of forwarding the King's interests before there is the strongest certainty of his army being in a condition to support them."[6]

To help control the situation, the British began enrolling loyalist militias and then, on 3 June 1780, Clinton made perhaps the biggest strategic blunder of the war. He issued, and Cornwallis tried to enforce, but then repealed, an

*Lt. Gen. Charles Cornwallis (1738–1805), commander of the British army at Guilford Courthouse. Oil painting by Thomas Gainsborough (1783). NPG 281. © National Portrait Gallery, London.*

edict requiring paroled prisoners to join the British militia or be treated as outlaws. Already-paroled Whigs, including militia leaders Andrew Pickens and Thomas Sumter, had basically opted out of the war, content to salvage what they could. However, Whig depredations committed between 1775 and 1780 had so rankled the Tories that many of them tried to turn the tables and punish the Whigs. After their properties were vandalized, many Whigs like Sumter and Pickens went back into the field. Under the threat of the Clinton proclamation, they saw no recourse but to fight or flee. Given the property confiscations and threat of death, Whigs had little to lose by fighting on after 3 June. Of course, they probably knew this after Waxhaws, but now it was "official."[7]

In North Carolina, there remained a small, yet capable Continental force. The Maryland-Delaware Division, eight regiments under Maj. Gen. Jean, Baron DeKalb, had been sent south to reinforce Charleston. They were too late but continued marching in slow increments as they waited for the commander who would lead a new army. When Gen. Horatio Gates finally reached North Carolina, he immediately opted for a march against the British stronghold at Camden, South Carolina, the keystone to the British fortification ring around the outlying regions of South Carolina. Despite severe supply problems, Gates marched toward the British post in July.

The British sallied out of Camden under Gen. Charles, the Earl Cornwallis. They met Gates's force north of Camden in the night and then fought an intense but short battle on 16 August 1780. Largely because the American militia fled, along with their commanding general, the Continentals were slaughtered, suffering some 50 percent casualties in the forty-five minutes of fighting. Gates reached Hillsborough to "rally his forces" in early September, with various Continentals straggling in two and three weeks later. In the meantime, many American prisoners taken at Camden were offered a choice between being incarcerated in prison ships or joining the British army. Over 120 Maryland and Delaware Continentals enlisted in the British Legion alone. Some joined the British to avoid the prison ships and attempt a future escape. Others may genuinely have changed their allegiance, inasmuch as some of them were still with the British Legion after Yorktown.[8]

The British Legion nearly doubled in size after Camden and, coupled with backcountry militia that were raised, provided a screen of light troops to help secure the frontier and stabilize it. The Whigs, now seen increasingly as outlaws, spoiled British intentions with raids on their supply lines. In response, Lt. Col. Patrick Ferguson moved rapidly north and west from the British stronghold at Ninety Six and on into North Carolina. Here he issued a proclamation ordering the "overmountain men" to cease raiding in the Carolinas and to stop harboring raiders who fled to them.

The "overmountain men," an unstructured group of settlers from western North Carolina, Virginia, and what is now Tennessee, responded by calling up their forces and moving immediately to solve the problem. As word of their approach reached Ferguson, he withdrew and took a position at Kings Mountain. Here, on 7 October 1780, he was attacked and his force totally destroyed by the overmountain men, as well as more local Carolina militia. As a result, Cornwallis had lost half his light troops and a western protective screen. He evacuated Charlotte, North Carolina, and took position at Winnsboro, South Carolina, until he could refit his army. For the Whigs, Kings Mountain was a wonderful victory, but it came with a price. State legislatures, especially the one in South Carolina, seemed to think the war could be won by militia alone and there was no longer a need to rebuild their state's Continental regiments. The lack of regular troops would hinder Continental efforts to reestablish state government, and the militia would be a constant source of problems and exasperation for Continental army leaders sent to the Carolinas and Georgia.[9]

While legislatures debated, Whig partisans continued raiding. Tarleton tried to bring them down and had limited success. Even his defeat by Gen. Thomas Sumter's militia at Blackstock's could be seen as something of a minor victory because Sumter was knocked out of action with a severe wound. After Blackstock's, some of the fire seems to have left Sumter, except when he didn't get his way. Known as the "Gamecock" for his fiery temper and unwillingness to compromise, Sumter continued to argue with any Continental or militia officer who stood in the way of his personal ambitions.

When Congress eventually learned of the Camden debacle, Gen. George Washington was allowed to pick a replacement, and he sent Gen. Nathanael Greene, the man who had organized Washington's northern Continental army's logistical affairs. As quartermaster general, Greene had created an effective supply system under poor circumstances. What he would find in the South would be far worse. As soon as he reached North Carolina, he began to study the landscape. By mid-December 1780, his grasp of the river system was remarkable. His understanding of the strategic situation was even better. The combination of supply shortages and what he perceived to be an opportunity caused Greene to divide the army. Later historians have challenged Greene's decision, based on the principles of war. However, the Western versions of these principles were largely derived from the Napoleonic Wars, and Napoleon did say that an army divides to live (in this case, eat) and unites to fight.[10] Greene clearly pointed out his strategic situation in a letter sometime between 26 December 1780 and 23 January 1781:

> I am well satisfied with the movement [division of the army], for it has answered thus far all the purposes from which I intended it. It makes the most of my inferior force, for it compels my adversary to divide his, and holds him in doubt as to his own line of conduct. He cannot leave [Brig. Gen. Daniel] Morgan behind him to come at me, or his posts of Ninety Six and Augusta would be exposed. And he cannot chase Morgan far, or prosecute his views upon Virginia, while I am here with the whole country open before me. I am as near to Charleston as he is, and as near to Hillsborough as I was at Charlotte; so that I am in no danger of my being cut off from my reinforcements, while an uncertainty as to my

future designs has made it necessary to leave a large detachment of the enemy's late reinforcements in Charleston, and move the rest up on this side of the Wateree. But although there is nothing to obstruct my march to Charleston, I am far from having such a design in contemplation in the present relative positions and strength of the two armies.[11]

While Greene's division of forces represented a logistical solution for the Whigs, the different units operating against the British posed a major strategic problem for Cornwallis. Greene couldn't support his whole army in one place. By dividing them, he could feed his men, and by moving them independently of one another, he caused problems for scattered British garrisons that could hardly allow the Americans under Brig. Gen. Daniel Morgan, Lt. Col. Henry "Light Horse Harry" Lee, Lt. Col. William Washington, and numerous partisans to ramble about the countryside. In effect, Greene created rallying points for the backcountry partisan bands.

After the Clinton proclamation was issued, backcountry fighting escalated, and the British could do little about it. It's hard to see what they could have done. If they had managed to restrict the activities of their own provincials and maintained order, they might have succeeded in holding on to the South. But with the call to paroled prisoners to enlist and the unchecked Tory raiding, the Whigs had nothing to lose by resisting. The rebellion fed upon itself in a series of raids and bitter reprisals by both sides. For the British leadership, there was no clear focal point to attack. Local militia leaders hid out, emerging when the tactical situation was favorable to conduct raids. This partisan economy of force compelled the British to deploy detachments vulnerable to partisans. Greene exploited the situation when he divided the Southern Army in the face of Cornwallis's larger British army. The result was Cowpens.

Greene had intended on harassing the local Tories, exploiting the British inability to protect them, while at the same time rallying the backcountry South Carolina Whigs. Before moving to a camp along the Pee Dee River, he ordered Morgan to the west with instructions to "spirit up the people, to annoy the enemy in that quarter; collect the provisions and forage out of the way of the enemy. . . . You will prevent plundering as much as possible . . . giving receipts for whatever you take to all such as are friends to the independence of America." Even so, a typical Tory claim after the war stated, "the Rebel Genl. Morgan took possession of my plantation before Col Tarletons

Defeat . . . they had used or destroyed my crop & took away almost every thing."[12]

Along with Morgan's force, Greene sent Lt. Col. William Washington with his 3rd Continental Light Dragoons. Washington immediately went on a raid against Tories assembling just north of Ninety Six. He smashed the Tories and then burned a Tory post at Williamson's Plantation, a short distance from Ninety Six. He then retired to Morgan's main camp, followed by Col. Andrew Pickens with his South Carolina State Troops. In one stroke, Morgan had exacerbated the problem posed to Cornwallis when Greene divided his forces, and he also "spirited up the people" enough to bring militiamen rallying to his camp. To stop Morgan's raiding and secure Ninety Six, Cornwallis ordered Tarleton to "push Morgan to the utmost."[13]

On 17 January 1781, Tarleton caught up with Morgan at the Cowpens, a well-known crossroads with adjacent springs and some forage. Tarleton didn't catch Morgan, for the "Old Wagoner," as he was known, had turned and placed his mixed group of Continentals, state troops, and militia into an effective formation that devastated Tarleton's 1,200 men. When what was arguably the finest American tactical effort of the Revolutionary War was over, less than a half hour later, 800 of Tarleton's men were dead, wounded, and/or taken prisoner.

After Cowpens, the British were faced with a major problem. Despite the army's being recently reinforced, nearly 1,000 British and provincial soldiers were prisoners of war in North Carolina. Cornwallis moved swiftly to recapture them and, more important, in his own mind, to cut off supplies flowing into the Carolinas from the north. He also wanted to bring the Americans to battle while they were divided. To do so, he turned his entire army into a light force and burned his supply wagons at Ramsour's Mills, North Carolina.

The pursuit began when the British crossed the Catawba River, starting the initial phase of what became known as the "Race to the Dan." Ultimately, the American withdrawal was successful in getting the Continentals and their prisoners to safety. For the British it was an impending disaster because Cornwallis marched his army into a logistical trap as both forces moved rapidly through a zone that the Americans swept almost clear of food and forage. From late January to early February, the British army began to slowly starve because retreating Americans took all readily available forage and food in their front and flanks. The British, moving rapidly through the same area, found very little left for their use. The key elements in this chase across North

Carolina and subsequent maneuvering are virtually unknown today, but they are a clue to Greene's strategic success in bringing the southernmost colonies back into the United States and sending Cornwallis and his army to York-town. The "Race to the Dan" and the prebattle maneuvering in early March set the stage for the battle of Guilford Courthouse.

*It was resolved to*
*follow Greene's army*
*to the end of the World.*
—BRIG. GEN.
CHARLES O'HARA,
*Brigade of Guards,*
*20 April 1781*

CHAPTER ONE THE RACE TO THE DAN

The "Race to the Dan" began shortly after the battle of Cowpens ended. During the early morning of 17 January 1781, Brig. Gen. Daniel Morgan had destroyed a British expeditionary force led by Lt. Col. Banastre Tarleton in less than one hour. Morgan, along with his army and nearly 600 British prisoners, immediately marched north, crossing the Broad River and bivouacking. Convinced that Cornwallis, learning of Tarleton's defeat, would come after him to free the prisoners, Morgan set a furious pace and led by example, despite his deteriorating health. The "Old Wagoner" had his army moving up the road before dawn on 18 January.[1]

That same morning a dejected Tarleton rode into Cornwallis's camp along Turkey Creek, South Carolina, delivering news of the disaster. Nearly one-quarter of Cornwallis's army had been killed or captured. His lordship was in an extremely difficult position, having lost two expeditionary groups from his main force: one, chiefly provincials, to backcountry riflemen at King's Mountain; and the other, his light troops, at Cowpens to Morgan's Continentals and militia. Cornwallis confessed in a letter to Lord Francis Rawdon four days later that "the late affair has almost broke my heart."[2]

On the day Tarleton arrived, Cornwallis wrote his superior, Gen. Sir Henry Clinton, in New York, letting him know that he refused to "give up the important object of this Winter's campaign." That object, he later noted to Lord George Germain, was "to penetrate to North Carolina, leaving South Carolina in security against any probable attack in my absence." Refusing and ignoring orders to remain near Charleston, Cornwallis marched north after Morgan and did not write Clinton for nearly three months.[3]

Late in the evening of 18 January, Cornwallis received some 1,200 reinforcements brought up from Charleston by Maj. Gen. Alexander Leslie. With these men, Cornwallis now fielded an army of nearly 2,500 soldiers, including more than 2,000 regulars. The next morning, he set out after Morgan, who by that time was twenty miles north of Cowpens at Gilbert Town, near present-day Rutherfordton, North Carolina. Cornwallis's later writings indicate that he severely miscalculated not only Morgan's position but also the influence of the numerous fords and rivers in southwestern North Carolina:

> I decided to march by the upper, in preference to the lower roads leading
> into North Carolina, because fords being frequent above the forks of
> the rivers, my passage there could not easily be obstructed; and General
> Greene having taken post on the Peedee, and there being few fords in
> any of the great rivers of this country below their forks, especially in,
> winter, I apprehended being much delayed; if not entirely prevented
> from penetrating by the latter route.[4]

Cornwallis correctly noted that fords above the forks were more numerous and, thus, less likely to be strongly held by defenders. While he attributed winter problems to the lower river zones, he seems to have forgotten that rivers could rise even more rapidly above the forks. If his letter was an honest assessment of his preinvasion planning, Cornwallis made a serious miscalculation by not considering the upper rivers' potential for flooding.

Coupled with that error, Cornwallis also failed to understand the road network as it related to the rivers and weather. Several participants left accounts of their travels through the region, but no one gave as succinct an overview as Benson J. Lossing, who passed through on a historical tour nearly seventy years later and remarked that "no one can form an idea of the character of the roads in winter . . . where the red clay abounds, without passing over them. Until I had done so, I could not appreciate the difficulties experienced by the two armies in the race toward Virginia, particularly in the transportation of baggage wagons or of artillery." Written long after the war's conclusion, when roads should have been better, Lossing's account provides a fairly accurate assessment of conditions sixty-eight years earlier when redcoats and rebels passed over the same roads.[5]

From 19 to 22 January, Cornwallis marched north, using intelligence gathered by patrols sent out under Tarleton's command. Most of the British Legion dragoons had survived the fiasco at Cowpens, and now they played a major role in searching for Morgan's whereabouts. Tarleton's reports "induced Earl Cornwallis to cross Buffaloe creek and Little Broad river, in hopes of intercepting General Morgan." Tarleton continued, "Great exertions were made by part of the army, without baggage, to retake our prisoners, and to intercept General Morgan's corps on its retreat to the Catawba; but the celerity of their movements, and the swelling of numberless creeks in our way, rendered all our efforts fruitless."[6]

The British discovered that Morgan had crossed the Catawba River at Sherrald's Ford, while sending his prisoners farther north to cross at Island Ford. Having done so, Morgan pushed northward, keeping the swollen river between himself and his British pursuers. Still in pursuit, Cornwallis's men encamped at Ramsour's Mill on 25 January. Far from moving speedily, they had taken three days to cover thirty miles. Here, Cornwallis made another fateful decision and burned his wagon train. He reported,

> As the loss of my light troops could only be remedied by the activity of the whole corps, I employed a halt of two days in collecting some flour, and in destroying superfluous baggage and all my wagons, except those loaded with hospital stores, salt, and ammunition and four reserved empty in readiness for sick or wounded. In this measure, though at the expense of a great deal of officers' baggage, and of all prospect in future of rum, and even a regular supply of provisions to the soldiers, I must, in justice to this army, say that there was the most general and cheerful acquiescence.[7]

Brig. Gen. Charles O'Hara, commanding the Guards who came with Leslie's reinforcements, wrote his friend the Duke of Grafton, that "Lord Cornwallis sett [sic] the example by burning all of his Wagons, and destroying the greatest part of his Baggage, which was followed by every Officer of the Army without a murmur." No other British officer in America had taken such drastic action, and Cornwallis's troops must have seen it as a combination of bravado and necessity, although many rankers probably cringed when

Cornwallis proclaimed, "The Supply of Rum for a time will be Absolutely Impossible." O'Hara summarized the British situation: "Without Baggage, necessaries, or Provisions of any sort for Officer or Soldier, in the most barren, inhospitable unhealthy part of North America, opposed to the most savage, inveterate perfidious cruel Enemy, with zeal and with Bayonets only, it was resolved to follow Greene's army to the end of the World."[8]

Cornwallis readied his regiments for the forced march that lay before them. Having found "a sufficient quantity of leather to complete the brigade in shoes in this village," Cornwallis had shoes "soled and repaired" and ordered that each man take "one pair of spare soles." As well as preparing equipment, his men conducted foraging on a large scale to obtain the necessary food for soldiers and horses. These localized expeditions required protection in the hostile environment, and a fairly large detachment was created to "cover the foragers of the different corps."[9]

Having taken nearly three days to complete these preparations, Cornwallis's army finally marched on 28 January and encamped near Beattie's Ford the next day. By now, the Catawba River had risen so much it was completely impassable. Morgan meanwhile had been "collecting the Militia" and "filling all the Private fords to Make them Impassable." Morgan wrote Greene from Sherrald's Ford that he "was a Little Apprehensive, that Lord Cornwallis intends to Surprise me . . . but if the Militia don't Decieve me who I am Obliged to Trust as guards up and down the River I Think I will put it out of his Power." He also dispatched Brig. Gen. William Lee Davidson, a former Continental officer, with 800 North Carolina militiamen to Beattie's Ford.[10]

Although Greene considered striking south from Cheraw toward British outposts near Charleston and Savannah, he opted to reunite the main army with Morgan's "Flying Army." Leaving his Continentals along the Pee Dee River under Brig. Gen. Isaac Huger, with orders to march north to Salisbury, Greene set out with a guide and three dragoons on the more than one-hundred-mile-long journey across the south central part of North Carolina on 28 January. He wrote Huger, "I am not without hopes of ruining Lord Cornwallis, if he persists on his mad scheme of pushing through the Country. . . . Here is a fine field and great glory ahead."[11]

Exactly how Greene got to Beattie's Ford remains something of a mystery. It is quite likely that he rode north into Anson County before turning northwest through present-day Stanly, Montgomery, and Cabarrus Counties. This route would have taken him across Rocky River at ferries located at Colson's Ordinary or Robert Lane's Ordinary. He could just as easily have headed west

*Maj. Gen. Nathanael Greene
(1742–86), commander of the
American army at Guilford
Courthouse. Oil painting
by Charles Wilson Peale.
Independence National
Historical Park.*

across present-day Union and Mecklenburg Counties. Regardless of which route he took, the fact that he found Morgan's army without being attacked by Tories or intercepted by a British patrol borders on the miraculous.

A day after reaching Morgan on 30 January, Greene held a council of war at Beattie's Ford with Morgan, Davidson, and cavalryman Lt. Col. William Washington. Capt. Joseph Graham, a North Carolina militiaman who was present, remembered that the four officers sat down on a log a few hundred yards from camp and decided on their plans. As they discussed the situation, a party of British dragoons appeared across the Catawba, and one officer, who they presumed was Cornwallis, appeared to watch them with a spyglass. The rain had stopped, and the river level was falling. Greene was convinced that it would be fordable soon. Davidson later told Graham that, "though General Greene had never seen the Catawba before, he appeared to know more about it than those who were raised on it."[12]

Greene realized that he had only Morgan's Flying Army and Davidson's 800 militiamen to defend the numerous fords between the British army and Salisbury, where Greene initially expected Huger's men to rendezvous with Morgan's force. Greene's plan was simple. Morgan's men were to hold Sherrald's Ford. Davidson and his militia would hold the lower fords as long as possible and then fall back to Salisbury. A major supply and manufacturing center for the southern Continental army, Salisbury would provide much-needed equipment, food, and ammunition to Greene's retreating men. They would need to evacuate the small garrison and many prisoners of war, as well as the artisans who worked in the military manufactories located in the town.

While Greene met with his war council, Cornwallis was finally moving again. Determining that both Sherrald's Ford and Beattie's Ford were too heavily guarded, Cornwallis sent a feint led by Lt. Col. James Webster and the 33rd Foot toward Beattie's Ford and then "marched at one in the morning with the brigade of guards, regiment of Bose, 23rd, 200 cavalry, and two 3-pounders, to the ford fixed upon for the real attempt," a smaller crossing four miles south, known as Cowan's Ford. When word came that Cornwallis was at Cowan's Ford, Webster's force "made demonstrations of attacking the post at Beattie's." One British company actually entered the water and fired a volley toward the Americans. Capt. Joseph Graham described how the artillery pieces "fired smoothly for thirty minutes, and his [Cornwallis's] front lines kept firing by platoons as in field exercises." They caused little damage, but the reports of the weapons were "like repeated peals of thunder . . . heard all over the country."[13]

Davidson guessed at Cornwallis's intentions and deployed 250 militia and several dozen dragoons under Capt. Joseph Graham at Cowan's Ford. Among the militia were Robert Beatty, a local schoolmaster, and his charges. They took their "stand" opposite the lower, or wagon, route at Cowan's Ford. There were actually two ways across Cowan's, a wagon ford and a horse crossing. The remainder of Davidson's force stood on a small bluff above the horse ford. The entire party was apparently asleep when the British arrived in the predawn hours of 1 February. Sixteen-year-old Robert Henry, one of Beatty's boy soldiers, later claimed that a local Tory, "Dick Beal, being deceived by our fires had led them into swimming water."[14]

The British entered the river, following their commander's example. Sgt. Roger Lamb reported that "Lord Cornwallis, according to his usual manner, dashed first into the river, mounted on a very fine, spirited horse, the brigade of guards followed, two three-pounders next, the Royal Welch fuzileers after them." In the darkness, Lamb may have mistaken the Guards' forty-five-year-old Lt. Col. Francis Hall for Cornwallis. North Carolinian Joseph Graham claimed, "Col. Hall was the first man to appear on horseback . . . and was distinctly heard giving orders." The noise of the horses in the water woke militiaman Joel Jetton, who ran to the water's edge, found the sentry asleep, and promptly kicked him into the river. The terrified youngster then ran back into camp yelling, "The British! The British!"[15]

Nature aided the American cause, as the swift current swept away several British soldiers. Maj. Gen. Alexander Leslie's horse tripped, throwing its rider into the torrent, as did Brig. Gen. Charles O'Hara's stallion that "rolled with him down the current near forty yards." Both men survived and were rescued. Many enlisted men on foot were not so lucky. A Tory "saw 'em hollerin' and a snortin' and a drownin'." Sgt. Roger Lamb of the 23rd Foot barely rescued an artilleryman who had been swept off his feet. Exactly how far the British traveled crossing the ford is unknown; the ford no longer exists, but 500 yards appears reasonable.[16]

The Whigs ran to the water's edge and began firing on the advancing redcoats. The first man shot down was Lieutenant Colonel Hall. Graham saw Hall killed and reported that as he went into the swirling waters, "two or three soldiers caught him and raised him up." Cornwallis's horse was hit several times by musket fire but bravely carried the commander to the opposite bank before collapsing. Robert Henry "fired and continued firing until I saw that one on horse-back had passed my rock in the river, and saw that it was Dick Beal. . . . I ran with all speed up the bank." At the top, he heard Colonel Polk shouting, "Fire away, boys! Help is at hand!" "I saw my lame schoolmaster, Beatty, loading his gun by a tree. I thought I could stand it as long as he could and commenced loading. Beatty fired, and then I fired, the head and shoulders of the British being just above the bank. They made no return fire. . . . I observed Beatty loading again. I ran down another load. When he fired, he cried, 'It's time to run, Bob.'"[17]

The British did not return fire because they had been told to advance without shooting. Cornwallis "ordered them to march on, but to prevent confusion not to fire until they gained the opposite bank." Concerning the Guards, Cornwallis wrote, "Their behaviour justified my high opinion of them, for a constant fire from the enemy in a ford upwards of five hundred yards wide, in many places up to their middle . . . made no impression on their cool and determined valour nor checked their passage." Roger Lamb noted that advancing in the chest-high water with an unloaded musket "urged us on with greater rapidity, till we gained the opposite shore, where we were obliged to scramble up a very high hill under a heavy fire."[18]

After gaining the Whig side, the Guards loaded and fired one volley, ac-

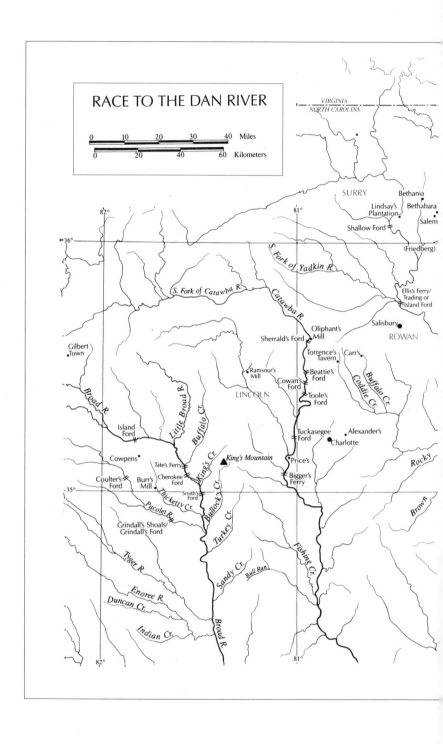

# RACE TO THE DAN RIVER

0    10    20    30    40  Miles
0      20      40      60  Kilometers

VIRGINIA
NORTH CAROLINA

SURRY

Bethania

Lindsay's
Plantation
Bethabara

Salem

Shallow Ford

(Friedberg)

82°

81°

36°

S. Fork of Yadkin R.

S. Fork of Catawba R.

Catawba R.

Ellis's Ferry/
Trading or
Island Ford

Salisbury

Oliphant's
Mill

ROWAN

Sherrald's Ford

Gilbert
Town

Torrence's
Tavern

Carr's

Buffalo Cr.

Ramsour's
Mill

Beattie's
Ford

Coddle Cr.

Broad R.

Little Broad R.

Buffalo Cr.

Cowan's
Ford

LINCOLN

Toole's
Ford

Island
Ford

King's Cr.

Tuckasegee
Ford

Alexander's

Charlotte

Cowpens

Tate's Ferry

King's Mountain

Price's

Rocky

Coulter's
Ford

Burr's
Mill

Cherokee
Ford

Bigger's
Ferry

35°

Thicketty Cr.

Smith's
Ford

Bullock's Cr.

Brown

Pacolet R.

Grindall's Shoals/
Grindall's Ford

Turkey Cr.

Tyger R.

Sandy Cr.

Bull Run

Fishing Cr.

Enoree R.

Duncan Cr.

Indian Cr.

Broad R.

82°

81°

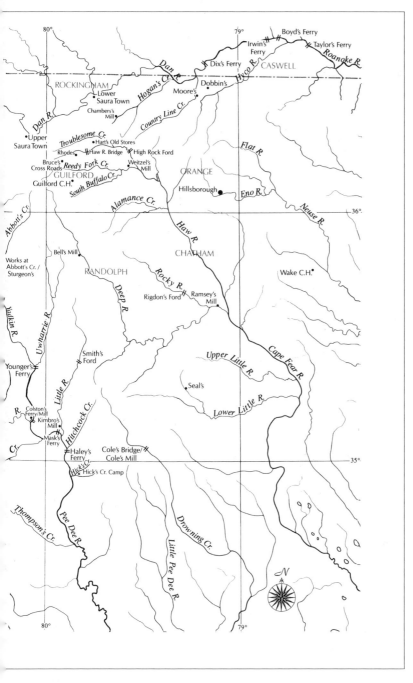

**MAP TWO** *Race to the Dan River. From Showman et al.,* The Papers of General Nathanael Greene, *vol. 7 (1994). Courtesy of the Rhode Island Historical Society.*

cording to Robert Henry, who avoided being hit by straightening "myself behind a tree." Beatty, his teacher, was not so lucky. Shot in the hip and crippled, Henry last saw him "hallowing for me to run." A single shot, which Joseph Graham attributed to a local Tory named Frederick Hager, killed Gen. William Lee Davidson, who had ridden to the wagon ford from the upper horse crossing. Davidson died instantly from a ball in his chest, and as he fell from the saddle, most militiamen broke and fled. Two days later, Greene wrote to South Carolina militia leader Thomas Sumter, "The loss of General Davidson is a great misfortune at this time."[19]

British losses at Cowan's Ford are unknown. Cornwallis stated that he lost four killed, including Lieutenant Colonel Hall, and thirty-six wounded. However, Robert Henry recorded that the day after the battle, he and several friends found fourteen dead men, most of "whom appeared to have no wound, but had drowned," lodged in a set of fish traps below the ford. All along the river, locals found bodies "lodged on brush, and drifted to the banks." American losses are similarly uncertain but were substantially lighter than those incurred by the British. Tarleton claimed the Americans lost "about forty men killed and wounded." Joseph Graham put the figure at four; among the dead was schoolmaster Robert Beatty.[20]

The British wasted little time getting organized after crossing over Cowan's Ford. Cornwallis had gotten the majority of his army across, and Lt. Col. James Webster's force rejoined the main column after Davidson's remaining men fled Beattie's Ford. Rain began falling again, slowing Cornwallis's progress, but the British army managed to reunite and made a wet camp six miles from Beattie's Ford during the evening hours of 1 February. Before setting out from Cowan's Ford, Cornwallis dispatched Tarleton with the 23rd Foot and his legion dragoons to discover Greene's location, seemingly unaware that the Continentals had fallen back to Salisbury.

Tarleton left the 23rd about five miles east of Beattie's Ford due to "heavy rain and bad roads" and continued on with his horsemen. Capt. Joseph Graham's North Carolina militia light horse company barely escaped Tarleton's men by hiding in a "swampy branch" along the road. At first, Graham's men thought the passing dragoons were Whigs, until they saw "the tails of their horses being docked square off, which all knew was the mark of Tarleton's Cavalry." "Bloody Ban" Tarleton and his legion failed to notice the rain-soaked North Carolinians and kept riding. Tarleton's party went three miles further, where he "gained intelligence that the fugitives from the fords . . . were to assemble at two o'clock in the afternoon at Tarrant's [Torrence's] tavern." He realized that, although likely outnumbered, he had two advantages: the element of surprise and the weather. Or as he put it, the "time was advantageous to make impressions upon the militia; [and] the weather, on account of a violent rain, was favourable for the project." With the rain, most of the militia's powder would be soaked and therefore unusable.[21]

Greene intended Davidson's militia to fall back to Salisbury, but several dozen militiamen halted ten miles from Beattie's Ford at a small tavern owned by the Torrence family. They were joined by hundreds of fleeing refugees, mostly women and children, their wagons piled high with belongings. Many militiamen apparently got drunk, as pitchers of whiskey and other spirits were liberally passed through their ranks. The Whigs had no idea that nearly 200 dragoons of the British Legion were riding in their direction.[22]

Tarleton arrived shortly after 2:00 P.M. What happened next remains something of a controversy. Several postwar accounts claim that Tarleton found the militia in complete distress, many of them drunk, and completely incapable of fighting back. Joseph Graham, who did not witness the event firsthand, stated, "The wagons of many of the movers with their property mixed in the lane, the armed men all out of order, and mixed with the wagons and people, so that the lane could scarcely be passed, when the sound of alarm was given from the west end of the lane, 'Tarleton is coming!'" Tarleton claimed, "The militia were vigilant, and were prepared for an attack," a sentiment echoed by Cornwallis's description of the event afterwards as an "attack on a large body of infantry posted behind rails & in strong houses."[23]

Whether the North Carolinians were intoxicated or "prepared," or a combination of the two, remains unknown, but Tarleton "resolved to hazard one charge" and implored his dragoons to "remember the Cowpens." His men charged "with excellent conduct and great spirit" and quickly cut down the Whigs. Militiaman Elisha Evans described how, "After we were driven from the Catawba we were overtaken in a lane called Tarrance's Lane and here we had a sharp engagement and were defeated." One young officer, Capt. Salathiel Martin, saw Tarleton's men approaching and tried in vain to rally his men to stand along a rail fence, but he had his horse shot from under him. Entangled in the horse's tack, Martin was captured. One of his men, Jonas Clark, recalled that "at Mrs. Torrens we had a sharp skirmish and our Captain Martin had his horse killed and him taken prisoner." Tarleton claimed little loss and credited his men with killing forty to fifty Whigs and capturing an unknown number. Joseph Graham claimed Whig casualties were closer to ten. The British "made great destruction of the property in the wagons

. . . ripped up beds and strewed the feathers, until the lane was covered with them."[24]

The impact of Davidson's death and the havoc wreaked at Torrence's had considerable impact on the local populace. According to Cornwallis, "This stroke, with our passage of the ford so effectually dispirited the militia that we met with no further opposition on our march to the Yadkin." The British soldiers were hardly peaceful. In addition to strewing the road with bed feathers and civilian property, they also burned the home of local Whig John Brevard and Torrence's Tavern. Cornwallis attempted to quell such activity, stating that he was "highly displeased that Several Houses was set on fire during the March this day." He threatened to punish "with the Utmost Severity any person or persons who shall be found Guilty of Committing so disgracefull an Outrage." Three days later, he repeated his threats against the "most Shocking complaints of the Excesses Committed by the Troops" and called on the officers of his army to "put a Stop to this Licentiousness, which must Inevitably bring Disgrace & Ruin on his Majesty's service."[25]

After learning of Davidson's defeat at Cowan's Ford, Greene evacuated Sherrald's Ford and sent word to the remaining North Carolina militia to gather at David Carr's, on the road between Beattie's Ford and Salisbury, since defending the fords was "of no further use." Exactly how many joined him is unknown, but in a later aside, Lt. Col. John Eager Howard placed Rowan County's militia commander at home during this crisis. Francis Locke "was not at the Catawba but at his own house when we passed and to the best of my recollection & belief, he was there taken by the enemy with Greene's letter of the 31st in his pocket. If he ever deserved the title of gallant colonel, he forfeited it by his conduct on this occasion." If their commander stayed home, it is no wonder his troops did not turn out.[26]

While the militia scattered across the countryside, Morgan and the Flying Army successfully executed their own withdrawal. Howard pointed out, "Sherards [Sherrald's] is not nearer to Salisbury than Beatty's [Beattie's]." Sgt. Maj. William Seymour of Kirkwood's Delaware Continentals noted, "We remained on this ground till the first February, waiting the motion of the enemy, who this day crossed the river lower down than where we lay, and coming unawares on the militia commanded by Genl. Davidson, on which ensued a smart skirmish in which General Davidson was killed, and a great many more killed and wounded, upon which the militia retreated off in great disorder."[27]

Once the British forced the crossing at Cowan's, the Continentals had no recourse but to move rapidly. The Continentals marched toward Salisbury by a more northerly route. Howard noted, "We retreated by a different road than that by Torrances [Torrence's]." It had taken some time for Morgan to learn about the debacle at Cowan's Ford. According to Seymour,

> Morgan did not leave the river until 10 or 11 o'clock on the 1st [2d] of February after it was known that the enemy had crossed and that Davidson had been defeated; then it was that Genl. Greene ordered the retreat. We marched all night in the rain & mud, and a most fatiguing march it was. We arrived at Colonel Lock[']s 4 miles short of Salisbury, at sun rise on the 2nd & halted to get dry and for the men who had fallen out of the ranks from fatigue, to come up. . . . We marched off this place for Salisbury on the evening of the first February, and continued our march all night in a very unpleasant condition, it having rained incessantly all night, which rendered the roads almost inaccessible. Next day, being the 2d, we arrived at Salisbury.[28]

The following day, 2 February, Greene evacuated Salisbury. Wagons were loaded with all the food, ammunition, and weapons stored in the town. Of the latter, Greene found 1,700 militia muskets that were so rusted as to be completely useless. He exploded in a rage: "These are the happy effects of defending the Country with Militia from which the Good Lord deliver us!" The wagons loaded, Greene ordered them to Trading Ford on the Yadkin River and dispatched another flurry of letters. He ordered Huger to hurry his men along. With the same express, he urged Henry Lee to join the main army as soon as possible, stating that his "anxiety to collect the cavalry is very great" since he could not challenge Tarleton's operations unless he had a "superiority in cavalry." Maj. Ichabod Burnet, Greene's aide, wrote Lee that if he did not hurry, he would "lose the opportunity of acquiring wreaths of laurels." In the meantime, the Flying Army was already moving: "Next day, being the 2d . . . crossed the River Yatkin [Yadkin], which the enemy approached on the 3d."[29]

In the early morning hours of 3 February, Greene and Morgan rode to Trading Ford and watched the army crossing in the almost constant rain. The river was rapidly rising. Delaware Lt. Thomas Anderson reported "every step being up to our knees in mud [and] it raining on us all the way." A small group of Virginia militia commanded by Brig. Gen. Edward Stevens was already at the ford. Stevens wrote Thomas Jefferson several days later that the "rain that fell the night before raised the river in such a manner as made it difficult to cross even in boats." Greene and Morgan were running out of time. Even with the river up, the knowledge that Cornwallis was only a day's march behind meant the Whigs had no choice but to risk the crossing.[30]

Greene's presumptions about Cornwallis were correct. The British rested on 2 February, but the following morning marched for Salisbury. They entered the town that afternoon and halted to pillage any food and supplies left by Greene's army. Cornwallis's men also freed a number of prisoners held in the Salisbury jail and later wrote to Greene protesting their condition, stating they had evidently been held without "common sustenance."[31]

At midnight on 3 February, the British van led by Brigadier General O'Hara reached Trading Ford. The men had marched all day, nearly twenty miles in rain and mud. In the darkness, they stumbled upon baggage wagons stuck in the mud. A small party of North Carolina militia, including Capt. Joseph Graham, remained on the west side of the river, but Greene, Morgan, and the Continentals had crossed. On the eastern bank, the boats they had used were tied to shore, safely out of British hands. Graham's party ambushed the British, firing "two or three volleys," and then fled "two miles" down-river, where they crossed. Graham's men "took out the horses" as they passed bogged-down wagons, taking away any possibility the British could put them to use. Mother Nature had played her hand against Cornwallis again.[32]

As Greene and Morgan rested safely north of the river, Cornwallis's artillery fired a few errant rounds across, but they did little damage. The exhausted British army camped and spent the remainder of 4 February resting. The Americans did not. Morgan, despite a severe bout of rheumatism and debilitating "piles," marched for Guilford Courthouse with his Continentals. Sergeant Major Seymour noted, "On the 4th we received intelligence that the enemy had crossed the river at a shallow ford above where we lay, upon which we marched all that night, taking the road towards Guilford Court House, which we reached on the 6th." Despite constant rain, Morgan's men covered the forty-seven miles in just forty-eight hours. Greene remained behind at the Yadkin with a small detachment, watching Cornwallis. On 5 February he followed Morgan and wrote Huger again, ordering him to abandon hope of uniting with Greene's army near the ford, but to rendezvous at Guilford Courthouse. He noted that the "contempt he [Cornwallis] has for our Army . . . may precipitate him into some capital misfortune."[33]

Greene continued sending letters to the region's militia commanders. He first dispatched an express to Col. James Martin, commander of the Guilford

County militia, urging him to gather men and supplies and to send Greene the "most intelligible man . . . well acquainted" with the local roads, distances, and settlements. Greene then requested commanders of the "militia in the rear of the British army" to unite, attempt to get around the enemy, and join him. His request ended up in the hands of Rowan County militia commander Francis Locke, whose men made a brief, but determined stand against a party of Tarleton's dragoons along Second Creek near Salisbury on 5 February.[34]

On 6 February, Cornwallis headed north for Shallow Ford, twenty-five miles above Trading Ford. His men, growing accustomed to the rain pelting them as they struggled over the wet, red clay roads, made the distance and crossed the ford by the following morning. Since both armies were experienced campaigners, marching at the rate of only one mile an hour is a telling commentary on what the men endured. It was slow, tough slogging in miserable, cold, wet, conditions. They passed through the Moravian communities including Bethania, Bethabara, and Salem. The Moravians, a pacifist religious sect that originated in Bohemia and Moravia in the present-day Czech Republic, had settled in the North Carolina Piedmont in the 1750s, having migrated south from several Pennsylvania communities they had established in the 1740s. Tarleton wrote admiringly of the "mild and hospitable disposition of the inhabitants, being assisted by the well-cultivated and fruitful plantations in their possession, afforded abundant and seasonable supplies to the King's troops during their passage through this district." The Moravians may not have had the same cheery view as Tarleton; Whig militia had been plundering the area in the weeks prior to the British arrival. Two days previous to the British arrival in Bethania, a party of "Liberty Men arrived, who had been driven out of Georgia and South Carolina," and demanded food in a rough fashion.[35]

The British army arrived at Bethania, a small community of 91 people, "about noon" on 9 February. Several officers were quartered in the village, including a commissary named Knecht from Switzerland and a German Reformed preacher, who may have been the chaplain of the Von Bose Regiment. The British also requisitioned cattle, and "more than sixty were killed during the day, of which about thirty were seized here; this did not include the sheep, geese and chickens which they took." Maj. Richard England, Cornwallis's quartermaster general, also impressed seventeen horses for the artillery, although Moravian Johann Jacob Ernst noted somewhat gloatingly that "six of these had been taken secretly from English teamsters." A company of the

British Legion was sent to nearby Bethabara, a similarly small village of only 81 inhabitants, where "100 gallons of brandy, more than 300 lbs. of bread, and all the meal that was ready" were requisitioned.[36]

Cornwallis's army left Bethania at 7:00 A.M. the following morning and arrived at Bethabara. According to the journal of Lorenz Bagge, the "English army was passing through our town from eight o'clock in the morning until nearly two in the afternoon." Cornwallis must have been wary of his men's need for rum, for Bagge noted that "good order was maintained, and a guard was stationed near the tavern, where the road turns toward Salem, and another guard was placed in front of the tavern. Another guard was placed at the still-house." The British took the goods they had earlier requisitioned, as well as "eighteen of our largest oxen."[37]

Passing through Bethabara, the British moved on to Salem, a small town of 167 inhabitants and the center of the Moravian settlements. Advance elements began arriving at 10:00 A.M., and "the entire army followed in irregular order, continuing until four o'clock in the afternoon." A large party of refugees followed them. Salem diarist Johann Michael Graff wrote that among the army were "many people who to save their lives had placed themselves, their wives and children under the protection of the army." Graff was quite critical of these individuals, noting, "The people who followed the baggage stole various things at the store and in the houses." Cornwallis, several of his officers, and exiled Royal governor Josiah Martin met with the town's leading men for a short time before rejoining the column. The British camped outside the town on the plantation of Friedrich Müller, their encampment reportedly extending "about two and one half miles." Cornwallis was now in an excellent position to place his forces between Greene's army and the Dan River, the next major watercourse before the Virginia line.[38]

Greene and Morgan reached Guilford on 7 February. Morgan and the Flying Army were already there, and the next day Huger came up from Cheraw. Sergeant Major Seymour recorded, "General Greene's Army assembled on the 5th from Chiraw [sic] Hills, and in a most dismal condition for the want of clothing, especially shoes, being obliged to march, the chief part of them, barefoot from Chiraw Hills. Here however the men were supplied with some shoes, but not half enough." For a member of the Flying Army to comment on the "dismal condition" of the main army, as Seymour did, provides sufficient evidence that marching around North Carolina in the winter wore out men, clothing, and equipment.[39]

Huger and Lee arrived and camped "in the woods a few hundred yards in the rear of the courthouse," along the Reedy Fork Road. The Southern Army was reunited, but Greene had only a few more than 2,000 exhausted men, 600 of whom were "poorly armed" militia. The Continentals were immediately placed on their usual footing and issued orders to clean and mend their gear. Greene's orders to Williams's men stated, "The officers will please to be particularly attentive to the care of their men[']s arms and ammunition. The Musketts are not to be unbreach'd, nor the locks taken to pieces. . . . Cleaning the locks is more Servicely and affectually done by boiling them in clean water and brushing out the dirt with a bunch of Hoggs Bristles or Feathers, and applying a little Neatsfoot Oyl." In the army, life continued more or less as normal, despite the pressures of the pursuit, especially when officers were attentive to the little details.[40]

The morning of 9 February, Greene wrote Thomas Sumter, "If I should risque a General Action in our present situation, we stand ten chances to one of getting defeated, & if defeated all the Southern states must fall." Despite his known aversion to councils of war, Greene called a meeting of his principal commanders that afternoon. Noting the terrible strategic position they were in, and taking into account the condition of the 1,426 "badly armed and distressed for want of clothing" Continentals with the army, Greene and his officers agreed that they had to "avoid a General Action at all Events, and that the Army ought to retreat immediately over the Roanoke River."[41]

Greene organized a light corps to serve as both a decoy and a blocking force to delay and harass Cornwallis's army, thereby allowing the American main force time to reach the Dan. The first thing was to build up the strength of the Flying Army companies that had been worn down by the Cowpens campaign and subsequent marching. To bring them back up to sixty men, "the First Battalion of Maryland Troops is to furnish Twenty five Privates, and the second Battalion thirty five privates for Light Infantry to fill up the Companies agreeable to General orders of Yesterday—they are to be detail'd from the Companies from which they were before drafted according to the strength of each." The larger number of men supplied by the 2nd Battalion reflects the heavy casualties (25 percent) suffered by Kirkwood's Delawares at Cowpens.[42]

Greene intended to give this command to Morgan, but upon his leaving the army, the honor went to Col. Otho Holland Williams. Williams had 700 men under his command: William Washington's horsemen from the 1st and 3rd Continental Light Dragoons, Henry Lee's Partizan Legion infantry and cavalry, a 280-man detachment of Virginia, Maryland, and Delaware light infantry under Lt. Col. John Eager Howard, plus 60 Virginia riflemen led by Capt. David Campbell.[43]

Greene planned a rapid withdrawal to the Dan River, where his men would be taken across on boats collected by Lt. Col. Edward Carrington. The ferries Greene intended to use were actually northeast of Guilford Courthouse. Dix's Ferry was near modern-day Danville, Virginia. Twenty miles east (downstream) of Dix's stood Irwin's Ferry (also known as Irvine's), and four miles downstream was Boyd's Ferry. Carrington reported that he had found six boats between Irwin's and Dix's. Greene sent word to assemble every boat, canoe, and anything else that floated and could hold men at the two lower ferries. Greene would march the main army toward the lower ferries, while Williams made a feint toward the upper crossings to mislead Cornwallis. For his part, Cornwallis had no knowledge of Carrington's efforts to bring the boats to a single location and felt that Greene would only be able to cross at the shallower fords, located in the upper reaches of the Dan nearer Salem.[44]

After the council ended, Greene sent letters to supply officers ordering them to move all baggage and supply wagons over the Dan River into Virginia. Patrick Henry received a plea from Greene to raise 1,500 militiamen from Virginia counties bordering North Carolina. Baron Von Steuben, commanding American forces near Richmond, was requested to begin "preparing musket cartridges" at Prince Edward Courthouse. Greene also sent expresses back to Francis Locke and Thomas Polk ordering them to "hang upon the enemies['] rear," harassing and delaying the British column. He also wrote North Carolina governor Abner Nash, stating, "Should I leave the state, I shall return the moment I find the army in a condition to take the field." He also admonished Nash on the condition of the state's militia and their arms. "I cannot stop this letter without one observation. Such a waste of arms and ammunition as I have seen in different parts of this state is enough to exhaust all the Arsenals of Europe." In a 10 February letter to Greene, the Marquis de Malmedy, a French mercenary organizing North Carolina dragoons in Halifax, indicated that Nash and other government officials severely underestimated the threat at their doorstep. He claimed the North Carolina leadership simply dismissed suggestions to raise more Continental troops, and "the opinion of the majority is that Lord Cornwallis has crossed the Catabaw [Catawba] only in order to retake the prisoners of General Morgan."[45]

Greene then said good-bye to Daniel Morgan. Morgan had survived a flogging by the British during the French and Indian War, fought nearly five years as a Continental officer, including an extended period on a prisoner-of-war hulk, taken part in nearly every northern campaign, and destroyed Tarleton's force at Cowpens. In the end, no British ball or blade, but instead rheumatism and failing health, finally wore him down. The "Old Wagoner" was put into a carriage and taken home to his farm in the Shenandoah Valley. After Morgan's departure, Greene supposedly stated, "Great generals are scarce—there are few Morgans to be found."[46]

While Greene said his good-byes, Cornwallis determined his own course of action. After arriving in Salem and encamping at Friedrich Müller's, the British could have marched northeast in an effort to block Greene from the fords along the Dan. Cornwallis, unaware that Huger's division had already reached Greene's forces, chose instead to march southeast in a misguided effort to block the two columns from uniting.[47]

While the British camped at Müller's farm, Greene dispatched Colonel Williams's light corps to Bruce's Cross Roads, roughly seven miles northwest of Guilford Courthouse. Their sense of normalcy changed the next day when Greene headed the main force toward the Dan River while Colonel Williams was "ordered to take command of the Light Infantry, Cavalry, etc, which form'd the Light Army on the Retreat to Dan River." Sergeant Major Seymour recorded the following in his journal:

> We marched from here on the ninth inst., taking the road towards
> Dan River, which we reached on the fourteenth, after a march of two
> hundred and fifty miles from the time we left our encampment at Pacolet
> River. By this time it must be expected that the army, especially the light
> troops, were very much fatigued both with traveling and want of sleep,
> for you must understand that we marched for the most part both day
> and night, the main army of the British being close in our rear, so that
> we had not scarce time to cook our victuals, their whole attention being
> on our light troops.

Williams's orders were to deceive Cornwallis and draw the British away from Greene's main force. The Marylander sent the light horse of Washington's Continental dragoons and Lee's Legion further west and northwest to make contact with the British army. Lt. Col. Henry Lee later described the effect of Williams's movements as "judicious" and said that they "checked the rapidity of his [Cornwallis's] march to give time for his long extended line to condense."[48]

On 11 February, Cornwallis marched east, but upon reaching Abbott's Creek Meeting House and Idol's Tavern, he learned Huger had reached

Greene. Realizing their mistake, the British turned northeast and began marching along the Salisbury Road. Local Whigs spotted the British forces, and one rode into the American light infantry camp to give Williams and Lee the news. Later that afternoon, Williams reported to Greene that, "Accident informed me the Enemy were within six or Eight miles of my Quarters. I detached Col. Lee with a Troop of Dragoons & put the rest of the Light Troops in Motion to Cross the Haw River at a Bridge." Seymour noted, "We marched from here, General Green's Army taking one road and the light troops another, being joined the next day by Colonel Lee's horse and infantry. This day we received intelligence that the British Army was advancing very close in our rear, upon which Colonel Lee detached a party of horse to intercept them, who meeting with their vanguard, consisting of an officer and twenty men, which they killed, wounded and made prisoners, all but one man."[49]

Lee, whose troopers were enjoying a late-morning breakfast, in turn dispatched a troop of the legion commanded by Capt. James Armstrong along with the local Whig to find the British. As the remainder of his men finished what they could of their meal and gathered their gear, he ordered them to follow Armstrong's detachment.[50] Lee caught up with Armstrong after only a mile, having sent word to him to proceed slowly. The young Virginian, spotting no sign of the British, "began to believe that his guide, however well affected, was certainly in mistake." Lee ordered Armstrong to remain with three dragoons and the local, and then the rest of his force went "to return to breakfast." The local protested that his "meager poney" was not capable of continuing on, so Lee ordered his bugler, James Gillies, to exchange horses with the man. Lee then sent Gillies back in advance of the legion to inform Williams of his position.[51]

As Lee rode back to his camp, gunfire in his rear announced that Armstrong and his small picket had indeed run into the British. Lee took the legion into a patch of woods along the road and watched as first Armstrong and then Capt. Patrick Miller's troop of Tarleton's Legion rode by, Lee being "unperceived by the pursued and the pursuers." Dispatching a lieutenant with several men to guard their rear, Lee set out in pursuit of Miller's dragoons, thus placing himself between the British dragoons and their main force. Armstrong's men escaped the British troopers, but young Gillies did not. Unable to escape on the local man's worn-out horse, the young bugler was "immediately unhorsed and sabered several times while prostrate on the ground." Lee described Gillies as "one of the band of music, and exclusively

*Col. Otho Holland Williams (1749–94), Maryland Continental Brigade. Oil painting by Charles Wilson Peale. Independence National Historical Park.*

devoted in the field to his horse, used in conveying orders. Too small to wield a sword, he was armed only with a pistol." Lee pointed out that Gillies had no weapon to defend himself from the British dragoons, as his pistol was with the "countryman mounted on his horse."[52]

Enraged by the assault on Gillies, Lee charged directly into Miller's troopers. "The enemy was crushed on the first charge: most of them were killed or prostrated; and the residue, with their captain, attempted to escape." Lee sent Lt. Stephen Lewis in pursuit with orders to give no quarter. Lewis soon returned with Miller and several dragoons who were "cut in the face, neck, and shoulders." Lee reprimanded Lewis for not killing them and then told Miller to "prepare for death." Miller pleaded with Lee, telling him that he gave orders to save the bugler but that his dragoons "being intoxicated, all his efforts were ineffectual." The British captain then temporarily swayed Lee, proclaiming that his humane actions at Waxhaws had "been acknowledged by some of the Americans who escaped death on that bloody day." Going to the mortally wounded bugler's side, Lee asked him what had happened, which "confirmed the former impressions of Lee." The Virginian angrily handed Miller paper and pencil, ordering him to "note on paper whatever he might wish to make known to his friends," fully intent on hanging him in a nearby field.[53]

Before Lee could effect Miller's execution, the remainder of Tarleton's British Legion arrived. Miller and the other prisoners were sent on to Williams under guard, with Lee and his legion following a short distance behind. Precise casualty figures for the brief, bloody skirmish at Bruce's Cross Roads remain unknown. Lee claimed he left eighteen British Legion dragoons dead, although another account put the figure at seven. Lee lost only Gillies, who died shortly after telling his version to Lee. At 3:00 P.M., 11 February, Otho Holland Williams wrote Greene that he was sending the British prisoners on to headquarters and that the light corps had crossed the bridge over the Haw River.[54]

What occurred over the next few days remains debatable. Lee's version of events erroneously placed the Bruce's Cross Roads fight on 13 February and claimed that the Americans continued marching until they spotted campfires they believed to be Greene's main army in their front. They discovered that the fires had been lit by Greene on 11 February, according to Lee, and that the locals had kept them burning as a guide for Colonel Williams's light corps. Some historians have argued that the skirmish at Bruce's Cross Roads actually took place on 12 February, but Williams's letter describing the skirmish to Greene was written on the afternoon of 11 February. Greene wrote a letter on 12 February from "Caswell County," notifying North Carolina militia commander John Butler that he was retiring "as fast as I can towards Boyd's Ferry."[55]

Greene's army began crossing the Dan on 13 February. In a letter to Williams written that morning, Greene related that, "The night before last, as soon as I got your letter, I sent off the baggage and stores, with orders to cross as fast as they got to the river." He wrote dejectedly that the "North Carolina militia have all deserted us, except about 80 men. Majors and captains are among the deserters." Greene warned Williams, "You have the flower of the army, don't expose the men too much, lest our situation should grow more critical." Williams replied that evening at 7:00 P.M., stating that he had written Greene that morning from "Harts old Stores" and also from Chamber's Mill imploring his commander to march as hard as possible for the fords. The tone of Williams's letter is quite dejected and demoralized, evidenced by his statement that "My Dr General at Sun Down the Enemy were only 22 miles from you and may be in motion now or will most probably by 3 o[']Clock in the morning." He advised Greene, "Their intelligence is good. They maneuvered us from our Strong position at Chambers Mill and then mov'd with great rapidity." He closed the letter, "I'm confident we may remain in the State but whither it will not be at the risque of our Light Corps and whither we shall not be wasted by continual fatigue you can determine."[56]

Greene spent the night of 13 February supervising the crossing at Boyd's and Irwin's ferries. At 4:00 A.M., he sent word to Williams to march for the crossings with his light troops. He admitted that he "had not slept four hours" since he last saw Williams on 10 February and was preparing "for the worst." When word arrived at Williams's camp, he roused his men and had them on the road shortly thereafter. At 2:00 P.M., Greene sent a dispatch stating that the "greater part of our wagons are over, and the troops are crossing." Three and a half hours later, Greene sent another letter proclaiming that the army was across and jubilantly stating, "the stage is clear." According to historian William Gordon, as word of Greene's crossing passed along Williams's column, the cheers of the Americans could be heard by Cornwallis's van, led by O'Hara and Tarleton.[57]

As Greene completed crossing, Williams was pushing his men even harder. They were nearly thirty miles from Irwin's and had to set an incredibly fast pace. Cornwallis's advance troops were right on their heels. Williams's infantry and William Washington's dragoons arrived at Irwin's Ferry in the early evening hours. The exhausted men began crossing under torchlight. Greene apparently waited until Williams arrived and then crossed with him. Lee's Legion crossed at Boyd's Ferry, the men in boats and the horses swimming. Lee later claimed that the last men to cross were himself and Lt. Col. Edward Carrington, the unsung hero of the river crossing.[58]

O'Hara later claimed he arrived twelve hours after the Americans crossed. Cornwallis had ordered his main force to march at 4:00 A.M. on 15 February with "no more baggage than their canteens, and the men will leave their packs behind them." Tarleton claimed his dragoons arrived much earlier than O'Hara's infantry, finding "some works evacuated, which had been constructed to cover the retreat of the enemy, who six hours before had finished their passage, and were then encamped on the opposite bank." If the last of Greene's men got across by midnight on 14 February, then the British likely arrived around 7:30 or 8:00 A.M. Bloody Ban, who rarely offered compliments to his American enemy, stated of Greene's retreat, "Every measure of the Americans, during their march from the Catawba to Virginia, was judiciously designed and vigorously executed."[59]

One reason Cornwallis's army may have lost the race was the large number of prisoners and camp followers associated with the column. Provost marshal records indicate that nearly one hundred American prisoners, many of them captured at Torrence's Tavern, were being marched with the army. These, along with the large number of women, were mouths to feed that didn't carry muskets. They took up provisions and undoubtedly marched slower than the infantrymen. On 30 January, Cornwallis had ordered, "When the Brigade Marches the Women, Sick & Weakly Men, will March in the Rear of the Second Battalion . . . and form a Guard to the Baggage." He also had major discipline problems with the female camp followers, noting that they were "the sources of the most infamous plundering." Greene had his camp followers and prisoners as well, but there is no record left of any disciplinary or logistical problems associated with them.[60]

With the army having made it across the swollen Dan, and with all nearby boats on the north side, Greene could finally get a few hours' rest. The next morning, Maj. Ichabod Burnet penned a jovial letter proclaiming Greene's army "safe over the river and . . . laughing at the enemy who are on the opposite side." There is no written record of Cornwallis's thoughts upon hearing of Greene's crossing. In a letter to Secretary of State Lord George Germain written a month later, Cornwallis blamed his inability to intercept Greene on "defective" intelligence, "bad roads, and the passage of many deep creeks and bridges destroyed by the enemy's light troops." He had pursued Greene's army for three weeks, covering some 250 miles over muddy, frost-encrusted roads, in torrents of rain and sleet, crossed several major waterways, and fought numerous skirmishes. The Race to the Dan was over, and Nathanael Greene had won.[61]

CHAPTER TWO **FROM THE DAN TO
GUILFORD COURTHOUSE**

On 19 February 1781, advance portions of Maj. Gen. Nathanael Greene's
Southern Army crossed the Dan River, carrying the war back into North
Carolina. He sent word ahead to Brig. Gen. Andrew Pickens ordering him
to utilize his militia forces to harass Cornwallis's army. Pickens had been
appointed overall commander for the Mecklenburg and Rowan county militias. This positioned him over Col. Francis Locke, who nominally led the
Yadkin Valley militia after William Lee Davidson's death at Cowan's Ford. In
response, Locke and most of the militia of Mecklenburg and Rowan Counties had gone home, but Pickens did have nearly 150 militiamen from Surry
and Wilkes Counties under Col. John Armstrong and Maj. Joseph Winston,
as well as nearly 100 Caswell County militiamen under Col. William Moore.
In addition to the North Carolinians, Pickens led several South Carolina and
Georgia companies. He reported to Greene that his 700 men would follow
their orders although they were "universally bent" on an "expedition into
South Carolina" and that the Rowan County militiamen were deserting in
droves. Pickens referred to the fugitives as being "among the worst Men" he
had ever commanded.[1]

Initially, Greene sent an advance party of Lee's Legion with two Maryland Continental companies to operate with Pickens. The two forces united 23 February when Pickens's men almost fired on Lee's men, mistaking their green coats for those of Tarleton's British Legion. Capt. Joseph Graham, a North Carolina militiaman, reported that his men, fearing Tarleton was upon them, decided "too late to retreat, so prepared to fight," but the situation was resolved before bloodshed occurred. Greene appeared that evening with a small escort, gave his commanders their orders, and then returned across the Dan.[2]

That evening, Lee and Pickens learned that Tarleton's British Legion was encamped nearby. Cornwallis, whose men had arrived in Hillsborough on 20 February, had sent "Bloody Ban" with 200 dragoons, 150 infantrymen of the 33rd Foot, and 100 Ansbach *Jägers* (jaegers) west of the Haw River to protect local loyalist militiamen hastening to join the British army. Lt. Col. Henry Lee later recalled that the countryside through which Tarleton passed had been completely plundered, and that local women told him the Tories were organizing between the Haw and Deep Rivers.[3]

For two days, Pickens and Lee followed Tarleton. On 25 February a party of nearly 400 Tories under the command of Col. John Pyle, a local doctor, ran into advance elements of Lee's Legion. Mistakenly thinking the green-jacketed men before them were the British Legion, Pyle's Tories calmly moved to the roadside, waiting on "Tarleton's" passage. Lee rode the entire length of the Tory line "dropping occasionally expressions complimentary to the good looks and commendable conduct of his loyal friends." Lee argued that fighting began as he was shaking hands with Pyle and preparing to reveal his true identity. However, North Carolinian Joseph Graham argued that it started when legion major Joseph Eggleston asked a Tory, "Whose man are you?" The man answered, "A friend of his majesty," and Eggleston cut him down.[4]

The Whigs made quick work of Pyle's force. At least ninety Loyalists were sabered to death. The remainder, most of whom were wounded, fled. Pyle, seriously injured, supposedly hid in a nearby swamp, with only his nose above the water. Lee lost only one horse in the engagement; a small price for what many of his men saw as revenge for Tarleton's reputed actions against Col. Abraham Buford's Virginia Continentals at Waxhaws the previous year. Many of Buford's men had reportedly been killed after surrendering. Pyle's men paid for Tarleton's indiscretions. Moses Hall, a North Carolina militiaman, remembered seeing six Tory prisoners "hewed to death with broadswords" when a Whig shouted, "Remember Buford!"[5]

Pyle's Defeat, as the event became known, proved devastating to Cornwallis's ability to gather loyalist support. A large force of Tories, directly under the supposed protection of Tarleton, had been slaughtered. The disaster was made worse when several of Pyle's men, having escaped Lee, approached Tarleton's camp, where they were mistaken for Whigs and cut down. British captain Forbes Champagne of the 23rd Foot optimistically wrote, "this unparalleled cruelty serves only to make our friends more steady and zealous in assisting us to restore their former legal and constitutional government." Champagne could not have been more wrong. After the debacle, Cornwallis retained little hope of a mass loyalist uprising in the Carolina Piedmont. Andrew Pickens succinctly summed up the impact of the rout, claiming, "It has knocked up Toryism altogether in this part."[6]

In the evening hours following Pyle's Defeat, a party of approximately 300 Virginia riflemen from Montgomery and Botetourt Counties under the command of Colonels William Preston and Hugh Crockett were also maneuvering after Tarleton. Preston's men, most whom were veterans of King's Mountain, had intended to join Greene's main army but could not find it along the Haw River. The Virginians had been marching for several days and had passed through Bethabara, where they "behaved very well, according to their Colonel's orders, and by 9 o[']clock in the evening it was so quiet that no one would have known that so many men were in the town." Preston and Crockett finally located Pickens and Lee in the early morning hours of 25 February. Pickens apparently split the Virginians into two halves, sending William Preston with 150 men and a small group of Guilford County militia under Lt. Col. John Paisley south of the Haw River to pursue Tarleton as well as a second group of loyalists reported to be assembling. Crockett was sent with 160 men "well fixd with Riffles" to find Greene. Crockett wrote Greene on 26 March that he fully expected a detachment of nearly 400 men to join him in "two or three days," although exactly who those individuals were remains uncertain. He joined Otho Holland Williams's light infantry that evening. A letter from Williams to Greene sent after Crockett's arrival likely indicates why Crockett's men were split off from Preston's detachment: the Marylander noted that the Virginians had no provisions or ammunition and pleaded with Greene to send "with all possible dispatch powder and Lead for 500 rifles."[7]

While Crockett's men marched for Greene's army, the detachment under Preston and Paisley located Tarleton's force; but before they could launch an attack, rifleman John Ewing noted, "a tory deserted from our army and

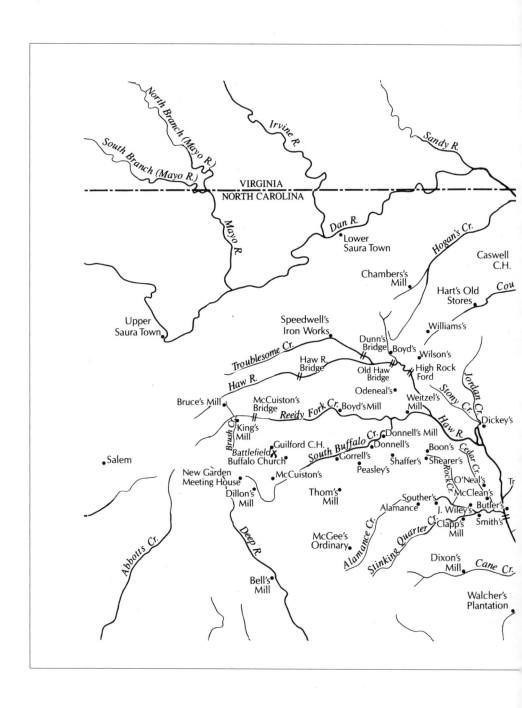

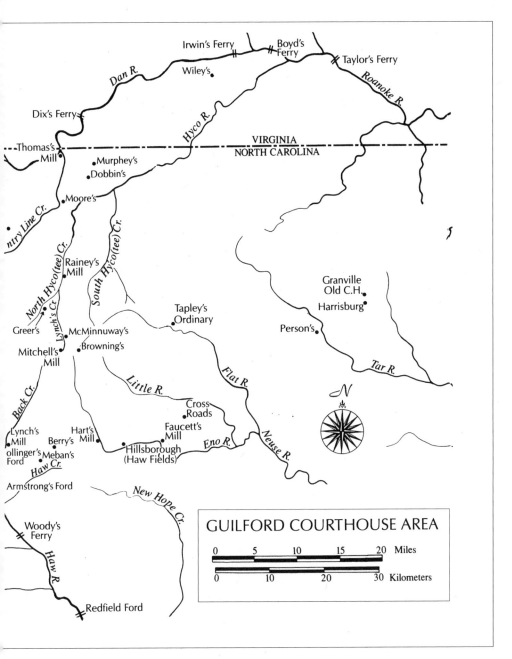

Irwin's Ferry
Boyd's Ferry
Taylor's Ferry
Dan R.
Wiley's
Roanoke R.
Dix's Ferry
Hyco R.
VIRGINIA
NORTH CAROLINA
Thomas's Mill
Murphey's
Dobbin's
ntry Line Cr.
Moore's
North Hyco(tee) Cr.
South Hyco(tee) Cr.
Lynch's Cr.
Rainey's Mill
Granville Old C.H.
Harrisburg
Tapley's Ordinary
Person's
Greer's
McMinnuway's
Mitchell's Mill
Browning's
Tar R.
Little R.
Flat R.
Back Cr.
Cross Roads
N
Lynch's Mill
Hart's Mill
Berry's
Faucett's Mill
ollinger's Ford
Meban's
Hillsborough (Haw Fields)
Eno R.
Neuse R.
Haw Cr.
Armstrong's Ford
New Hope Cr.
Woody's Ferry
Haw R.
Redfield Ford

## GUILFORD COURTHOUSE AREA

| 0 | 5 | 10 | 15 | 20 | Miles |
| 0 | | 10 | 20 | | 30 | Kilometers |

MAP THREE *The Guilford Courthouse area. From Showman et al.,* The Papers of General Nathanael Greene, *vol. 7 (1994). Courtesy of the Rhode Island Historical Society.*

gave information of the contemplated attack and Tarleton left his camp in the night & crossed the Haw River at a place called the High Rock Ford [in Rockingham County]." Ewing contended that the riflemen pursued Tarleton until they received word from Lee and Pickens, who "informed us we must retreat, for we were in the vicinity of Cornwallis' main army." Preston's detachment then rejoined Pickens and Lee. Tarleton's version claimed his forces were preparing to attack the American encampment when an express arrived ordering him to return to the main army.[8]

Cornwallis recalled Tarleton because Greene's army began moving across the Dan on 22 February. For over a week, Greene had rested his army and replenished supplies in Halifax County, Virginia. At the same time, Virginia governor Thomas Jefferson granted Greene permission to "take horses to mount your cavalry, and I will attempt to have it justified." Greene had already ordered Lt. Col. William Washington to "impress a sufficient number of good Dragoon horses to mount all the men in your detachment who are dismounted."[9]

Greene also received word of reinforcements. Brig. Gen. Edward Stevens was marching toward Greene with "several hundred" Virginia militia from the western half of the state, fresh from delivering the Cowpens prisoners. On 25 February Jefferson wrote Brig. Gen. Robert Lawson, ordering him to move forward with his command to meet Greene and reporting that he had "ordered out all the militia of Cumberland, Powhatan, Chesterfield, Dinwiddie, Amelia, Lunenberg, and Mecklenburg who could be armed and a fourth part of Washington, Montgomery, Botetourt, Henry and Pittsylvania." He also noted that the Charlotte and Halifax militia were already in the field, and Col. Charles Lynch had raised a corps of Bedford County riflemen. In addition, word arrived of "1,000" riflemen from the Shenandoah under Col. William Campbell who were likewise headed south.[10]

Cornwallis responded by moving his army west of Hillsborough. In part, he was reacting to Greene's movements, but his army also greatly wanted provisions, having consumed all Hillsborough could produce. Cornwallis wrote that he was "amongst timid friends and adjoining inveterate rebels." The army's ration of spirits had run out, prompting several desertions. On 22 February the men were warned, "It is with great concern that Lord Cornwallis hears every day reports of Soldiers being taken by the Enemy, in consequence of their straggling out of camp in search of whiskey." Three days later, as Pyle's men died at the hands of Lee's Legion, Cornwallis established camp on the south side of Alamance Creek, between the Haw and Deep Rivers.[11]

Learning of Cornwallis's movements, Greene ordered Col. Otho Holland Williams's light troops to coordinate with Lee, Pickens, and Preston to shield the main army from the British. For the next three weeks, the armies were almost never still. Delaware captain Robert Kirkwood served under Williams and recorded that his men marched a total of 230 miles, including 60 miles in one two-day span. The weather during this period consisted of late winter rains and sleet that clogged the roads with mud, exacerbating the hardship of both armies' soldiers.[12]

Several small skirmishes occurred between American and British patrols. On 26 February, a British attack on American pickets at Fletcher's Mill along Alamance Creek killed Maj. Micajah Lewis of the North Carolina militia, a former Continental officer. Lewis, commanding militiamen of Surry and Wilkes Counties from Col. Benjamin Cleveland's regiment, died after being shot through "both thighs while on a stratagem towards the enemy's piquet." Shortly afterwards, Pickens and Lee united their forces with those under Williams.[13]

Col. Williams sent Lee's Legion, some of Preston's riflemen under Maj. Thomas Rowland, as well as the Rowan, Lincoln, and Mecklenburg militias under Captains Joseph Graham and Joseph Dixon to patrol along Alamance Creek on 2 March. In addition to the Continentals and militia, a small party of Catawba Indian scouts under Capt. Michael Boykin accompanied the force. Following closely as a reserve were Williams's Continental light infantry, Preston's main body, William Washington's Continental light dragoons, and the remainder of Pickens's militia. A foraging party under Capt. Richard Hovenden of the British Legion spotted Lee's men and relayed the information to Tarleton. The British leader advanced a portion of the legion, the light infantry company of the Guards Brigade led by Capt. Francis Dundas, and 150 men from Webster's Brigade under Captains James Ingram of the 33rd and Forbes Champagne of the 23rd.[14]

Lee prepared an ambush for Tarleton. Capt. Michael Rudolph positioned a number of dragoons behind a double-pen barn, while the riflemen and militia advanced through the underbrush toward the British. Graham noted that the forest was so thick that the "foe could not be seen until they were within 60 or 70 steps [50 yards] of him when a heavy fire commenced." The Catawba, "who had hitherto been very alert could not stand it[,] turned and took off like a Turkey." Most of the Americans fired at least three rounds before a bayonet charge by the 33rd Foot forced the riflemen to retreat. Tarleton's dragoons evidently engaged some North Carolina militia, as one, Robert

Harris, lost his right hand to a saber cut. As the militia, riflemen, and dragoons retired, they were covered by fire from Capt. Robert Kirkwood's Delawares and Capt. Edward Oldham's Marylanders.[15]

When the American detachment fell back to the protection of Williams's Continentals, Tarleton's men broke off the pursuit. At least ten Americans were killed and several more wounded. Many casualties were transported to the Moravian settlements. Johann Michael Graff recorded meeting some on the road from Salem to Bethabara, "many with empty horses returning from a skirmish which had been on the 2nd. Some wounded were also brought to Salem." British losses are unknown, but one account places them at seventeen dead. A local farmer, Barney Clapp, reported to Greene that he watched the British carry off one officer dead and bury several enlisted men; however, no known officer was killed. Capt. James Ingram of the 33rd Foot was wounded, as was Lt. Thomas Chapman of the 23rd. The next day, Capt. Joseph Graham returned to the battlefield and noted that the British had buried their dead but not the Americans.[16]

The following days proved quite disappointing for Greene, now headquartered in Guilford County, only six miles from Cornwallis's army. Greene had severe problems to face because his remaining North Carolina militia were grumbling that their tours of service were up. Despite the entreaties of Greene and fellow officers for them to stay just one more week, the men deserted in droves. Some Virginia riflemen under Williams refused to serve under a Continental, as "they say they are Volunteers, and shod be treated with distinction." Henry Lee reported that "the militia company now with me have furnished twelve riflemen to act with me for three months, on condition that the remainder be discharged. I have bargained with them on these terms." Greene sent the small contingent to join Williams's light troops south of the Haw River along with Surry County, North Carolina, militia under Maj. Joseph Winston.[17]

The majority of the Virginia riflemen were mounted, and their horses severely taxed the Southern Army's supply base. When Williams and Lee proposed that the militia horses be sent home, the suggestion was met with utter contempt. Nevertheless, Greene approved the order. Johann Michael Graff noted that on 4 March, "Today and the following day about a hundred and fifty horses passed, returning from the army for lack of forage" through Salem. That same evening Lorenz Bagge of Bethabara recorded, "one party after another came from the army with riderless horses. It was said that these were all Colonel Preston's horses and about fifty of his men."[18]

Further demonstrating Greene's problems with the militia, Col. William Campbell appeared on 5 March with just 60 men from Washington County, far short of the 1,000 riflemen that had been promised. As with Preston's and Crockett's detachments, Campbell had passed through the Moravian settlements, where he quickly took control of deteriorating relations between plundering Whig militias and the local citizens. For two weeks after the British had marched through the area, roving bands of marauders and North Carolina militia had terrorized the Moravians, claiming that by aiding Cornwallis they had proven themselves true loyalists. Capt. William Lenoir of Wilkes County had "declared roundly that we were his enemies." At one point the Salem congregation was told, albeit falsely, that the town was to be burned by Maj. Joseph Winston, who instead offered them as much protection as he could in the form of a written guarantee of protection. However, Winston's order was largely ignored. Upon arriving, Campbell reestablished order, going as far as to give "emphatic warning to Captain Lenoir of Wilkes, concerning the bad behavior of himself and his men."[19]

Despite his disappointment at Campbell's small numbers, Greene realized a more pressing issue was the deteriorating situation between his regulars and militia. If things seemed bad, they would worsen tenfold the next day. At 3:00 A.M. on 6 March, Cornwallis sent a large force under Lt. Col. James Webster and Tarleton toward Weitzel's Mill near Reedy Fork. Sgt. Roger Lamb, 23rd Foot, claimed that Cornwallis gave orders "to beat up the American post at Reedy Fork" in an effort to "allure Greene, who lay in the direction of Guilford Courthouse, to a general engagement." At that moment, Colonel Williams's detachment was posted well south of the Haw River, while the remainder of Greene's army was north of it. Williams had no idea Cornwallis was moving, writing Greene in the early morning hours of 6 March, "The British Army, about Seven miles off, remains where it is. While Lord Cornwallis keeps his present position, like a Bear with his Stern in a corner, I cannot Attack him but with tooth and nail." While Williams wrote, Cornwallis moved. His lordship had a perfect opportunity to destroy a sizable portion of Greene's army if Webster's and Tarleton's men could position themselves between the river and Williams's rear. Luckily for Williams, a patrol spotted the British advancing through the early morning fog about 5:30 A.M. and correctly guessed their intentions. For the next several hours the two detachments raced for the ford over Reedy Fork Creek.[20]

Williams's force included the Maryland Light Infantry, Kirkwood's Delaware company, Lee's Legion, and William Washington's dragoons. Williams also had Pickens's South Carolinians, Georgians, and the North Carolina militia companies from Mecklenburg, Lincoln, and Surry Counties. Rounding out his force were approximately 410 Virginia riflemen led by Colonels Preston, Crockett, and Campbell. The British force racing Williams for Reedy Fork included the 23rd and 33rd Regiments, the 2nd Battalion, 71st Highlanders, and a company of Ansbach jaegers under the command of Lt. Col. James Webster, 33rd Foot. They were augmented by the Guards Light Infantry Company, led by Captains John Goodricke and Francis Dundas, and four field pieces commanded by Lt. John McLeod. Seventy-four British Legion dragoons under Lt. Col. Tarleton provided an advance party guarding against surprise.

Williams won the race, although it was close. As his Continentals began crossing Reedy Fork, the British appeared. Williams posted Pickens's militia and Preston's and Campbell's riflemen south of the ford to provide covering fire while the Continentals crossed to set up another battle line. Williams was under direct orders from Greene to protect the Continentals and dragoons at all costs. By all accounts, the riflemen acquitted themselves well, pouring an effective fire into the advancing British. In the low river bottom, gun smoke became so thick that little of the action could be seen. Joseph Graham, sitting atop the ridge, north of the ford, reported, "The air was calm and dense, then the militia were seen running down the hill from under the smoke. The ford was crowded, many crossing the watercourse at other places. Some, it was said, were drowned."[21]

The Continentals provided some covering fire for the militia and riflemen to escape. The 33rd and Guards Light Infantry forded the river in pursuit as the riflemen retreated. When one group of British soldiers faltered, Lt. Col. James Webster personally rode his horse into the river, admonishing them and ordering them forward. According to Lt. Col. Henry Lee's *Memoirs*, twenty-five riflemen, veterans of King's Mountain personally selected by Lee, were posted in an old log schoolhouse near the ford, whose entire purpose was to "hold themselves in reserve for particular objects." Lee claimed that each man "singled him [Webster] out as their mark," but every shot missed him. As the 33rd and Guards Light Infantry crossed, they were followed by the 23rd and 71st, but Williams successfully withdrew the Continentals and dragoons.[22]

In the evening after the skirmish at Weitzel's, Kirkwood made a reconnaissance toward Tarleton's camp. Tarleton's pickets challenged Kirkwood's men, exchanged gunfire, and then retired into their camp. The Americans reported that the British quickly retreated "in great confusion towards the main army . . . about two miles from this place; when, meeting a party of Tories and mistaking them for our militia, he [Tarleton] charged on them very furiously, putting great numbers to the sword. On the other hand, they taking Colonel Tarleton for our horse and infantry, there commenced a smart skirmish, in which great numbers of the Tories were sent to the lower regions." Having caused Tarleton some consternation, Kirkwood's men, "marched for camp which we reached about daybreak after a very fatiguing journey, having marched all night through deep swamps, morasses and thickets, which rendered our marching unpleasant and tiresome, twenty-six miles."[23]

Casualties for the day's fighting were relatively light. Thirty British soldiers were killed or wounded in exchange for two dead Continentals, eight dead Virginia riflemen, and twelve wounded. Many casualties were again transported to the Moravian towns. On 7 March, Johann Michael Graff recorded that "Captain Ewing and Lieutenant Kinder and one with 15 wounds were brought to Salem." The following day he recorded that "more of Preston's men arrived who had been wounded," and on 9 March that "Colonels Crockett and Preston returned, with some of their own men, and a wounded lieutenant named Sawyer who had been shot in the side." Preston and Crockett remained in the settlements looking "after the wounded with all love and faithfulness." The Virginians departed on 11 March for their home state, leaving $240 in Continental money in the town's poor box.[24]

The way Williams fought the skirmish resulted in greater losses for Greene's army. Many militiamen, with some justification, felt they had been sacrificed protecting the Continentals and that the "burthen, and heat of the day was entirely thrown on them." The militia's anger, combined with Greene's decision to send their horses home, resulted in the mass desertion of several units, including virtually all of Preston's riflemen and Pickens's militia. Others, including Private John Scott of Campbell's riflemen, lost their horses at Weitzel's Mill after having been ordered to dismount. Scott stated that the British "took sum horses, and mine was one of them appraised to Sixty dollars together with my Saddle and bridle all which I lost on that day." Scott decided to return home on account of "the weather being Blustary and cool & and we having lost our Blankets." Pickens similarly argued that his South Carolina and Georgia militias had served long enough and far from their homes. There was little Greene could do. Within a few hours on 6 March, numbers of his soldiers began departing for home. Thomas Jefferson summed up the situation: "They seem only to have visited and quitted him."[25]

Despite such losses, Greene continued marching along the eastern bank of the Haw River, with Cornwallis following a parallel course on the west bank a dozen miles behind. On 10 March, Greene reached High Rock Ford and was greeted by the arrival of reinforcements. More than 1,000 were North Carolina militia formed into two brigades. Brig. Gen. John Butler led one brigade, consisting of men from Caswell, Granville, Guilford, and Orange Counties. Brig. Gen. Thomas Eaton commanded the other brigade of militiamen from Franklin, Halifax, Nash, and Warren Counties, as well as a company or two from parts further east. Pension records indicate the majority were draftees serving one- to three-month tours.[26]

A second large contingent was several hundred men under Brig. Gen. Edward Stevens from western Virginia. Many carried rifles and were transferred to Col. William Campbell. Unlike the North Carolinians, pension accounts for Stevens's men show that they were largely willing volunteers enlisted for three-month tours. Some were also Continental veterans, including at least two who had fought with Daniel Morgan at Quebec. One of the new arrivals, Rockbridge County's Samuel Houston, kept a vivid journal of his unit's march south. He set out from Rockbridge County on 1 March, drawing a ration of liquor and paying a Mrs. Brackenridge fifteen dollars for beer before commencing a seventeen-mile march. He noted the following day that several men were drunk. Like any proper soldier, Houston hated fatigue duty, and when ordered to drive steers on 4 March, he recorded that "happily they had broken out of pasture." Houston's journal mentions several desertions as well as disciplinary measures. Two men received whippings for stealing. However, Houston records no such action taken against the "boys who set the woods on fire" on 9 March. He stated that they reached Greene's army on 10–11 March.[27]

Problems retaining the militia still existed. Maj. Charles Magill, Greene's aide and a spy of sorts for Jefferson, wrote the Virginia governor, "The Militia are daily joining but heretofore in no regular Bodies, a number from different counties, who turned out Volunteers on the first approach of the British, finding the life of a Soldier by no means an agreeable one, thought proper to take a hasty leave of their brother Sufferers." Houston's journal, as well as several pension accounts, indicates that many men simply drifted off in the night, never returning to their units.[28]

Regardless of Magill's complaints, militia *were* coming in. Shortly after the arrival of Stevens's men, another large body of Virginia militia under Brig. Gen. Robert Lawson arrived, followed by Bedford County riflemen under

Col. Charles Lynch. The next day, a detachment of 400 Virginia Continentals led by Lt. Col. Richard Campbell came in carrying muskets they had just received at Hillsborough. Several companies of light dragoons from North Carolina and Virginia appeared as well. The new men swelled Greene's army to well over 4,000 troops.

On 12–13 March, Greene continued integrating the militia into his army and explained the tactical maneuvering they would be using. He then provided practical instruction as they paraded and drilled in the open fields above High Rock Ford. Samuel Houston wrote, "We paraded several times, and at last fired in platoons and battalions; in doing which one of the North Carolina militia was shot through the head; a bullet glancing from a tree, struck Geo. Moore on the head of our battalion. In the evening we marched from Haw River about three miles, and encamped." Despite such accidents, Greene's men, with full stomachs, were ready. On 13 March, Magill wrote to Thomas Jefferson, "Since the arrival of a Detachment of North Carolina Militia, those [Virginians] under General Lawson, and the Regulars under Col. [Richard] Campbell, nothing is talked of but a General Action and every preparation is making." The following day at 6:00 A.M. Greene marched the remaining ten miles toward Guilford Courthouse.[29]

While the Southern Army absorbed reinforcements, Cornwallis was attempting to feed his army. Two months of maneuvering by two large armies had exhausted local forage. Charles O'Hara wrote his friend the Duke of Grafton that his lordship's army was "completely worn out, by the excessive Fatigues of the Campaign in a march of above a Thousand Miles, most of them barefoot, naked and for days living upon Carrion . . . and three or four ounces of unground Indian Corn." The officer's account is confirmed by 33rd Foot private John Shaw, who later recollected, "At this time the scarcity of provisions was so great that we had but one pound of flour for six men per day with very little beef, and no salt the half of the time." One British officer noted that Cornwallis had no intelligence regarding Greene's movements and that he had determined to march to Wilmington to resupply. Cornwallis himself confirmed this in a 17 March letter to Lord Germain, stating that he had determined to "maintain communications with our shipping at Wilmington" on "account of the sufferings of our army."[30]

Following the engagement at Weitzel's Mill, Cornwallis's army had camped at local farms and mills, foraging for whatever provisions could be found. On 8 March, they encamped near Guilford Courthouse before moving on to Dillon's (or possibly Dixon's) Mill, where on 11 March, his men received a small amount of cornmeal. While at Guilford Courthouse, John Shaw and a private from the 23rd Foot were captured while conducting their own private foraging expedition through the stratagem of a Major Bell's wife. The following afternoon, the British marched again past Guilford Courthouse and, according to Charles Magill, "filed off down the Hillsborough Road, awaiting an opportunity to attack." Cornwallis's men encamped at the Deep River Meeting House, nearly twelve miles southwest of the courthouse.[31]

Still hoping to feed his troops, Cornwallis immediately dispatched "one officer and fifty privates of the Brigade of Guards to parade immediately and march to Mendenhall's Mill." These men may have been attacked en route. Sgt. Maj. William Seymour recorded that Lee's Legion engaged and captured nearly thirty British soldiers, presumably a foraging party, on 12 March. Nevertheless, some British reached the mill, because Cornwallis sent a sergeant and twelve men to escort grain wagons on 14 March. According to Mendenhall family tradition, British soldiers also absconded with the family cow, although upon the daughter's protestations, Cornwallis returned the animal.[32]

Magill's quote about Cornwallis's intentions to attack are intriguing. Greene surely believed the British would go on the offensive. British accounts, however, indicate that Cornwallis was expecting Greene to pursue. Cornwallis wrote, "I was determined to fight the rebel army if it approached me." St. George Tucker, a major in Lawson's Virginia militia, wrote home on 14 March while marching toward Guilford Courthouse: "We are at this moment marching to attack Cornwallis with a force which I am in hopes is full able to cope with him." Furthermore, the British were completely unaware of the actual number of men Greene had. Maj. Johann Christian Du Buy, commander of the Hessian Von Bose Regiment, placed the number at 9,000 men, while British commander Cornwallis guessed 7,000 militia and Continentals. The Americans may have had a much better account of British strength than the enemy had of the Americans, because "Light Horse Harry" Lee and Otho Holland Williams blocked all roads toward Greene's army.[33]

When scouts reported the American army at Guilford Courthouse in the evening hours of 14 March, his lordship quickly sprang into action. Cornwallis had chased Greene for nearly two months, and now only twelve miles stood between him and the Americans. At 2:00 A.M., he ordered the baggage, pack horses, wounded, and sick sent to Bell's Mill with a detachment consisting of Lt. Col. John Hamilton's loyalist Royal North Carolina Regiment and 117 British regulars led by Capt. Charles Horneck of the Guards Brigade and

Capt. Henry Broderick of the 33rd Foot. The remainder were roused from their slumber and ordered to advance along the Great Salisbury Road (now the New Garden Road) at 5:30 A.M.[34]

Although Greene had no advance knowledge of Cornwallis's intentions, he guessed correctly that an attack was imminent. Greene ordered Lee's command, consisting of the legion of about 150 mounted dragoons and infantry, as well as 60 Virginia riflemen under Col. William Campbell and Capt. James Tate detached to Lee, to camp three miles west of Guilford Courthouse on the Great Salisbury Road. Lee, in turn, ordered a small mounted detachment under Lt. James Heard to "place himself near the British camp, and to report from time to time what occurrences might be heard." At 2:00 A.M. Heard reported movement in the British camp. Two hours later Heard sent word that the sound of numerous wagon wheels indicated a "general movement." The noise was the British baggage train nonetheless leaving for Bell's Mill, but Lee sent word to Greene. Lee had his subordinates awaken the remainder of his men, and he ordered them to "take breakfast as quickly as possible."[35]

Shortly after Lee's men finished eating, a message arrived from Greene directing Lee to advance toward Cornwallis and ascertain whether it was a "general movement." Lt. Col. "Harry" Lee, twenty-five years old and impetuous, complied, and his dragoons trotted down the road, followed as quickly as possible by the legion infantry, Virginia riflemen, and a company of Virginia Continentals under Capt. Andrew Wallace. Headed up the road in Lee's direction were the advance elements of Cornwallis's army, led by Banastre Tarleton, nearly 300 men of the British Legion, as well as 100 British Guards Light Infantry and 84 Ansbach jaegers.[36]

Some four miles west of the courthouse, Tarleton's dragoons gingerly approached the New Garden Meeting House. A ragged volley suddenly erupted from the underbrush on both sides of the Great Salisbury Road, followed by the hurried sound of hoof beats scattering into the distance. Lieutenant Heard's videttes had opened fire on Tarleton's men before retiring toward Lee's main detachment. Tarleton suffered no loss and recorded the incident simply as "the light troops drove in a picket of the enemy." Nevertheless, the first shots of the battle had been fired.[37]

*If they fight, you*

*will beat Cornwallis;*

*if not, he will beat you.*

— DANIEL MORGAN *to*

NATHANAEL GREENE,

*20 February 1781*

CHAPTER THREE **GREENE'S ARMY**

After firing their volley, Lieutenant Heard's men dashed east along the Great Salisbury Road. They met Lieutenant Colonel Lee's column about four miles from Guilford Courthouse. Having confirmed that Cornwallis's entire army was indeed on the move, Lee ordered an aide to deliver the word to Greene. He then ordered his men to retire toward his supporting infantry. While retracing their steps to the east, Lee's men found themselves in a long, straight portion of road bordered by high fences on either side. Lee realized that he could position his column so as to bottleneck the British forces within this "lane."

Tarleton was as impetuous as Lee, if not more so. He saw the Virginian's withdrawal and promptly ordered his legion dragoons to charge after them. Lee's rear guard, commanded by Capt. James Armstrong, wheeled about and repulsed two charges by Tarleton. The head of Tarleton's column and the rear of Lee's, with some four men abreast, fought hand-to-hand with one another, while other dragoons fired their pistols and carbines over and around their comrades. The melee must have resembled the phalanxes of ancient Greek warfare crashing into each other, except this situation involved men on horseback carrying firearms as well as blades. Lee's account states that "the whole of the enemy's front section was dismounted and many of the horses prostrated, some of the dragoons killed, the rest made prisoners: not a single American solider or horse was injured." Armstrong's men then counterattacked, and Lee reported, "Tarleton retired with celerity."[1]

Tarleton's men fled down the Great Salisbury Road and then took a secondary road that branched to the southeast. The route, evidently passing over territory now occupied by Guilford College, allowed Tarleton to travel along the Hillsborough Road on his way to the New Garden Meeting House, where he expected to meet the infantry of Cornwallis's advance guard. Lee went straight down the Great Salisbury Road toward the Quaker grounds, where the Guards Light Infantry under Capt. John Goodricke surprised him.

The Guards deployed into line from the road and fired a volley that knocked down several dragoons, including Lee. Apparently only a few had actually been shot. Sgt. Peter Rife of the legion stated that, as Lee's men charged, the sunlight glistening off the "British armor, which was burnished very bright," caused such "a flash of light to be thrown back on the American horses, as they approached, that it frightened them and caused a momentary disorder." Lee's men were charging west, and the British would have had the sun directly in their eyes, as Rife describes its being "about an hour high, and shining with unclouded splendor." Rife watched as Lee himself was thrown from his horse, "a fine chestnut sorrel," only to be saved when one dragoon, "instantly alighted, and putting the Colonel on his horse, undertook to shift for himself in the best way he could, which he did by falling in with the legion or Campbell's riflemen."[2]

Rife's account provides several important details. First, his comment about the sun's position provides a time for the engagement. The average sunrise on 15 March in Guilford County, North Carolina, occurs at 6:30 A.M. If the sun was "an hour high," the skirmish in the lane took place at roughly 7:30 A.M. Second, the comment concerning Lee's rescuer joining the infantry indicates how close the foot soldiers were to the dragoons at this stage in the engagement. This means that Lee, although he later claimed he came at the British at "full speed," allowed time for his panting and footsore infantry to catch up with him.[3]

Shortly after the British volley, and as the Guards Light Infantry continued to deploy, Lee's Legion infantry, under Capt. Michael Rudolph, "came running up at trail arms, and opened a well aimed fire on the guards, which was followed in a few minutes by a volley from riflemen under Campbell, who had taken a position left of the infantry." Lee recorded, "it was now about one hour after sunrise . . . the sun had just risen above the trees." His statement supports Rife's claim about the time of the engagement. Pursuing Tarleton after the skirmish in the lane, Lee's men could have easily covered the distance to New Garden Meeting House in only a few minutes.[4]

The skirmish became quite "general" as more troops began arriving around the meetinghouse. The Ansbach jaegers appeared on the field, as did part of the 23rd Foot. Now outnumbered, Lee ordered his cavalry to stand their ground while the infantry and riflemen retreated seven-tenths of a mile east to a wooded area along the Great Salisbury Road called "Cross Roads." The position was roughly midway between the first encounter at the lane and the second at the New Garden Meeting House. The British pursued, although constantly harassed by intermittent rifle and carbine fire. Along the road, the sixteen-year-old son of a local Quaker named Hunt shot a British dragoon from his horse. Although some accounts label this man an officer, the only dragoon officer wounded that day was Tarleton, and contrary to several accounts it was not at the New Garden skirmish but in the actual battle at Guilford. The account distinctly mentions the victim in a red uniform, indicating he was probably a member of the 17th Light Dragoons.[5]

Lee fought another delaying action at the new site that was mostly an infantry fight, as the wooded and broken terrain prevented Lee's Legion and Tarleton's dragoons from operating effectively. According to Lee, the skirmish lasted some thirty minutes, before he retired to the safety of Greene's army. Casualties among the officers were fairly high. Capt. John Goodricke of the Guards, cousin of the famous Dutch astronomer, died in the fighting, as did Capt. James Tate, commanding a company of Virginia riflemen detached from Col. George Moffett's Virginia militia regiment. Lt. Jonathan Snowden of Lee's Legion was wounded. Tarleton reported, "Captain Goodricke of the guards, a promising young officer, fell in this contest, and between twenty and thirty of the guards, dragoons, and yagers were killed and wounded." A reasonably accurate figure for British casualties for the three skirmishes lies between thirty and forty men.[6]

Americans recorded their losses as well. Tate's company took severe losses, as John Wason stated: "Tate's company was discharged some short time after the battle, in consequence as was supposed of its having suffered excessively in bringing on the general engagement at that place, not more than 20 or 25 men having survived." One of those who fell was Frederick Fender, who "received a musket ball in the elbow of the left arm that produced total dis-

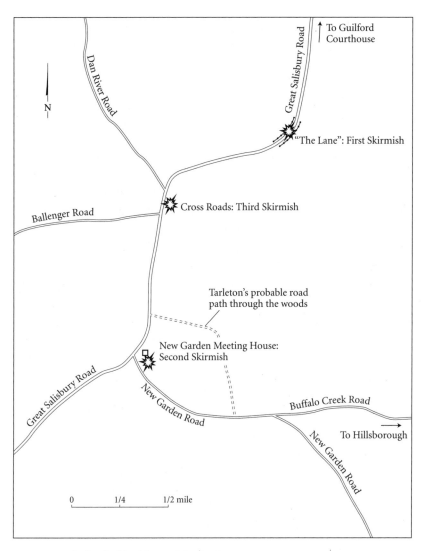

To Guilford
Courthouse

Great Salisbury Road

Dan River Road

N

"The Lane": First Skirmish

Ballenger Road

Cross Roads: Third Skirmish

Tarleton's probable road
path through the woods

New Garden Meeting House:
Second Skirmish

Great Salisbury Road

New Garden Road

Buffalo Creek Road

To Hillsborough

New Garden Road

0    1/4    1/2 mile

**MAP FOUR**  *Prebattle skirmishes, 15 March 1781, 7:00–10:00 A.M.*

ability." Peter Rife claimed that Lee's Legion lost seventeen men before they reached Greene's army. Isaac Sampson, an eighteen-year-old private of Lee's dragoons, lost an eye in the skirmishing, while Pvt. John Garner, age twenty-three, lost two fingers to a saber cut, confirming there was close in, hand-to-hand combat in addition to small arms fire. Those losses, combined with the estimated number of Virginia losses, put the American casualties for the morning skirmishes at probably thirty-five to forty.[7]

The outlying fighting was a running skirmish, with peaks of activity at the initial ambush, the lane, the meetinghouse, and at the lane again. Lee's delaying actions provided Greene time to organize and deploy his army. The initial encounter between Heard and Tarleton occurred shortly after dawn, and the skirmish at the lane took place about 7:30–8:00 A.M. The time it took Lee to reach the New Garden Meeting House is uncertain, although he likely covered the distance in only a few minutes. Some scholars have estimated that the meetinghouse skirmish lasted between twenty and thirty minutes. Lee then retreated half the distance to the lane, where he made another thirty-minute stand, before retreating the full distance to Greene's army, likely another ten to fifteen minutes, depending on how long it took to cover his infantry's withdrawal. This time frame indicates that the entire New Garden skirmish scenario may have lasted nearly two hours.

Greene spent the two and a half hours Lee gave him deploying his army in the dense woods west of the courthouse. The general had chosen the precise site just west of the courthouse the day before, but he had thought about fighting on this ground in early February. The terrain consisted of a gently sloping rise from west to east along the Great Salisbury Road, broken by several small ravines and swales. The western end of the battlefield along the road included open areas that were freshly plowed fields and one or two others referred to in pension declarations as "oldfields," indicating they were likely fallow or in stubble. The remainder of the area was a smattering of dense forest and undergrowth combined with broken terrain. The far eastern portion consisted of an open vale with its slopes covered in trees and brush. The British *Annual Register for 1781* described the area as "a wilderness, covered with tall woods, which were rendered intricate by shrubs and thick underbrush; but which was interspersed here and there by a few scattered plantations and cleared fields."[8]

Greene positioned his men based loosely on the tactics Brig. Gen. Daniel Morgan had used at Cowpens. Morgan's surprisingly daring use of untested militia proved that even an army composed largely of undisciplined troops, if properly handled, could defeat a professional force. On 17 January 1781, Morgan had utilized a defense in depth against Tarleton that involved advanced skirmishers, then a main line of militia, supported by a second line of bayonet-armed Continental infantrymen. The "Old Wagoner," Morgan, also placed dragoons to cover his rear and flanks. Knowing the limits of his militia, he ordered them to fire two shots and then fall back behind the Continentals. His tactics worked brilliantly, and even when a misunderstood order sent the Continentals into a withdrawal, Morgan's able subordinate, Lt. Col. John Eager Howard, quickly corrected the situation in time to fire a devastating, close-range volley into the surprised faces of the pursuing 1st Battalion, 71st Foot.[9]

Before Morgan left the Southern Army due to ill health, he noted that nearly half of Greene's men were militia. Militia—citizen soldiers usually called out for three- and six-month tours—had little experience and less military discipline. Often led by local politicians, the militia carried an odd assortment of personal weapons, from fowling pieces to old smoothbores and often rifles. Few, if any, had access to bayonets. As a result, militiamen had a reputation for running in the face of a British bayonet charge. Most Continental officers had low expectations of militia, especially after the collapse of most of the Virginia and North Carolina militia at Camden the previous August. Drafted militia often gave a particularly poor performance compared to those who volunteered. Thirty-nine percent of the North Carolina and 15 percent of the Virginia militia Guilford veterans whose pension files were used in this study had been drafted.

Continental service, depending on the state of enlistment, could range anywhere from nine months, to three years, to the duration of the war. Examinations focusing on the social history of the Continental Line have demonstrated that while Continental officers were often second and third sons from good families who proudly identified themselves as gentlemen by their rank, the enlisted Continentals were generally men from the lower classes. In the early months of the war, a period some historians have argued was a *rage militaire*, men from all levels of society joined the Continental army. By 1781, the ranks were composed of men who typically did not own land and were generally less economically advantaged than those in the militia. Muster rolls of Continental units from various states, and specifically those of the South, indicate a large number of farm laborers but also include men from all walks of society, including large numbers of tradesmen whose livelihoods were circumvented by the war. Most of the Continentals serving with the Southern Army under Greene and Morgan were veterans of nearly five years of service who had proven themselves on numerous battlefields. The American commanders looked to them as the proverbial rock upon which the army's success or failure rested.[10]

Morgan left Greene with his analysis of the militia: "If they fight, you will beat Cornwallis; if not, he will beat you, and perhaps cut your regulars to pieces, which will be losing all our hopes." Morgan offered Greene an important suggestion. Discovering that many former Continentals were serving with Greene's militia, Morgan stated, "I think it would be advisable to select them from among the militia and put them in the ranks with the regulars." He continued, "put the riflemen on the flanks, under enterprising officers who are acquainted with that kind of fighting, and put the militia in the center with some picked troops in the rear with orders to shoot down the first man that runs." Morgan closed his suggestions, stating, "If anything will succeed, a disposition of this kind will."[11]

Greene acted on several of Morgan's suggestions, but he did not pull the former regulars out of line and place them in Continental regiments. Instead, he made sure that former Continental officers as well as supernumerary active duty officers were placed in command positions. North Carolina militiaman Jeremiah Gurley reported, "Greene put most of the militia under regular officers, and our men were under Col. Eaton." An analysis of identifiable North Carolina militia field-grade officers shows that 5 of 9 battalion commanders were Continental veterans (55 percent), although the brigade commanders were not. Gurley's claim is thus verified at the regimental level. Still, only 2 of 9 majors or lieutenant colonels were Continental veterans (22 percent). A similar investigation into the 66 identifiable North Carolina militia company-grade officers indicates only 6 with prior Continental service (9 percent).[12]

In comparison, both Virginia brigade commanders were former regulars, but only 2 of 7 Virginia militia battalion commanders (28 percent) and 3 of 9 majors or lieutenant colonels were Continental veterans (33 percent). Of 47 identifiable Virginia militia company commanders, only 4 had regular experience (8.5 percent). Although Charles Lynch did not serve as a Continental, 4 of his 7 rifle company commanders did (57 percent). Only 2 of the 9 rifle company commanders under William Campbell, a former regular, had prior experience in the Continental army (22 percent). Overall, 14 percent of the North Carolina militia officers had regular army experience, compared to 20 percent of the Virginians.[13]

Although Continental army experience did not automatically equal battlefield capability, such service likely factored into unit and officer performance. Several studies have claimed that a large percentage of the enlisted Virginia militiamen were former Continentals. Guilford pension declarations qualify, if they do not directly challenge, this claim, inasmuch as perhaps one-tenth of the Virginia militia were former regulars. Of 133 Virginia militiamen and 58 riflemen whose pensions were studied, only 10 militiamen (8 percent) and 6 riflemen (10 percent) claimed prior Continental service. Seven of these former Continentals served in Stevens's brigade, with the remaining 3 under Lawson. The riflemen were split evenly between Lynch and Campbell. In comparison, only 6 of 182 North Carolina militia pensioners (3 percent) indicated prior service in the Continental army. Four of these men served in Eaton's brigade, the remaining 2 with Butler. These numbers hardly suggest a leavening of Continental experience was to be found among the militiamen, even if many had seen prior militia service.[14]

The terrain and the sheer size of Greene's force dictated that he develop a three-line system instead of Morgan's two battle lines. (See Appendix A, "Order of Battle.") Greene positioned two militia lines, one North Carolina, one Virginia, supported by a third line comprised of his Delaware, Maryland, and Virginia Continentals. However, as Morgan suggested, Greene placed riflemen and light troops on each flank. Dragoons covered the extreme flanks, and Greene positioned his artillery in two sections, one at the center of the first line, and one at the third. Although he did not place skirmishers in advance of his army, the argument could be made that the deployment of Lee's Legion, the riflemen, and the light infantry companies served that purpose. Greene also ordered Lt. Col. Edward Carrington, his adjutant general and senior artillery officer, to "lay off" the battlefield for distances to help Capt. Anthony Singleton range his cannon. A seventy-year-old Guilford County native, Thomas Moody, who had worked the fields nearby all his life, helped pilot Singleton's guns to the first line and helped Carrington determine the best position for the artillery.[15]

Greene's first militia line consisted of the two North Carolina brigades. North of the Great Salisbury Road, Greene placed Brig. Gen. Thomas Eaton's Halifax District brigade, consisting of approximately 500 to 600 men. Eaton was forty-two years old, a wealthy planter from Warren County, who had been a politician and paper soldier. Although appointed the Bute County militia commander during the War of Regulation in 1771, Eaton had not seen action. His only combat experience had been the disastrous American defeat at Briar Creek, Georgia, in March 1779. Command of his district's brigade originally had been offered to Brig. Gen. Jethro Sumner of the North Carolina Continental Line, but Eaton had successfully wrangled political favors to gain the command.[16]

Pension accounts allow a reconstruction of Eaton's brigade organization north of the road. Farthest to the north, on the American right flank and partially hidden within a copse of woods, Eaton posted the Warren and Franklin county militias under Colonels Benjamin Williams and Pinkatham Eaton. Both Williams and Eaton (who was Thomas Eaton's cousin) were Continental veterans and had served at Brandywine, Germantown, and Monmouth. Pinkatham "Pink" Eaton had been wounded leading a militia regiment at Briar Creek in 1779. South of the Franklin militia, along a rail fence and facing west into the recently plowed, muddy fields stood the militiamen of Nash, Edgecombe, and Halifax Counties under the overall command of Col. William Linton. In addition, at least two companies from Martin and Northampton Counties also served under Linton, although their place in the line is unknown. Like Williams and Eaton, Linton had nearly two years' prior service as a Continental company commander in Washington's army.[17]

South of the Great Salisbury Road, Greene placed Brig. Gen. John Butler's Hillsborough District brigade, consisting similarly of 500 to 600 men. Butler was a politician like Eaton, having served in the Provincial Congress and the General Assembly. Butler had much more combat experience than his fellow brigadier. In 1776, he led a regiment in the Moore's Creek Bridge Campaign. Three years later, the fifty-year-old Butler received praise for his performance leading a militia brigade at Stono Ferry, South Carolina, and again the following year during the American defeat at Camden. One of his soldiers described him quite simply as an "old man wearing a hunting shirt."[18]

Pension declarations place the Caswell County militia, commanded by Col. William Moore, on the brigade's right, bordering the road. Like the men just across the road, the Caswell militia rested themselves on the rail fence, facing west. Moore, a county politician, had little previous military experience. However, several pension accounts indicate that Maj. Henry "Hal" Dixon, an experienced North Carolina Continental serving as inspector general of the North Carolina militia, took charge during the engagement. South of the Caswell County troops, Butler placed the Granville County militia, led by Col. Joseph Taylor, a planter with little military background. Two Orange County militia regiments, including a small detachment of Wake County men, stood to the left of Taylor's regiment. Col. Thomas Farmer and Col. John Taylor, both Camden veterans, commanded these units. A third, smaller detachment led by Col. Robert Mebane may have also been present. Standing to their left were small contingents, probably platoon-size formations numbering about twenty-five men each, from Rockingham, Randolph, and Chatham Counties. Further south, Butler posted the Rowan, Mecklenburg, and Guilford militias. The majority of the Rowan and Mecklenburg militias under Col. Francis Locke had previously left Greene's army, but pension accounts place approximately fifteen to twenty-five men, a small company, on the field under Capt. James Billingsley and Lt. Robert Walker. These last men were partially hidden in woods, with some standing behind the rail fence that ran the length of the field to their north.[19]

Guilford County pension files indicate that many local militiamen evidently avoided service with Greene. Whether they had previously seen service with the Salisbury District militia, and thus refused to serve another tour, or simply refused to leave their firesides is unclear. At the time of Guilford Courthouse, three Guilford companies were in the field. Henry Weitzel, owner of Weitzel's Mill, commanded a company composed of the county's German speakers, while Arthur Forbis commanded an "English company." For whatever reason, Weitzel's men never arrived at Guilford Courthouse, although Forbis's men did. Forbis had little previous combat experience and had only commanded men in the field once before. A smaller detachment under Capt. Henry Connelly was also present. Connelly, a veteran of Cowpens, arrived shortly before daybreak with twenty men.[20]

Forbis and Connelly came under the overall command of Col. James Martin, Lt. Col. John Paisley, and Maj. James Hunter. Paisley, a capable militia officer with combat experience, was incapacitated by smallpox. In his pension declaration, Martin claimed that shortly after the engagement began, he and Major Hunter were "ordered" by General Greene to leave their troops in the first line, retire to the courthouse, and wait there to rally fleeing militia. Martin certainly did not fight on the first line, although the veracity of his statements concerning why he didn't seems very suspect. No other North Carolina militia officer was ordered to the rear during the battle, and it is highly unlikely Greene specifically ordered a field officer to abandon his command in the beginning of an engagement.[21]

In the center of the road, Greene posted two six-pounder field pieces, commanded by Capt. Anthony Singleton of the 1st Continental Artillery, a highly capable officer with several years' experience. Greene had two companies of artillery present at Guilford Courthouse. According to February muster rolls, Singleton's company had himself, two captain lieutenants, and thirty-eight enlisted men, almost all of whom were Virginians. At Guilford, however, he may have only had one subordinate officer, as Greene had furloughed Capt. Lt. William Poythress on 5 March. The identity of the other subordinate remains unknown, and exactly who served under Singleton remains something of a mystery. According to Lt. Edmund Brooke of the 1st Continental Artillery, "Not long before the invasion of Virginia by Cornwallis, the companies composing the Regiment aforesaid were consolidated into two full companies, marched to South Carolina, and merged in the army commanded by Nathanael Greene." He continued, "Captains Coleman, Dix, Miller, Bohannon, and myself and all the other officers of Harrison's regiment except those who marched to the South with the two companies aforesaid remained in Virginia and took command of captain's quotas of militia drafted to fill in the ranks of said regiment."[22]

To support Singleton, Greene positioned a company (possibly several small companies) of at least forty North Carolina Continentals who had avoided capture at Charleston the previous year. Most had been guards and artisans at the Continental laboratory at Salisbury under the command of Capt. Edward Yarborough and Lt. John Campbell. Yarborough had evacuated his men and joined Greene's army on the Race to the Dan. In addition to Yarborough, pension accounts indicate the possible presence of Captains Clement Hall and Reading Blount and Lt. Col. Archibald Lytle. These men arguably held the most exposed position on the first line and likely stood behind and to the flanks of Singleton's artillery, serving as both infantry support and substitute matrosses.[23]

On the north flank of the first line, Greene posted Col. Charles Lynch's Virginia riflemen, Capt. Robert Kirkwood's Delaware company, Capt. Phillip Huffman's Virginia company, Lt. Col. William Washington's Continental dragoons, and at least two mounted companies of militia dragoons, one from Virginia and one from North Carolina. A more likely interpretation is that Lt. Col. William Washington's Continental dragoons were not on this flank due to the heavy brush and the lack of any pathways adequate for horsemen. It is possible they were in the open space north of the courthouse when the army camped in early February. Lynch, a forty-five-year-old tavern owner, judge, and planter, led 150 riflemen from the mountains of Bedford County. He is perhaps best known as the originator of the term "lynching," from his version of justice, known as Lynch law, for dealing with Tories.[24]

Capt. Robert Kirkwood, known affectionately by his men as "Captain Bob," would serve in thirty-two Revolutionary War battles, including almost

*Lt. Col. William Washington
(1752–1810), 3rd Continental
Light Dragoons. Oil painting
by Charles Wilson Peale.
Independence National
Historical Park.*

every campaign of George Washington's army. Beloved by his men, Kirkwood could be a strict disciplinarian. When the 2nd Platoon of his company held back from a charge at Camden, Kirkwood "stepped directly in front of them, and, raising his sword menacingly, said, 'By the living God, the first man who falters shall receive this weapon in his craven heart!'" The Delawares, including many Irish immigrants, were widely considered among the toughest veterans in the Continental Army. The majority had seen service since 1776, and, with the 1st Maryland men, were the most experienced American infantry on the field. The Delaware Regiment lost so many soldiers at Camden that the battalion had been reduced from eight companies to two. Dressed in blue regimentals faced with red, the Delawares wore distinctive yellow binding around their cocked hats. Greene, watching Kirkwood's men festively fiddling and carousing in camp in early February, commented, "I like to witness a scene like this, captain, for it prevents the spirit of the army from flagging. Ha! Your soldiers are singular fellows, they fight all day and dance all night!"[25]

Lt. Col. William Washington, second cousin to George, had been in service since 1775 and was a veteran of the most important battles of the war.

He had been awarded a silver medal by Congress for his actions at Cowpens. Washington's command, seriously under strength, included eighty veterans from the 1st and 3rd Continental Light Dragoons, as well as thirty light horsemen from Prince Edward County, Virginia, commanded by Capt. Thomas Watkins. Watkins's troop included a twenty-year-old, six foot six, 260-pound giant named Peter Francisco. A native of the Azores, the young man was already a legend in the Southern Army for his bravery at the battle of Camden in 1780.[26]

Greene also posted a forty-man North Carolina company commanded by the Marquis de Bretigny with Washington. Bretigny, formerly a French cavalry officer and rumored to be an illegitimate brother of Louis XVI, had sailed for America in 1777. A Royal Navy vessel captured the brig he sailed in, and Bretigny spent a year in a St. Augustine prison. He had appealed unsuccessfully for a commission from Congress but finally received a militia or state troops appointment from North Carolina governor Richard Caswell.[27]

One of Bretigny's troopers was twenty-six-year-old George (Jorge) Farragut, born in Minorca, Spain, who had served aboard a fireship in the Russian navy, fighting against the Turks at the battle of Chesma in July 1770, and sailed around the world as a merchant seaman before arriving in Charleston in 1776. He served as an officer aboard a privateering vessel in 1776–77 and as a sailor in the South Carolina State Navy before being captured at the siege of Charleston in 1780. After his exchange, Farragut enlisted as a private in Bretigny's corps. With Farragut, Washington's small cavalry battalion included a Spaniard, a Portuguese, and a Frenchman.[28]

Greene anchored the southern flank with William Campbell's Virginia riflemen, Joseph Winston's Surry and Wilkes County, North Carolina, riflemen, and Lee's Legion dragoons and infantry. Thirty-six years old and six foot six, Campbell led Washington County, Virginia, riflemen at the battle of Kings Mountain. He had several small companies from Washington, Augusta, and Rockbridge Counties under his command at Guilford. His men included Capt. David Gwin, a Welshman who fought at Fort Necessity under George Washington in 1754, and Pvt. Isaac Robinson of Capt. Henry Paulding's company, who had "visible marks to his face and perforated ears" from his eight years of captivity with the Shawnee Indians. The British feared Campbell's men for their aim with the long rifle. Cornwallis referred to them as "mountain men," and Johann Christian Du Buy, commander of the Von Bose Regiment, called them the "Blue Mountain Men," likely referring to the Blue Ridge Mountains.[29]

Maj. Joseph Winston, age thirty-six, commanded at least three small companies of riflemen from Wilkes and Surry Counties. There has been considerable debate over whether these men were attached to Butler's North Carolina militia or Campbell's riflemen, but pension accounts conclusively show that Winston's men were attached to the Virginians. John Stonecypher remembered that Capt. Richard Allen's company "was attached to Col. Campbell's riflemen." Benjamin Jones served with Capt. Minor Smith and stated that he "was under Major Joseph Winston but under overall command of William Campbell on the day of the battle." Capt. James Gaines, a former Virginia Continental, commanded the third company. Capt. James "Jesse" Franklin and Lt. Robert Taliaferro were also present but without command. Two other Surry County companies were present but not engaged. Capt. Arthur Scott's men were detailed to guard Greene's baggage, and Capt. Abraham Bostick left the army with his entire company after becoming quite "ill" the night before the engagement, according to pensioners.[30]

Lee's Partizan Legion, commanded by twenty-five-year-old Lt. Col. Henry "Light Horse Harry" Lee, had served from 1776 to 1778 with the 1st Continental Light Dragoons before being detached as the 2nd Partizan, or Partisan, Corps. The regiment, consisting of three twenty- to thirty-man dragoon troops and three similar-sized infantry companies, wore green jackets that mimicked the uniforms of the British Legion, although they may have been wearing drab jackets at Guilford. Lee's cavalry commanders included Joseph Eggleston, Ferdinand O'Neal, and James Armstrong, while his infantry commanders included Michael Rudolph, Patrick Carnes, and George Handy. Michael Rudolph's brother John, known as "Fighting Jack," served as Lee's major and second in command. A North Carolina militiaman who witnessed Lee's men in action, stated, "These veteran troopers attracted much attention from the militia, who judging them, though inferior in numbers, to be far superior in effectiveness to British cavalry, were inspired with a confidence they had hitherto not possessed."[31]

Greene posted the Virginia militia roughly three hundred yards behind (east of) the North Carolinians in a dense tangle of underbrush and woods. North of the road Greene positioned Brig. Gen. Robert Lawson's brigade of Virginians, comprised of men from the central and eastern part of the state. Born in Yorkshire, England, Lawson had migrated to America in 1769, become an attorney in Prince Edward County, and served in the 1775 Virginia Convention. In 1775, he was appointed major of the 4th Virginia, followed by promotions to lieutenant colonel and eventually colonel. He fought at Trenton, Princeton, Brandywine, and Germantown before resigning his commission in December 1777. Thomas Jefferson appointed him brigadier general of militia in 1781, shortly before ordering him to raise troops for Greene's aid.[32]

Lawson assigned Col. Beverley Randolph's regiment, consisting of men from Powhatan, Amelia, and Cumberland Counties, to the brigade's northern (right) flank. Randolph, a twenty-six-year-old graduate of the College of William and Mary and a prominent Virginia politician, had never seen action, although his second in command, Maj. William Cunningham, served as a Continental captain from 1775 to 1778. South of Randolph stood Col. John Holcombe's regiment, a composite of men from Amelia, Charlotte, Mecklenburg, and Powhatan Counties. Holcombe served as a captain in the 4th Virginia Continentals under Robert Lawson (then a colonel), until being wounded at Germantown in October 1777. His second in command, Maj. St. George Tucker, operated as brigade major. Born in Bermuda in 1752, Tucker studied law with George Wythe in Williamsburg, befriended Thomas Jefferson, and was brother-in-law to Beverley Randolph. The smallest regiment in Lawson's brigade, consisting of only a few companies from Mecklenburg, Powhatan, and Brunswick Counties, held the position closest to the road. The unit had marched to Guilford under the command of Col. Robert Munford, a forty-four-year-old playwright and poet from Williamsburg. Munford, suffering from gout, had relinquished command to Maj. Henry Skipwith. Although not an experienced soldier, Skipwith made one of his company commanders, Capt. Thomas Hubbard, his aide. Skipwith chose well, for Hubbard had extensive prior experience as a sergeant major and regimental quartermaster in the 13th Virginia Continental regiment in 1776–78.[33]

Brig. Gen. Edward Steven's brigade, generally men from the lower Shenandoah Valley, stood south of the Great Salisbury Road. Stevens, age thirty-six, had raised a Culpepper County militia battalion that fought at Great Bridge in 1775. Afterwards, he received a commission as colonel of the 10th Virginia Continentals. He led his regiment at Brandywine and Germantown before resigning in January 1778 during Valley Forge. Stevens accepted a position as brigadier general commanding Virginia militia in Horatio Gates's army in 1780 and was horrified when his command fled in panic during the battle of Camden. Still humiliated from that event and determined to regain his honor, Stevens posted marksmen ten yards behind his line with orders to shoot down "the first man who flinched."[34]

Closest to the road and south of Skipwith's men, Stevens placed Col. Peter

Perkins's Pittsylvania County regiment. Perkins, considered a highly capable officer, had led militia since 1777. Berry Hill, his plantation, served as a Continental army hospital throughout the war. Perkins arrived at Greene's army with eight small companies; however three of them, made up of riflemen, had been detached for service with Charles Lynch. South of Perkins's men, Stevens placed Col. Nathaniel Cocke's regiment. The majority of Cocke's companies came from Lunenburg County, but the regiment included two companies from Halifax County and one from Prince Edward. Cocke had served briefly as a captain in the 7th Virginia in 1776. His second in command, Lt. Col. Haynes Morgan, first cousin of the "Old Wagoner," had perhaps more experience that any other American soldier at Guilford Courthouse. Born in 1730, Morgan had served six years in the British army as sergeant major of the 80th Foot, a provincial light infantry unit organized around a nucleus of officers from Roger's Rangers. Commanded by Col. Thomas Gage, who later served as Massachusetts governor under the Coercive Acts, the 80th Foot unit saw extensive combat in New York and at Montreal during the French and Indian War and at the defense of Detroit in 1763, during Pontiac's Rebellion. After his discharge in 1764, Morgan returned to Virginia. He fought against the Shawnee at Point Pleasant in 1774 and raised a battalion of minutemen in 1776. Morgan served as commander of Virginia state troops and militia from 1776 to 1778. The regiment's major, Henry Conway, had been a captain in the 14th Virginia and fought at Brandywine and Germantown.[35]

South of Cocke's men, Stevens positioned Col. George Moffett's Augusta County regiment. Like Munford, Moffett claimed sickness the day of the engagement and relinquished command to Maj. John Pope, who served as a lieutenant in Stevens's 10th Virginia until July 1777. Capt. James Tate, the Cowpens veteran who died earlier that morning at New Garden Meeting House, had served as a company commander under Moffett. The southernmost unit of Steven's brigade was the regiment from Rockbridge and Augusta Counties under Col. Samuel McDowell, whose more famous cousins, Capt. "Pleasant Garden Joe" and Col. "Quaker Meadows Joe" McDowell led North Carolina troops at Kings Mountain and Cowpens. McDowell's regiment stands out for not having any former Continentals among the officers. His second in command was Maj. Alexander Stuart, and the major's son Archibald served as quartermaster. On the day of the battle, McDowell fell quite sick, and Stuart actually commanded the regiment. Many men from Rockbridge and Augusta Counties were experienced combat soldiers and had participated at Kings Mountain and Cowpens.[36]

Samuel Houston, one of McDowell's men, provided probably the best physical description we have of the Virginia militia from the western half of the state, as well as Lynch's and Campbell's riflemen:

The men generally wore hunting shirts of heavy tow linen; died brown with bark; they were open in front and made to extend down near to the knee and belted round the waist with dressed skin or woven girths. The sleeves were large, with a wrist band round the wrist and fringed over the upper part of the hand as far as the knuckles. Under the hunting shirt was a jacket made of some finer materials, and breeches of dressed buck or deer skin to just below the knees, with long stockings and moccasins of deer leather, and underneath the jacket or vest was also their linen which was made of the finer kinds of flax cloth. The hats were imported from England, Ireland or Scotland or as they said then "from home"—the crown was low round and fitted the head, with a broad brim which by loops through the crown could be drawn up and made a three cornered or cock'd hat . . . profane language was very little used and continued to be so until the return of the soldiers and militia from the army of the revolution; after their return however it became very prevalent and I believe was much used for many years afterward.[37]

Houston also provides a very telling statement concerning the tree cover along the second line as well as how the Virginia militia south of the road fought. He stated, "When we marched near the ground we charged our guns. Presently our brigade major came, ordering us to take trees as we pleased. The men run to choose their trees, but with difficulty, many crowding to one, and some far behind others. Presently the Augusta men, and some of Col. Campbell's men fell in at right angles to us." Houston's version suggests that the tree cover south of the road may have been less thick where McDowell was stationed and also indicates that the Virginia militia fought not in a linear formation but as skirmishers.[38]

Greene's third line, posted more than five hundred yards to the east, behind the Virginians, consisted of Maryland, Delaware, and Virginia Continentals under Col. Otho Holland Williams and Brig. Gen. Isaac Huger. Unlike Morgan at Cowpens, Greene could not see the entire battlefield. This situation would affect both the outcome of the engagement and Greene's comprehension of what actually took place. Greene and his staff sat on their horses behind the third line near the courthouse, sixty yards to the rear of the 1st Maryland. His "family," as he affectionately called his aides, included deputy adjutant general Lt. Col. Edward Carrington, commissary general Col. William R. Davie, as well as aide-de-camps Lt. Col. Lewis Morris Jr., Maj. Ichabod Burnet, and Capt. William Pierce.[39]

The Maryland brigade, consisting of Col. John Gunby's 1st Maryland and Lt. Col. Benjamin Ford's 2d Maryland, was commanded by thirty-two-year-old Col. Otho Holland Williams. Williams had seen service since the 1775 siege of Boston and had been captured at Fort Washington in 1776 while acting as major of a combined Maryland-Virginia rifle regiment. Promoted to colonel of the 6th Maryland Regiment while still a prisoner, he was later exchanged and fought at Monmouth. He served as adjutant general of the Southern Army, serving under Gates at Camden and then taking command of Greene's light corps when Morgan was invalided and returned home in early February. Williams was a masterful commander, with an acute understanding of infantry tactics.[40]

The 1st Maryland, posted within a copse of woods on the slopes of the slight ridge in the center of the Continental line, was perhaps the most experienced regiment in the Continental army, having been involved in nearly every important engagement since August 1776. From orderly books and accounts by Howard and others, it is evident the 1st Maryland was arranged along the lines of the September 1780 reorganization following Camden. The right four companies represented the old 1st, 3rd, 5th, and 7th Maryland Regiments and had originally been under Maj. Archibald Anderson, but just before the battle, he was reassigned to the 2nd Maryland. The left four companies were made up from the Camden survivors of the Delaware regiment, plus the 2nd, 4th, and 6th Maryland Regiments, from right to left, under Maj. Henry Hardman. The 1st Maryland provided four companies for Morgan's Flying Army, and they performed distinguished service at Cowpens. Many observers considered them the elite of the Continental army. They would have another opportunity of demonstrating their prowess on 15 March.[41]

Col. John Gunby and Lt. Col. John Eager Howard led the 1st Maryland at Guilford Courthouse. Gunby, age thirty-six, had enlisted as a militiaman in 1775. When admonished by his father for his choice, Gunby replied that he would "rather sink into the grave of a patriot than wear the crown of England." Receiving a Continental commission, Gunby served with Washington's army until the Marylanders were sent south in 1780. He commanded the 7th Maryland at Camden and had been in charge of the American supply depot at Hillsborough, North Carolina, before being ordered to Prince Edward County, Virginia, to oversee supplies moving to Greene's army. He left Prince Edward on 12 March and had only recently taken charge of the regiment.[42]

John Eager Howard, twenty-eight years old, had established a solid reputation as a Continental officer in the northern campaigns. He commanded the 2nd Maryland at Camden and afterwards the Maryland-Delaware Light Infantry Battalion at Cowpens, where he had distinguished himself. For his actions at Cowpens, Congress awarded him a silver medal. He was a superb commander, perhaps the finest battalion commander in the Continental army, and Greene would later write, "Howard, as good an officer as the world affords. He has great ability and the best disposition to promote the service."[43]

Greene posted the 2nd Maryland closest to the Great Salisbury Road with its left flank turned at a right angle from the crest of the ridge to the roadbed. The 2nd Maryland, formerly the Maryland Regiment Extra, was practically the complete opposite of its fellow Maryland regiment. Although much larger than the 1st, but with fewer company officers, only a handful of men in the regiment had combat experience. Even their uniforms, brown coats faced red, contrasted with the blue regimental coats of the 1st Maryland. The unit had been organized in the summer of 1780 with recruits from across the state. The Regiment Extra, so called because it was in addition to those Congress had called for, marched south during October 1780 and reached North Carolina in December. The regiment refused to join the main army because of disputes over rank between the new officers and the veteran Maryland-Delaware Division officers.[44]

The dispute was not a petty argument. Continental officers jealously guarded their rank and seniority within the line. When the Regiment Extra appeared in North Carolina, veteran officers without commands felt they deserved to lead the new troops on the basis of their seniority. The Regiment Extra officers felt that since they had raised and commanded the men for nearly six months they should remain in command. After all, they would themselves be without commands if the veterans took command of the regiment.

Greene remained loyal to his veterans. He sought the Maryland Council's permission to replace the new officers with veterans based upon the formal organization of seniority and regimental assignments established in January 1781. Before receiving permission, Greene dismissed the Regiment Extra officers with the provision that they would receive one year's pay and expenses, but no pension. Veteran officers took charge of the unit, which then became

the 2nd Maryland. In addition, some noncommissioned officers were transferred to the 1st Maryland.[45]

Command of the 2nd Maryland went to Lt. Col. Benjamin Ford, who had served since January 1776 and led the 5th Maryland at Camden. His second in command was Maj. Archibald Anderson. It is likely that the company commanders were veteran Captains Horatio Claggett, Edward Edgerly, Edward Oldham, Perry Benson, Capt. Lt. James Bruff, and 1st Lt. Gassaway Watkins. This analysis is based on paper transfers to the 5th Maryland, effective January 1781. Other officers probably with the 2nd Maryland were Lieutenants John Lynn and Roger Nelson. The newly designated 2nd Maryland consisted of nearly 400 men on 15 March. As of 17 February, Greene had thirteen cap-

*2nd Maryland Continental infantryman. Painting by Don Troiani, www.historicalimagebank.com.*

tains, one captain-lieutenant, twelve lieutenants, and six ensigns in the Maryland brigade. By all accounts the regiment was understaffed at the company level.[46]

The Virginia brigade consisted of the 1st and 2nd Virginia Regiments of 1781, which are often, but erroneously, listed as the 4th and 5th Virginia. These regiments were similar to the Marylanders in that they included new levies as well as battle-seasoned veterans. Brig. Gen. Isaac Huger, a thirty-nine-year-old South Carolinian who had been wounded at Stono Ferry, led the brigade. During the siege of Charleston, Huger commanded light infantry forces outside the city. On 14 April 1780, at Monck's Corner, Lt. Col. Banastre Tarleton routed and destroyed Huger's force. Shortly afterwards, Huger fell ill and thus avoided being surrendered when the city fell. He took command of the Virginia brigade in February 1781.[47]

Similar to the 1st Maryland, the 1st Virginia consisted of a conglomeration of men, including many survivors of Buford's Massacre and those who had otherwise escaped capture at Charleston. Greene positioned them furthest north of the road, hidden within the woods along the west-facing slope. Since the vale bulges east at this point, they were well to the rear of the 1st Maryland's axis. They must have appeared quite ragged, as Greene wrote to Jefferson on 24 February complaining that "many of them are so ragged that it is painful to exact common duty on them. Even those of the last detachment who had short Jackets being made so bad, the shoulders of them were not lined and the rubbing of the musket has worn them to pieces."[48]

These men, roughly 450 in number, were under the command of Col. John Green, a fifty-year-old former Quaker, who had served as a captain in the 1st Virginia from September 1775 until his promotion to colonel of the 10th Virginia and subsequent transfer to the 6th Virginia in 1777–78. Green distinguished himself in the northern campaigns and had received a sword from Congress for his service at Brandywine and Monmouth. Lt. Col. Henry Lee referred to him as "one of the bravest of the brave." After the consolidation of the Virginia regiments, he was left without a command until ordered south in 1780 to take command of the remaining Virginia regulars. During the Race to the Dan, Nathanael Greene admonished the colonel upon finding him taking a nap: "Good heavens, Colonel, how can you sleep with the enemy so near, and this the very hour of surprise?" Green replied, "Why General I knew that you were awake." Greene later recalled that it was the greatest compliment he received during the entire war.[49]

Green's second in command was Lt. Col. Richard "Dick" Campbell, twenty-six years old, who had served as a captain, major, and lieutenant colonel of the 8th and 13th Virginia Regiments since 1776. In 1779–80, Campbell served on the western frontier at Fort Pitt, commanding the 13th Virginia, which was redesignated the 9th Virginia Regiment. In February 1781, Campbell requested and received a transfer to the 4th Virginia and was put in charge of new levies raised in the fall and winter of 1780–81 at Chesterfield Courthouse. Campbell collected nearly 400 new troops, including many who had prior Continental service, and marched them to Greene's army, where they became the 2nd Virginia. Campbell may have hoped to command them, but since Lt. Col. Samuel Hawes of the 6th Virginia had seniority, he was given command, and Campbell took his place as Green's subordinate.[50]

The 2nd Virginia was positioned between the 1st Virginia and 1st Maryland, facing northwest along the slope bordering the southern edge of the vale's eastern extension. The regiment consisted almost entirely of new levies, much like the 2nd Maryland. Many of these men, however, did have prior Continental experience. Also similar to the 2nd Maryland, there was a shortage of company officers. On 17 February 1781, the Virginia brigade had seven lieutenants and six ensigns, but only two captains. Pension records indicate that Campbell may have brought seven more captains and a handful of lieutenants and ensigns from Chesterfield Courthouse. Nevertheless, they did not have enough captains for both regiments, and pension declarations reveal that lieutenants commanded many Virginia companies at Guilford. They received uniforms before departing Virginia and drew muskets in Hillsborough. Unfortunately, the clothing's quality was defective, and the regiment likely looked quite ragged at Guilford, as reflected in Campbell's 3 April letter to Jefferson:"When I marched from the state of Virginia to join the Army I received a Pare of Overalls for Each soldier, made of Osnabrigs which did not last them more than two or three weeks, and also a shirt for Each soldier which are intirely worn out and them distressed for every kind of Cloathing Except coats."[51]

The Virginians Campbell led south provide an insight into the social background of Continental recruits in the winter 1780. The majority of these men are listed on the "Chesterfield Supplement of 1780–1781," a descriptive list of the men who passed through the Continental recruit depot at Chesterfield County Courthouse, many of whom became part of the 400-man detachment sent to Greene. The group included men who had been born in nearly every North American colony, as well as a large number from Britain, France, Germany, and even three Italians. Their average height was five foot six, with the tallest individual being six foot three and the smallest four foot three. The Chesterfield men's median age was twenty-one years, with the eldest being sixty and the youngest only thirteen. A full 51 percent of the 877 men whose ages are known were under twenty-one, with 132 of them under seventeen. Fifteen men gave their ages as over forty-five. Fully one-third of the eldest were foreign born.

Most intriguingly, considering these were Continentals from a southern state, is that descriptive records of the men concerning their hair and eye color as well as complexion indicate possibly as many as 110 African Americans were among the group. If these individuals were all truly black, it would mean they comprised more than 12½ percent of the recruits of a southern state's Continental line recruited at one particular station in 1780–81, likely reflecting a ratio consistent with other recruitment centers and possibly the state's regulars as a whole.

Many of these individuals are listed outright as having black hair, black eyes, and black complexion. Others are listed as mulatto, yellow, or swarthy, with black hair and black eyes. Still others are listed with black hair, black eyes, and "dark" complexions. This of course assumes that African Americans would have been listed with black hair and black eyes. John Chavis, a known African American who later became a prominent schoolteacher in North Carolina, is listed as having brown eyes, black hair, and a swarthy complexion. If we had not had prior knowledge of him as an African American Virginia Continental, he might have been omitted in this examination. What is more striking about the possibility that these men were African Americans is that they are obviously not slaves, because Virginia required black recruits to present a freedom certificate from their local justice of the peace. Most were farmers, but their records also reflect a wide variety of occupations, including individuals listed as blacksmiths, sailors, and carpenters. The enlistment of slaves and free blacks into the Virginia line of the Continental army likely says something about the desperate need for recruits in the turbulent years of 1780–81 and also illuminates an enlistment pattern often ignored in research of the southern regiments. At least one of the black men, Isaac Brown, was a sergeant and would have overseen white privates and corporals, a quite remarkable situation within a southern unit.

Study of this detachment's descriptive records also indicates the impact of the British blockade on the Chesapeake. A large number of those individuals whose occupations were recorded worked in maritime enterprises, including sailors, shipbuilders, and caulkers, as well as rope and sail makers. The list of occupations also indicates a major decline in small-scale manufacturing employing bricklayers, stonemasons, artists, papermakers, weavers, and shoemakers. Their ranks included twenty-one tailors, two schoolmasters, two silversmiths, a bookbinder, and one man who gave his occupation as "ditcher." However, as with all eighteenth-century armies, the majority of the men had been in agricultural pursuits. Of the nearly 900 men who provided their occupation, 592 gave their occupation as either farmer or planter. These men's occupations, ages, and places in society provide us with an interesting and rare glimpse into the livelihood and possible motivations of the eighteenth-century recruit.[52]

Between the Virginia regiments, Greene positioned a section of artillery. Capt. Lt. Ebenezer Finley commanded these two six-pounders along with two lieutenants and twenty-six enlisted men. Finley, a former Baltimore attorney who also served as deputy judge advocate general of Greene's army, had served as an artillery officer since 1777. As with Singleton's company, Finley's men are somewhat difficult to track. The men were Marylanders who had served in Capt. Richard Dorsey's artillery company at Camden. Most of Dorsey's company had been killed or captured there, and the terms of service for those who survived ended in the fall of 1780. Finley, an officer in Dorsey's company, remained with a small cadre of men who reenlisted or whose enlistments were not up yet. John Clark, one of Dorsey's men, was captured at Camden "but made his escape and rejoined his company then commanded by Lt. Ebenezer Finley and later by Captain James Smith." At the time of Guilford Courthouse, Smith was in Baltimore on recruiting duty.[53]

Several smaller militia units, most of them light horse, were operating in the Guilford Courthouse vicinity. Col. James Read, a former North Carolina Continental, had a battalion of dragoons near Greene's army, but pension declarations indicate they were not involved in the battle. Another mounted detachment, roughly one hundred men under Col. François Lellorquis, the Marquis de Malmedy and Baron de Gloeback, were north of the courthouse. Pvt. Sam Shepherd, a Wilkes County veteran of Malmedy's detachment, said that they heard the "first cannons, but did not arrive in time of the fight." Other accounts place Malmedy's men arriving at the battlefield just as the battle was ending and credit his unit with the loss of one man killed.[54]

Two companies of Virginia militia, commanded by Captains Ambrose Nelson and James Franklin, were also nearby but not involved. William and Henry Cashwill of Franklin's company reported that "we were within ten miles of Greene's army when we heard the guns but did not arrive in the time of the battle." Franklin was relieved of command shortly after the engagement when his men accused him of cowardice. Nelson's men similarly arrived after the battle concluded and were not involved in the fighting.[55]

Pension accounts suggest that Guilford County supplied at least two light horse companies commanded by Captains Thomas Cook and Daniel Gillespie that were foraging nearby but similarly did not take part in the battle. Both Samuel Gann and John Gibson, serving with Cook, claimed they were in charge of driving cattle for Greene's army. Several Guilford County men also claimed they had served as pilots for Lee's Legion under a Capt. Andrew Wilson. One, seventeen-year-old Solomon Mitchell, stated that he would have been at Guilford "but for the entreaties of my dear mother."[56]

Local individual volunteers appeared during the battle, falling in with different units as they found them. Several men joined Lynch's riflemen and Kirkwood's Delaware company on the northern flank. John Larkin, a young Guilford County Irishman, arrived with "a spit of meat in one hand and his rifle in the other." Receiving permission to fall in with Kirkwood's men, Larkin calmly "sat down, striking his spit into the ground beside him. He calmly ate from the meat while preparing his rifle for the oncoming battle." Others, such as Robert Rankin, provided similar service with Campbell's riflemen on the southern flank. Gideon Johnson "was at home plowing in his field when he heard the firing of the cannon and platoons at the battle of Guilford on 15th of March 1781, he immediately took out his horse, seized his gun and hastened hither though not himself in service."[57]

By 11:00 A.M., Greene's men were in position. With subtractions for those guarding the baggage train and the men who had fallen at the New Garden skirmishes, Greene had over 4,000 men on the field. All that remained was to sit and wait. Maj. Richard Harrison of the Granville County militia penned a quick note to his pregnant wife: "It is scarcely possible to paint the agitations of my mind . . . struggling with two of the greatest events that are in nature at the same time: the fate of my Nancy and my country. Oh, my God, I trust them with thee; do with them for the best." Referring to his unborn child, Harrison continued, "This is the very day that I hope will be given me a creature capable of enjoying what its father hope[s] to deserve and earn—the sweets of Liberty and Grace." The monotony was broken when Greene rode up and down the first line, imploring the militia to "fire two volleys and then retire." As he spoke of honor and liberty, several accounts mention Greene doffing his hat and mopping his forehead, indicating that by midday temperatures may have been quite high.[58]

Greene retired to the third line after giving his speech. Shortly afterwards, Lee's men came riding in, and the young Virginian, likely unaware of Greene's oratory, decided to give his own speech to the front line North Carolinians. Guilford County's William Lesley remembered how Lee called upon them:

"My brave boys, your lands, your lives & your country depend on your conduct this day—I have given Tarleton hell this morning & I will give him more of it before night" & speaking of the roaring of the British cannon he said "you hear damnation roaring over all these woods & after all they are no more than we" & we went on to flank the left of the American army — this deponents place in the battle was on the left of the artillery.

David Williams, an Orange County militiaman, reported that Lee appeared before the line "in a great rage for battle, and that he told them that it would be sufficient if they would stand to make two fires." Williams noted that there "appeared to be blood on his sword." Lee and his men then rode to their position on the south flank, suggesting that there was possibly a lane, or path, at the first line fence and that this connected to the southeast trending road just beyond the left flank.[59]

Around 11:30 A.M., the North Carolina militia spotted "scarlet uniforms, burnished armor, and gay banners floating in the breeze" 400 yards to the west. The citizen soldiers watched anxiously as a long column of British soldiers advanced "with a firm step and full confidence in their prowess" down the descent and across a small creek toward Joseph Hoskins's house. The wait was over. Cornwallis had arrived.[60]

*This day we fought*
*men, for some days*
*before we were*
*fighting with hunger.*
—SGT. ROGER
LAMB, *23rd Foot*

CHAPTER FOUR **THE BRITISH ARMY ADVANCES**

Cornwallis's army took nearly two hours to reach Greene's battlefield. The British likely spent half that period resting and collecting the wounded and dead. The Guards light infantry and jaegers probably replenished their ammunition. By 10:00 A.M., the column had been on its feet for nearly five hours. The men were likely tired, definitely hungry, and probably well splattered with mud. While American prisoners were marched to the rear and interrogated as to Greene's dispositions, the British evacuated their wounded to the New Garden Meeting House. Many of Cornwallis's men perhaps took the opportunity to eat their last "unground corn." After roughly twenty minutes' rest, British and German officers had their sergeants yelling for the men to fall in. Cornwallis had finally "caught" Greene, and the decisive battle that he had been seeking was at hand.

Ahead of Cornwallis's main column marched an advance party of jaegers, Guards Brigade light infantry, and the British Legion cavalry. Overall command of this advance guard fell upon Lt. Col. Banastre Tarleton. The twenty-six-year-old son of the mayor of Liverpool, Tarleton had studied law at Oxford before purchasing a commission in the 1st Dragoons. He came to America as a volunteer in December 1775 and a year later made his name by capturing Gen. Charles Lee in a nighttime raid at Basking Ridge, New Jersey. In 1778, he helped organize the British Legion, a mixed provincial unit of infantry and cavalry comprised of loyalists from New York, Pennsylvania, and New Jersey. Tarleton earned a reputation for cruelty and brutality at the Waxhaws in May 1780 when his men reputedly massacred Virginia Continentals after they had surrendered. On 17 January 1781, Daniel Morgan destroyed an expeditionary force led by Tarleton at Cowpens, South Carolina, that included the loss of the 7th Foot, the 1st Battalion of the 71st Foot, four companies of light infantry, and the majority of the British Legion infantry. Humiliated, Tarleton never forgot, nor forgave, the defeat.[1]

Tarleton's Legion dragoons, who had been held in reserve, then refused to charge, and thus escaped at Cowpens, now consisted of 272 men including Lieutenant Colonel Tarleton, 6 captains, 8 lieutenants, 3 ensigns, 20 sergeants, 5 drummers, 6 other staff, and 223 rank and file. The majority were long-term combat veterans, although at least one troop was formed from southern loyalists in February 1781. In addition to Waxhaws and Cowpens, the green-jacketed dragoons had seen action at Camden, Blackstock's, Hanging Rock, and Torrence's Tavern as well as many smaller skirmishes prior to Guilford. The cavalry also included a number of former legion infantrymen who had been mounted after Cowpens and a troop of the 17th Light Dragoons. The 17th Light Dragoons served throughout the war. At Cowpens, the forty-man detachment led by Capt. Lt. Henry Nettles saved Tarleton by charging, although outnumbered, into William Washington's cavalry. They lost several men, including Nettles, who was wounded, and Cornet Patterson, who was killed. At least two dozen men of the 17th Light Dragoons served at Guilford, although it is unclear who led them if not Nettles. Prior to Guilford, the proud regulars declined an offer to replace their tattered red regimentals with surplus British Legion green jackets.[2]

The jaegers, Germans fighting in the pay of the British army, were serving as light infantry alongside the British Legion. In 1775, Germany consisted of over 300 independent states, duchies, princedoms, bishoprics, and landgraviates. The leaders of these various courts often hired out their military units to foreign powers. After the House of Hanover ascended the British throne in 1714, Hessians served Britain during the War of Austrian Succession as well as on the battlefield of Culloden in 1746. It was no great leap for George III to turn to the Germans again to supplement his 20,000-man army in 1775. The British king struck his first deals with Charles I, Duke of Bruns-

*German jaeger. Painting by Don Troiani, www.historicalimagebank.com.*

wick, and Frederick II, Landgrave of Hesse-Cassel, in January 1776. These acquisitions were followed by deals with Hesse-Hanau, Ansbach-Bayreuth, Waldeck, and Anhalt-Zerbst. For a going rate of roughly £17 4s. per year, per man, the German states provided 30,000 men for the British army. The largest proportion came from Hesse-Cassel, so "Hessian" became synonymous for all George III's German soldiers.[3]

The jaegers who fought at Guilford Courthouse appear to have been a single Ansbach-Bayreuth company under the command of Capt. Friedrich Wilhelm von Roeder. Two such companies served in the British army during the war as part of, or attached to, the Hesse-Cassel *Jägerkorps*. Evidence also suggests the von Roeder company may have included a few Hessians as well. Consisting of one captain, one lieutenant, one sergeant, three drummers, and seventy-eight rank and file, the unit may have included an Ansbach-Bayreuth and a Hessian platoon. Jaegers (the word *Jäger* means "hunter" in German) were foresters and game wardens in their native provinces and were recruited for their prowess with the short, .54 caliber rifles, also known as Jägers, and unconventional fighting styles. Well respected by both sides, the jaegers acted as light infantry in nearly every campaign after 1775. Von Roeder arrived in America in 1778 and took command of his company in December 1779. He came from a Silesian military family, and his father was a Prussian colonel who served in the Seven Years' War.[4]

The Guards Light Infantry Company was a composite formation of the fastest, most agile men who were pulled from the two-battalion Brigade of Guards, which had itself been created for North American service by drafting men from each of the three Guards regiments in Britain. Each British army infantry regiment had two specialized "flank" companies. One was composed of grenadiers; the other was light infantry, chosen for their endurance and agility. The only British unit with flank companies present at Guilford was the Guards. Those companies represented both battalions. The light infantry company consisted of roughly 100 men, but they had suffered losses at New Garden earlier that morning. They originally may have numbered 150, but losses during the Race to the Dan, as well as at Weitzel's Mill and Clapp's Mill, had taken their toll. After Captain Goodricke's death at New Garden, command passed to Capt. Francis Dundas of the 1st Foot Guards.[5]

Next in column was Webster's brigade, consisting of about 580 men of the 23rd and 33rd Regiments of Foot. Forty-year-old Lt. Col. James Webster, the field commander of the 33rd, was the son of a prominent Edinburgh minister named Alexander Webster. A fine soldier, Webster was considered Cornwallis's right hand, and Gen. Henry Clinton, commander of all British forces in North America in 1781, recalled him as "an officer of great experience on whom I reposed the most implicit confidence." Tarleton, a man who rarely agreed with Clinton or Cornwallis, concurred that Webster "united all the virtues of civil life to the gallantry and professional knowledge of a soldier." Webster had served in America since 1776 and had distinguished himself at Monmouth. His brigade had routed Gen. Edward Stevens's Virginia militia at Camden.[6]

The 23rd Foot, known as the Royal Welch Fusiliers, had served in North America since 1773. They took part in the Lexington and Concord campaign as part of Lord Percy's relief column. The light infantry and grenadier companies distinguished themselves at Bunker Hill. In 1777, the regiment took part in the Philadelphia campaign, and in 1778, Monmouth. Shortly thereafter, they were deployed with the Royal Navy serving as marines in several inconclusive engagements with the French fleet. From late 1778 until spring 1779, the 23rd served in New York, fighting along the Hudson River. Trans-

*Infantryman of the 23rd Regiment of Foot, the Royal Welch Fusiliers. Painting by Don Troiani, www.historicalimagebank.com.*

ferred to the southern colonies as part of Gen. Sir Henry Clinton's army, the 23rd took part in the siege of Charleston and served the remainder of the war with Cornwallis.[7]

At Guilford Courthouse, the 23rd consisted of 238 men, including 3 captains, 8 lieutenants, 1 staff officer, 12 sergeants, 2 drummers, and 212 rank and file, led by Capt. Thomas Peter. Peter, described as an "attentive officer," divided the regiment into two wings, one commanded by Capt. Thomas Saumarez and the other by Capt. Forbes Champagne. Peter was an experienced soldier and had been wounded at Brandywine. Saumarez, only twenty years old, was a native of Guernsey and the son of an admiral and the brother of a Royal Navy captain and future admiral. Champagne, a twenty-nine-year-old

*Infantryman of the 33rd Regiment of Foot, Cornwallis's regiment. Painting by Don Troiani, www.historicalimagebank.com.*

Irishman of Huguenot ancestry, had previously served in the 4th Regiment of Foot. At least one subaltern, a sergeant, a corporal, and twenty to twenty-two privates were detailed to the baggage train.[8]

The 33rd Foot, considered by several observers to have been the finest drilled regiment in the army, was Cornwallis's regiment, a colonelcy he held until his death. Lord William Howe, after inspecting them in 1774, declared their discipline and drill, "established upon the truest principles, far superior to any other corps within my observation." Sgt. Roger Lamb of the 23rd Foot reported the "33d was in a high state of appointment, and exceedingly well disciplined, by that able disciplinarian Colonel Webster. I never witnessed any regiment that excelled it in discipline and military appearance." The regiment, one of only two in the British army wearing redcoats faced red, came to America with Webster and took part in the unsuccessful attack on Charleston in 1776, as well as the British victories at Long Island and Fort Washington. In 1777, the 33rd fought at Brandywine and Germantown and the following year played an important role at Monmouth. Two years later, the 33rd was sent south and helped besiege Charleston, the city that they failed to take in 1776. Afterwards, they took part in every campaign of Cornwallis's army and fought courageously at Camden under Colonel Webster's direction.[9]

At Guilford, the 33rd consisted of 234 men, comprised of 1 lieutenant colonel, 3 captains, 4 lieutenants, 4 ensigns, 1 staff member, 8 sergeants, and 213 rank and file under the overall command of Lieutenant Colonel Webster. Since Webster commanded the brigade, the officer assignments meant that a senior captain actually led the regiment, which was divided into two wings, each consisting of two companies. As with the 23rd, the two junior captains of the 33rd commanded the wings, with the companies each led by a lieutenant and an ensign. The regiment had many veteran company commanders but was likely led by Capt. Frederick Cornwallis, the army commander's nephew. Capt. Henry Broderick was also a member of the 33rd but had been detached to serve as Cornwallis's aide-de-camp. At least one subaltern, a sergeant, a corporal, and twenty to twenty-two privates were detached to the baggage train. Sgt. Roger Lamb of the 23rd recorded, "The Royal Welch fuzileers were brigaded with the 33d during the entire of the campaign in South Carolina; both regiments were well united together, and furnished an example for cleanliness, martial spirit, and good behaviour."[10]

The muster rolls of the 33rd Foot provide a representative group for the British soldiers who fought at Guilford. Their ages averaged in the late twenties, and the regiment's ranks included men who had ten and fifteen years' service. The majority of the men who marched toward Guilford that morning had been in the unit since before 1775. They were comrades who had shared their struggles in the war for nearly six years. Ensign John Fox was something of a rarity in the British army. Formerly a sergeant major with nearly thirty years' service, Fox had been commissioned for his bravery at Camden in August 1780. The ranks of the 33rd included several sets of brothers and at least one father and son. As several studies have shown, group cohesion is a vitally important, perhaps the most integral, factor influencing a unit's performance in battle. The long service records and bonds of brotherhood that had developed among the men of the 33rd evidenced in the regiment's muster rolls may explain their outstanding record during the southern campaign. Their experience and combat effectiveness were likely mirrored by the 23rd and 71st, as well as the Guards Brigade.[11]

Following closely behind Webster's men was Maj. Gen. Alexander Leslie's brigade. Leslie had the 2nd Battalion of the 71st Foot and a Hessian musketeer regiment, the Von Bose. Leslie, a fifty-year-old widower and single parent, was lieutenant colonel of the 64th Foot, an Irish regiment that served in Boston during the turbulent early 1770s. The son of the Earl of Levin, Leslie entered the army as a Guards officer in 1753 and took part in the Seven Years' War as a captain in the 64th before being promoted to lieutenant colonel. When the Revolution broke out, the 64th was detailed to guard the approaches into Boston harbor and missed several of the early engagements. During the Siege of Boston, the 64th was the last regiment evacuated. Shortly thereafter, Leslie was promoted to brigadier general and took command of the British army's three light infantry battalions. Promoted to general in 1779, he was detached to take part in the southern campaign and played a significant role at Charleston. Known for his kindness, Leslie was described by Anne Delancey Cruger, wife of one of New York's leading loyalists, as "the most friendly easy great man I have seen." John Peebles, an officer in the 42nd Foot who served with Leslie in the campaigns around New York, described him quite succinctly as "a genteel little man, lives well and drinks good claret."[12]

The elite unit in Leslie's command was the 2nd Battalion, 71st Foot, known as Fraser's Highlanders, or the "Scottish Whites." Raised in 1775 at Inverness, Edinburgh, and Glasgow, the regiment received 2,340 recruits, forcing the commanders to organize the unit as two regiment-sized battalions. The regiment was raised "for rank," meaning that unlike the traditional method of purchasing commissions, potential officers in the 71st earned their rank based on the number of men they recruited. The 71st arrived in America in the late spring of 1776. Several 2nd Battalion companies were captured aboard their transports by American vessels. As the first "foreigners" involved in the war, the 71st became the "hirelings" mentioned in the Declaration of Independence. The 71st saw extensive service in the north and became known as an "elite" unit. In December 1778, they expanded on their reputation for using the bayonet at Savannah and repeated their performance on 3 March 1779 at Briar Creek. They fought at Stono and the Siege of Savannah in 1779 and then took part in the Siege of Charleston. At Camden, the regiment played a major role in the destruction of the Maryland-Delaware Continental Division. The Marylanders returned the favor five months later at Cowpens, where they de-

*Infantryman of the 71st Regiment of Foot, Fraser's Highlanders. Painting by Don Troiani, www.historicalimagebank.com.*

stroyed the 249-man 1st Battalion. Only one officer out of the sixteen present on 17 January survived without being killed or captured.[13]

At Guilford, the 244 men of the 2nd Battalion were seeking revenge. Led by Capt. Robert Hutcheson, the battalion included some survivors of the 1st Battalion under Ens. Edward Fraser, who escaped Cowpens while serving as Tarleton's baggage guards. Captain Hutcheson had served with the 2nd Battalion since 1775, obtaining his captaincy in August 1778. He fielded a battalion consisting of 3 captains (including himself), 6 lieutenants, 5 ensigns, 1 staff member, 25 sergeants, 10 drummers, and 194 rank and file. The numbers suggest that, like the 23rd and 33rd, Fraser's Highlanders fought in two wings at Guilford. Each wing likely consisted of three companies under lieu-

*Hessian musketeer of the Von Bose Regiment. Painting by Don Troiani, www.historicalimagebank.com.*

tenants, with the two junior captains each leading a wing under Hutcheson's overall command. Although distinguished by their continued use of the Scottish bonnet, the 71st had long since discontinued wearing kilts in favor of overalls or trousers and wore redcoats faced white.[14]

Leslie's other regiment, the musketeers of the Von Bose Regiment, came to America in 1776 as a portion of the "Hessian" mercenaries hired by George III. German regiments were named for their commanding officers, or *chefs*, and the Von Bose first arrived in America in 1776 as the Von Trumbach Regiment under Maj. Gen. Karl Levin Von Trumbach. On 19 October 1778, Lt. Gen. Karl von Bose, formerly colonel of the Ditfurth Regiment, replaced Trumbach, and the unit became the Von Bose. From 1776 to 1780, the regiment was garrisoned in New York, taking part in several small skirmishes and playing a minor role in Clinton's 1777 Hudson River expedition. In April 1780, the regiment took part in the successful raid on Paramus, New Jersey, and the following October set sail with 17 officers and 580 men with Leslie, first for Virginia and then Charleston.[15]

The Von Bose joined Cornwallis's army in December 1780 and suffered severely throughout the Race to the Dan. Regimental records indicate a large number of desertions and deaths by disease in January and February. Clothed in blue coats faced white, with red turnbacks, not too unlike the uniforms of the Virginia and Maryland Continentals, the regiment numbered 321 men consisting of 1 major, 4 captains, 4 lieutenants, 2 ensigns, 1 staff member, 35 sergeants, 18 drummers, and 256 rank and file on 15 March. One subaltern, a sergeant, corporal, and twenty privates were detached with the baggage train, although as with the 23rd Foot, 33rd Foot, and 1st Guards, it remains unclear whether they were included in the 15 March field return figures. Although administratively the regiment was divided into five companies, the even number of captains and lieutenants suggests that they fought at Guilford in wings, each consisting of two companies, with the men of the fifth company possibly divided, a platoon going to each respective wing. The regimental rolls illustrate that they had field musicians consisting of drummers, but no fifers, and also a band of oboists.

The Von Bose were led by Maj. Johann Christian Du Buy, a forty-four-year-old native of Dresden who had spent thirty years as a soldier and fought in thirteen battles during the Seven Years' War. Baron von Knyphausen referred to him as "a most capable, gallant, and meritorious man." Du Buy led the raid on Paramus, about which John Graves Simcoe commented, "Major DuBuy seemed to be a master of the country through which he had to pass." Most of the other officers and a large proportion of the enlisted men had also served in the Seven Years' War. The average age of Von Bose soldiers whose dates of birth are known was thirty-three at the time of Guilford Courthouse. For those Americans used in this study, the average age was twenty-three, and although much less available for the British soldiers, statistics suggest that their average age was roughly twenty-eight. Many Germans who fought in America were draftees in 1776; however, most probably had prior military experience.[16]

The Hessian muskets may have been almost as old as the men carrying them. Although many German soldiers carried Prussian weapons produced at Potsdam, most Hessian soldiers apparently shouldered .72 caliber muskets made at Schmalkalden. These weapons, some of which were nearly thirty years old, were replaced at Wilmington after the Guilford campaign. In an April 1781 letter to Landgrave Frederick II, Du Buy "could not refrain from mentioning that all our guns were in a very bad condition and almost useless as we had been obliged to leave our gunsmith behind on account of illness when we left New York, and that consequently we had not been able to have anything done to them for the last seven months, and that I was, therefore, very anxious that we should be supplied with English guns." He noted that senior ordnance officer Lt. John McLeod of the Royal Artillery should "take the old ones instead and give them to the Provincial troops, who would only desert with them and make little use of them."[17]

Marching behind Von Bose was the Brigade of Guards, the elite of Cornwallis's army. The British army had three regiments of Foot Guards who could trace their lineages to the 1660s. These units were considered the elite of the British military and given the finest clothing, weaponry, and training possible. Only recruits of the finest order were allowed in, and officers who obtained commissions in the Guards held one rank above their status within the Guards when serving with non-Guard regiments. Not surprisingly, many Guards officers came from the highest strata of British society.[18]

The British war ministers authorized formation of a detachment from the three Foot Guards regiments to serve in America on 13 February 1776. Each of the sixty-four Foot Guards companies provided fifteen privates. The regiments also provided officers, noncommissioned officers, and musicians. In addition, a surgeon, mate, and chaplain were recruited. The men were then divided into eight line companies, one light infantry company, and one grenadier company. Each company had nearly 100 men. The brigade was placed under the command of Brig. Gen. George Mathew of the Coldstream Guards and set sail for America on 2 May 1776.[19]

The Guards arrived off Long Island in August 1776. The brigade was divided into two battalions of five companies each, and the traditional Guards parade uniform was given up in favor of a campaign dress consisting of trousers, eighteen yards less of white lace on the coats (with the exception of the 1st Battalion's shoulder straps), and the cocked hats of the line infantry were cut down and turned up on one side. Officers were ordered to "wear the same uniform as the common soldiers, and their hair to be dressed in the like manner, so that they may not be distinguished from them by the riflemen, who aim particularly at the officers." On 27 August 1776, five days after first setting foot on American soil, the brigade saw its first combat at Long Island. They participated in the 1776 New York campaigns and in 1777 took part in the Philadelphia campaign. The following year, the Guards fought at Monmouth and then became part of the New York garrison until 1780, when they were ordered south, joining Cornwallis's army in January 1781.[20]

The Guards Brigade received a restructuring in command upon joining Cornwallis's force. Recalled to England in late 1780, Brig. Gen. George Mathew had temporarily been replaced by Brig. Gen. John Howard of the 1st Foot Guards. Howard, the fifty-year-old son of the Earl of Suffolk, had served in the British army since 1756 and saw extensive combat during the Seven Years' War. He had been in America since 1777, seeing action throughout the northern campaigns. In January 1781, Brig. Gen. Charles O'Hara, senior to Howard in time served, arrived from England with orders to take command. Howard stepped aside but remained with the army as a "volunteer."[21]

The Guards' new commander was a larger-than-life figure. Charles O'Hara was born in 1739, the son of James O'Hara, Lord Tyrawley, a British field marshal who served as British envoy to both Portugal and Russia and was best known for his licentiousness. Horace Walpole noted Tyrawley's return from Portugal, stating that he had brought "three wives and fourteen children; one of the former is a Portuguese with long, black hair plaited down to the bottom of her back." Charles was the issue of James O'Hara and Walpole's Portuguese woman, Donna Anna. His half-siblings included fellow future British officer James O'Hara Jr. and the well-known actress George Anne Bellamy.[22]

Sent to Westminster School as a boy, Charles entered the army as an ensign in the 8th Foot at age eleven in 1751, followed by an appointment as a cornet in the 3rd Dragoons the following year. Four years later, he was appointed a lieutenant in the Coldstream Guards, his father's regiment. He served briefly in the Seven Years' War, seeing little action but still achieving promotion to lieutenant colonel. In 1765, O'Hara was made governor of Senegambia and commandant of His Majesty's African Corps of Foot, a penal detachment of delinquent soldiers offered pardons in exchange for life service in Africa. During the next eleven years, O'Hara managed to completely alienate the civil authorities through his inattention to administrative duties. In addition, he nearly lost his entire command to disease. In September 1776, the British Board of Trade recalled him. Shortly thereafter, he shipped for America, where he arrived in March 1777.[23]

O'Hara spent the next two years in a series of administrative positions dealing with such things as prisoner exchange. Following his father's example as a lover of wine and women, O'Hara developed quite a reputation while stationed in Philadelphia. He helped organize Lord William Howe's departure party, or "mischianza," in May 1778. George III once said of O'Hara, an inveterate gambler, that "though a very clever man, he is not the best economist." Tired of administrative duty, O'Hara returned home in February 1779 but was called back in October 1780 to command the Guards Brigade. O'Hara likely saw this as an opportunity to make his name, considering he had spent nearly thirty years in the army and only been in action on a few, minor occasions. Some officers obviously felt that he lacked any military acumen. John Graves Simcoe once remarked to Henry Clinton that O'Hara was "the person one would wish at the Head of the Enemy's Army."[24]

At Guilford Courthouse, O'Hara's command consisted of nearly 530 men divided into two battalions of two companies, plus the grenadier and light infantry companies. On 1 March, the brigade reported 605 men present for duty, but they lost 71 men during the skirmishing prior to Guilford. Cornwallis's morning report for 15 March gives the brigade's total strength as 481, although it is unclear whether or not this figure includes the 2 sergeants, 2 corporals, and 35 enlisted men detached to the baggage guard. The figure may include the light infantry and grenadier companies, and if so, this means each company of the Guards Brigade fielded roughly 80 men. Lt. Col. Chapple Norton, a twenty-year veteran of the British army whose father was a member of Parliament, led the 1st Battalion, and Lt. Col. James Stuart, the son of a Scottish earl and twenty-five-year veteran with service in the Seven Years' War, commanded the 2nd. Capt. Napier Christie, an American by birth and son of British general Gabriel Christie, and Capt. William Home, 2nd Earl of Dunglass, led the Guards Grenadier Company. Several other notables served with the Guards at Guilford, including Pennsylvania-born Capt. Francis Richardson; Brig. Gen. George Mathew's son and namesake, Lt. George Mathew; Capt. William Schutz, the son of the Coldstream Guard's commander; and Ens. John Stuart, the son and namesake of the British superintendent of Indian Affairs in the southern colonies.[25]

Cornwallis's artillery consisted of four six-pounders and two three-pounders from the 4th Battalion, Royal Artillery. Orderly books indicate that the artillery was divided into three two-gun sections. The company consisted of 3 lieutenants, 7 sergeants, and 40 matrosses. Exactly which officer was in charge of the entire company is unknown, but considering the Royal Artillery served the majority of the war in detachments scattered at various posts, it was not uncommon for sections to be grouped together as they were

*Royal Artilleryman. Painting by Don Troiani,*
*www.historicalimagebank.com.*

in Cornwallis's army. The three officers were Lieutenants John McLeod, John Smith, and Augustus O'Hara, Brigadier General O'Hara's nephew.[26]

Cornwallis and his staff remained close to the artillery but in the rear of the main line. His aides included his adjutant general, Maj. John Despard of the Volunteers of Ireland; quartermaster general Maj. Richard England of the 47th Foot; and his secretary, Maj. Alexander Ross of the 45th Foot. Capt. Henry Broderick, 23rd Foot, served as Cornwallis's aide-de-camp. Immediately before Guilford Courthouse, Broderick was involved with an American, Lt. Col. Edward Carrington, in trying to arrange a prisoner exchange. The British general also had the services of Ens. Henry Haldane, Royal Engineers, who provided the first published map of the battle of Guilford Courthouse.

Exactly how Despard, England, and Ross were chosen to accompany Corn-wallis's army is unknown, since none of their parent regiments were present. Thirty-nine-year-old Ross was a close personal friend of Cornwallis before the war. England had suffered a severe wound at Bunker Hill in 1775 and likely received the appointment as a personal favor from Cornwallis. Despard, a career soldier, had been captured in 1775 and spent a year in a Whig prison. After his exchange, he rejoined the army and in 1778 had been put in charge of the Volunteers of Ireland, a loyalist corps raised by Lord Francis Rawdon. The following year he had became deputy adjutant general of the British army in North America.[27]

Cornwallis wasted no time in situating his forces upon discovering Greene's troops blocking the road. He ordered Leslie, Webster, and O'Hara to advance and deploy into line north and south of the road. The anticipation of the coming fight had to weigh heavily on the British soldiers' minds, most of whom were exhausted and starving. Sgt. Roger Lamb of the 23rd Foot, recalling the events of that morning in later life, stated, "This day we fought men, for some days before we were fighting hunger." As each unit crossed Horsepen Creek, they deployed into the woods, assuming their linear for-mations to the left or right about a hundred yards west of Joseph Hoskins's house. They did so under a bombardment of solid shot fired by Anthony Singleton's artillery that had moved forward, several yards in advance of the North Carolina militia line. Jeremiah Gurley, a Johnston County militiaman, later recalled, "Affiant and his company were near the center of Greene's line, which opened at the center & the artillery passed through, formed in front & returned the cannonade." Utilizing the ranges provided by Edward Carring-ton that morning, Singleton began inflicting discomfort and some injury to the British. Because of the dense woods adjacent to the road, Singleton's shot would only fall on the head of each British regiment as it turned to de-ploy.[28]

Anxious to answer the American artillery, Cornwallis ordered Lieutenants McLeod, Smith, and O'Hara to advance their pieces to the front and return fire. Exactly which guns were brought forward remains a mystery. Tarleton claimed they were three-pounders, but if so they would have been badly outranged by Singleton's six-pounders. It is more likely that the British used their own six-pounders in the long-range artillery duel, as Cornwallis re-ported. Further confusion exists about the number of British guns employed in the preliminary bombardment. Tarleton's map shows three guns. Logic and regulations state that there should have been a fourth, but no record of what happened to it exists. Room to maneuver in the roadbed may have been tight with two guns, let alone three or four, and it is likely they did not attempt to deploy the guns in the adjacent woods. Perhaps the fourth simply could not maneuver, or it may have been dismounted by a lucky American shot.[29]

The artillery duel lasted at least twenty minutes but inflicted only minor casualties on each side. Firing one shot per gun every minute would mean the Americans got off some twenty to thirty rounds, the basic load in their ammunition boxes. The British probably fired a few less, as they began firing after the Americans revealed their presence. The Americans then apparently withdrew their guns, as there is no evidence suggesting their active participation in repelling the British attack on the first line. A variety of reasons explain Singleton's withdrawal. His horses may have been dead by this point, and it would have taken considerable time to move the guns up the road by hand. Singleton had orders to fall back to the third line and join the Continentals, and he likely realized that if he remained in place he would lose his guns upon the first line's expected collapse. Singleton also may have run low on ammunition. Exactly how many rounds the first line American artillery had is unclear, but they could easily have expended their ready supply, unless their ammunition wagon came forward with them to the front line, an unlikely situation since it was planned for them to withdraw to the third line.

There is no official record of British losses while deploying, beyond the comment that an American solid shot killed Lt. Augustus O'Hara, a "spirited young officer . . . whilst [he was] directing the three-pounders before the line was ready to move on." American casualties were light, although Singleton's artillery horses were killed or maimed. A few North Carolina militiamen were struck down. One, a young man named Pinkerton, was "killed by the last cannonball, supposed to be from a six-pounder, thrown from the British artillery." The "ball struck him in the head, and as he was resting on one knee to keep himself more steady, which made his posture coincide with the parabolic curve of the descending ball, it tore out the spine the whole length of the body."[30]

Under the cover of the bombardment, Cornwallis deployed his forces with "the utmost rapidity." North of the road, he placed Webster's brigade, with the 33rd Foot holding the left flank and the 23rd Foot the right. South of the road stood the 71st Highlanders and the Von Bose Regiment. Johann Christian Du Buy reported that "the 71st regiment received the order to move into the forest to the right and draw up *en battaille* [line of battle]. Immediately afterwards I received the order that the Von Bose regiment was to draw up on the right wing in a line with the 71st regiment." The Hessian major noted that they "hastily laid aside their knapsacks and everything that could inconvenience a soldier" and fell into line.[31]

Supporting the main line, Cornwallis positioned the Guards Grenadiers and 2nd Guards Battalion across the road, centered behind the 23rd and 71st. Farther south, he placed the 1st Guards Battalion to support Major General Leslie and the right wing. Behind the 2nd Guards, north of the road, Cornwallis stationed the jaegers and the Guards light infantry. Across the lane from them stood Tarleton's British Legion and the 17th Light Dragoons in column as a reserve.

Cornwallis explained his plan in an after-action report: "The woods on our right and left were reported to be impracticable for cannon; but as that on our right appeared more open, I resolved to attack the left wing of the enemy." He presumably was referring to a second, smaller, open field in front of the American left flank, but his statement may also reflect that the woods south of the road were less dense than those to the north, thus agreeing with Samuel Houston's account from the American second line.[32]

Shortly after 12:00 noon, the British army started forward through the dense underbrush and woods toward Greene's first line. Few British soldiers could see the Americans. Johann Du Buy noted that, "As the whole country is covered with woods and forests, it was impossible to see the enemy, much less their position." Within minutes, the 23rd and 71st came into the open, entering the plowed fields roughly four hundred yards from the North Carolina militia line. The 33rd on the far northern flank marched forward the best they could within the woods, as their front did not extend into the field. Similarly, on the far southern side of the battlefield, the Von Bose Regiment was hidden from American sight within the woods.[33]

When the 23rd and 71st reached the clearing, the sight before them must have been quite stunning. Four hundred yards away, across a recently plowed field, "wet and muddy from the rains which had recently fallen," were several hundred militiamen with "their arms presented and resting on a rail fence." The regiments would have to cross two fence lines before reaching the Americans, the first located on the western skirt of the clearing, and then a second fence roughly 200 yards from the American line north of the road, and 150 to 175 yards south of the road. The 33rd Foot and Von Bose likely saw very little to their respective fronts other than thick woods. The 33rd's right wing companies may have entered the field's northern edges for a few brief mo-

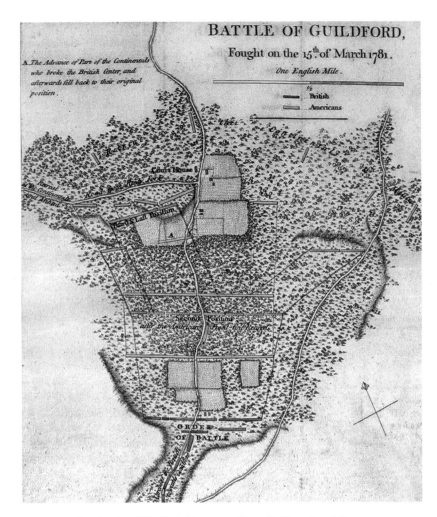

MAP FIVE *"Battle of Guildford." By Lieutenant Henry Haldane, Royal Engineers.*
*Published in Banastre Tarleton,* A History of the Campaigns of 1780 and 1781
in the Southern Provinces of North America *(1787).*

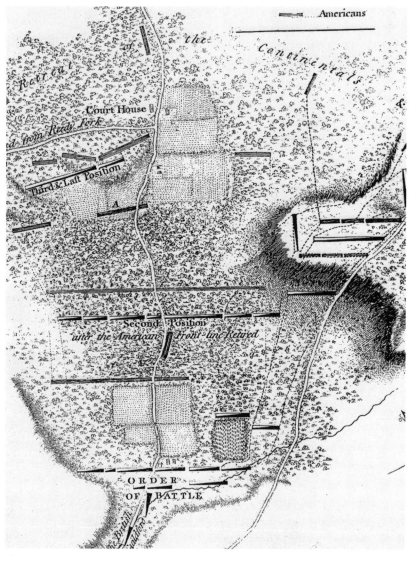

MAP SIX "*The Battle of Guildford.*" *By Charles Stedman. Published in Charles Stedman,* The History of the Origin, Progress, and Termination of the American War *(1794).*

ments. Similarly, the right half of the Von Bose Regiment would be exposed in a second soggy field roughly 300 yards south of the road that opened about 150 to 200 yards west of the southern flank of Butler's North Carolina Militia Brigade. Despite the obvious psychological, physical, and geographical difficulties before them, the veteran British and Hessian soldiers wasted no time advancing toward the North Carolina militia with "steadiness and composure." The attack on the American first line had begun.[34]

*The part of the British
line at which they aimed
looked like the scattering
stalks of a wheat field,
when the harvest man
has passed over it with
his cradle.* — WILLIAM
MONTGOMERY,
*North Carolina militia*

CHAPTER FIVE **THE FIRST LINE**

Finally seeing British soldiers advancing toward them with fixed bayonets, the North Carolina militiamen were justifiably nervous. The moment of truth was now less than ten minutes away. Officers would have been shouting encouragement to their men, reinforcing what Greene and Lee had said a few minutes earlier. The psychological impact of the advancing redcoats must have been quite dramatic for the militia. After waiting nearly two hours for the British approach, they were probably stiff and tired from inactivity. Pension accounts that mention the weather suggest humidity increased throughout the day, adding to the unpleasantness of the situation. Those nearest the road had been under artillery fire, albeit ineffective, for nearly twenty minutes, and they likely witnessed Singleton retiring up the road with the Continentals assigned to his guns after the British crossed the midfield fence line. Although many North Carolina militiamen carried muskets issued from military stores in Hillsborough, few had bayonets. And Greene's command was "fire two volleys and then retreat," so bayonets were not part of the first line's tactical plan. Veterans of previous campaigning, and the Continental officers turned militia leaders, likely attempted to alleviate the militiamen's nervousness.[1]

Exactly how long the British took to cross the 330 yards of open field north of the road is uncertain. The British army typically had three marching speeds. With the first, known as the ordinary or common step, covering "the space between [the] two feet of a man in walking, usually reckoned at 2½ feet," a British soldier advanced roughly 1 yard per second, or 75 paces in a minute. At the quick step of 120 paces per minute, a man covered roughly 5 feet, or 1⅔ yards, in the same time. The British almost always opened their advances at the quick step, according to historian Matthew Spring. The third step, basically a run, was reserved for the actual bayonet charge. Using these figures as a starting point, it is estimated that the 23rd Foot arrived at the fence dividing the northern fields in less than two minutes at the common step, and 1¼ minutes (75 seconds) at the quick step. The larger, more easterly section north of the road was 220 yards, a furlong wide and long. To cross this space without halting would take almost 3½ minutes. At the quick step, the distance would be closed more rapidly, in about 2¼ minutes. At either pace, there was adequate time to fire and reload.[2]

These ideal figures do not consider the existing conditions described by Capt. Thomas Saumarez: "The Royal Welch Fusiliers had to attack the enemy in front, under every disadvantage, having to march over a field lately ploughed, which was wet and muddy from the rains which had recently fallen. The regiment marched to the attack under a most galling and destructive fire, which it could only return by an occasional volley." The wet field undoubtedly slowed his men. He also implied that they stopped to fire back, another delay. Consequently, the British infantry could not have reached the North Carolinians in less than five minutes at the common step, especially when they had to go over a fence, re-form, halt, fire, reload at least once, and then come to a spontaneous halt before actually charging, at a distance of less than forty yards.[3]

South of the road, Hessian Berthold Koch stated, "General Leslie commanded our right wing. We advanced against the enemy without a shot coming from the enemy against us." Here, the 71st had about 170 yards to march across an open field before reaching the midfield fence. The Highlanders could cover the distance in 5 minutes at common step, or a little over 1½ minutes at the quick step. At that point, they had to clamber over a fence and reorder their ranks before stepping off again, this time facing the same distance as the 23rd Regiment north of the road. At the same time, the Hessians were moving southeast to come on line with the Highlanders.[4]

The 23rd and 71st had to keep their respective flanks aligned with the 33rd to the north and the Von Bose to the south, both of whom moved much more slowly through wooded areas. Had the 23rd and 71st Foot not done so, they would have exposed their flanks to enfilading fire. If it is assumed that they approached the middle fence at the common step, and the pace at which the flanking regiments advanced is taken into account, a proper estimate would be that the British arrived along the middle fence line in approximately 3 minutes, if not more.

According to Greene, Tarleton, and Lee, the militia first fired at 140 to 150 yards, which would have been about 75 seconds after the British crossed the middle fence lines. Lee specifically noted that the range was nearly excessive but that the firing was done on orders, presumably by riflemen: "When the enemy came within long shot, the American line, by order, began to fire." The distance is controversial. First, the earliest reference to this distance is Greene's statement, but he was with the Continentals on the third line. Tarleton, who wrote six years after the battle, was posted behind the British infantry battle line and may not have had an accurate picture of the initial range. Lee, who published his book thirty years after the war, was posted along the flank with riflemen who may well have fired sooner and at that distance.

The effective "killing range" of a smoothbore musket, with which the British, Hessians, and a majority of the North Carolina militia were armed, is about forty yards. It is highly unlikely that the senior militia officers, many of whom were Continental veterans, would have given an order to fire at a distance over three times the muskets' effective range. Morgan's order to the militia at Cowpens was to "pour but two volleys at a *killing* distance," which the "Old Wagoner" determined was inside "50 yards." Accounts by those British and Americans actually engaged at the first line suggest the main volley came at approximately 35–50 yards, further supporting the idea that the firing Greene, Tarleton, and Lee mentioned was by riflemen raking the British flanks as the redcoats re-formed after passing over the middle fences. At that range they would have been tempting targets.[5]

William Campbell, leading the Virginia riflemen on the southern flank, presents a slightly different view. According to him, the British deployed, "then immediately advanced upon our Troops, upon which the firing of small Arms began." Campbell, who was in a position to know, thus indicates that firing commenced as soon as the British began "advancing." This seems to imply that, as the British came out of the western tree line, crossed the far western fences bordering the fields, and began moving through the open, "firing" began. Campbell does not claim this was volley fire and seems to be reporting that the flankers were shooting at targets of opportunity, beginning the attrition process that would cost the British a quarter of their manpower before the day was over.[6]

The first men shot down on the British line may have been Hessians entering the southwestern field. They would have been the first to enter within range of Campbell's rifles and were in an open field with an exposed flank. They were also within 220 yards of the North Carolina line. Von Bose's commanding officer, Maj. Johann Du Buy, stated that, as the Von Bose moved through the woods before entering the open field, they found

> a deep ravine in front of us with high banks filled with water. We crossed
> it with much difficulty and then came to a fenced-in wheat field, on the
> other side of which was the enemy consisting of about 1,500 Continental
> troops and militia *en ligne*. We tore down most of the fences on our side
> and jumped over the others without, however, being inconvenienced
> by the enemy, although they were not more than 300 yards distant. I
> formed the battalion into line with the utmost dispatch and ran to meet
> the enemy in tolerable order.

The "deep ravine" encountered as they moved through the woods was probably the lower, western end of a watercourse that now ends in a pond on the Tannenbaum Park property. The leftmost companies of the Von Bose regiment entered the southernmost field about 220 yards west of the first line, but their right flank companies were exposed and within range of Campbell's Virginia riflemen posted on the ridgeline just beyond the southern edge of the field and those riflemen positioned on the first line's southern end. Although Du Buy's distances are apparently off, he suggests that they did not receive much initial fire from riflemen. Sgt. Berthold Koch claimed the Americans opened a destructive fire at 100 yards. If Koch's company was posted on the Von Bose left flank in the open, and Du Buy's on the right in the woods bordering the field, it becomes clear that perceptions of casualties relate to location. Men in the open were shot; those in the woods were not subjected to such galling fire.

Some North Carolinians under Eaton and Butler did carry rifled weapons, and they may have opened fire at the longer distances Koch reports. James Martin recalled that he was standing next to Capt. Arthur Forbis, watching the British advance. When the enemy came within 100 yards, they spotted a "British officer with his sword drawn, driving up his men." Martin challenged Forbis, who had a rifle, to "let him come another fifty yards, then take him down, which he did." The officer was likely Lt. Archibald McPherson of the 71st, who was killed at the first line. Forbis, armed with a rifle, waited till the enemy was within 50 yards, and Martin makes no statement about firing at 150 yards. Virginian Samuel Houston, who climbed into a tree to see the first line fighting, said the North Carolinians waited till the British were "very near" before they fired. Royal Welch sergeant Roger Lamb put the distance of the militia volley at 40 yards, stating that the militia were "taking aim with the nicest precision," and one Scottish account places the distance at "30 to 40 paces," or about 30 yards. Taken together, these accounts show that the rifle-armed flanking parties engaged the British much earlier, and at longer range, than the rifle-armed first line militia, but the majority of the first line militiamen fired well within "killing distance" for their muskets.[7]

Having crossed the middle fences, the British north of the road had another 200 yards to pass over before reaching the militia line. Despite being harassed by rifle fire, they advanced with an "order and coolness" that "could not sufficiently be extolled," according to Tarleton. According to Lamb, the 23rd broke into a "sharp run with weapons charged," likely meaning they trailed their muskets and moved forward, either at the quick step or the double-quick step, probably leaving their left flank open to enemy fire and possibly their right flank as well, if the 71st did not advance with them. Tarleton noted they were under fire, and this may indicate that the 23rd responded to rifle fire by an immediate assault on the "riflemen," as they had been taught.[8]

Despite their impetuous charge, when the Welch Fusiliers came within range of the North Carolinians' muskets, the veteran redcoats balked at the sight of so many muskets loaded with buck and ball aimed at them. As Lamb recalled it, "a general pause took place; both parties surveyed each other a moment with the most anxious suspense." Quickly sizing up the situation, their brigade commander, Lt. Col. James Webster, rode to the front of the 23rd and yelled, "Come on my brave Fusileers!" Instantly they broke into a "run" toward the enemy's line. According to Lt. Harry Calvert of the Royal Welch, the Americans held their fire until the redcoats were "within 50 yards."[9]

The weapons of the North Carolina militia erupted into a sulfurous cloud of smoke and fire, an image that Roger Lamb later put into poetry: "Amazing scene! What showers of mortal hail! What flaky fires!" The volleys' effects were devastating, and Capt. Thomas Saumarez reported the 23rd received "a

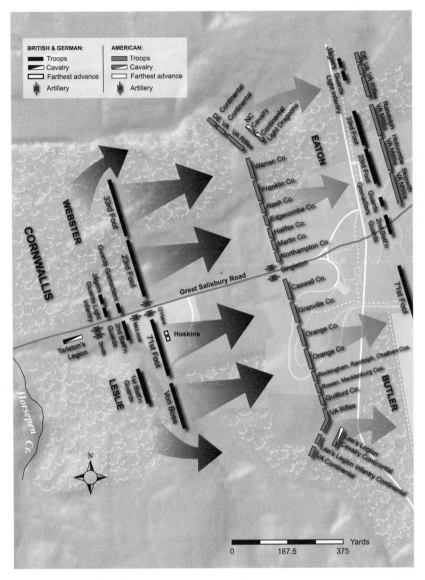

BRITISH & GERMAN:
- ▬ Troops
- ▨ Cavalry
- ▭ Farthest advance
- ⚏ Artillery

AMERICAN:
- ▬ Troops
- ▨ Cavalry
- ▭ Farthest advance
- ⚏ Artillery

CORNWALLIS

WEBSTER

33rd Foot

Guards Grenadiers
23rd Foot
Jägers Light Infantry
2nd Batt'n Guards
O'Hara
McLeod
Smith
Tarleton's Legion

Hoskins

1st Batt'n Guards

LESLIE

71st Foot

Von Bose

Horsepen Cr.

N

DE Continental
VA Continental
VA Rifles
NC Cavalry
Continental Light Dragoons

Warren Co.
Franklin Co.
Nash Co.
Edgecombe Co.
Halifax Co.
Martin Co.
Northampton Co.
Singleton
Caswell Co.
Granville Co.
Orange Co.
Orange Co.
Rockingham, Randolph, Chatham Cos.
Rowan, Mecklenburg Cos.
Guilford Co.
VA Rifles

EATON

Jägers
Guards Light Infantry
33rd Foot
23rd Foot
Grenadiers
2nd Batt'n Guards

DE VA VA Rifles
Randolph VA Militia
Holcombe VA Militia
Skipwith VA Militia

71st Foot

BUTLER

Lee's Legion Cavalry
Lee's Legion Cavalry Continental
Lee's Legion Infantry Continental
VA Continental

Great Salisbury Road

Yards
0    187.5    375

MAP SEVEN  *The first line. By Mark A. Moore, North Carolina Department of Cultural Resources. See pp. 2-3 for the full map showing the sequence of battle lines.*

*Lt. Harry Calvert (1763–1826)*
*of the Royal Welch Fusiliers.*
*Drawing by Richard Golding,*
*after line engraving by Thomas*
*Phillips.* NPG D32541. © *National*
*Portrait Gallery, London.*

most galling and destructive fire." Another officer reported that "Col. Webster was equally fortunate in the repulse of the force immediately in his front," an indication that the North Carolina fire was just as devastating as Lamb and Saumarez reported.[10]

The British losses and North Carolina militia's performance are related to time, space, and the American cartridge. Continental infantrymen had been using buck and ball cartridges since roughly 1778. This was a lethal combination of one large ball with at least three buckshot in the .30 caliber range. North Carolina militiamen used seven buckshot in their buck and ball loads as early as 1760 and were using the same load at Camden in August 1780. Modern experiments we conducted with buck and ball loads demonstrate that even inexperienced shooters quite easily hit a man-sized target with the big ball at 50 yards, but often none of the buckshot hit home, either falling to the ground or flying wide at that range. In the hands of an experienced shooter working with only three buckshot, at 45 yards the big ball hit every time, but only one buckshot hit a man-sized silhouette while another hit a similar target to the right. This sequence was repeated at 40 yards and 35 yards, with all the large shot and increasing numbers of buckshot hitting the

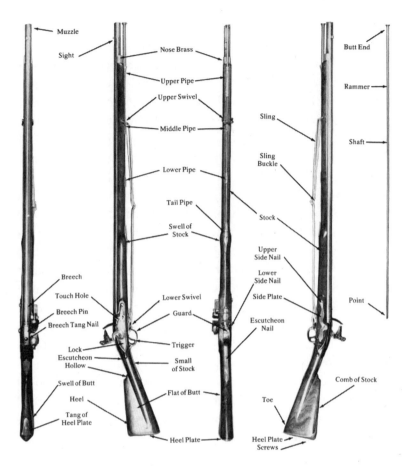

*Musket nomenclature. From* The Exercise of Arms in the Continental Infantry *by Ernest W. Peterkin, courtesy Museum Restoration Service.*

targets. At 30 yards, the range effectively known as the "whites of their eyes," the center silhouette was hit dead center on the cross belts, and there was a buckshot in each arm. At 25 yards, the ball hit dead center and all three buckshot hit, including two buckshot that penetrated a strap of harness leather and then went through the ⅜-inch silhouette board. Under 25 yards, everything hit. Test firing with seven buckshot and one ball was equally instructive. At 30 yards, six of the seven buckshot hit the torso; at 20 yards, all seven hit home.[11]

It is important to note that, if the North Carolina militia were using buck and ball, the British halted at the extreme range of buckshot's effectiveness, took their fire, and then charged. The distance was great enough that, if trained troops were reloading, they could get off another shot and then "charge" their bayonets—that is, bring the musket down from the shoulder and hold it against the hip, with the attached bayonet facing outward—to resist the British attack. If the North Carolinians fired at 100 yards and then again at 30–40 yards, they would still have had some twenty seconds before their opponents reached the fence line. Most North Carolina militiamen were not experienced with live firing, however, and the British bayonets got too close before they could finish reloading, so they ran. Still, Lamb makes it clear that the British had fairly high casualties north of the road.

Positioned to the 23rd's right, the 71st crossed 150 yards of open field before they received a substantial volley. Granville County militiaman John Watkins wrote that along the left of the American line "orders were given not to fire until the Enemy passed two dead trees standing in the field through which they was to approach us, about 100 yards from the fence." Ens. Dugald Stuart of the 71st reported, "In the advance we received a very deadly fire from the Irish line of the American army, composed of their marksmen, lying on the ground behind a rail fence." He continued, "One-half of our Highlanders dropped on that spot. There ought to be a very large tumulus on that spot where our men were buried." William Montgomery of Forbis's Guilford company later recalled, "the part of the British line at which they aimed looked like the scattering stalks of a wheat field when the harvest man has passed over it with his cradle." Sam Houston, watching from his treetop, claimed the effect on the British left was "very deadly."[12]

The Germans to the 71st's south suffered as well. Hessian sergeant Koch, even allowing for exaggeration in his account, confirms this: "About 100 yards from the enemy line, they delivered a general fire and 180 men of our von Bose Regiment immediately fell." Nathan Slade, a Caswell County militiaman, remembered the British fired a second time and then a third, so at least one volley was presumably associated with halting and reloading while coming across the field, as Saumarez reported the 23rd did north of the road. The amount of time involved is reasonably plausible, even if the British moved at the double-quick step, still taking about a minute to cover 100 yards.[13]

Obviously stunned, the British and Hessians dressed their lines and returned fire. It is uncertain if Leslie and Webster coordinated the volleys of the 23rd, 71st, and Von Bose in front of the North Carolina militia. Doing so would have been quite difficult, and the British regiments likely responded as they could, rather than as a single volley or sequence of firing. During the volley firing at the first line, the 33rd probably did not fire at the first line mili-

*Capt. Thomas Saumarez (1760–1845) of the Royal Welch Fusiliers. Oil painting by unknown artist. Collections of the Royal Welch Fusiliers Museum, Caernarfon, United Kingdom.*

tiamen, because they were in the woods north of the fields, already engaged with Washington's flankers and wheeling north to engage Lynch's Bedford County riflemen and the Continental infantry under Capt. Robert Kirkwood and Lt. Philip Huffman.

The British volleys, while not as effective as the American fire, caused casualties. It is uncertain which units fired a second volley, since neither Tarleton nor Cornwallis mentioned a second British volley. The 23rd's Thomas Saumarez provides a clue, stating that the regiment advanced under fire, "which it could only return by the occasional volley," thus apparently corroborating what Slade said of the British gunfire. Saumarez further stated, "they never returned the enemy's fire but on word of command," and that when "they got within a few yards of the Americans' first line they gave a volley, and charged with such impetuosity as to cause them to retreat." Saumarez's account indicates that the 23rd may have fired at least three volleys before they charged upon the first line. Lt. Harry Calvert's account differs slightly; he reported that his men "instantly returned it [the initial volley] and did not give the enemy time to repeat their fire but rushed on them with bayonets." Several North Carolinians opposite the 23rd fell, including Jeremiah Gurley's brother William, who was killed, and William Griffis of Halifax County, who survived a "severe wound to the head." Most pension accounts indicate that the 23rd likely fired low. Militiamen John Dowtin, Peter Bailey, Elijah Hooten, and Howell Harton were all shot in the lower extremities.[14]

Those North Carolina militiamen facing the 71st and the Hessians also suffered casualties. Since the 71st was the unit facing Slade's militia regiment, the Highlanders may have followed the 23rd's example, volleying once or twice as they approached the last fence. The Hessians further toward the American left also "sent a volley after them, jumped over the fences, formed the battalion into line and followed the fugitives at double-paced march." Capt. John H. Graves of Caswell County fell, as did Capt. Arthur Forbis and Lt. William Wiley of Guilford County. Several enlisted men were shot down, including William Boyce, who lost two brothers in the same volley, and Eles Chaffin, who fell with a wound to the leg. The exact number of North Carolinians killed or wounded by the initial British fire is unknown because some continued fighting on the flanks, masking the true impact of the first line.[15]

Whether the North Carolinians fired a second volley or not has become a controversial issue. In his 16 March report to Samuel Huntington, president of Congress, Greene stated that "the North Carolina Brigades . . . waited [for] the attack until the enemy got within about one hundred and forty yards, when part of them began a fire, but a considerable part left the ground without firing at all; some fired once, some twice, and none more, except a part of a Battalion of General Eaton's brigade." Two days later, Greene's letter to Joseph Reed, president of the Pennsylvania Council, stated that the North Carolinians "had the most advantageous position I ever saw, and left it without making scarcely a shadow of opposition." On 20 March he wrote Daniel Morgan, stating that Eaton's and Butler's men had "deserted the most advantageous post I ever saw & without scarcely firing a gun." Over four days, Greene had gone from reporting that some North Carolinians fired as many as three times to saying that most fled "without scarcely firing a gun." However, Greene was not on the first line, and therefore his opinion could only have been developed through secondhand knowledge, and it is possible that he was also posturing to advocate regenerating the southern states' Continental lines instead of continuing to rely on large bodies of militia.[16]

"Light Horse Harry" Lee echoed Greene's statement that part of Eaton's brigade stayed and fought while the others fled, but nearly everything in Lee's account is suspect, if not erroneous, perhaps due to the lapse of thirty years between the actual event and his written account. First, he described part of Eaton's brigade "who clung to the militia under Clarke; which, with the legion, manfully maintained their ground." The brigade closest to Lee's Legion was commanded by Butler, not Eaton. There was no militia officer by the name of Clarke on the southern side of the road, and the only North

Carolinians who can positively be identified as fighting alongside the legion and Campbell's riflemen were Joseph Winston's Surry and Wilkes county men. Furthermore, Lee erroneously claimed that the North Carolinians fled in an "unaccountable panic; for not a man of the corps had been killed, or even wounded." Lee appears simply to have copied Greene's 16 March statement about Eaton's men, and these statements call his full account into serious question. He may simply have forgotten the militia officers' names, or he may in fact have been "embellishing" the story.[17]

British accounts shed little light on the issue. Cornwallis tersely stated that he broke the American first line quite easily. Tarleton claimed that the North Carolina militia fired at 150 yards, and that "some of them repeated their fire." Sergeant Lamb never really comments on the issue. Hessian accounts suggest that Americans on the far southern flank did not fire a second volley at the fence, but retreated a short distance and then fired. Du Buy reported the Americans "did not have time to reload," a sentiment echoed by Bernard Koch's statement that "before they could reload, we charged them with the bayonet." However, Du Buy's account does show that the militia, "profiting by all the advantages offered by the ground, halted and discharged their pieces at us. We dislodged them every time." The second half of his statement suggests there may have been more than just one or two volleys.[18]

Exactly what happened as the first line's citizen soldiers faced their moment of truth is unclear. A great many North Carolina militiamen broke and ran. Seventeen-year-old John Warren, a Northampton County militia private under Col. William Linton, admitted in his pension application, "Colonel Linton and his men broke and left the field in disorder, deponent returned as far as Halifax where he met some of the Regiment returning under Colonel Linton." Just as surely, some men, perhaps those closest to the flanks, within the woods, and near the protection of Continental bayonets and Virginia rifles, fought on quite courageously. Virginia's Samuel Houston spelled it out clearly: "Some made such haste in retreat as to bring reproach upon themselves as deficient in bravery, while their neighbors behaved like heroes." Houston, watching from his treetop perch above the second line, asserted that some North Carolinians within his view fired at least twice. "According to orders the Carolina line, when the enemy were very near, gave their fire, which on the left [sic] of the British line was very deadly, having repeated it, retreated; some remained to give a third fire." Nearer the road, Nathan Slade reported that he was reloading after his first fire, when he broke his ramrod. He immediately asked for one from the man to his right and was in the process of ramming another round home, when he realized the British were too close to fire a second round and fled. However, he claimed, "Many of the men on both sides of him did give two fires."[19]

The North Carolinians directly in the Hessian line of attack were elements of the Guilford militia and likely some from Randolph, Wilkes, and Surry Counties. Peter Rife, a Lee's Legion infantryman, declared that he witnessed North Carolina militia "clubbing their guns and beating back the Hessians from the fence." The North Carolina militiamen were using clubbed muskets because the Hessians were on them "before the enemy could reload." Rife's account contradicts Du Buy's statement about the North Carolinians fleeing, but not Koch's account, which includes the statement that "everyone was bayoneted." Rife reported that the North Carolinians fired a second volley and actually forced the Hessians to retreat forty yards. The Von Bose then charged again, but were met with a third volley that momentarily disrupted them. This sequence matches what Houston saw.[20]

Rife may have witnessed the last few moments of Arthur Forbis's command. Henry Connelly's Guilford company "all broke near the first charge in a panic and fled," although he stayed and fought, being "unable to rally them." Forbis's men stood until only four men remained who were not hurt. Forbis himself was severely wounded in the thigh and abdomen in the first British and Hessian volley and then bayoneted as the enemy passed over their position. Lt. William Wiley, his second in command, was shot down. William Paisley, one of the last four stalwarts, turned to run, when, "looking underneath the smoke, the British were so near there seemed no chance of escape; and dropping to the ground he lay with his face in the leaves as if he were dead." Luke Sartain, another young militiaman, followed Paisley's example. He was in the process of loading his weapon a second time when a bullet grazed his forehead, knocking him to the ground. Sartain "lay there flat on the ground, pretending to be dead, in which he acted his part so well that the enemy did not think worth while even to give him a push of the bayonet."[21]

On the northern flank, the "battalion of Eaton's brigade" mentioned by Greene was likely Benjamin Williams's Warren County militia, the regiment closest to Kirkwood and Lynch. Several secondary sources suggest that Greene officially commended Williams for his actions at Guilford Courthouse, and one work states that he received a sword for his courage. No primary record confirming this exists; however, Williams's position on the northern flank, shielded in woods, probably allowed his men to stay and fight longer than Eaton's other regiments. If so, this may explain Greene's quote concerning one of Eaton's battalions as well as indicate the origin of the claims concerning Greene's supposed commendations of Williams. Unfortunately, none of the Warren County pensions identified so far clarify this issue.

Despite the courageous actions of small groups of North Carolina militia, the majority broke in the face of British and Hessian bayonets. Militiamen along the road were particularly hard-pressed. William Lesley, a Guilford County militiaman, stated that the intended objective of the 23rd and 71st "appeared to be the artillery" that was retreating eastwards, probably after firing into the advancing British infantry as they re-formed after crossing the middle fence lines. In pension accounts taken nearly fifty years after the battle, many North Carolinians were brutally honest about their flight. Orderly Sgt. Elihu Ayers stated that "at the battle of Guilford this applicant was one of the North Carolina militia who got panick struck and ran from the scene of action." John Amos, a Wake County man, reported that the "militia were dispersed and scattered in every direction." Westwood Armistead's pension application similarly stated that his entire company fled as the British charge began. Many men ran directly to the rear, moving through Lawson's and Stevens's brigades. The Virginians had received orders to open their lines and let the North Carolinians pass through so they could re-form near the courthouse. Other militiamen made their way to the northern and southern flanks and disappeared into the woods beyond, as the British "charged with such impetuosity as to cause them to retreat, which they did to the right and left flanks."[22]

Greene later asserted, "The General and field Officers did all they could to induce the Men to stand their Ground, but neither the advantages of the position nor any other consideration could induce them to stay. They left the ground and many of them threw away their arms." Lee claimed that he had even ridden among the men, attempting to rally them and "threatening to fall upon them with his cavalry." Again following Greene's lead, Lee stated, "every effort was made by the generals Butler and Eaton, assisted by colonel Davie, commissary general, with many officers of every grade, to stop this unaccountable panic." Davie disagreed with Lee and Greene, arguing that the militia, "never were so wretchedly officered as they were that day." Nathan Slade agreed, and in his pension application stated, "the general who had immediate command of the portion of troops I belonged to was Butler—an officer in whose courage and skill I then had no confidence and have now but little respect for his character." Davie also disputed Greene's claim concerning the advantageous nature of the North Carolina position, offering his own opinion that the fence "was a cover too insignificant to inspire any confidence." However, Saumarez, whose men stormed that fence, felt the North Carolinians "were most advantageously posted on a rising ground and behind rails." Davie further challenged Greene's tactical deployment, writing that "his 2nd line was too remote from the 1st to give it any support, and the position of the Continentals forbade any movement that could succor the 2nd line or second their efforts."[23]

As the 23rd and 71st broke through the North Carolina center, the 33rd and Von Bose turned their attention to the flanks, attacking Kirkwood and Lynch on the northern flank and Campbell, Winston, and Lee on the southern. As these units moved after the flankers, they began separating entirely from their brigades. As the 33rd advanced to the northeast, the 23rd, attempting to maintain their brigade's alignment, was drawn to the north as well, resulting in a large gap developing in the British center. In response, Brigadier General O'Hara led the 2nd Battalion of Guards under James Stuart and the Guards Grenadier Company into the space. Cornwallis also sent the light infantry of the Guards and the jaegers into the woods to support the 33rd's northern flank. For the Von Bose Regiment, O'Hara advanced the 1st Battalion of Guards under Chapple Norton to cover the Hessians' right flank. Greene's "Corps of Observation" had successfully forced the British to extend their battle line and commit their only reserves.[24]

After firing on the initial British advance, the flankers' activity consisted of a long fighting withdrawal. From the beginning of the battle, Lynch's Bedford riflemen north of the road, and Campbell's and Winston's riflemen on the southern flank harassed the British and Hessians. Delaware Continental sergeant major William Seymour said that the "riflemen and musquetry behaved with great bravery, killing and wounding great numbers of the enemy." He claimed that the men under William Washington were "attacked by three British regiments," presumably meaning the 33rd, the Guards light infantry, and the jaegers. The dense woods dictated that the northern flank fighting took place at a much more personal range, even though both sides had numerous riflemen who were apparently assigned to kill officers. John Larkin, a Guilford County man who volunteered to serve alongside Kirkwood's men, said they received orders not to fire until the British were within "sixty steps [50 yards]." He also noted that Kirkwood's men were not in a linear formation but had chosen trees to stand behind. Shortly after the North Carolina line collapsed, Kirkwood and Lynch began a fighting withdrawal to the east, drawing the jaegers, the Guards light infantry, the 33rd, and eventually the 23rd northward.[25]

When Webster found "that the left of the 33rd was exposed to a heavy fire from the right wing of the enemy, he changed his front to the left." At the same time, "the Yagers and light infantry of the Guards" moved with the 33rd, something they had done together as early as the 1776 New York campaigning. Together, they "attacked and routed" the flanking parties, at least according to Cornwallis. As the 33rd moved across the stream and attacked east along the ridgeline, the Guards Grenadier Company and 2nd Guards Battalion moved northeast to fill the gap between the 71st and the 23rd. With the exception of the British Legion dragoons, the entire British force was now on line, moving through the dense woods toward the Virginians.[26]

A similar situation occurred on the British right. Here the Hessians had been badly handled, first by Campbell's riflemen, then by the North Carolina militia. To cover the right flank and continue the attack where "the British right became so injured by the keen and advantageous contest still upheld by Campbell and the legion," Cornwallis or O'Hara told "Leslie to order into line the support under lieutenant colonel Norton." Cornwallis reported, "Major-General Leslie after being obliged, by the great extent of the enemy's line, to bring up the first battalion of Guards to the right of the regiment of Bose, soon defeated everything before him." It is unclear whether Cornwallis meant that the 1st Guards Battalion moved beyond the Hessian right flank and then drove Campbell's riflemen and the legion infantry away during the assault on the first line, or whether this shift occurred after the first line broke. Certainly, the map drawn by Charles Stedman, the commissary general of Cornwallis's army (see Map 5, Chapter 4), seems to imply that the 1st Guards were on the battle line during the assault against the North Carolina militia.[27]

As the Guards came on line, Campbell and Lee withdrew southeast to a position well south of their intended post on the second line's flank. Exactly why they did this is unknown. One of Campbell's riflemen, Rockbridge County's Andrew Wiley, offered a partial explanation, declaring, "when the Carolinians retreated, the British forces came down upon the ridge between the riflemen of the left wing and a company of riflemen commanded by Col. Campbell." The statement appears to indicate that the British managed to exploit a terrain feature separating the two bodies of troops, and that Campbell and Lee, apparently following level ground, drifted away from the main army's flank. Lee's men, especially his dragoons, may have oriented themselves on the road that bordered the southern edge of the battlefield. This would have allowed them to maneuver on horseback and cover that flank. Wiley must have been referring to the Guards, as the Hessians were still bogged down with the remaining North Carolinians.[28]

Pension declarations and postwar memoirs indicate that the British did not stop after breaking the first line but continued advancing "in their eagerness to go at the Virginia line." Their blood was up from breaking the North Carolinians, and Cornwallis did not want to lose momentum. Having driven one militia line out of the way, the British were about to face a much longer and bloodier fight against the second American line.

*The roar of musquetry*
*and cracking of rifles*
*were almost perpetual*
*and as heavy as any I ever*
*heard.* — COL. OTHO
HOLLAND WILLIAMS,
*Maryland Continental*
*Brigade, 16 March 1781*

CHAPTER SIX THE SECOND LINE

Exactly how long each British unit took to cover the 400 yards between the first and second lines cannot be determined precisely, because each unit moved at a different pace due to variations in ground cover, terrain, and American resistance. North of the road, the 33rd Foot was in woods from the time they formed their battle line, following a stream on their left and trying to maintain contact with the 23rd Foot, which moved across open fields, while fighting off a swarm of Virginia riflemen blazing away at their left flank and front. Even before they passed the axis of the first line, the 33rd had been forced to cross the stream and start fighting along the northern ridge. Once on the slope and crest, the 33rd turned east and began driving the flankers toward the rear. By the time they passed the now abandoned first line, the light infantry and the jaegers were covering the 33rd's left flank as they drove against Kirkwood's Continentals, scattered pockets of North Carolina militiamen, and, eventually, the fringes of the second line Virginia militia.

The Virginians along the second line could not see the advancing British army but were well aware of what had taken place on the first line. They heard the artillery exchange, and several cannonballs had fallen along their line.

Capt. William Dix, positioned near the south side of Great Salisbury Road, had his horse killed by a ball, but somehow he escaped injury. North of the road, St. George Tucker observed that Maj. Henry Skipwith's regiment was "in the express Direction of the Shot," although Tucker himself "was in perfect security during the whole time except from a few shot which came in the Direction towards me." These shots were likely overshoots or ricocheted rounds bouncing through the woods, as the British guns were positioned nearly 850 yards away. Eighteenth-century testing demonstrated that solid shot could travel fairly great distances and heights after falling out of its trajectory and striking the ground.[1]

The men of the second line would have then heard rifle fire and thunderous musket volleys, the screams of the wounded, officers giving orders, and the shouts of men both advancing and withdrawing. Shortly afterwards, they would have seen the North Carolina militia, some with expressions of pure terror, streaming toward them, first as individuals and small groups and then as a massive wave. The Virginia officers would have tried to calm their men, with some Virginians probably jeering the Carolinians as they ran through their open ranks. The right flank companies of Beverley Randolph's regiment may have seen Kirkwood's Delawares and Lynch's riflemen taking new positions in the trees to their right, while the men of Samuel McDowell's regiment on the far southern flank could only hear Lee and Campbell moving in the woods off to the south.

North of the road, Lawson personally ordered Randolph's and Holcombe's regiments forward upon spotting the advancing redcoats. This suggests that the 33rd made slower headway in the woods than the 23rd—not surprising, given that the 33rd had been marching through woods since advancing on the first line. The Virginians' right front would have thus overlapped the Fusiliers' northern flank and may have prompted Lawson's order. According to St. George Tucker, as soon as the "cannonading ceased, orders were given for Holcombe's regiment and the regiment on the right of him [Randolph's] to advance and annoy the enemy's left flank." Several of Lynch's riflemen witnessed Lawson personally giving the order to Randolph's regiment. The position of Lynch's riflemen and the fact that they witnessed Lawson ordering an attack against the 23rd prior to themselves being engaged further indicates that the British advance on the far northern flank, although now including the Guards light infantry and the jaegers, struggled in the broken terrain.[2]

Lawson's order created a near disaster. At the very moment Randolph's and Holcombe's regiments approached the left flank and front of the 23rd, the

Guards grenadiers and 2nd Guards Battalion advanced to fill in the British battle line and stepped into the widening gap between Skipwith and Holcombe. The Guards Grenadier Company angled north and struck Holcombe's left flank, "rolling up" the Virginians. Seeing the British in their rear "threw the militia into such confusion, that, without attending in the least to their officers who endeavored to halt them, and make them face about and engage the enemy, Holcombe's regiment and ours instantly broke off without firing a single gun, and dispersed like a flock of sheep frightened by dogs." John Chumbley, a private in Randolph's regiment, said the Virginians "withstood the enemy for some time under a severe fire," but he admitted that "the right wing to which this applicant was attached gave way first, and perhaps to[o] did not act so gallantly or fight so obstinately as the left." Chumbley seems to be referring to both regiments, rather than companies in his own unit.[3]

The battle for the second line's northern half rapidly dissolved into a series of sharp skirmishes as small squads and platoons of Virginians and British infantrymen slugged it out in the dense underbrush. Tucker reported that "with infinite labor Beverly and himself rallied about sixty or seventy of our men, and brought them to the charge." Holcombe was not so successful. He "could not rally a man though assisted by John Woodson, who acted very gallantly. With the few men we had collected, we at several times sustained an irregular kind of skirmishing with the British, and were once successful enough to drive a party for a very small distance." Tucker and Holcombe may be describing the same event when their combined pressure forced the British back. William Ligon of Randolph's regiment referred to the fighting as a "most desperate engagement." Lawson barely escaped death when a British musket ball slammed into the head of his horse, killing it instantly. Pension accounts place him on foot, exhorting his men to stand and fight.[4]

The British and Virginians exchanged numerous volleys, and Tucker later claimed that his men "fired away fifteen or eighteen rounds & some twenty rounds a man, after being put into such disorder. Such instances of the militia rallying and fighting well are not very common I am told—perhaps it is more honourable than making a good stand at first, & then quitting the Field in Disorder." The number of rounds fired by Tucker's Virginians provides some information about the length of fighting and helps explain why those militiamen who did fight finally had to withdraw. A musket flint was good for about fifteen shots. Once a flint wore down, it no longer produced sparks to ignite the priming, and the firelock became unreliable, if not useless. Consequently, Tucker, perhaps unconsciously, reported that those fighting militiamen were at a stage when they had to replace their flints, thus leaving themselves at the mercy of advancing British infantry's bayonets. Already engaged in the dense woods and now without reliable weapons, they opted to withdraw rather than take time to replace the flint, an operation of at least a minute or two, far too much time to be "naked" in the woods fighting.[5]

Seizing their opportunity, the 23rd Foot and Guards grenadiers rolled up the Virginians from south to north, then moved east, turning Skipwith's right flank and forcing it backwards while encountering the scattered clusters of Virginians who had not yet quit. Going through woods with a dense brush understory, engaging small militia groups that constantly turned and fought back, unit cohesion in the 23rd broke down, as described by Sergeant Lamb: "In fighting in the woods the battalion manoeuvering and excellency of exercise were found of little value. To prime, load, fire and charge with the bayonet expeditiously were the chief points worthy of attention."[6]

The British also expended a great deal of ammunition. Sergeant Lamb eventually became separated from his regiment while attempting to replenish his ammunition, indicating that by the second line fighting he had expended some twenty-six rounds, the typical load carried in the British cartridge pouch. One reason Lamb fired so many times is that he had learned nontraditional fighting methods more suited to the North American woods while serving with the 9th Regiment of Foot during Burgoyne's campaign that ended at Saratoga. He stated, "It was our custom after loading and priming, instead of ramming down the cartridge, to strike the breech of the firelock to the ground, and bring it to the present and fire." A loading procedure such as Lamb describes would enable far more rapid firing that would leave undisciplined soldiers without adequate ammunition at a key moment. It is likely that many men in the 23rd used similar loading methods in the second line fighting. Firing as individuals and reloading as rapidly as possible lest they be caught defenseless, soldiers of both sides, alone or in small groups, soon found their cartridge boxes running low.[7]

Capt. Thomas Saumarez recalled that the 23rd Foot obliqued north to engage a party of Virginians "formed behind brushwood." The regiment "were obliged to take the ground to their left to get clear of the brushwood. They then attacked the enemy with the bayonet in so cool and deliberate a manner as to throw the Americans into the greatest confusion and disperse them." John Chumbley may have been among these men because he fell in with a party hidden by the "cover of our undergrowth." Most of these Virginians soon joined in the flight, and the fusiliers bayoneted those who remained.

The 23rd gained the upper hand and surged forward in squads and sections, making ground where they could, moving through gaps in the broken Virginia line. Conflict became fiercer "before [the second line] was completely routed." When the Virginians who resisted began to melt away, Sergeant Lamb charged after a fleeing militia officer and was "gaining on him, when, hearing a confused noise on my left, I observed several bodies of Americans drawn up within the distance of a few yards." Under their fire, Lamb barely escaped death before "I saw a company of Guards advancing to attack these parties." Lamb must have been on the far southern flank of the 23rd, because his saviors were likely Guards grenadiers advancing northeastward after having brushed aside Skipwith's right flank. He also replenished his ammunition from a dead Guardsman, further indicating his position on the battlefield.[8]

Both sides suffered in the confusing give-and-take fighting for the woods. Tucker recorded passing "eight or ten killed or wounded" during his regiment's short-lived "drive" of the enemy unit. He also rode "over one of the haughty British officers who was lying prostrate by the Root of a Tree, genteelly dressed. One of our soldiers gave him a dram as he was expiring & bade him die like a brave man—How different this conduct from that of the Barbarians he had commanded!" As Tucker would have been facing the 23rd, it is quite likely that the man he saw was Lt. William Robins, the only fusilier officer killed at Guilford, although he may have seen Capt. Thomas Peter, who was wounded, and mistakenly thought that he expired.[9]

Along the road, Skipwith's right flank caved in but maintained unit cohesion while the grenadiers pushed by and the 2nd Guards Battalion assaulted its front and lapped around it. When the second line finally gave way, these right flank companies were aligned east and west and firing north. Skipwith was caught in a maelstrom as fire came in from front and flank. The fighting in this sector, described by Pvt. Thomas Berry as "a warm contest," appears to have been particularly intense. Skipwith's battalion was the smallest in Lawson's brigade and suffered serious harm at the hands of the grenadiers and the 2nd Guards Battalion. Pension declarations indicate the Guards fired low and then followed their volleys with the bayonet. Six of the eight identifiable wounded men from Skipwith's battalion fell with lower-body injuries. Pvt. Bartlett Cox was shot through the knee, a wound that later led to amputation. Ens. Jeremiah Dupree, the regimental color-bearer, fell with a "severe wound to his thigh," but apparently he somehow saved his flag, as there is no record of the British capturing any colors at Guilford.[10]

This interpretation is supported by archaeological evidence. The one large cluster of musket balls found on the battlefield is in the area where Skipwith's men were bent back but did not initially break. Several accounts indicate that they put up a fight before withdrawing. The 2nd Guards Battalion and the Guards Grenadier Company suffered severe casualties as well. Brig. Gen. Charles O'Hara received a ball in his thigh and temporarily relinquished command to Lt. Col. James Stuart. Capt. William Home, 2nd Earl of Dunglass, collapsed from a severe wound while leading the grenadiers, and his command fell upon Capt. Napier Christie. Christie himself may have been slightly injured; as Tarleton claimed, "all their officers were wounded." Fighting along the north side of the road became so intense, Lt. Col. John Eager Howard reported, that "Lord Cornwallis, finding Stevens' men fought bravely, and that it was difficult to force them, put himself at the head of the grenadiers and second battalion of guards, and by a vigorous charge broke the line; and that he had two horses shot under him." Howard's account is important for several reasons. First, it implies that Cornwallis saw a crisis developing, perhaps due to a shortage of officers, and rode forward to lead the attack personally. Second, Howard either mistook Lawson for Stevens, or the Guards were deployed on both sides of the road and actively engaged Stevens's northern flank. Finally, his comments about Cornwallis having horses shot from underneath him corroborates a long-disputed statement made by Sergeant Lamb:

> I saw Lord Cornwallis riding across the clear ground. His lordship
> was mounted on a dragoon's horse (his own having been shot), the
> saddlebags were under the creature's belly, which much retarded his
> progress, owing to the vast quantity of underwood that was spread over
> the ground; his lordship was evidently unconscious of the danger. I
> immediately laid hold of the bridle of his horse, and turned his head.
> I then mentioned to him, that if his lordship pursued in the same
> direction, he would in a few moments have been surrounded by the
> enemy, and, perhaps cut to pieces or captured. I continued to run along
> side the horse, keeping the bridle in my hand, until his lordship, gained
> the 23rd regiment, which was at that time drawn up in the skirt of the
> woods.[11]

Shortly after the Guards Grenadier Company turned Holcombe's flank, the 33rd, the jaegers, and the Guards light infantry engaged Lt. Col. William Washington's "Corps of Observation" on the northernmost flank. The terrain along the northern flank consisted mostly of dense woods. Washington posted himself and Lynch's rifles "on a height covered with thick woods; and had drawn up his cavalry and continental infantry about one hundred yards in their rear."[12] The dragoons were probably farther back and north of the courthouse.

Some of the most terrible fighting took place along this flank. Lynch's Virginians were completely outnumbered by the redcoats but made a brave, if not futile stand. As the jaegers came on line, the action became rifle against rifle, and casualties indicate the Germans had orders to shoot officers. Four of Lynch's eight known company commanders fell to enemy fire. Captains William Jones and Thomas Helm were both killed. Capt. David Beard was shot in the arm, and Capt. Jacob Moon "was mortally wounded, having received a ball through the left side that he caught in his hand as it passed through his right side, exclaiming to Michael Gilbert, his brother-in-law, that he had received a mortal wound." Thomas Brown, Edward Burress, and Nathanael Harris carried Moon from the field. John Bryan carried Capt. James Dixon, "a lame man," from the field on his back after Dixon's horse was killed. During their escape, Bryan received a ball that tore a hole through his shirt, burning the skin but doing no serious damage.[13]

Lynch's enlisted men suffered as badly as their officers. Pension accounts identify eleven killed and several wounded. As with the Guards grenadiers and 2nd Battalion of Guards, the British and Hessians apparently fired low. Private Henry Brown of Moon's company fell with "a wound in the thick part of my thigh." His cousin, Hubbard Brown, was shot through the hand "leaving me a cripple." Sixteen-year-old Moses Hendricks received a ball in the left leg, while Isaac Ready and Robert Church were both crippled with gunshot wounds to their hips. None ever fully recovered, but they did receive compensation for their injuries from the Virginia legislature in 1782.[14]

Under cover of the jaegers' rifle fire, the 33rd and light infantry advanced on the riflemen. Faced with the daunting prospect of defending against bayonets with clubbed rifles, Lynch's Virginians finally withdrew. As they did, Robert Kirkwood and Phillip Huffman stood firm with their Delaware and Virginia Continentals. The two regular companies fought courageously for several minutes, driving the British and Germans back at least once. As Lawson's brigade collapsed, the Continental officers knew they would soon be outflanked and began their own fighting withdrawal toward the third line.

All accounts suggest a vicious struggle on the northern flank as the Continentals and Lynch's regiment withdrew. Both sides suffered numerous losses along the second line. Although the names of many wounded and killed from the American and British units that were engaged are known, in most cases precisely where they received their injuries remains uncertain. As these units fought on all three lines, and some in the New Garden skirmishes, there remains no way of knowing exactly when or where an individual was hit. For example, Abraham Hamman of Phillip Huffman's company was wounded at Guilford serving with Kirkwood, however his pension declaration does not indicate precisely where on the field. Similarly, four jaegers, including a non-commissioned officer and a musician, were killed and three were wounded, but when and where these casualties occurred cannot be established. In addition to the losses among Lynch's officers, Lieutenant Huffman was killed shortly after the Continentals entered the fight at the second line.[15]

South of the road, Cornwallis's army had a much more difficult time pushing back Stevens's brigade. As the 23rd and Guards grenadiers overwhelmed Holcombe and Randolph, the 2nd Guards Battalion straddled the Great Salisbury Road in their assault on Stevens. Cornwallis reported that "the 71st regiment and Grenadiers, and second battalion of Guards, not knowing what was passing on their right, and hearing the fire advance on their left, continued to move forward, the artillery keeping pace with them on the road, followed by the cavalry." The 71st, who began the day with only 212 men and likely lost 20–30 soldiers on the first line, would have only taken up a small portion of Stevens's front. Therefore, it is quite possible that Howard's quote concerning the Guards meant that part of the 2nd Battalion overlapped the road and engaged Stevens's right flank and Skipwith's remaining men. South of the 71st, the Von Bose faced Stevens's extreme left flank while the 1st Guards Battalion followed the southeasterly path taken by Lee's Legion and Campbell's rifle-men.[16]

Stevens's brigade exchanged several volleys with the 71st and portions of the 2nd Guards. As with fighting to the north, the struggle south of the road soon became a contest of small squads and platoons fighting intermixed throughout the woods. Near the road, Peter Perkins's battalion struggled against the Guards' onslaught. According to Samuel Houston, "close firing began near the centre, but rather toward the right, and soon spread along the whole line." Phillip Russell was shot "in the side," and Nathan Rowland was shot while turning to run. In his disability affidavit made in 1787, Russell claimed the ball was still lodged in his foot. Pittsylvania County brothers James and John Atkinson fell with severe wounds, James having his thigh broken and John losing several fingers on his right hand. After Capt. Joseph

Morton collapsed with a wound, his company fell apart. Lt. Thomas Gaines attempted to rally his platoon "after some 30 or 40 of the company retreated." One of his men, Thomas George, "slapped him on the back and told him he would stand by him as long as there was a pea in the dish." Shortly thereafter, the dish ran out of peas, as the majority of Perkins's men fled.[17]

Fighting along the road became intense, Col. Otho Holland Williams recalled: "The Virginia Brigades of militia commanded by Generals Stevens and Lawson gave the enemy so warm a reception, and continued their opposition with such firmness . . . during which time the roar of musquetry and cracking of rifles were almost perpetual and as heavy as any I ever heard." Coming from a veteran of several of the war's most ferocious engagements, Williams's comment about the noise is testimony to the volume of fire along the second line.[18]

Near the center of the line, an equally vicious battle erupted between Nathaniel Cocke's and George Moffett's regiments and the 71st Foot. Thomas Anderson of Cocke's regiment stated that he fired his gun until the barrel became "so hot that he could scarcely hold it." Depending on the outside temperature, a musket barrel usually becomes quite hot after five or six rapid shots, so Anderson's statement corroborates fellow militiaman Isaac Grant's claim that he "fired his musket six or seven times." Several American officers were shot down. John Arrington and John Blankenship noted that Capt. John Thompson of Halifax County was killed near them. Lt. James Speed of Sylvanus Walker's company was "wounded by a ball in his left side that destroyed two or three ribs." "Lt. Speed received a wound through his right side a little below his ribs and Lieutenant [Matthew] Maury a ball through his left hip but by the vigilance of friends both were brought off the field of action." Cocke himself had his horse killed and he nearly died when a British musket ball knocked his hat from his head. The fire was too much for Maj. John Williams, as Samuel Houston noted: "Our brigade major, Mr. Williams, fled."[19]

The American enlisted men suffered too. Joseph Ligon, one of John Thompson's men, received a musket ball in his right shoulder. Edward "Ned" Tuck of Capt. Byrd Wall's company received a wound, the "British ball boring completely through his body," and was captured. Reese Gullet was shot in the thigh and then cut across the face by a Highland officer's broadsword. Eighteen-year-old Joseph Forsyth received a bayonet in the side. George Anderson of Moffett's regiment was shot through the neck, as was Frederick Burkett, but both somehow survived. Another miraculous recovery was that of William Gaulding, who survived a ball that "entered his head and exited in front of his nose." Sgt. William Harris of James Tate's company fell with wounds in both thighs. Harris had taken command of the company after the captain's death that morning at New Garden Meeting House. He had only been an American for six years when the Revolution broke out, having emigrated from London in 1769 after serving several years in the British army.[20]

As with the British north of the road, determining how many casualties the 71st Foot and 2nd Guards Battalion suffered on the second line is impossible. Charles Stedman later referred to the woodland fighting as an "action of almost infinite diversity" and described the Americans' "fierce and fatal fire." The 71st had already been hurt on the first line and probably lost several more men engaging the Virginians. The Guards took severe losses in their struggle with Perkins and Skipwith. In addition to O'Hara, Dunglass, and possibly Christie, Capt. Thomas Swanton received a wound, as did Capt. William Schutz, who was "shot through the bowels." In short succession, the Guards Grenadier Company may have lost all their officers, while the 2nd Battalion lost half their company-grade officers.[21]

The Virginians' moment of crisis came when Brigadier General Stevens was wounded. Lee later wrote that Stevens "received a ball through his thigh, which accelerated not a little the retreat of his brigade. The militia no longer presented even the show of resistance." Having already had his horse killed underneath him, Stevens was within "15 or 20 feet" of Peter Perkins's regiment near the road when he was wounded. After Stevens fell, he gave the command to fall back, and the Virginia militia south of the road began streaming rearward, beginning with the center regiments and then extending to the southern flank. Christopher Hand of Moffett's regiment said that his men "held their ground until their brave commander Gen'l Stevens ordered them to retreat."[22]

Determining Stevens's position at the time of his wounding is important for understanding the fighting at the second line's center. Exactly what took place near the road is impossible to know; however, the very fact that the Guards grenadiers and 2nd Guards Battalion struggled so much with Skipwith's and Perkins's Virginians and that Cornwallis, O'Hara, and Stevens were present indicate something dire happened there. The latter two being wounded and the former having two horses killed underneath him indicates that a ferocious fight took place. It may also indicate that the North Carolina Continental Company withdrawing up the road made a stand between Perkins and Skipwith, buying Anthony Singleton time to get his guns back to the third line. The fact that the British units in the center advanced briskly toward the guns on the first line, combined with Virginia militia accounts stating that men had to "help with the cannon," lends further credence to this argument. The majority of the North Carolina Continental pensioners who can positively be identified as having fought at Guilford were wounded in the engagement, at least two with bayonets. It seems likely that some of these men fell in this brief but deadly encounter in the center of the second line.[23]

When the northern half of Stevens's brigade began retreating, the far southern battalion, where Samuel McDowell's men fought under Maj. Alexander Stuart, stood their ground. Although they surely could hear the fighting and see the smoke of gunfire to their right, Stuart's men could see no one advancing toward them. According to Samuel Houston, two men appeared and told them "the British had fled." What apparently took place is that the British unit to their front, the 1st Guards, had followed natural terrain lines, where several slight ridges run east-southeast, in their pursuit of Campbell's riflemen and Lee's Legion. The men who appeared before Stuart's battalion stating the British had retreated were likely North Carolinians who had taken part in the fighting against the Von Bose Hessians. At any rate, their story validates Koch's claim concerning the Hessians being driven back. These men likely took part in that action and were under the impression the Hessians had retreated.[24]

Their statement implies that the Hessians became bogged down and may have indeed "clubbed muskets" with a party of North Carolinians, delaying them and preventing their reaching the second line together with the 71st Foot or 1st Guards Battalion. The 1st Guards, already engaged with Campbell's riflemen and Lee's Legion, continued to pursue them to the southeast, unaware that the Hessians had not kept up, thus exposing their left flank. Seizing the opportunity, Stuart's regiment of Rockbridge County and Augusta County militiamen struck the Guards directly in their left flank. Stuart's men eventually fell, along with Campbell and Lee, into a desperate "battle within the battle" on the American army's extreme right flank.

With the movement of Hessians and the 1st Guards Battalion to the southeast, Greene's defense in depth had succeeded in breaking up the British attack formations and causing casualties. The Virginia militia had stood their ground. Charles Magill later noted, "The greater number from Virginia behaved in such a manner as would do honor to Veterans, but were at last compell'd to give way by Superior numbers." Still, the collapse of Lawson's brigade prompted William R. Davie to state that Greene "attributes the glory acquired by Stevens to the whole of the Virginia militia, when the truth is, Lawson's brigade fought as illy as the North Carolinians. The only difference was they did not run entirely home." Otho Holland Williams later credited the success to the flanking parties, stating, "our light troops kept up a lively fire upon each flank," and despite the fact "that the fate of the day was dubious for a long time, at length their discipline prevailed."[25]

Because of the Virginians' stand and the flanking parties' resistance, the British infantry were now on slightly different axes of attack and not advancing at the same rate. Two battalions were far to the south, in continuous contact and in danger of being overwhelmed. Two had a difficult linear firefight south of the Great Salisbury Road before forcing Stevens back. The 23rd had initial success in rolling up Lawson's brigade, but many Virginians then fought on in small parties, delaying the Royal Welch Fusiliers, grenadiers, and light infantry and forcing them to expend much of their ammunition. In contrast, the 33rd Foot and the jaegers had a relatively easy time of it. They pursued Washington's flankers in a rugged give-and-take as they drove the Americans eastward. The end result of the second line fighting was that tired, numerically weakened British battalions with diminished ammunition supplies, and most important, fighting as individual units, came upon fresh Continental infantry. The result had the potential for a British disaster.

*The enemy . . . still
did us much injury from
behind the trees in the
thick wood, took advantage
of the above, and surrounding
our left flank, came on our
rear.* — MAJ. JOHANN
DU BUY, *Von Bose
Regiment, 20 April 1781*

CHAPTER SEVEN   THE BATTLE
WITHIN A BATTLE

Once the British forces moved beyond the first line, the fighting on the
southeastern flank developed separately from the main engagement. Nearly
a quarter mile south of the main line, the Von Bose and 1st Guards Battalion
became embroiled in an extremely bloody, confused fight with elements of
Maj. Alexander Stuart's Virginia militia, Col. William Campbell's riflemen,
Lt. Col. Henry Lee's Legion infantry, and Capt. Andrew Wallace's Continentals. The divergence from the main fighting occurred as Henry Lee's flank
detachments withdrew from the first line and moved along the road running southeast because it allowed his cavalry to maneuver as a solid unit.
The British extreme right flank under Maj. Gen. Alexander Leslie followed
them. Tarleton stated that "the right wing, from the thickness of the woods
and a jealousy for its right flank, had imperceptibly inclined to the right, by
which movement it had a kind of separate action after the front line of the
Americans gave way."[1]

The British, Tarleton explained, became "engaged with several bodies of
militia and riflemen above a mile distant from the center of the British army.
The 1st Battalion of Guards commanded by Lieutenant-Colonel Norton, and

the regiment of Bose, under Major De Buy [*sic*], had their share of the difficulties of the day, and, owing to the nature of the light troops opposed to them, could never make any decisive impression." While Tarleton misstated the distance from the main fighting at the end of the battle, he provided clues about the nature of the fighting. The Americans, largely without bayonets, tried to stand off and engage with rifle fire, while the Guards and Hessians tried to close with the bayonet. The result was a near disaster for both British battalions.[2]

The Hessians were initially delayed briefly by diehard parties of North Carolinians who fought them hand to hand with clubbed rifles and muskets. The 1st Guards advanced alone, stepping off obliquely toward Lee and Campbell, who were already moving southeast, in part because Lee's dragoons were confined to operating on a road that became the battlefield's de facto southern border. As they chased Lee's flankers, the Guards' left flank became exposed too, and they unwittingly came within range of Stuart's militia from Rockbridge and Augusta Counties. This was an ideal target for the riflemen. Samuel Houston almost gloated in reporting that "soon the enemy appeared to us; we fired on their flank, and that brought down many of them; at which time Capt. Tedford was killed." Charles Stedman confirmed this: "At one period of the action the first battalion of Guards was completely broken. It had suffered greatly in ascending a woody height to attack the second line of Americans." Houston described pursuing the Guards up this "woody height": "We pursued them about forty poles [220 yards], to the top of a hill, where they stood." After an impetuous chase, the Guards rallied on a low ridge and repulsed the Virginians, who "retreated from them back to where we formed. Here we repulsed them again." Once again, the Virginians went after the Guards, who retreated, then rallied, and "they a second time made us retreat back to our first ground." In this give and take, Stuart's Virginia regiment must initially have been on a small ridge, because Stedman reported that "the second line of Americans, strongly posted upon the top of it, who availing themselves of the advantages of their situation retired, as soon as they had discharged their pieces, behind the brow of the hill, which protected them from the shot of the guards, and returned as soon as they had loaded, and were again in readiness to fire."[3]

Eventually, the Guards drove Stuart's men from their position: "Notwithstanding the disadvantage under which the attack was made, the guards reached the summit of the eminence, and put this part of the American line to flight." Their success was misleading because, "no sooner was it done, than another line of the Americans presented itself to view, extending far beyond the right of the guards, and inclining towards their flank, so as to almost encompass them. The ranks of the guards had been thinned in ascending the height and a number of officers had fallen."[4]

The new line of Americans must have been Lee and Campbell coming back into the fight. Their attack must have commenced during what Houston described as the Virginians pursuit of, and repulse by, the Guards because he mentioned also encountering the Hessians. Hit in the front and flank, with casualties mounting, the Guards, perhaps the finest troops in the entire British army, began collapsing. "The great extent of their line, being poured in not only on the front, but flank of the battalion, completed its confusion and disorder, and notwithstanding every exertion made by the remaining officers, it was at last entirely broken." Every company-grade officer in the 1st Guards was struck down. Capt. Augustus Maitland was wounded, retired to the rear, had the injury dressed, and returned to the battle line. Capt. William Maynard was not so lucky. "Naturally of a cheerful disposition and great hilarity," Maynard was a man who had shown "great Gallantry," but became "possessed in his mind" of a "certain presentiment of his fate on the day of action." Maynard approached Lieutenant Colonel Norton "two or three times ... [saying] that he felt himself very uncomfortable and did not like the business at all." Norton "endeavoured to laugh him out of his melancholy ideas," but "even after the cannonade began he reiterated the forebodings of what he conceived was to happen." Wounded in the leg, Maynard asked Sgt. Maj. Robert Wilson, the battalion adjutant, for his horse, to ride to the rear. In mounting the horse, "another shot went through his lungs, and incapacitated him."[5]

Ens. John Stuart, Maitland's second in command, lay nearby, bleeding profusely from a horrible wound to the groin and lower abdomen. With Stuart wounded, the Guards battalion was without officers except Lt. Col. Chapple Norton. Adding insult to injury, one Guards officer lost a piece of his uniform as well. Virginia militiaman Samuel Kennerly took a "cocked hat & his feather from a wounded British officer as he lay on the ground."[6]

The Hessians rescued the Guards. The Von Bose "advancing in a firm and compact order" struck Stuart's Virginians in their right flank, driving them away from the Guards. While the Hessians may have refused to adopt the open order used by the British, at this point in the battle, their tighter formation saved the Guards. The Von Bose also surprised the Virginians because, in the confusion of the woods, the Virginians mistook the Hessians' regimental

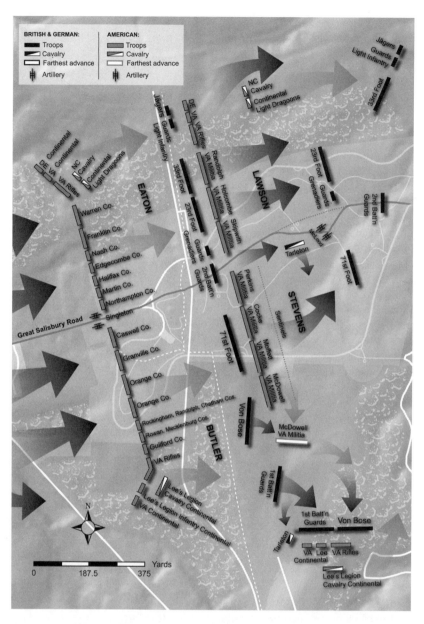

BRITISH & GERMAN:
▬ Troops
◪ Cavalry
▭ Farthest advance
⚏ Artillery

AMERICAN:
▬ Troops
◪ Cavalry
▭ Farthest advance
⚏ Artillery

Jägers
Light Infantry

NC Cavalry
Continental Light Dragoons

33rd Foot

DE VA VA Rifles

Jägers Guards
Light Infantry

DE Continental
Continental
DE VA VA Rifles
NC Cavalry
Continental Light Dragoons

39rd Foot

EATON

23rd Foot

Randolph VA Militia
Holcombe VA Militia
Skipwith VA Militia

LAWSON

23rd Foot Grenadiers
Guards Grenadiers
2nd Batt'n Guards

Warren Co.

Franklin Co.

Nash Co.

Edgecombe Co.

Halifax Co.

Martin Co.

Northampton Co.

Great Salisbury Road  Singleton

Caswell Co.

Granville Co.

Orange Co.

Orange Co.

Rockingham, Randolph, Chatham Cos.

Rowan, Mecklenburg Cos.

Guilford Co.

VA Rifles

Grenadiers Guards 2nd Batt'n

71st Foot

Perkins VA Militia
Cooke VA Militia
Moffett VA Militia
McDowell VA Militia

McLeod
Tarleton

71st Foot

STEVENS
Sentinels

Von Bose

McDowell VA Militia

BUTLER

1st Batt'n Guards

Lee's Legion Cavalry Continental
Lee's Legion Infantry Continental
VA Continental

1st Batt'n Guards  Von Bose

Tarleton

VA Lee VA Rifles
Continental

Lee's Legion Cavalry Continental

N

Yards
0    187.5    375

MAP EIGHT *The second line and the southern flank fighting. By Mark A. Moore, North Carolina Department of Cultural Resources. See pp. 2-3 for the full map showing the sequence of battle lines.*

coats for Continentals': "We were deceived by a reinforcement of Hessians, whom we took for our own, and cried to them to see if they were our friends, and shouted Liberty! Liberty! And advanced up till they let off some guns; then we fired sharply on them."[7]

Lieutenant Colonel Norton "thought the fortunate arrival of the regiment of Bose presented a favorable opportunity for forming again his battalion, and requested the Hessian Lt. Col. to wheel his regiment to the right, and cover the guards whilst their officers endeavored to rally them." Under the cover of the Hessian muskets, Norton realigned the Guards, who probably now numbered only a small fraction of their original strength. Then, having reorganized his men, Norton led his battalion off the knoll and into the woods. Charles Stedman stated, "The battalion again being formed, instantly moved forward to join the Hessians: the attack was renewed, and the enemy were defeated." However, "no sooner had the Guards and Hessians defeated the enemy in front, than they found it necessary to return and attack another body of them that appeared in the rear; and in this manner they were obliged to traverse the same ground in various directions; before the enemy were completely put to rout." As the Hessians and British moved back and forth, breaking their ranks in the thick woods, the Virginia militiamen, now joined by Campbell's riflemen, Lee's Legion infantry, and Wallace's Virginia Continentals, pulled back and enfiladed the British forces from all sides.[8]

The new American attack was made possible, although inadvertently, by Stuart's moving northeasterly, as Campbell and Lee pulled further south and southeast. The Von Bose and Guards simply advanced into the dense woods, exposing their respective left and right flanks. As Tarleton stated, "the Americans gave ground in front, and inclined to their flanks." The fighting became quite confused, with American units attacking both Von Bose and the Guards from nearly every possible angle. Stedman later stated, "As one party had disregarded the retreat of their comrades, the other had not followed the advance of their's, and they were left to decide a distinct contest." Lee stated that Stuart's men somehow linked with Campbell and the legion and that the two forces actually moved so far to the south that it "brought the combatants almost at right angles to their first formation." While Lee and Campbell faced north, "at length the Germans and the riflemen, the guards and the legion were respectively opposed." In this position, the combatants could indeed have been perpendicular to the original second line, but the Rockbridge and Augusta men who once composed the second line's left flank were not yet out of the fight. Stuart's Virginians, formed in small groups, simply drifted out of the Hessians' path and took position, first on their flank, then on their rear.

British and Hessian accounts are quite clear that they were being hit on all sides and not engaged in a linear firefight. Du Buy claimed, "The enemy, who was fortunately no longer together, but who still did us much injury from behind the trees in the thick wood, took advantage of the above, and surrounding our left flank, came on our rear." Tarleton reported that the "1st battalion of Guards and the Regiment of Bose were warmly engaged in front, flank, and rear, with some of the enemy that had been routed on the first attack and with part of the extremity of their left wing which by the closeness to the wood had been passed unbroken."[9]

Sgt. Berthold Koch reported that "the regiment had to divide into two parts. The second, commanded by Major Scheer, had to attack toward the rear, against the enemy, who were behind us, and forced them again to take flight." Major Du Buy confirmed Koch's story, explaining that "I was obliged to make the two companies of the left wing wheel around to the right in order to defend our flank and rear. The 1st Battalion of Guards, whose right wing was also flanked, lost many men and a little ground." The "front facing" Hessians continued forward, trying to engage Campbell's men with their bayonets. "In this extremity I advanced with the three companies of the right wing" against Campbell's riflemen, which "gave the Guards time to form into line and advance." The rear-facing Hessian companies held off Stuart's Virginia militia, buying time for Norton to re-form his guardsmen.[10]

The Hessians paid a heavy price in the intense fighting. Senior Capt. Johann Eichenbrodt, commanding the 2nd Company, fell wounded, as did Lt. Johann Schweiner and Lt. Phillip Ernst Geise of the 1st and 3rd Companies. Presumably, the first three companies were engaged with Campbell, and his riflemen definitely appear to have targeted Hessian officers. The rearward-facing companies also suffered, as Capt. Alexander Wilmousky, commanding the 4th Company, and Ens. Phillip von Trott both fell mortally wounded. In total, the Hessians lost twenty-two killed in action and thirty-eighty wounded. Adding to their misery, smoldering cartridge papers, floating down into the wet leaves after a Hessian volley, set the woods ablaze in front of the Von Bose regiment. "The enemy retreated back into the bushes behind them. The small arms fire from the enemy and us began in earnest. This firing ignited the foliage of the bushes and many of the wounded died in the fire."[11]

The Hessians and the Guards also had a few men taken prisoner. Andrew Wiley of Campbell's riflemen recalled, "the British forces came in on the ridge between the riflemen and a company of [illegible] . . . Campbell then of Augusta County had formed upon the rear of the left wing. But all were cut off by the Virginia forces to which this applicant belonged. They generally formed in columns of 12 & 16 men deep: but were cut off and compelled to ground arms." Here Wiley points out that Campbell's men were farther east, "upon the rear of the left wing." Wiley's account also suggests that some Guardsmen advanced in a column of platoons or squads and were isolated by Campbell's advance. The Guards as a whole claimed twenty-two men missing after the battle. Twelve Hessians from the Von Bose can positively be identified as being captured at Guilford, although there were likely more.[12]

On the American side, the fighting seemed just as bloody. Robert Rankin, a young North Carolinian fighting with Winston's withdrawing riflemen, told one commentator after the war that he stood behind a tree and fired two or three times before "the Hessians retreated, and they pursued, until they delivered their fire, when they had to retreat in turn. The Hessians then fired, raised the shout, and charged with the bayonet, driving the Americans before them until they could reload. This alternate advancing and retreating continued, the Americans driven a little further every time by the use of the bayonet." Samuel Houston later claimed that he had fired his rifle fourteen times in this fluid fight. This number of shots corresponds nicely with Tucker's comments concerning the number of shots north of the road on the second line. Houston may have stopped firing when his flint wore out.[13]

A number of Americans fell in the intense fighting. Captain Maynard of the Guards was not the only officer that day to predict his own death. Capt. Andrew Wallace, commanding the Virginia Continentals assigned to the southern flank, "that morning expressed a mournful presage that he would fall that day. In the course of the action, he sheltered himself behind a tree, with some indications of alarm. Being reproached, he immediately left the shelter, and in a moment received his death wound." Wallace was one of three brothers who died in the war. Capt. Alexander Telford of Stuart's regiment fell dead shortly after the fighting began, as did Ens. Robert Moore, and Capt. John Paxton received a musket ball in the foot. Capt. David Gwin, the Welshman who fought with Washington at Fort Necessity, caught a British musket ball in the stomach while commanding some of Campbell's riflemen but survived. Several enlisted men fell as well. James Braden, one of Campbell's men, was shot in the leg, and Samuel Kirkpatrick received "numerous wounds." Private Matthew Amix of Henry Paulding's company fell with "a ball between my shoulder and elbow that rendered my arm useless," while

Joshua Davidson of Lee's Legion infantry had his ankle shattered by a round. Samuel Kennerly may have regretted wearing the cocked hat with a feather he took from a British officer, because soon afterwards a British soldier shot him in the head. He survived but bore the scar the rest of his life.[14]

Several men also claimed they had close calls as bullets were "shot through their clothing," including Isaac Robinson, the orderly sergeant with facial markings from several years' captivity with the Shawnee, who said "some balls shot on that day in the action cut his hair and clothes." He also stated that his "captain left the company, the lieutenant staid with the company and this applicant personally saw and heard on that day Colonel Campbell giving directions to the Lieutenant when and where and how to retreat." Another rifleman claimed "Col. Campbell the officer acted well."[15]

The "battle within a battle" lasted at least thirty minutes and continued even after the main fighting ended on the third American line. Charles Stedman later reported that "the firing heard on the right, after the termination of the action in the center, and on the left, induced Lord Cornwallis to detach Tarleton with part of the cavalry, to gain intelligence of what was doing in that quarter, and to know whether general Leslie wanted assistance." Tarleton obeyed, and leaving nearly half the British Legion dragoons in the Great Salisbury Road west of the vale. Cavalry could not have operated in the dense woods and steep, broken terrain south of the Great Salisbury Road immediately west of the vale. Nor is it likely that Tarleton took his cavalry down into the vale and then south because he mentions freeing prisoners held by small parties of Americans. It is more likely that Tarleton took his men back to the first line arena and then followed the same path used by Lee after speaking to the first line militia to reach the south road. The British dragoons rode across ground already fought over as "the British cavalry, on their way to join them, found officers and men of both corps wounded, and in possession of the enemy: The prisoners were quickly rescued from the hands of their captors, and the dragoons reached General Leslie without delay."[16] Tarleton's having freed prisoners suggests that there were pockets of American resistance scattered all through the woods on the south flank and that the fighting was extremely spread out. The scattered POWs and their wardens may have been bypassed by the 71st to the north and by the Von Bose and Guards to the south. The amount of time it took Tarleton to traverse the battlefield and reach the Von Bose indicates that fighting on the south flank, the "battle within a battle," continued for quite some time after Greene's infantry left the field.

Upon Tarleton's arrival, "the guards and the Hessians were directed to fire a volley upon the largest party of the militia, and under the cover of the smoke, Lieutenant-Colonel Tarleton doubled round the right flank of the guards and charged the Americans with considerable effect. The enemy gave way on all sides and were routed with confusion and loss." Stedman erroneously reported that, "before Tarleton's arrival on the right, the affair was over, and the British troops were standing with ordered arms." In a letter written to the Hessian landgrave shortly after the battle, Johann Du Buy stated that the Hessians had pushed back Campbell's riflemen, and that "Lieutenant-Colonel Tarleton, whom Lord Cornwallis had sent with a body of his dragoons to inquire how we were getting on, came jus a'propos to rout the fugitives entirely." However, while visiting his former enemy, John Eager Howard, after the war, Du Buy admitted that the Hessians were on the verge of destruction when Tarleton's cavalry rescued them. He told Howard that Tarleton's cavalry arrived just in time to save the Von Bose, who were being 'eat up' by the American riflemen.[17]

Tarleton's men rode down and sabered many Virginia and North Carolina riflemen. He was able to do so unimpeded, because shortly before his arrival Henry Lee had withdrawn his legion to the north in an apparent effort to reinforce Greene. Lee later claimed that

> Lt. Col. Norton determined to unite with that part of the British line which by successive detachments had reached and engaged the conti- nentals. He therefore drew off in that direction, and all apprehensions of a defeat in this quarter being removed by his disappearance, Lt. Col. Lee directed his cavalry to repair to the left of the Continentals, there to act until further orders; and turning with his infantry upon the regiment of Bose, with which the riflemen were engaged, the Germans fell back, and were pursued by Colonel Campbell; when Lee with his infantry, and one company of riflemen, pressed forward to join the Continentals and take his appropriate station on their left. In this progress he again encountered the guards under Norton and passing to the right of the British, after Greene had retreated, joined his cavalry near the courthouse.[18]

Lee's account poses several problems. How did Lt. Col. Chapple Norton pull the remnants of the 1st Guards Battalion out of line and move them north? Did Lee initially send only his dragoons, while remaining with "his infantry upon the regiment of Bose," who withdrew? After the "Germans fell back," how could Lee and his infantry, along with "one company of riflemen," press toward the third line and engage Norton's battalion attempting to reach the British right? Lee's men, delayed by fighting with Von Bose, could hardly have caught the Guards on their march toward those few Continentals still remaining on the field. Lee's statement does not present an accurate evaluation of the actual situation. While his account might be a reflection of a failing memory, it might also be an attempt to save face. It is possible that as his men were retreating from the field they actually spotted the 2nd Guards Battalion near the courthouse where they had halted after the third line fighting, as the remainder of the American army retreated from the field.

There is no primary evidence suggesting the 1st Guards made any movement toward the north or northeast. Several postwar historians, including Benjamin Lossing and Eli Caruthers, suggested that Norton did indeed attempt to move the 1st Battalion of Guards northward, but both writers were simply echoing what Lee wrote. It is inconceivable that General Leslie would have ordered the 1st Guards to abandon the Von Bose on the southeastern flank. Furthermore, to do so in their regimental alignments, Norton would have had to pull the Guards from the Hessian right and maneuver around the Von Bose rear, leaving Von Bose terribly exposed.

Lee also reported that he engaged the 1st Battalion of Guards in the woods where Lawson's brigade had fought earlier. Lee surely mistakenly placed Lawson where Stevens had battled, south of the road, but it is highly improbable that Lee moved west to meet the 1st Guards moving west, or north, considering that would have placed him in the rear of Cornwallis's whole battle line. In order to reach the retreating elements of Greene's army, Lee had to move east by northeast and not due north, much less west.

Lee's timing of his departure from the Virginia riflemen is very debatable. Campbell reported that Lee left just as Tarleton approached, not before, as Lee later wrote. Another commentator stated, "the Legion infantry had retreated, and only a few resolute marksmen remained in rear of Campbell who continued firing from tree to tree," which indicates that Lee indeed left with both his cavalry and infantry. Tarleton makes no mention of any legion infantry being present. It is possible that Lee's dragoons left first, followed very shortly thereafter by his infantry, before the British Legion arrived. To do so without meeting Tarleton on his way south suggests that Lee's men were not in the vale's bottomland, but on its eastern slope, in the woods, perhaps following a path that led to the courthouse area between the fields and approximating modern Nathanael Greene Avenue. This could be construed as "passing to the right of the British," if the British were moving north, while Lee, avoiding contact, moved to reach the Continental left. It is also possible that Tarleton, to reach the southern flank, rode back down the Great Salisbury Road, then turned to the south along the same path that Lee seems to have taken after speaking to the first line militiamen. That would place him on the southeast-trending road bordering the battlefield that Lee's dragoons had moved down earlier.

Whatever Lee's intentions or actions, he left Campbell still engaged with at least the Von Bose Regiment, and without consulting him. As Tarleton's British Legion bore down on Campbell's men, the riflemen could do little but fire parting shots and run for their lives. Without the protection of Continental bayonets or dragoon sabers, the riflemen were virtually defenseless in the much thinner woods south of the courthouse. It was only because these woods were less dense that Tarleton's cavalry could chase after them.

After the Hessian volley described by Du Buy and Tarleton, the British dragoons swept down upon the Virginians, slashing down any militiaman unlucky enough to be caught in the open. Fleeing up the eastern slope of the ridgeline, the Virginian and North Carolinian foot soldiers stood little chance of outrunning the British Legion's horsemen. Samuel Houston later stated that Stuart's men were "obliged to run, and many were sore chased and some were cut down." North Carolinians Jesse Franklin and Robert Taliaferro sprinted for their horses, tied to trees nearly fifty yards in the rear of their position. They made it, but as both men mounted, a British dragoon shot Taliaferro in the back, killing him instantly. Unable to save his friend, Franklin cut the reins binding his horse to the tree and escaped. Virginian David Gamble later claimed that all but seventeen of the men in his company were killed or wounded. References to saber wounds in the pension declarations of Stuart's and Campbell's riflemen confirm that Tarleton's dragoons exacted a heavy toll.[19]

One British dragoon hacked Virginian David Steele across the head with his saber. The young man's friends helped him from the field. Steele survived, to the amazement of his friends, after undergoing an emergency trepanning and insertion of a silver plate over the injury to his skull. The Marquis de Chastellux met Steele in April 1782 and described him:

He was a young man, twenty-two years of age, . . . [with a] charming face, fine teeth, red lips, and rosy cheeks. . . . His walk and carriage did not however correspond to the freshness of his looks, for he appeared sluggish and inactive. I inquired the reason, and he told me he had been in a languishing state ever since the battle of Guilford Courthouse, where he had received fifteen or sixteen sword wounds. . . . He had a piece of his own skull, which his wife brought out to show me. . . . I was the most touched to learn that it was after he had received his first wound, and was made prisoner, that he had been thus cruelly slashed. This unfortunate young man related to me how, when beaten down and bathed in blood, he had still presence of mind enough to think that his cruel enemies would not want to leave any witness or victim of their barbarity, and that there remained to him no other way of saving his life than to pretend to have lost it.[20]

Many other Virginians fell. The young commissary, Archibald Stuart, escaped, but his father, Maj. Alexander Stuart, was cut down and taken prisoner. He later recalled, "his captors plundered him and left him standing in his cocked hat, shirt, and shoes." Many Americans threw down their weapons and surrendered. Some were spared the fate met by Virginia Continentals at Waxhaws the previous May when Tarleton's men ran amok in a frenzy of bloodletting. Pvt. Joseph Horton "gave up" to two dragoons who cornered him against a tree. Others did not quit so easily. Pvt. Samuel Steele shot one British dragoon who was pursuing him, but two others quickly overcame him. He refused to deliver up his weapon, however, and as he was being led to the rear, leapt between two fallen trees and opened fire on his would-be captors, killing one and driving the other off.[21]

Exactly how many British Legion dragoons were killed or wounded by Campbell's riflemen is impossible to know. Only a few are listed among the wounded left at New Garden Meeting House, and it is unclear whether these men were hit during the morning skirmishing or in the afternoon fighting. One parting shot struck Banastre Tarleton. While traditional postwar accounts, using Lee as a source, suggest Tarleton was wounded in a morning skirmish, Maj. Johann Du Buy was present at Tarleton's wounding. Du Buy stated shortly after the battle that Tarleton "had the misfortune to lose two fingers on his right hand by a shot from a rifleman" while engaged in the flank fighting.[22]

Surviving Virginia and North Carolina riflemen, as well as what remained of Stuart's militia regiment, fled east in the general direction of the courthouse. Tarleton's men halted their pursuit, and Major General Leslie ordered the Guards and Von Bose to march northeast, up the vale toward the third line and Reedy Creek Road. Little is known of Leslie's role in the southern flank fighting. He apparently was present and surely played a role in rallying the Guards, but there remains no extant statement about his actual activities. As the British moved north and surviving Americans fled to the east, fighting along the southeastern flank died out. The "battle within a battle" ended with a whimper, as British dragoons continued to run down and saber any men unable to reach the cover of the heavy woods to the east and south.

*Leaping a ravine, the
swords of the horsemen
were upon the enemy, who
were rejoicing in victory
and safety; and before they
suspected danger, multitudes
lay dead.* — LT. PHILEMON
HOLCOMBE, *Virginia militia*

CHAPTER EIGHT **THE THIRD LINE**

The Continentals had been waiting for nearly an hour and a half, quietly
scanning the fields down in the vale and the woods beyond the western
slopes. Separated by nearly 600 yards from the second line, the regulars saw
none of the fighting to their front and could only nervously wait, listening
to the roar of battle edging closer to them by the minute. General Nathanael
Greene, "well pleased with the present prospect, and flattering himself with
a happy conclusion, passed along the line exhorting his troops to give the
finishing blow." Greene had good reason to be optimistic as "his continental
troops were fresh, in perfect order, and upon the point of engaging an enemy,
broken into distinct parts, and probably supposing the severity of the action
to be over."[1]

Looking west, Lt. Col. John Eager Howard recollected, "the first [Mary-
land] regiment under Gunby was formed in a hollow, in the wood, and to the
right [west] of the cleared ground about the Court house. The Virginia Brigade under Genl. Huger were to our right. The second [Maryland] regiment
was at some distance to the left of the first, in the cleared ground, with its

left flank thrown back so as to form a line almost at right angles [to the] 1st regt." Howard's description suggests that the 2nd Maryland was largely south of the Great Salisbury Road, with only a segment, perhaps two companies (a division), facing west from the north side of the road. Howard also implies there was a gap between the Maryland battalions. This ground was wet and covered with a densely wooded copse, uncut because it was centered on a gully and not suitable for farming.[2]

It is likely that given the shortage of officers the 2nd Maryland was arranged into three divisions, each consisting of two companies. Two sixty-man companies would easily cover eighty yards, the distance from the Great Salisbury Road nearly to the gulley running down into the vale from a point northwest of the courthouse. Between one division positioned north of the road and the other two south of the road were posted the surviving North Carolina Continentals and Singleton's two six-pounders, positioned to fire west down the Great Salisbury Road, the probable axis of a British attack. More important, they were also located to fire across the open fields south of the courthouse and enfilade the open vale south of the road.

The Virginia regiments were aligned behind the front, or western, edge of the terrace on which they were positioned, somewhat out of the line of sight from the vale. They were virtually hidden in the woods that extended down into the vale. Lt. Col. Samuel Hawes's men were facing somewhat to the northwest, following the terrace around to the east, while Col. John Green's regiment was perhaps seventy yards further east, positioned on the slope above a wood-covered eastern extension of the vale. Numerous Virginia militiamen retreating from the second line fell in alongside Hawes's and Green's regiments. St. George Tucker reported, "Our Militia join'd the Virginia Regulars [1st Virginia] under Col. Campbell," the second in command to Green.[3]

Beyond the vale's eastern extension is a westward-leading ridge where Col. Charles Lynch's riflemen and Capt. Robert Kirkwood's Delawares took their positions. The Delawares were augmented by Capt. Phillip Huffman's surviving Virginia Continentals, who were now under Kirkwood's command because Huffman had fallen earlier in the fighting. The flanking units had already conducted a fighting withdrawal, commencing well in front of the first line and being almost constantly engaged with the 33rd Foot, the jaegers, and the light infantry of the Guards. These tired men took a position along the nose of a ridge north of the Virginians. Where the ridge joins the terrace, Washington's dragoons had immediate access to the Reedy Fork Road that ran south toward the courthouse behind the Continental infantry. They were ideally situated to react to any crisis on the third line because the road allowed rapid cavalry movement, something missing almost everywhere else on the battlefield. Capt. Lt. Ebenezer Finley's two six-pounders were situated on the terrace's southwest corner, overlooking the vale's extension and its northern extremity. The guns were positioned to fully enfilade any assault following the low ground toward Green's Virginians, yet they could still fire across the vale toward the two likely avenues of approach created by ravines heading east, off the western plateau, and down into the vale.[4]

As the last remnants of the second line withdrew across the vale, the Marylanders and Virginians steeled themselves for engaging the British infantry. Whether Greene intended it or not, the British battle line had been broken into six separate elements that would arrive at different times. The rested Continentals were being given an opportunity to closely engage a tired foe with their fresh and superior numbers. Still, the developing tactical situation held promise for both sides. If the Continental infantry held, then Greene would have a victory. If the British broke any Continental regiments, they stood a good chance of carrying the field.

The third line fighting is, on the face of it, the easiest to understand because a sequence of engagements occurred as the British infantry made their assaults across the open vale. The 33rd Regiment arrived first and immediately attacked, only to be driven back by massed Continental infantry and artillery fire. The 33rd recoiled and took a high-ground position from which they could not be dislodged. The 2nd Battalion of Guards then rushed across the vale and routed the 2nd Maryland, taking Singleton's guns in the process. The 1st Maryland and Washington's 3rd Continental light dragoons, as well as the Marquis de Bretigny's North Carolina and Thomas Watkins's Virginia horsemen, then piled into the Guards. The melee eventually drifted west. As Washington led his dragoons toward a cluster of British officers on the western heights, Lt. John McLeod's Royal Artillery section fired on them. As these events transpired, Greene opted to ensure his army's survival and ordered a withdrawal. While Green's Virginians moved to cover the withdrawal, the 23rd and the 71st Regiments entered the fight. Together with the 2nd Guards Battalion and the Guards grenadiers, these regiments moved toward the courthouse, trailed on their left by the 33rd. After a short pursuit that was checked by Green's Virginia Continentals, the British broke off pursuit, allowing Greene an unimpeded march to Troublesome Creek.

The 33rd appeared first across the vale from the Continentals. They were flanked by the Ansbach jaegers and the Guards light infantry to their north. The light infantry and jaegers probably just kept moving forward, simply continuing their running fight with Kirkwood and Lynch. Webster, spotting Finley's artillery on the terrace, and possibly not seeing many Virginia infantrymen in the woods, led his men in sliding and stumbling down the steep slope into the vale, where they re-formed and charged forward, "unsupported, the troops to his right not having advanced from inequality of ground or other impediments."[5]

Webster's impetuousness is, at first look, curious. By the third line, the 33rd certainly numbered less than 250 men and were thus completely outnumbered by Hawes and Green, let alone the 1st Maryland. The only explanation for the very experienced Webster's forward rush is that he may not have seen Hawes or Green, as their regiments were undoubtedly partially hidden behind the military crest of their terrace and in fairly thick woods. From his earlier experience fighting Americans, Webster knew a bayonet charge often won the day. So, assuming he spotted two cannon apparently only lightly defended, or possibly undefended, his apparently rash decision to charge makes more sense. Halfway across the field, Webster probably discovered his mistake. The 33rd received a volley from Hawes's troops as Finley's two guns fired case shot, and then the 33rd was struck in their right flank by volleys from the 1st Maryland. The 33rd's left front was probably also shot up by Green's men. Under this heavy fire, "with equal rapidity he [Webster] was compelled to recoil from the shock."[6]

The American pursuit across the vale was not an all-out effort. The 2nd Virginia, Green's regiment, composed almost entirely of new levies brought south by Campbell, "were repeatedly led up to action by Genl. Greene in person, and could not be induced to stand the fire of the enemy: the presence of the general seconded by the exertions of Huger, Hawes & Campbell." It seems that when Webster recoiled, Greene, Huger, and senior Virginia officers tried to rouse their men to an all-out pursuit, but Hawes's men were not willing to assault the new British position on the vale's steep western slope. Certainly, the two Virginia regiments did something here, because they both suffered casualties.[7]

Further north, the jaegers and the Guards light infantry were heavily engaged with Kirkwood, who was positioned well forward of the 2nd Virginia's right flank. The British and Germans were in open order because this part of the vale was heavily wooded. Using the trees as protection, they crossed the vale and started up the eastern slope. Firing in this sector became quite intense. Sgt. Maj. William Seymour of Delaware claimed,

> Colonel Washington's Light Infantry on the right flank was attacked by three British regiments, in which they behaved with almost incredible bravery, obliging the enemy to retreat in three different attacks, the last of which they pursued them up a very steep hill, almost inaccessible, till observing the enemy, who lay concealed in ambush, rise up, and pouring in a very heavy fire on them, in which they were obliged to retreat, having suffered very much by the last fire of the enemy.[8]

Seymour's description requires some explanation. His three British "regiments" were Webster's 33rd, the jaegers, and the light infantry of the Guards. It may be that, in addition to the jaegers and the light infantry, Webster's left flank, after crossing the vale, became engaged with the American flankers. Certainly, some 250 men, in slightly open order, would cover the space from Kirkwood's position south to beyond Finley's guns. If this is correct, then the 33rd was conceivably fired upon by four different American groups plus Finley's artillery. Seymour's "three different attacks" probably refers to the first and second lines and the continuous fighting back to the third line. He is clear that the third attack was the assault across the vale, because he links it with the British withdrawal to the very steep western slope across from Kirkwood's position.[9]

Once on the western terrace above the vale, Webster seemingly ordered his men to lie down, possibly to avoid case shot fired by Finley, as Seymour says that they "lay concealed in ambush" and had to "rise up" to fire. The statement also suggests that Kirkwood, and probably the survivors of Huffman's company, as well as some of Huger's Virginia Continentals, pursued the British to the lower western slope, where they received a volley from which they "suffered very much." Here, something of a stalemate ensued. The mortally wounded Webster was waiting for support while the Americans held their positions. As Howard noted, "We had been for some time engaged with a part of Webster's Brigade, though not hard pressed, and at that moment their fire had slackened." It is unlikely the 1st Maryland moved very far down into the vale at this time in the battle. British accounts say they were concealed from the Guards, something that would not have been possible were they in the vale's open field below their initial position. They were immediately engaged with the Guards after they turned and faced to the rear, confirming they had not moved far, if at all, in pursuit of Webster. The lack of pursuit by the Mary-landers helps explain why Greene and senior Virginia officers were trying to get the Virginia Continentals moving after Webster.[10]

As the Virginians, 1st Maryland, and Kirkwood's Delawares repulsed Web-ster, the 2nd Guards Battalion exited the woods, entering the clearing via the slope where the Great Salisbury Road dropped down into the vale. The climactic moment of the engagement was now at hand. In the next few min-utes, roughly 600 fatigued and anxious men would decide the outcome of the battle of Guilford Courthouse. Personally led by Brig. Gen. Charles O'Hara (who had his wound dressed and then returned to the fight), Brig. Gen. John Howard, and Lt. Col. James Stuart, the Guards charged across the open vale directly toward Singleton's artillery and the 2nd Maryland. Cornwallis stated, "The second battalion of Guards first gained the clear ground near Guilford Court-house, and found a corps of Continental infantry, much superior in number, formed in the open field on the left [north] of the road." The Con-tinentals were the 2nd Maryland, arrayed in the open, with most of the men facing south. "Glowing with impatience to signalize themselves, they [the Guards] instantly attacked." Col. Otho Holland Williams, the Maryland bri-gade commander, "charmed with the late demeanor of the first regiment, has-tened toward the second, expecting a similar display, and prepared to com-bine his whole force with all practicable celerity; when, unaccountably, the second regiment gave way, abandoning to the enemy the two field pieces."[11]

Faced by the onrushing Guards, the 2nd Maryland crumbled and then broke. Their right flank was located above the vale, facing west, and separated "some distance" from the 1st Maryland. Their left flank was posted parallel to the Great Salisbury Road, facing south, and extended almost to the court-house, guarding against an attack coming north up the vale's eastern slope. Because these Marylanders were positioned along the road, any British pro-jectiles passing through the woods or up the road enfiladed the regiment. Some stray rounds almost certainly came their way and likely inflicted in-juries. Six hours of waiting, with stray rounds falling around them during the last hour, must have been unnerving. Compounding their problems, the men were led by unfamiliar officers who had been in command less than a week. Some of the regiment's noncommissioned officers had been transferred to make up deficiencies in the 1st Maryland shortly before the battle.[12]

Another reason for the unit's breakdown might be seen as social. This late in the war, the majority of the Maryland troops were from the lowest social classes. Many men were drafted, and others were substitutes hired by drafted men seeking to escape military service. The companies of the Regiment Extra had been raised all over Maryland rather than in a single county, so few of the men knew one another prior to joining the regiment. Unlike the 1st Maryland, they were not a group bound together by shared danger and experiences. The discipline and sense of command authority that had been instilled over the last seven months had been shaken by leadership changes within the last five days.

Command changes and shaky morale do not fully account for their performance, however. Lt. Col. John Eager Howard provided some additional explanations: "The guards . . . pushed into the cleared ground and run at the 2d regiment, which immediately gave way, owing I believe to the want of officers & having so many new recruits." Howard did not say that the regiment was under fire, but their left flank was wide open, in the air, on open ground, and at right angles to the rest of the American battle line.[13]

Even positioning two six-pounders in the middle of the regiment did not help. The artillerymen had been fighting for almost two hours, shifting one gun rearward at a time and avoiding being overrun. The artillery horses had already been killed, so the North Carolina Continental infantrymen assigned to protect the guns helped manhandle them back to the third line, under a constant fire that inflicted casualties.

When the 2nd Guards Battalion came out of the western woods and descended into the vale, they had to re-form before crossing the open space created by the old fields in the bottomland. They then advanced at a trot across the vale, halting and firing a series of platoon volleys before finally charging. The Guards maneuvered while Maryland leaders were rearranging the 2nd Maryland's line to confront them. Seeing the Guards coming across the vale, Lt. Col. Benjamin Ford brought his men on line to face them, so they could resist a bayonet charge. Most of the Marylanders had to be moved from their original position, facing south, so they would all be facing west. This meant, in effect, wheeling the regiment to the right, a maneuver that could occasion disorder. It is not likely the regiment actually wheeled to the right because there were fence lines and buildings in the way. It is more likely that the 2nd Maryland companies already facing south faced to the right, moved west along the road, and then turned south at a fence line at the edge of a terrace that probably had cleared space along it. The movement would have been done as rapidly as possible.

Confusion definitely ensued. According to Col. William R. Davie, "Ford ordered a charge, that proceeded some distance, and were halted by Colo.

Williams." The charge may have been an interpretation of the maneuver to face left, or it may have followed the realignment. Due to apparent disorder in the ranks, the regiment was halted and was "ordered again to fall back and dress with the line." While these adjustments occurred, "The British continued to advance." But they must have halted at least once to open fire, because the Marylanders re-formed their line: "under a heavy fire—when the men were again ordered to advance they all faced about, except a single company on the left which I think was Capt. [Edward] Oldham[']s."[14]

The eyewitness accounts provide a good explanation for the 2nd Maryland's breakdown. To confront the Guards' threat from the west, Ford ordered his regiment to shift its front by moving to face west. He probably ordered his men to move rapidly, a factor in splitting the men apart from each other. Then, when they came on line with the regiment's right division that was already facing west, they were ordered to charge. At this time, Williams probably halted the charge because he had almost certainly seen disorder in the ranks. The regiment's battle line was then ordered to dress its line preparatory to engaging the Guards. They even gave one "disorderly fire," an attempted volley, or more likely a series of platoon volleys, into the advancing Guards. By the time they fired, the Guards were already beyond the creek and fence line, in the middle of the vale, moving forward in a charge and probably within twenty-five yards. Even if the 2nd Maryland's volley had been a precise, simultaneous firing, at the ranges involved and shooting downhill, it might not have done the trick. As a "disorderly," scattering fire, it probably had little impact.[15]

For the 2nd Maryland, fighting their first battle, the mental and physical stress involved in being under fire and doing nothing, then moving, stopping, regrouping, and then trying to move forward again must have been tremendous. The situation is similar to combat problems reported in World War II: "If a skirmish line was halted two or three times during an attack by sudden enemy fire, it became impossible to get any further action from the men, even though none had been hurt. . . . Attacking companies were being drained of their muscle power by the repeated impact of sudden fear." A similar breaking point was noted in the Civil War by a Texan: "We were the reserve, which is a dreaded position when kept up for you will hear the roar of the battling front . . . being exposed to shell, grape or canister shot; and as one has ample time for reflection, they can well feel the seriousness of the surroundings with all its horrors."[16]

In their open position above the vale, the 2nd Maryland had ample opportunity to see North Carolina and Virginia militia withdrawing toward the courthouse behind their position. Because some Virginians conducted a fighting withdrawal, shot continued to fly. Many militiamen, ranging from generals to privates, were wounded. No doubt the troops of the 2nd Maryland felt the same stresses of waiting for the fighting to come to them that have been experienced by combatants in other wars. Once the Guards arrived opposite them, more shot came their way, even as they tried to maneuver.

An added problem was that the second in command, Maj. Archibald Anderson, was killed and at least one other officer, Roger Nelson, wounded. Seeing a senior officer go down would hardly have encouraged lowly privates worrying about their own survival. Whatever the exact reason, the 2nd Maryland "broke in confusion." Williams, echoing comments by Howard, reported, "The Second has but 8 comm'd officers to 6 comp'ys and has a large proportion of State troops. I can give no better reason why that regiment refused to charge when it was ordered." Another officer, Capt. James Armstrong, made note that the regiment suffered "a deficiency of platoon officers." Given Williams's comment about there being only eight officers, there were no platoon officers in the 2nd Maryland, only a company commander instead of a commander, two platoon leaders, and an ensign. The Guards, aided by the collapse of the 2nd Maryland, "defeated them, taking two 6-pounders, but, pursuing [them] into the wood[s] with too much ardour," the Guards bypassed the left rear flank of the 1st Maryland, which was concealed by a "copse of woods." As the Guards surged forward, driving the 2nd Maryland north into the courthouse area with what Cornwallis deemed "too much ardour," they overran and captured Singleton's two cannon. The Guards probably did not spike the guns, but they might have rendered them inoperable by breaking the rammers and sponges. It is also possible that the increments of the assaults on the Continental line occurred in such rapid fashion that there was no time to do anything to the guns.[17]

There is at least one additional clarification about the capture of the guns that must be made to give credit where it is due. "In the center the 2nd battalion of guards, commanded by Lieutenant Colonel Stewart [sic] . . . made a spirited and successful attack on the enemy's six pounders, which they took from the Delaware Regiment." The men described as defending the six-pounders were most certainly not Kirkwood's Delawares, as those men were on the right flank, well to the north. Nor were they Capt. Peter Jacquett's Delaware Company that was now part of the 1st Maryland. Tarleton labeled these men "Delawares" because something about them was unique to the Delawares. He had fought Kirkwood's Delawares on many occasions and knew they had distinctive gold binding on their hats. Tarleton claimed the Continentals fought to save Singleton's guns before the 1st Maryland charged, and these individuals were surely not the fleeing 2nd Maryland. The 1st Maryland and the Delawares wore blue coats faced red, while the 2nd Maryland wore brown coats faced red. The only obvious difference between the 1st Maryland and the Delaware companies was the gold binding on their hats.[18]

Tarleton likely spotted the remaining members of Capt. Edward Yarborough's beleaguered band of North Carolina Continentals. In January 1781, North Carolina Continentals at Salisbury and those attached to the Southern Army were issued clothing from the Maryland and Delaware depot in Hillsborough. The men Tarleton saw were most likely North Carolinians wearing blue coats with red facings and cocked hats with the distinctive "Delaware" gold edging. Further evidence supporting this argument can be found in the pension applications of former North Carolina Continentals who reported enlisting during the winter of 1780–81 and who served with Captain Yarborough. They claimed in their sworn accounts to have been bayoneted or otherwise wounded at Guilford Courthouse. North Carolina privates Zachariah Jacobs, a black man, and Zachariah Elliott were both wounded in the legs, the latter by a bayonet, while Thomas Ralph reported being wounded "severely in both arms." Yarborough earlier had led North Carolina Continentals who fought as artillery supports at Camden the year before Guilford Courthouse and would again at Eutaw Springs six months after Guilford. Several North Carolina Continentals who enlisted in the months previous to the battle turned up among Cornwallis's wounded Guilford prisoners.[19]

The Guards were now beyond the right rear of the 1st Maryland, but "this transaction [taking the guns] was in great measure concealed from the 1st regiment by the woods and the unevenness of the ground." The Guards were on a slightly higher terrace, but still below and west of the courthouse clearing. A copse of trees stood between them and the slope below, concealing them from the 1st Maryland. Before the Guards reached the courthouse clearing, Stuart recognized there was a problem to their left and rear. "The guards were soon called from the pursuit of the second Maryland regiment, and led by Lieutenant Colonel Stuart against the first." Word also reached the 1st Maryland. Lt. Col. John Eager Howard's "station being on the left of the 1st regt. . . . next to the cleared ground," he heard about it when "Capt. Gibson, Deputy Adjutant General rode to me and informed me that a party of the enemy, inferior in numbers to us, were pushing through the cleared ground and into our rear, and that if we would face about and charge them, we might take them." Howard "rode to Gunby and gave him the information. He did not hesitate to order the regiment to face about." It is important that Howard says "face about" and not "wheel." Facing about made an immediate battle line facing in the opposite direction, even if it did reverse the usual order of the companies. Howard noted that as soon as the 1st Maryland faced about and started forward, "we were immediately engaged with the Guards," demonstrating that they had not moved a long way in pursuit of the 33rd Regiment.[20]

When the Marylanders got within range, "our men gave them some well directed fires." While the 1st Maryland came up on the Guards' left and rear, the redcoats were already trying to face west. Maintaining platoon integrity while individuals, groups, and sections turn to face another direction and then extend into an approximate battle line while reloading and firing was not something described in the manual. Switching the front under these circumstances could not be planned but rather was improvised, especially with veteran soldiers. Given the disorder caused by their reorientation, it is not surprising that the Guards "were thrown into confusion by a heavy fire."[21]

After the initial firing, probably by platoon or division, the Marylanders "advanced and continued firing." The Guards return fire was effective: "At this time Gunby's horse was shot, and when I met him some time after he informed me that his horse fell upon him, and it was with difficulty he extricated himself." From near the courthouse, North Carolina militiaman Nathaniel Slade noted that "this conflict between the brigade of Guards and the first regiment of Marylanders was most terrific, for they fired at the same instant, and they appeared so near that the blazes from their guns seemed to meet." Slade indicates that the Marylanders' advance almost certainly triggered the Guards' moving downslope and facing west. It is quite possible that the first Guardsmen facing west, those originally on the battalion's left flank, fired a platoon or company volley to buy time for the rest of the Guards. Gunby's horse was killed under him, and command fell to Lieutenant Colonel Howard. Whether Howard saw Gunby go down or not, as a mounted leader, he was almost certainly now in front of the regiment, even if not in the center, leading them on.[22]

The Guards reacted well, as might be expected of a veteran unit, despite changing their front to the west and being "thrown into confusion by a heavy fire" by effective Maryland volleys, Cornwallis reported. As the 1st Maryland emptied their muskets and then charged toward the Guards' left flank,

*Lt. Col. John Eager Howard (1752–1827), 1st Maryland Continental Regiment. Oil painting by Charles Wilson Peale. Independence National Historical Park Collection.*

Lt. Col. William Washington attacked the Guards from the rear. While the Maryland threat came first and occupied the Guards, the situation allowed Washington's dragoons, having ridden over from behind the American right flank, to aid the 2nd Maryland, thundering down onto the Guards' right flank and rear. British cavalry leader Banastre Tarleton must have appreciated what happened as "the Maryland brigade, followed by Washington's cavalry, moving upon them before they could receive assistance, re-took the cannon, and repulsed the guards with great slaughter." The sequencing and the opportunity afforded Washington was clearly seen by Cornwallis, who noted the 2nd Guards Battalion was "immediately charged and driven back into the field by Colonel Washington's dragoons, with the loss of the 6-pounders they had taken."[23]

A key element for the Americans' retaking the cannon is that Washington acted appropriately under the circumstances by getting into a position from which he would "be able to charge them should an occasion offer." While sporadic infantry fighting continued on the northern flank against Webster, Washington started moving his mounted men along the Reedy Fork Road, preparing to make use of the open spaces around the courthouse if a crisis developed. North Carolina militiaman John Watkins, who had halted at the courthouse after fleeing the first line fighting, watched as "Colonel Washington's horse [cavalry] . . . formed and rode over the Branch to the opposite Hill where the battle was raging and charged the enemy." Howard explained Washington's actions thus:

> Finding that the British were carrying every thing before them I think his eagerness to seize an opportunity to make a charge and if possible to turn the fate of the day was the cause of his moving that way and I think that our fire led him to the place where he met with the guards. . . . Gunby's regiment formed the right [*sic*] of the line, and Washington's proper place was then near us. Our own fire no doubt influenced his movement which brought him to the place where he met with the guards.[24]

Washington's dragoons, amalgamated with mounted militia under the Marquis de Bretigny and Virginia militia captain Thomas Watkins, stormed into the Guards. Watkins's lieutenant, Philemon Holcombe, recalled, "leaping a ravine, the swords of the horsemen were upon the enemy, who were rejoicing in victory and safety; and before they suspected danger, multitudes lay dead." The ravine the dragoons jumped is hardly visible today, but it does appear on topographic maps at the head of a westward-leading, intermittent watercourse about ninety yards north of the Great Salisbury Road, just west of the courthouse site. Erosion since the battle, and a 1790s county public project, filled it in to such an extent that it no longer resembles what Holcombe saw. The gulley was associated with the copse that kept the Guards from seeing the 1st Maryland until they charged.[25]

Washington was successful in part because the 2nd Guards had already turned to face the 1st Maryland's bayonets. It also helped that the same copse that initially blocked the Marylanders' view of the Guards likewise blocked the view up Reedy Fork Road, down which Washington was moving. The dragoons were not visible when the Guards began shifting their front to cope with the 1st Maryland and left themselves vulnerable to Washington's cavalry. This observation provides an inkling of how rapidly the sequence of charges and counter charges on the third line occurred. The dragoon charge was a brilliant, though fortuitous, coordination by two of the most accomplished officers in Greene's command.

Through the smoke of their volleys, some of Lieutenant Colonel Howard's men saw the cavalry attack develop after they fired. "We were advancing upon them but were 30 or 40 yards from them when the horse charged. . . . As we advanced I observed Washington's horse, and as their movements were quicker than ours they first charged and broke the enemy." The Marylanders likely fired their last volley inside the killing distance of forty yards and then let out a yell as they advanced, further distracting the Guards just before their mounted comrades began "charging through them and breaking their ranks three or four times." Washington's dragoons turned about and charged through the Guards a second and then possibly through the fringe elements a third time, before moving westward across the vale. Large numbers of Guardsmen were struck down, Howard recalled, "many of whom had been knocked down by the horse without being much hurt. We took some prisoners, and the whole were in our power."[26]

The melee between the 1st Maryland and 2nd Guards Battalion was the climactic moment of the battle. Two of the best, perhaps the finest, veteran battalions in the British and Continental armies were locked in a brief, bloody, hand-to-hand combat. This engagement inside a battle captures the imagination because it involves two nearly identical units with outstanding combat records striving for victory at a key moment that will determine the campaign's result. Many things hung in the balance, but the combatants were almost certainly only trying to survive the encounter.

The two regiments *were* remarkably similar. The 2nd Battalion of Guards was a composite unit drawn from the three home regiments and sent overseas. Composed of men from the 1st Regiment of Guards, the Coldstream Guards, and the 3rd, or Scots, Guards, the unit had a proud heritage dating back to the English Civil War and very high morale. The leaders were men of quality who would have a future impact if they survived. The men were battle hardened, some arriving in New York in July 1776 and campaigning ever since. They came from all over the British Isles as well as other European countries.

On the other side was the 1st Maryland, arguably one of the finest regiments produced by the Continental army. Like the Guards, the 1st Maryland fought in the 1776 New York campaigns. Some were survivors of Smallwood's Maryland Battalion and the Maryland Flying Camp who covered the army's retreat from Long Island, a moment when George Washington allegedly exclaimed, "Good God, what brave fellows I must this day lose!" The regiment was now a composite force, made up of survivors from the one Delaware and seven Maryland regiments in the dark days following the battle of Camden, 16 August 1780. Each regiment was represented by a company in the new unit.

Officers and men knew each other well from their old regiments. There was a bond based on shared experiences going back nearly five years that could not be replicated in many other American units. The 1st Maryland officers were an elite group even without the noble lineages of many Guards officers, and several would go on to impact the new nation.

As the Guards officers gathered their men into a new line facing west and northwest and got them firing back, the Marylanders came on in a rush. The Guards responded largely without specific commands, being pushed by swords and muskets into an approximation of a battle line facing the oncoming Continentals, who fired several platoon volleys as they came. At a range of less than twelve yards, both lines fired again, so close that muzzle flashes overlapped into a wide sheet of flame and the heat from the volley could be felt in the cold, damp air.

Those hit by musket balls went down immediately. At this close range, the heavy lead balls used in the Charlesville and Brown Bess muskets smashed through bone, shattering it, and often passing through the body to exit on the other side. Those receiving the most serious head wounds were hit with catastrophic force that tore open large entrance wounds in the skull and destroyed the brain in a spray of bone, flesh, brain matter, and fluid. A soldier hit directly in the head at this range went down immediately, killed instantly.

A melee usually lasts only seconds, although in retrospect it is often described in such detail that it might seem like a long, drawn-out episode, one described by psychologist and author Dave Grossman as "an 'Intimate Brutality.'" Grossman provides considerable analysis of close-in fighting, noting that it is "psychologically easier to kill with an edged weapon that permits a long stand-off range" than one that requires close contact; and that it is "far easier to deliver a slashing or hacking blow than a piercing blow." He noted psychological factors at work during bayonet combat:

> The vast majority of soldiers who do approach bayonet range with the enemy use the butt of the weapon or any other available means to incapacitate or injure the enemy rather than skewer him. . . . When the bayonet is used, the close range . . . results in a situation with enormous potential for psychological trauma. . . . The resistance to killing with the bayonet is equal only to the enemy's horror at having this done to him. Thus in bayonet charges one side or the other invariably flees before the actual crossing of bayonets occurs.[27]

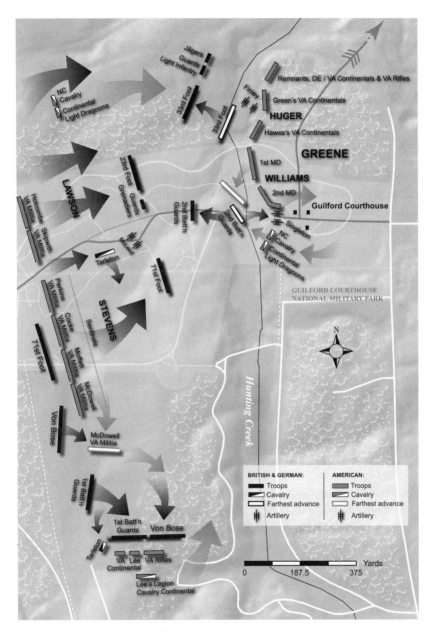

**MAP NINE** *The third line and the American withdrawal. By Mark A. Moore, North Carolina Department of Cultural Resources. See pp. 2-3 for the full map showing the sequence of battle lines.*

Grossman points out that the "thought of cold steel sliding into your guts . . . is more horrific and real than the thought of a bullet doing the same." Citing twentieth-century sources, he claims that "actual bayonet combat is extremely rare in military history," a point he reiterates by noting that "personal kills with a bayonet are so extraordinarily rare." His studies did not, apparently, include the Revolutionary War's southern campaigns, and 1st Maryland veterans would certainly have disagreed, as they had extensive combat experience with bayonets, including many with wounds from Camden and Cowpens. In the thirteen months from their first southern battle at Camden (16 August 1780) until Eutaw Springs (8 September 1781), the Marylanders and Delawares closed with the bayonet and engaged in a melee at least six times, including the initial fighting at Hobkirk's Hill and the "forlorn hope" assault at the Ninety Six Star Redoubt.[28]

From American pension accounts, it is clear that the British, be they Guards, line infantry, Scottish Highlanders, or in some cases provincials, also engaged in serious bayonet fighting. When the fear of death or injury does not cause the opposition to flee, there is a decided problem for both parties. The issue becomes one of survival; survival by killing as many of one's opponents, and as fast, as possible; or, as Thomas Hardy said so eloquently,

> . . . ranged as infantry,
> and staring face to face,
> I shot at him as he at me,
> and killed him in his place.

That is exactly what happened on the vale's eastern slope and bottom when the 1st Maryland and the 2nd Guards Battalion slugged it out. According to Otho Holland Williams, "the first Regiment embraced the opportunity and . . . they bayoneted and cut to pieces a great number of British Guards who had taken our field pieces." Greene himself witnessed the slaughter, stating, "The first regiment of Marylanders, commanded by Colonel Gunby, and seconded by Lt. Col. Howard, followed the horse with their bayonets; near the whole of the party fell a sacrifice."[29]

Perhaps the most famous incident in the entire battle took place during this melee. As the Guards and Marylanders struggled with bayonets, clubbed muskets, swords, and fists, the Guards' Lt. Col. James Stuart spotted Capt. John Smith of the 1st Maryland doing "great mischief" and attacked him. William R. Davie received this written account from Smith's postwar business partner, Samuel Mathis:

Smith and his men were in a throng, killing the Guards and Grenadiers like so many Furies. Colonel Stewart [*sic*], seeing the mischief Smith was doing, made up to him through the crowd, dust, and smoke, and made a violent lunge at him with his small sword. The first that Smith saw was the shining metal like lightning at his bosom he only had time to lean a little to the right, and lift up his left arm so as to let the polished steel pass under it when the hilt struck his breast, it would have been through his body but for the haste of the colonel and happening to set his foot on the arm of a man Smith had just cut down, his unsteady step, his violent lunge and missing his aim brought him with one knee upon the dead man, the Guards came rushing up very strong, Smith had no alternative but to wheel round to the right and give Stewart a back handed blow over or across the head on which he fell; his orderly sergeant attacked Smith, but Smith's sergeant dispatched him; a 2nd attacked him Smith hewed him down, a 3rd behind him threw down a cartridge and shot him in the back of the head, Smith now fell among the slain but was taken up by his men and brought off, it was found to be only a buckshot lodged against the skull and had only stunned him.[30]

The Smith/Stuart duel was arguably the most famous episode of the third line melee. Stuart, the son of a Scottish lord and member of the landed gentry, exemplified the British empire's time-honored traditions of nobility, peerage, and rank. His opponent, Smith, was the son of a wealthy, self-made Scots-Irish merchant from Baltimore. One intriguing note concerning this episode is the description of Smith being hit with buckshot, indicating that the British Guards were also using buck and ball. This assumption is further substantiated by the pension declaration of Pvt. Hezekiah Carr of Smith's company, who was wounded "severely by a ball and buckshot."[31]

About the time of Stuart's death, Brig. Gen. Charles O'Hara was rallying the 2nd Guards Battalion and suffered his second wound of the day, a gunshot wound to the chest. O'Hara may have even been briefly captured after being shot down, suggesting he may have been hit during the exchange of volleys between the Guards and Marylanders. During a meeting in Charleston after the war, Lt. John Linton of the 3rd Continental Light Dragoons told Cornet Alexander Garden of Lee's Legion "he had enjoyed the happiness of receiving General O'Hara's sword, who for some time remained his prisoner, though ultimately rescued by a superior force, which had rallied to save him." Neither O'Hara nor any other British officer made statements that would confirm

Linton's story, but it is possible he was telling the truth. If so, O'Hara's brief capture may explain why the Guards fought so courageously and did indeed surge back ("rallied") into the Marylanders. Having seen their popular leader shot off his horse, the 2nd Guards would have pressed forward to rescue him, becoming the "superior force, which had rallied to save him." The injury was almost certainly inflicted by a Maryland or Delaware infantryman, probably as the dragoons struck the Guards.[32]

Another event that later achieved legendary status, this one involving the young Portuguese dragoon Peter Francisco, occurred in the swirling melee of men and horses. According to one postwar account, the twenty-year-old giant "cut down eleven men in succession with his broadsword. One of the guards pinned Francisco's leg to his horse with a bayonet. Forbearing to strike, he assisted the assailant to draw his bayonet forth, when, with terrible force, he brought down his broadsword and cleft the poor fellow's head to his shoulders!" Despite this leg injury, Francisco supposedly remained in the battle until he was again wounded with a bayonet thrust "in his right thigh the whole length of the bayonet, entering above the knee and coming out at the socket of his hip."[33]

Francisco's own account of the fighting, given in 1820, dryly stated that "Colonel Washington, observing their maneuvering, made a charge upon them, in which charge he [Francisco] was wounded in the thigh by a bayonet from the knee to the socket of the hip and, in presence of many, he was seen to kill two men, besides making many other panes [sic] which were doubt-less fatal to others." Intriguingly, Francisco's account states that "after the action was pretty well over," Colonel Washington's dragoons charged "eight horses [eight dragoons] of the King's Guard [who had been] held in reserve to cut off the militia." Francisco may have mistaken Cornwallis and any staff members sitting on their horses near him for dragoons, or he possibly saw several British Legion dragoons who had not been sent to the southern flank. Regardless, Francisco played the episode down, only acknowledging two men, not eleven, and furthermore, he didn't directly state that he took lives, only that he was "seen to kill two men." Postwar Whig chroniclers later embellished the episode into legendary status, something a more reticent Francisco, who took part in some of the war's worst fighting before he was twenty-one years old, never claimed.[34]

With most of their officers down or walking wounded, the Guards fell back. The American dragoons charged after them. John Eager Howard wrote later that

Washington, after he had passed through the Guards into the ["old field" crossed out] cleared ground, observed an officer with several aid[e]s about him and supposed it was Cornwallis. He perhaps was prevented by [from] taking him by the following accident. He [Washington] lost his cap and there was some thing amiss with his saddle or bridle, I do not recollect what it was, but he was compelled to dismount, and the officer in front of his men, I think it was Capt. Fauntleroy, being shot through the body and disabled from guiding his horse, his horse carried him off the field. The officers and men followed of course without know the cause, and Washington was almost alone for some minutes.

Fauntleroy may have been struck by grapeshot or case shot, confirming a Cornwallis statement that "the enemy's cavalry was soon repulsed by a well-directed fire from two three-pounders just brought up by Lieutenant Macleod, and by the appearance of the grenadiers of the guards, and of the 71st regiment, which having been impeded by some deep ravines, were now coming out of the wood on the right of the guards, opposite to the court house." Capt. James Armstrong of Lee's Legion later wrote Brig. Gen. Mordecai Gist that Fauntleroy had "his thigh broke by a musquette ball," but he may have been describing a piece of case shot.[35]

The Washington and Fauntleroy incident is particularly intriguing because it explains an old tradition concerning the battle. Seeing the Guards locked in a desperate hand-to-hand struggle, Cornwallis supposedly ordered Lieutenant McLeod and his three-pounders to fire directly into the struggling mass of soldiers. When confronted by O'Hara with the fact that many British would die as well, Cornwallis bravely stated that it had to be done to save the army. The guns fired, and the Americans withdrew, saving what was left of the 2nd Battalion of Guards.

The story first appears in Henry Lee's *Memoirs*. Lee states that Cornwallis "seeing the vigorous advance of these two officers [Howard and Washington], determined to arrest their progress, though every ball, leveled at them, must pass through the flying guards." In a subsequent comment, Lee claims that

Cornwallis, seeing the discomfiture of one battalion of the guards, repaired in person to direct the measures for the recovery of the lost ground; when, by the dauntless exposure of himself, he was placed in extreme danger. It was upon this occasion that he ordered his artillery to open through his flying guards to stop Washington and Howard. Brigadier O'Hara remonstrated, by explaining, that the fire would destroy themselves. "True," replied Cornwallis, "but this is a necessary evil which we must endure to arrest impending destruction."[36]

Later authors, with varying alterations, basically copied Lee without taking into account that Lee himself was far to the south and engaged in his own battle with the Von Bose Regiment and the 1st Battalion of Guards when this supposed event took place. William Johnson, in his 1822 *Sketch of the Life and Correspondence of Nathanael Greene*, was just one of many authors who reproduced Lee's claims. Henry Lee Jr. included the incident, as did his half brother, Robert E. Lee, in their works on the family patriarch. William Gilmore Simms's *The Life of Nathanael Greene, Major General of the Revolution* repeated it, as did Eli W. Caruthers's *Revolutionary Incidents and Sketches of Character Chiefly in the Old North State*, and George Washington Greene's *The Life of Nathanael Greene*. Numerous secondary sources published in the twentieth and twenty-first centuries have followed their lead and repeated this story.

The image of a draconian Cornwallis ordering his guns to cut down his own elite Guards over the pleas of his courageous, wounded subordinate became legendary in the annals of Guilford Courthouse, despite the fact that neither Cornwallis nor O'Hara, nor for that matter any actual participant in the event, actually recorded its taking place. Cornwallis's account, as noted above, says nothing about O'Hara being present. Any account placing O'Hara on the scene would have to account for the severely wounded officer's rapid movement from the melee to McLeod's position. This movement would have taken place faster than the American dragoons or the "flying Guards."

It is unlikely the incident as it has come to be described ever happened and that it was either a rumor that Lee had heard or something that he developed in the interest of a good story. After all, he did not take part in the melee and most likely did not personally see the action, as he was involved in his own struggle more than a quarter mile away. What most likely happened was that Cornwallis ordered his guns to fire on Washington's cavalry and break up the attack, which they did by striking down Fauntleroy and other dragoons. In the process a number of the fleeing Guardsmen were possibly hit by grapeshot from their own guns.

As the American horsemen wheeled away to the rear, Lt. Col. John Eager Howard found the 1st Maryland in a precarious position. "After passing through the guards . . . I found myself in the cleared ground, and saw the 71st regt. Near the court house and other columns of the enemy appearing in different directions, Washington's horse having gone off, I found it necessary to retire, which I did leisurely, but many of the guards who were laying on the ground and who we supposed were wounded, got up and fired at us as we retired."[37]

One of the Guardsmen the Marylanders "supposed were wounded" was Lt. Col. Robert Lovelace. Lovelace, although technically second in command to Stuart, commanded the 3rd Company in the 2nd Guards Battalion. "There was a Captain Lovett, of the Guards, from whose fob a Maryland soldier found leisure on the field of battle to take a handsome watch. Washington purchased the watch from the soldier; and Lovett not being returned as killed or wounded, the conclusion was obvious. It afforded mirth to the American army, but is said to have compelled him to retire from the service." In the manuscript collections of the Historical Society of Pennsylvania there is a poem evidently written by St. George Tucker titled "To Col. Lovelace of the British Guards, who counterfeited Death at the battle of Guilford, March 15, 1781," that reads in part:

> Hail Lovelace, hail! Great Master of that Art,
> Which joins to Valour's better part,
> Who know from Instinct whether Danger's nigh,
> And whether prudence bids to fight or fly;
> Or when with subtle Wiles to cheat the Foe,
> And by dissembling ward the fatal Blow;
> By feigning Death arise again to Life
> When Danger's over from the doubtful Strife.

British accounts state that Lovelace apparently attempted to convince his fellow British officers the watch was stolen, but the ruse was quickly exposed. On 17 April 1781, he wrote to Cornwallis for permission to return home. As he was not at Yorktown, his departure must have been authorized.[38]

As the 1st Maryland withdrew toward the courthouse, the grenadiers of the Guards, 23rd Regiment, and 71st Foot entered the vale. "By the spirited exertions of Brig. General O'Hara, although wounded, the 2nd battalion of Guards was soon rallied and, supported by the grenadiers returned to the charge with the greatest alacrity. The 23rd regiment having arrived at that instant from our left, and Lieut.-Colonel Tarleton having advanced with part of his cavalry, the enemy was soon put to flight and the two six-pounders once more fell into our hands."[39]

The grenadiers of the Guards were not involved in the melee. Although

Tarleton wrote about "the repulse of the 2nd Battalion and the Grenadier company of the guards" by Washington's dragoons and the 1st Maryland, he also mentioned that the "grenadiers, after all their officers were wounded, attached themselves to the artillery and cavalry, who were advancing upon the main road." While Capt. William Home, Lord Dunglass, of the grenadier company was down, there is no evidence to suggest fellow officer Capt. Thomas Christie had been severely wounded. It is more probable that the grenadiers arrived with the artillery and were thus separated from the 2nd Guards Battalion. After O'Hara rallied the Guards, the grenadier company entered the fray alongside the regular Guards infantry. Cornwallis lends support to this scenario, stating that the dragoons were driven off by the arrival of the British artillery and the Guards' grenadier company. Tarleton is probably correct in reporting that the grenadiers were aiding the artillery because he was moving with the guns. Cornwallis also confirmed John Eager Howard's assertion that he withdrew the Marylanders after seeing the 71st and 23rd appear to his front and flank.[40]

As Howard moved toward the courthouse area, Greene was organizing the evacuation of the vale's eastern slope. When the 2nd Maryland collapsed, Greene mistakenly thought that the British had turned the army's southern flank, and that they were in behind the Virginians. In a 16 March letter, Greene summarized his view of the situation. "They having broken the 2d Maryland Regiment, and turned our left flank, got into the rear of the Virginia brigade; and appearing to be gaining on our right, which would have encircled the whole of the Continental troops, I thought it most advisable to order a retreat." In truth, Greene may have been shaken by a close escape of his own. At one point, British soldiers passed within "thirty yards of him," but a "copse of woods" intervened, and Greene was saved by "Col. Morris calling to me and advertising to me of my situation I had just time to retire."[41]

This incident probably occurred during the Guards' pursuit of the collapsing 2nd Maryland. Just as the Guards did not see the 1st Maryland or Washington's dragoons due to the thickness of the intervening copse, so Greene did not see how close he was to the onrushing Guards. It is likely that Greene was so focused on rallying the Marylanders that he forgot why they collapsed. The near disaster must have colored his view of the evolving situation on the third line's left flank.

Greene did not see the combined Howard/Washington assault on the Guards, although he later wrote that the Marylanders had nearly all fallen. He had initially ridden toward the northern edge of the third line, where he began urging the Virginians to counterattack Webster and the 33rd. Then, after he attempted to rally the 2nd Marylanders and was almost captured, he went back to the Virginians. That far north, in the woods, and on the eastern ridge above the vale, he was unable to witness the melee as Howard and Washington drove the Guards westward. Lee noted, "Ignorant or these facts [the Howard/Washington attack and pursuit], he persevered in his resolution, and directed a retreat, which was performed deliberately under cover of Colonel Green."[42]

The Virginians under Huger were under the same mistaken impression as Greene. Pvt. Lewis Griffin, serving in Hawes's regiment, reported, "At this juncture the battle became bloody, each party making an obstinate stand, but they were about to be surrounded and were ordered to retreat." Charles Magill, aide to Brigadier General Huger, reported to Virginia governor Thomas Jefferson that "the left of the Maryland Troops gave way. This and other concurrences gave the enemy possession of the ground and four Field Pieces all that were in the Action."[43]

Starting the withdrawal, Greene ordered Col. John Green to move his Virginia regiment back from the ridgeline and form a rear guard across the Reedy Fork Road. The Delawares and presumably what was left of Huffman's Virginians joined Hawes's right flank by withdrawing toward the east and then moving south along the terrace, filling the position vacated by Green. "General Huger, who had, throughout the action, given his chief attention to the regiment of Hawes', the only one of the two, constituting his brigade, ever engaged, and which, with Kirkwood's company, was still contending with lieutenant colonel Webster, now drew it off by order of the general." Nothing is known of the location of Ford's 2nd Maryland at this time, but it is likely they were re-forming, rallying around Captain Oldham's steady company north of the courthouse along the Reedy Fork Road in preparation for the retreat. Lee suggests that Otho Holland Williams organized the retreat by the American left. "Colonel Williams effected the same object in his quarter; both abandoning our artillery, as their horses had been mostly killed; and general Greene preferred leaving his artillery, to risking the loss of lives in drawing them off by hand." Williams later commented that "the artillery horses being shot, we were obliged to leave four six pounders in the field which was almost our only considerable loss. The General ordered the troops to retire which was executed with such good order and regularity." With the horses down, responsibility for pulling them from the field would have fallen on the artillerymen and their infantry supports. So many of these men were now casualties that it was impossible to retreat with the guns, especially out of the dense woods.[44]

From Cornwallis's vantage point, the moment of victory seemed at hand. With the arrival of the 23rd and 71st, and the rallied 2nd Guards Battalion, he had a relatively solid line of infantry ready to attack the disorganized American line. He ordered an advance, with the 23rd and 33rd Foot moving toward Hawes's regiment and Finley's artillery, and the 71st and 2nd Guards moving toward Howard and the courthouse. On the British left, Webster and the 33rd "recrossed the ravine and attacked Hawes' regiment of Virginia, supported by Kirkwood's company." In the fighting, Finley's guns fell to the 23rd Foot. According to one participant, "the Royal Welsh attacked and captured two brass six-pounders, having assisted in the attack and defeat of the third line and reserve of the Americans." The guns were lost along with their ammunition wagon, probably indicating that they were too far advanced in the dense woods and too far away from the Reedy Fork Road to be easily extracted.[45]

The brief, bloody struggle on the northern flank resulted in the wounding of both the American and British commanders in that sector. While leading his brigade forward against the Virginians, Lt. Col. James Webster fell with a severe leg wound that destroyed his kneecap and femur. Pvt. William Morton, a Charlotte County, Virginia, militiaman who joined Hawes on the third line, claimed the shot. Firing a round that consisted of "a ball and seven or eight buckshot," Morton took "deliberate aim at Webster and saw him fall." Brig. Gen. Isaac Huger, commanding the right flank, was also injured. Pvt. Lewis Griffin, serving in Hawes's regiment, saw Huger's wounding. "Gen. Huger was wounded in the right hand in his view. He saw him with his hand raised above his head encouraging his men when a shot penetrated his hand and his sword fell in his lap, which he caught up with his left, drew from his pocket a handkerchief, tied up his hand and moved on. Not long after this they were ordered to retreat." The apparently slight damage suggests that Huger was hit, either by buckshot or a rifle bullet. If hit by a rifle ball, it is likely the jaegers were still targeting American officers and, firing downhill, slightly overshot Huger's head. If it was buckshot, then Huger's injury indicates the 33rd, like the Guards, was firing buck and ball.[46]

Huger pulled the remainder of Hawes's regiment off the field, and they fell into column with the remainder of Greene's retreating army. Meanwhile, "the seventy-first and twenty-third, connected in their center by the first battalion and grenadiers of the guards," went forward as a solid battle line against Howard's retiring Marylanders. Otho Holland Williams claimed the withdrawal "was executed with . . . good order and regularity," and Charles Magill asserted that "never was ground contested for with greater Obstinacy, and never were Troops drawn off in better order." Some other accounts suggest Greene's men withdrawing along the road were quite disorganized. While "attempting to rally a party of regular Troops," St. George Tucker "received a wound in the small of my Leg from a soldier, who either by design or accident held his Bayonet in such a direction that I could not possibly avoid it as I rode up to stop him from running away." In the Virginia brigade, some problems arose because of the lack of company- and platoon-level officers noted by Charles Magill. "The Virginia Regulars with a sufficient number of Officers would have done honor to themselves, [but] that deficiency frequently created confusion."[47]

Cornwallis ordered the "23rd and 71st regiments, with part of the cavalry" to pursue Greene's forces. "Such men of the fusiliers and 71st as had strength remaining were ordered to pursue the dispersed enemy. This they did in so persevering a manner, that they killed or wounded as many as they could overtake, until, being completely exhausted, they were obliged to halt, after which they returned as they could to rejoin the army at Guildford Court House." The British were exhausted, and "the want of provisions, and the state of the wounded, dispersed over an extensive piece of ground, also prevented his lordship from following" the Americans further.[48]

As the foot soldiers gave up, British Legion dragoons continued the pursuit until a volley by Lt. Matthew Rhea's company of Green's Virginia Continental Regiment halted them in their tracks. St. George Tucker reported,

> Tarleton advanced to attack us with his horse, but a party of
> Continentals who were fortunately close behind us gave him so warm
> a reception that he retreated with some degree of Precipitation—a Few
> minutes after we halted by the side of an old Field Fence & observed him
> with his Legion surveying us at a distance of two or three hundred yards.
> He did not think proper to attack us again as we were advantageously
> posted and the Continentals who had encountered him just before were
> still in our Rear.

Since it is improbable that Tarleton had time to rejoin Cornwallis's main force after wreaking havoc on the Virginia riflemen, it is more likely Tucker saw one of Tarleton's senior captains, perhaps Richard Hovendon. If Tarleton had returned with the other half of his dragoons from fighting along the American left flank, it is more likely that he would have continued to harass the American line. Lacking his commander's impetuousness and vanity, the subordinate instead chose to fall back and not risk his men.[49]

Lee arrived near the courthouse after the last American units had left the clearing. Finding himself in front of the 71st Foot and 2nd Guards Battalions, Lee "retired down the great Salisbury road, until a cross-road enabled him to pass over to the line of retreat." Whether Lee knew that Greene had retired up Reedy Fork Road is impossible to know, and he may have assumed that the Americans had withdrawn along the Salisbury Road, only discovering along the way that he was actually moving away from the main column. Still, he extricated his infantry and dragoons without being pursued.

As Lee's Legion was leaving the field, they encountered a lone British "officer." Peter Rife of Lee's Legion told the story to Eli W. Caruthers:

> There were two Irishmen, one of whom belonged to the British and the other to the American army . . . for the sake of convenience we shall call the one belonging to the British O'Bryan and the other Jimmison. O'Bryan had been badly wounded; and from the intensity of his pain, without thinking or hearing where he went, he had strayed off so far from the corps . . . and towards the courthouse that he was near the road by which the Americans retreated. Being within a few steps and recognizing Jimmison as a countryman, he called to him, and begged for mercy's sake to give him a drink of water. He held in his hand a long round staff, resembling that on which the Ensign carries his flag, and had on the top of it a sharp iron, like that which we commonly see on the top of a flag staff. Jimmison happened to have some water in his canteen, stepped up very kindly and gave him a drink. When he turned to go away, and before he had got any distance, O'Bryan, so frenzied with pain and thirst, as Rife supposed, that he did not know what he was doing, threw his staff with all his remaining strength, at his benefactor, and the iron point struck him, but inflicted only a slight wound. Jimmison then turned back and drove his bayonet into O'Bryan's heart, which at once put an end to his life and his misery.[50]

The man Jimmison killed was probably carrying a spontoon and was possibly a British officer or noncommissioned officer, but most British officers and NCOs carried fusils, not spontoons. In the area around, or southeast, of the courthouse, it is more likely that Rife's victim was a common soldier who had been captured earlier and then left wounded near the courthouse when Greene's forces withdrew. It may be that this man was one of those Guards who had played dead when Howard and Washington overran them, but later rose to fire on them, causing the Marylanders to bayonet men on the ground. The question remains as to where he obtained a pole arm unless an American militia officer had discarded it. Whoever he was, "O'Bryan" may have the unfortunate distinction of being the last man killed at Guilford Courthouse. Pausing nearly three miles from the battlefield to look at his watch, Beverley Randolph reported to his men that "the general engagement including skirmishes of pickets and outpost continued 2 hours and 27 minutes." By 2:30 P.M., roughly two and a half hours after the first cannonade, and nearly seven hours after the first shots were fired at New Garden, the battle of Guilford Courthouse came to a close.[51]

*Such a complicated scene of*
*horror and distress, it is hoped,*
*for the sake of humanity, rarely*
*occurs, even in military life.*
— CHARLES STEDMAN,
*The History of the Origin,*
*Progress, and Termination of*
*the American War (1794)*

CHAPTER NINE  THE AFTERMATH

Ever the keen strategist, Greene retreated to a predetermined rally point he had chosen before the battle, fully prepared that things might go wrong. He led his men to Speedwell Ironworks along Troublesome Creek, where "our baggage was previously ordered . . . 13 miles from the place of the action, where our army encamped the same evening." Virginia militiaman John Chumbley wrote, "The army halted two to three miles from the battleground to take refreshment, and called stragglers, which being done, then proceeded through muddy roads . . . and cold driving rain 8 to 10 miles, to the iron works on what was called Troublesome Creek." The British regiments, battered and exhausted, could not keep pace with the American army. Otho Holland Williams stated, "the enemy did not presume to press our rear with any spirit they followed only three miles where the regular troops halted and a great many of the militia formed." Wary of a British attack, Greene ordered his army to construct earthworks. Officers were instructed to file reports of the men present and those missing, and the commissaries were ordered to distribute two days' rations, plus a gill of rum per man.[1]

Scattered parts of Greene's army made their way to the ironworks as best they could. While Lee escaped along the Great Salisbury Road, William Campbell's and Alexander Stuart's surviving riflemen and militia evaded their pursuers, as the exhausted 1st Guards Battalion, Von Bose Regiment, and Tarleton "followed us no farther than the Heights just above Guilford C House." Campbell reported that the "army retreated in good Order to Speedwell Furnace which is about ten Miles below, there the most of the Troops who were dispersed in the Action assembled next day." Among those who arrived at camp the next day was the young Virginian Samuel Houston.

> We all scattered, and some of our party and Campbell's and Moffitt's [sic] collected together, and with Capt. Moffit and Major Pope we marched for headquarters, and marched till we, about dark, came to the road we marched up from Reedy Creek to Guilford the day before, and crossing the creek we marched near four miles, and our wounded, Lusk, Allison, and James Mather, who was bad cut, were so sick we stopped and all being almost wearied out, we marched half a mile, and encamped, where, through the darkness and rain, and want of provisions we were in distress. Some parched a little corn. We stretched blankets to protect us from the rain.[2]

As terrible a night as the Americans moving to the ironworks underwent, the British suffered far worse. Having given up pursuit of Greene's army, Cornwallis and his men got what little sleep they could on the battlefield. His men were simply too exhausted to advance further or to fall back to their old camp at Deep River Meeting House. Hungry, surrounded by the dead and wounded, and exposed to a cold, incessant rain, the British soldiers attempted to settle in for the evening. Because of the weather, the redcoats weren't able to build proper fires to cook whatever food they had left or had discovered on the field. The men had last eaten at 4:00 P.M. on 14 March, consuming the last of their four ounces of beef and four ounces of bread per man. Since then they had marched nearly fifteen miles, fought several intense skirmishes, and engaged in a major battle.

British officers who were present spoke openly of the horrors of the night of 15–16 March. Charles Stedman, Cornwallis's commissary general, recalled, "The night was remarkable for its darkness, accompanied with rain which fell in torrents. Nearly fifty of the wounded, it is said, sinking under their aggravated miseries, expired before the morning. The cries of the wounded and dying, who remained on the field of action during the night exceeded all description. Such a complicated scene of horror and distress, it is hoped, for the sake of humanity, rarely occurs, even in military life." Charles O'Hara, suffering from two serious wounds, proclaimed, "I never did, and I hope never shall again, experience two such days and Nights, as these immediately after the Battle, [when] we remained on the very ground on which it had been fought cover'd with Dead, with Dying and with Hundreds of Wounded, Rebels, as well as our own—A Violent and constant Rain that lasted above Forty Hours made it equally impracticable to remove or administer the smallest comfort to many of the Wounded."[3]

All night long, men and women crossed back and forth over the field attempting to separate the living from the dead. If a man was lucky enough to be discovered that first night, he could hope to be taken to makeshift field hospitals the British established at the Joseph Hoskins house or other smaller dwellings and outbuildings in the area. Many more seriously wounded British soldiers were sent to New Garden Meeting House, while the Americans were placed in the courthouse. According to Cornwallis, "Between two and three hundred dead were left upon the field; many of their wounded that were able to move whilst we were employed in the care of our own escaped and followed the routed enemy and our cattle drivers and forage parties have reported to me that the houses in a circle of about 6 or 8 miles round us are full of others."[4]

The medical personnel attending to the wounded varied greatly in their training and experience. Those casualties who made it into the hands of the British field hospitals would have been in the care of Surgeons West Hill, 23rd Foot, William Cleland, 33rd Foot, Colin Chisholm, 71st Foot, John Rush of the Guards Brigade, and Konrad Wilhelm Worfelmann of the Von Bose, as well as a number of assistants. These individuals likely had some professional training, although it is known that Chisholm did not receive his medical degree till after the war. Regardless, the British surgeons had substantial experience in the field if not in the classroom. Those who found themselves being administered to by local Quakers would have had to rely on "country doctors" for their recovery. American "walking wounded" who managed to make the journey to Speedwell Ironworks with Greene's army came under the care of Surgeons Walter Warfield, Richard Pindell, and Levin Denwood of the Maryland Line, Reuben Gilder of the Delaware Regiment, and James Wallace of the 3rd Continental Light Dragoons. Several Virginia and North Carolina militia surgeons were probably present as well to help aid the wounded.[5]

Cornwallis stayed by his headquarters tent all night, receiving the good news that he had captured nearly 1,300 stands of small arms, as well as all four American six-pounders, two ammunition wagons, and sundry other articles. The returns also illustrated the casualty figures. According to his own field returns, Cornwallis led 1,924 men onto the field at Guilford Courthouse. Casualty reports showed that 93 had been killed, 413 wounded, and 26 were missing, a total of 532 men, or 28 percent of those engaged. Cornwallis had lost more than a quarter of his army.[6] (See Appendix B, "Battle Casualties.")

Hardest hit was the Guards Brigade, which went into the battle with 481 officers and men. The unit lost 37 killed in action, 157 wounded, and 22 missing, a loss of 45 percent of those engaged. Casualties were especially heavy among the officers and senior enlisted men. Brigadier generals Charles O'Hara and John Howard were both wounded, and Lt. Col. James Stuart was dead. Six of the brigade's ten captains had been killed or wounded. Capt. John Goodricke had been killed at New Garden, and captains William Schutz, William Maynard, and William Home later died of their injuries. Captains Augustus Maitland and Thomas Swanton survived their injuries, but neither took the field again during the American war. Adj. James Colquhoun was shot but recovered and was left in charge of the Guards wounded. Ens. John Stuart, the only officer of such rank in the brigade, survived a horrendous groin wound, but never returned to active duty. After the war, Stuart left former opponent Alexander Garden an interesting story illuminating the relationship between himself and Brig. Gen. John Howard.

> An Officer of the Guards, severely wounded at Guilford, was passing the tent of Colonel [Brig. Gen.] Howard, since Lord Suffolk, on a litter, the morning subsequent to the battle, when thus addressed by him, "Ha, Jack my good fellow, how do you find yourself today?" "In much agony Colonel, but I think likely to feel better, if favoured by a cup of the good tea which I see before you." "Why as to the tea Jack," said the Colonel, "you shall be welcome to it; but damn me if I would find sugar in this desolate wilderness for a brother."[7]

Webster's brigade took considerable casualties as well. The 23rd Foot (Royal Welch Fusiliers) entered the battle with 238 officers and men, while the 33rd Foot started the day with 234. The Royal Welch lost 13 men killed and 55 wounded (29%), proving Thomas Saumarez's assertion that "one-third of the Royal Welch fell" almost true; the 33rd Regiment lost 11 killed and 65 wounded (32 percent). Second Lt. William Robins of the 23rd died, as did

Ensign James Talbot of the 33rd. Capt. Thomas Peter of the Royal Welch was wounded. The 33rd Foot suffered a large number of officer casualties (two more than were officially reported), supporting the argument that Lynch commanded his riflemen to aim for the leaders. Among the 33rd's wounded officers were Capt. Lt. Charles Curzon, Lieutenants Arthur Beaver, James Harvey, Anthony Slavin, and George Wynard, and Ensigns John Fox, Ralph Gore, John Hughes, and John Kelly.[8]

Lt. Col. James Webster suffered from his leg wound for two weeks before succumbing to his injuries. He was buried on a plantation near Elizabethtown, a few miles outside Wilmington along the Cape Fear River. An officer respected for his courage and character by both American and British contemporaries, Webster's loss was much lamented. Sgt. Roger Lamb recorded that "it was reported in the army that when Cornwallis received the news of Webster's death, his lordship was struck with a pungent sorrow, that turning himself, he looked on his sword, and emphatically exclaimed, 'I have lost my scabbard.'" Cornwallis wrote to Webster's father, Dr. Alexander Webster of Edinburgh:

> It gives me great concern to undertake a task which is not only a bitter
> renewal of my own grief, but must be a violent shock to an affectionate
> parent. You have for your support the assistance of religion, good sense,
> and an experience of the uncertainty of all human enjoyment. You
> have for your satisfaction that your son fell nobly in the cause of his
> country, honoured and lamented by fellow soldiers; that he led a life
> of honour and virtue, which must secure to him everlasting happiness.
> When the keen sensibility of the passions begins a little to subside, these
> considerations will afford you real comfort. That the Almighty may give
> you fortitude to bear this severest of trials, is the earnest wish of your
> companion in affliction, and most faithful servant. Cornwallis.[9]

In Leslie's brigade, the 71st Foot carried 244 officers and men and the Von Bose fielded 321 Hessians. During the fighting, the 71st officially lost 13 killed in action and 50 wounded, not exactly the "one-half of the Highlanders" described by Ens. Dugald Stuart but still 26 percent of the regiment. Officer casualties were surprisingly light. Ens. Malcolm Grant was killed in action, as were Ens. Archibald McPherson and his kinsman, Ens. Donald McPherson; however, the latter two are not listed in official returns. The return of the Von Bose Regiment is likewise incorrect when compared to the actual monthly returns of the unit. Officially, the Von Bose suffered 11 killed, 66 wounded, and 3 missing. Analysis of the regimental records shows 15 killed in action, 8 more died of their wounds, 39 were wounded, and 12 were taken prisoner of war, a loss of 23 percent. Among the officer casualties, Capt. Alexander Wilmousky and Ens. Phillip Ernst Von Trott were mortally wounded, the latter dying in April aboard the transport *Lucretia* on his way to a Charleston hospital. Capt. Johann Eichenbrodt as well as Lieutenants Johann Schweiner and Phillip Ernst Geise survived their injuries.[10]

The other British units suffered too. The Von Bose's German brethren, the jaegers, took 84 men into the fight and lost 4 killed, 3 wounded, and 1 missing. Tarleton's British Legion, which skirmished heavily at New Garden but was kept out of the Guilford fighting until the closing moments, lost only 3 killed and 14 wounded out of an effective strength of 272. The legion's wounded included Tarleton, who lost two fingers. The Royal Artillery, with about 50 men present, lost 2 killed, including Lt. Augustus O'Hara, and 4 wounded.[11]

American casualty figures came in throughout the night and next morning. Officially, Greene's army fielded nearly 4,400 men and lost 79 killed, 184 wounded, and 1,046 missing. Adj. Gen. Otho Holland Williams broke the figures down further, stating that the militia lost 22 killed, 73 wounded, and 885 missing (chiefly North Carolinian militia who fled), and the Continentals lost 57 killed, 111 wounded, and 161 missing. These official statistics are virtually useless, because they are clearly inaccurate and incomplete. For example, Williams reported that the North Carolina militia suffered only 6 killed and 5 wounded. But pension records confirm that at least 24 North Carolinians were killed, wounded, or captured among the militia alone. Many more Virginia militia and rifle company officers are positively identified, by name, as casualties. Therefore, the losses are probably 15–20 percent higher than shown by official returns. If that is the case, then the actual casualty count (not including the missing) for the army stands at 90–94 killed and 211–20 wounded. Including the missing would mean that Greene lost 33 percent of his force. Omitting the missing, Greene's battlefield casualties consisted of only 7 percent of the army.[12]

Among the militia, casualty figures by unit are impossible to ascertain, but it is quite clear that certain groups suffered more than others. Along the North Carolina militia line, Benjamin Williams's regiment and Arthur Forbis's company had significant losses according to pension statements, indicating that those units on the flanks, closest to the Continentals and farthest into the woods, stood their ground longer. Only two North Carolina militia officers are known to have been casualties: Arthur Forbis and his second in command, William Wiley, were both shot down in their struggle against the Hessians. Wiley survived his injuries, but Forbis died shortly afterwards, having been taken home by his sister and wife, who found him lying on the battlefield, still alive two days after the engagement.[13]

Along the second line, regiments closest to the road obviously suffered the most. Unlike the first line, this had nothing to do with proximity to Continental regiments but instead concerns the breaking of Lawson's Virginia militia brigade by the Guards Grenadier Company and the actions of Gen. Edward Stevens near the Great Salisbury Road. Otho Holland Williams's report stated that Lawson's brigade lost only 1 rank and file killed; 1 major, 2 subalterns, and 13 rank and file wounded; and 1 subaltern and 86 enlisted men missing. The wounded major was undoubtedly St. George Tucker, who survived the bayonet wound to his leg. He wrote his wife, "I felt no inconvenience from it for some hours, but have since been obliged to hobble with the assistance of some person to lead me." Ens. Jack Smith Davenport of Skipwith's regiment was mortally wounded. It is unknown who the other wounded or missing subalterns were. Here again, Williams's figures are incomplete. Pension accounts of Lawson's brigade veterans, as well as Tucker's letters to his wife, all indicate much higher losses than simply 1 killed and 16 wounded.[14]

According to after-battle reports, Stevens's Virginia Militia Brigade had many more casualties. Williams reported 11 killed, 36 wounded, and 141 missing. He subdivided this to show that 2 captains and 9 enlisted men had been killed, and 1 captain, 4 subalterns, and 30 rank and file were wounded. In addition, 1 major, 1 captain, 3 subalterns, and 136 enlisted men were missing. Stevens survived the wound to his thigh and was even spotted riding alongside Greene on the retreat, acting as if nothing had happened. "The two generals were talking and laughing as pleasantly as if they had just finished a game of Fives," despite the fact that "blood was spouting from Stephens' thigh at every lope the horse made."[15]

The missing brigade major was Maj. John Williams, who Samuel Houston had seen fleeing the field. The two captains that were killed were James Tate of Moffett's regiment, who died at New Garden that morning, and Alexander Tedford of Stuart's regiment, killed fighting on the southern flank. Ens. Robert Dunlap of Moffett's regiment was also killed. Identifiable wounded officers include Capt. William Fitzgerald of Perkins's regiment, as well as Lt. Matthew Maury and Ens. James Speed of Cocke's regiment. Williams's numbers are skewed because Stuart's regiment suffered substantial casualties in the fringe engagement to the southeast. Aside from Capt. Alexander Tedford's death, Maj. Alexander Stuart himself was wounded and captured, and Capt. John Paxton was shot in the foot and disabled for life. Among the high number of missing, many may have been Stuart's men, who scattered after being assaulted by Tarleton's dragoons at the end of the battle.[16]

Compared to militia regiments, the rifle units had many more casualties per capita. On the northern flank, this was due to prolonged fighting against the 33rd, the light infantry of the Guards, and the jaegers, while Campbell's men on the southern flank likely suffered the majority of their casualties after being abandoned by Lee's Legion. It is quite apparent that the jaegers followed the pattern set by their American counterparts in targeting officers, as nearly every company commander under Lynch was wounded or killed. Williams's report puts both Campbell and Lynch together into the "rifle regiment," claiming they lost 2 captains and 1 rank and file killed; 1 captain, 1 subaltern, and 14 enlisted men wounded; as well as 94 missing. Capt. William Jones of Lynch's regiment was killed outright. Captains Thomas Helm and James Moon both died a few days later. A fourth, Capt. David Beard, survived his wounds. Campbell's regiment lost Capt. John Thompson, killed in action. Williams was fairly accurate concerning officers, but his figures on the rank and file were too low. Pension statements and postwar memoirs suggest that the Virginia riflemen suffered far more casualties than Williams credited them, especially among Campbell's men, who were hacked over by the British Legion dragoons.[17]

Casualty figures for Greene's Continentals are more reliable because these units were better organized than the militias and Williams had personal contacts and connections with most of the officers who provided him with reports on their losses. The Marylanders lost 15 killed, 42 wounded, and 97 missing. Maj. Archibald Anderson was dead, as was Capt. Samuel Hobbs. Lt. Roger Nelson was wounded but recovered quickly, as did Capt. John Smith, who was dragged back across the vale by his men after having being shot down during a "duel" with Lieutenant Colonel Stuart. The high number of missing reflects the 2nd Marylanders who fled when the 2nd Guards Battalion struck them. Williams put the total Delaware casualties at 7 killed, 13 wounded, and 15 missing. Kirkwood's light infantry company lost 4 killed, 5 wounded, including Lt. George Vaughan, and 15 missing, so the other 3 killed and 8 wounded must have been in Capt. Peter Jacquett's Delaware company in the 1st Maryland.[18]

Statistically, the Virginia brigade suffered higher casualties than the Marylanders. Williams credited them with losing 29 killed, 40 wounded, and 39 missing in action. At first glance, the statistics seemingly contradict the idea that the 1st Maryland did the majority of the fighting along the third line. These figures, however, include the companies of Captains Phillip Huffman and Andrew Wallace, who fought on the northern and southern flanks. Both Huffman and Wallace were killed, as was Ens. Alexander Brownlee, who fell alongside Wallace. Capt. Alexander Ewing, serving as one of Greene's aides, went down with a gunshot wound to the arm. Most of the Virginia casualties probably occurred among the flank companies, but pension accounts indicate several killed and wounded among both Lt. Col. Samuel Hawes's 2nd Virginia and Col. John Green's 1st Virginia regiments.[19]

The mounted arm of Greene's forces took severe casualties as well, both in Washington's attack on the 2nd Guards and Lee's fight at New Garden, the running fight along the southern flank. Williams stated that the "Cavalry" (Continental Light Dragoons) lost 3 killed, 8 wounded, and 3 missing. He further stated that the North Carolina cavalry under the Marquis de Bretigny lost 1 killed and 1 wounded. It is unclear whether Williams included the losses of Capt. Thomas Watkins's Virginia dragoons in the first count. The figures seem quite low, given the numerous charges that Washington's men made through the Guards. Among the wounded were Capt. William Barrett and Lt. Griffin Fauntleroy (called "Little Fauntleroy" by St. George Tucker). Both men were captured after being shot from their mounts. Barrett recovered, but Fauntleroy died shortly after the battle. Lee's Legion lost 3 killed, 9 wounded, and 7 missing, according to Williams, but it is unclear whether these figures include those lost in the New Garden skirmishing. It is further impossible to determine the breakdown of Lee's casualties between his infantry and dragoons. Only one of Lee's officers, Lt. Jonathan Snowden, was wounded during the fighting.[20]

The Continental Artillery and the North Carolina Continentals may have suffered the highest casualty rates per capita. Williams included no byline for the artillery on his return. This may indicate that the majority of both batteries were killed, captured, or missing, but it is possible that Williams simply lumped the Maryland and Virginia artillery casualties into their respective brigade figures. Both Capt. Lt. Ebenezer Finley's and Capt. Anthony Singleton's guns were taken in intense fighting, and several accounts suggest that Singleton's artillery suffered severely along the front line, during the withdrawal to the third, and in the third line struggle. Pensions from both Finley's and Singleton's sections include several men who were wounded. Comparing the names of North Carolina Continentals known to have enlisted in the fall of 1780 and January 1781 under Capt. Edward Yarborough with American prisoners taken by Cornwallis indicates that most of Yarborough's company was captured, some after being wounded. Further supporting evidence comes from the pension accounts of Yarborough's men. Five of eight pensioners who claimed service at Guilford with Yarborough also mentioned being wounded at the battle, and two mentioned being captured.[21]

For several days after the battle, the wounded were administered to and the fallen laid to rest. Local Quakers donated a variety of goods for the injured, including several fowls, hogs, and one sheep, as well as candles, eggs, flour, and milk. From the correspondence of both Cornwallis and Greene, it is quite obvious that neither army was even remotely prepared to handle the large number of casualties. On 16 March, Cornwallis wrote to Greene that he had "given orders to collect" the American wounded and that "every possible Attention shall be paid to them"; however, he asked that Greene "send immediately Surgeons to take care of them, & a Supply of Necessaries & Provisions." That same day Greene had sent Cornwallis an express asking permission to send Surgeon James Wallace of the 3rd Continental Light Dragoons to aid American wounded "who may be unhappily situated." By the late evening of 16 March, both American and British doctors were operating on their patients at New Garden Meeting House and at the Guilford Courthouse hospitals. Those who did not survive their injuries or were killed in the battle were often buried where they fell, although a great number may have been buried in a series of pits just west of the Hoskins house.[22]

In addition to the wounded and dead, both armies had to deal with the issue of prisoners. Before the battle had begun, both sides clamored for a prisoner exchange in order to lessen the logistical burden they presented. Exactly how many Americans were taken remains unknown, but Cornwallis later remarked, "We took few prisoners owing to the excessive thickness of the woods facilitating their escape and every man of our army being repeatedly wanted for action." Pension records indicate that most captured militiamen were paroled and sent home, as were a number of Continental soldiers. Others, such as Robert Fulton of Campbell's riflemen, were taken with Cornwallis's army to Wilmington and put aboard prison ships in the Cape Fear River. The few British soldiers who were captured included several former Continental soldiers. Sgt. Maj. William Seymour of the Delawares saw one, Solomon Slocum, formerly of the 2nd Maryland, executed on 25 March. A general court-martial on 31 March convicted three other men of the same offense, but Greene ordered them to receive one hundred lashes each and "make good the time" they were absent.[23]

On 18 March Cornwallis's army left the battleground and marched back to New Garden, following seventeen wagons full of wounded men sent the day before. The British rested at the Quaker community for two days. While there, Cornwallis issued a proclamation claiming "compleat victory" at Guilford Courthouse. The intention was to encourage the local loyalists to rise up and come out of hiding, the enemy army having been vanquished. As with most such British proclamations directed at loyalists, the effect was less than helpful. Cornwallis reported, "Many of the inhabitants rode into camp, shook me by the hand, said they were glad to see us, and to hear that we had beat Greene, and then rode home again."[24]

Realizing nothing more could be done, Cornwallis turned his hungry army toward Cross Creek, the Scottish Highlander community at the head of the Cape Fear River, where he hoped to find "some place for rest and refitment." Instead, "to my great mortification, and contrary to all former accounts . . . it was not possible to procure any considerable quantity of provisions." He also found that the surrounding countryside had been taken over by local patriot militias, and that navigation on the Cape Fear was "totally impracticable . . . the breadth of the river seldom exceeding one hundred yards." "Under these circumstances I determined to move immediately to Wilmington." On 7 April his battered and exhausted army arrived on the outskirts of the British-occupied town. Cornwallis had had enough of the Carolinas. That same day, Abner Nash wrote Greene, "you . . . possess the Peculiar Art of making your Enemies run away from their Victories leaving you master of their wounded and all of the fertile part of the Country." Shortly after arriving in Wilmington, Cornwallis wrote a short letter to Gen. William Phillips stating, "I assure you that I am quite tired of marching about the country in quest of adventures." His vision of conquering the Carolinas to end the war had faded, but he had not given up complete hope. Cornwallis now developed a new strategy that involved taking "our whole force into Virginia; we then have a stake to fight for, and a successful battle may give us America."[25]

The day before Cornwallis arrived in Wilmington, Greene, who had left the Guilford area shortly after the British and followed their army east, turned his army south and entered South Carolina, ordering his men to "march by the Right tomorrow at Noon." Although Henry Lee later claimed to have provided Greene with the plan for invading South Carolina in a spirited debate at a council of war on 5 April, Greene had already made his decision by then. On 29 March Greene wrote George Washington, "If the enemy falls down towards Wilmington they will be in a position where it would be impossible for us to injure them if we had a force. In this critical and distressing situation I am determined to carry the War immediately into South Carolina. The enemy will be obliged to follow us or give up their posts in that State." Recognizing the danger of moving away from his supply base, Greene noted, "The Manoeuvre will be critical and dangerous; and the troops exposed to every hardship. But as I share it with them I hope they will bear up under it with that magnanimity which has already supported them, and for which they deserve everything of their Country."[26]

Greene's army entered South Carolina two weeks later, and a little more than a month after Guilford fought a short, but fierce battle against a small British army led by Lord Rawdon at Hobkirk's Hill on the outskirts of Camden, South Carolina. Greene had marched into the interior of South Carolina hoping to capture the British posts of Camden and Ninety Six. Realizing that the British works outside Camden were too strong to assault and that he did not have enough men to invest the town by siege, Greene pulled his army back to Hobkirk's Hill, a pine-covered ridge a mile and a half from Rawdon's defenses and awaited reinforcements under Thomas Sumter. The night of 24 April an American deserter entered the British camp and told Rawdon of both Greene's weaknesses and the impending arrival of the American reinforcements. Although outnumbered by nearly 600 men, Rawdon decided to launch a surprise attack on Greene's position and attacked Greene's left flank the morning of 25 April.[27]

The two little armies slugged it out for nearly thirty minutes, until the 1st Maryland, in a moment reminiscent of the 2nd Maryland's flight at Guilford, broke and ran to the rear but then re-formed. Initially, the blame rested on the shoulders of Col. John Gunby who, Greene felt, gave an order that resulted in most of the regiment turning and withdrawing. The Marylanders were ordered to advance without firing and using only their bayonets. Gunby was accused of ordering half the regiment to halt in midcharge and then withdraw a short distance, resulting in a confused and disorderly retreat. The unit rallied, and Gunby was later exonerated.[28]

It appears that the actual confusion came from the death of Capt. William Beatty, who was "shot in the head in the field." Upon the captain's demise, his company fell apart, resulting in an accordionlike effect on the next company. Gunby pulled the other companies back on line, and more confusion resulted. Coupled with Lt. Col. Benjamin Ford's wounding and the disorder among the 1st Virginia, Greene ordered a withdrawal. As Greene's army retreated from the field, the general himself dismounted and helped the American artillery fall back, not wanting to risk the embarrassment of losing his guns to the British as he had at Guilford Courthouse. The Americans lost 19 killed and 115 wounded, as well as an unknown number of prisoners, compared to 38 British killed, 190 wounded, and 50 captured. Greene summed up the situation: "We fight, get beat, rise, and fight again."[29]

In the brief but bloody battle, a number of Guilford survivors were wounded or killed. Lt. Col. Richard Campbell, now leading the 1st Virginia, and Capt. Archibald Denholm were wounded. Aside from Captain Beatty, the Maryland brigade lost Lt. Col. Benjamin Ford. Ford, still embarrassed by his regiment's actions at Guilford, fell among his men in the thickest part of the action. His left arm shattered by a musket ball, Ford suffered through an amputation and languished nearly two months before dying in the army hospital at Charlotte, North Carolina. Capt. Lt. James Bruff was "shot through both ancles [sic]," and captured, as was 2nd Lt. John Trueman, who fell with a similar wound to his foot. The British also took Capt. John Smith, who had returned to duty after recovering from the head wound received on the third line at Guilford.[30]

Smith's actions at Hobkirk's Hill were no less heroic than those he exhibited at Guilford. As the American artillery became threatened, "General Greene galloped up to Capt. John Smith, who was leading his company as an immediate action reserve behind the Maryland brigade's center, and ordered him to fall into the rear and save the cannon." Smith and his men took hold of the cannon's drag ropes and began pulling the guns to the rear. British dragoons spotted Smith's men and charged. Seeing the oncoming horsemen, Smith ordered his company into line and fired a volley that halted the British advance. "This he repeated several times until they had got 2 or 3 miles from the field of action, here one of Smiths men fired or his gun went off by accident before the word was given which produced a scattering fire, on which the cavalry rushed in among them and cut them all to pieces." Smith and his men "fought like bulldogs" and were all killed or captured, but in their sacrifice saved the guns, which were subsequently pulled away by some of William Washington's dragoons.[31]

Smith surrendered and was immediately "stripped of everything he had on except his shirt and his commission which hung around his neck in his bosom." Confined in the Camden jail, Smith was informed that he was to be hung the next morning, although the guards refused to tell him for what crime. A British deserter who had seen Smith's situation informed Greene, who subsequently sent word to Rawdon asking if the tale was true and threatening retaliation if Smith was executed without explanation. Rawdon informed the American messenger that "2 or 3 women of the British Army had come from Guilford, North Carolina since the battle there (at Guilford Courthouse) and related that Capt. Smith had killed Col. Stuart of the Kings Guards in cold blood two hours after the battle on his knees begging for mercy." In a letter to Greene on 29 April, Maj. John Doyle stated that "several deserters and some American prisoners" reported that Smith had "inhumanly put to death a British officer and three privates" after their surrender at Guilford Courthouse. Smith himself wrote Greene the following day, stating that he had been accused by "Some deserters from our army" of having "Wantingly [sic] put to death" a British captain and several other soldiers "a Considerable time after they were made our prisoners." On 3 May Greene wrote to Rawdon regarding the charges, "Nothing can be more foreign from the truth than the charge. . . . Captain Smith no doubt did his duty in the action but he has too noble a nature to be guilty of such base conduct as you mention, nor did I ever hear an insinuation of the Kind in the army."[32]

Persuaded by Greene's statements, Rawdon released Smith on parole shortly thereafter. On 10 May the British evacuated Camden. North Carolina militia major Guilford Dudley recalled that the following day he breakfasted with Greene, who remarked, "wearing a smile of complacency . . . that 'Rawdon evacuated Camden yesterday afternoon,' and added in a facetious way, 'and has left Capt. Jack Smith commandant of the place, in care of his sick and wounded.'" Smith was indeed left in Camden with the wounded but then ordered on parole to Charleston 21 May. Remaining fearful of British reprisals, Smith wrote Otho Holland Williams that he still expected to "feel the Effects of British tiriny [sic]." Although none awaited him, Smith suffered from further humiliation on the road to the British-occupied town. Assaulted by rogues claiming to be Whigs, Smith's attackers "stripped him, bound him, and inflicted on him a barbarous castigation on the bare back."[33]

After the British evacuated Camden, Greene continued his operations against the interior of South Carolina by moving against Ninety Six. Before he had entered the state, Greene had dispatched Lee's Legion to join South Carolina militia leader Francis Marion in attacking several British forts along the Santee River. They captured Fort Watson on 23 April and after Rawdon's evacuation of Camden joined South Carolina militia in capturing British posts at Fort Motte and Fort Granby. By the third week in May, Greene's army had initiated a siege of the British works at Ninety Six. By then, Lee, with a detachment of Maryland Continentals, had joined Andrew Pickens's South Carolina and Georgia militias attacking three British forts near Augusta, Georgia. Fort Dreadnought fell on 21 May and Fort Grierson the following day, although the operation cost the life of Lt. Col. Pinkatham Eaton, who fell leading North Carolina Continentals. Fort Cornwallis fell on 5 June, effectively ending British rule in interior Georgia.[34]

The siege of Ninety Six lasted nearly a month. The small British garrison under Lt. Col. John Cruger proved much more stubborn than Greene anticipated. Having exhausted most of his provisions and learning of a soon-to-arrive relief force under Rawdon, Greene launched assaults against Ninety Six the evening of 18 June. These attacks were by Continentals under Richard Campbell, Henry Lee, and Robert Kirkwood. Fifty handpicked men, the "forlorn hope," charged directly into the Star Fort's ditch. Leading the "forlorn hope" were two Guilford Continental veterans: Lieutenants Samuel Selden of Virginia and Isaac Duval of Maryland. Captains Michael Rudolph and Robert Kirkwood assaulted another position on the other side of the town. After forty-five minutes of hand-to-hand combat, Greene called off the assault after losing nearly 150 men. Both Duval and Selden were shot down but evacuated by their men. Selden later lost his arm. Capt. George Armstrong of the Maryland Line was killed and Capt. Perry Benson severely wounded in the neck. Benson, a large, heavy man, was carried from the field by one of his soldiers, a black private named Thomas Carney.[35]

Greene withdrew to the High Hills of the Santee, where he remained until midsummer. Rawdon relieved the garrison at Ninety Six, then abandoned the post, and took position at Orangeburg, South Carolina. For nearly two months, the armies stood only sixteen miles apart, separated by the Congaree and Wateree Rivers. In July, Rawdon returned to Europe for health reasons, leaving Lt. Col. Alexander Stewart in command at Orangeburg. On 22 August Greene received reinforcements comprised of South Carolina militia and state troops, North Carolina militia, and a brigade of North Carolina Continentals that included many Guilford "runaways" under Brig. Gen. Jethro Sumner. Shortly thereafter, Greene advanced toward Orangeburg, prompting Stewart to move his small army forty miles southward to a plantation at Eutaw Springs.

On 8 September 1781, Greene's army fought its last major action in the southern campaign. The battle of Eutaw Springs ranks as one of the bloodiest per capita engagements of the entire American Revolution, as each side suffered nearly 25 percent losses. As at Guilford, Greene put his militia in the first line and his regulars in supporting positions. A British bayonet charge broke the militia, and the battle became a shifting struggle between British regulars, loyalist provincials, and American Continentals. One British party under Maj. John Majoribanks took a position within a thicket. In intense hand-to-hand combat and close-range volley firing, they managed to wound and capture William Washington and rout a portion of his Continental dragoons. The Virginia and North Carolina Continentals fought bravely, and the former runaway militiamen, having been drilled incessantly since early summer, performed well as regular soldiers, standing toe to toe and bayonet to bayonet with the British, losing nearly two-thirds of their number as casualties. North Carolina Guilford veterans on the field included Lieutenant Colonels Reading Blount and Henry "Hal" Dixon and Capt. Edward Yarborough. The Americans eventually pushed the British back through their camp, but the desire for plunder and provisions outweighed the Maryland Continentals' craving to destroy their foes. While many Continentals ransacked the British tents and baggage, Majoribanks (who was mortally wounded) and Stewart rallied their troops and counterattacked, driving the majority of the Continentals from the field.[36]

Greene had lost yet another battle, but he had delivered another fatal blow to a British army. Stewart lost 40 percent of his force: 85 dead, 351 wounded, and 257 missing. Greene lost 108 killed, 283 wounded and 39 missing. Among the dead were many who had survived Guilford. Lt. Col. Richard Campbell was shot down while leading his Virginians, as was Capt. Conway Oldham, who led Andrew Wallace's old light infantry company. Maj. Henry Dobson of the Maryland Continentals, who had been promoted following the death of Archibald Anderson at Guilford, was killed, as was Lt. Isaac Duval, the leader of the "forlorn hope" at Ninety Six. Numerous Guilford veterans were wounded, including Lt. Col. William Washington, who was also captured, and Lt. Col. John Eager Howard, who fell leading his Marylanders. British rounds wounded Lieutenants Clement Carrington and Laurence Manning of Lee's Legion as well.[37]

After Eutaw Springs, Greene moved his army toward Charleston. His men remained positioned outside the city until the British evacuated in December 1782. In ten months, Greene had fought three major battles, a siege, and numerous skirmishes. He had been defeated in nearly all of them. Yet his strategy of keeping his army alive and moving had worked. Describing the

Southern Army to Chevalier de La Luzerne, Greene stated, "We fight, get beat, Rise, and fight again. The whole Country is one continued scene of blood and slaughter."[38]

Cornwallis's fortunes were much different. After reaching Wilmington, Cornwallis refitted his army, sent the wounded to Charleston or to England, and made perhaps the most fateful decision of his military career. The earl decided to invade Virginia and join forces with Maj. Gen. William Phillips and Brig. Gen. Benedict Arnold, who had been raiding the Tidewater and eastern Piedmont since late March. Cornwallis had given up attempting to pacify the interior of North and South Carolina. By taking Virginia, Cornwallis felt that he could split the South and eliminate the supply networks that fed Greene's Southern Army. "I was firmly persuaded that until Virginia was reduced we could not hold the more Southern provinces; and that after its reduction they would fall without much resistance and be retained without much difficulty."[39]

Cornwallis wrote a series of letters to Lord Germain, British secretary of state for the American colonies, concerning his theories but discussed the matter little with the overall British commander in North America, Gen. Sir Henry Clinton, before marching. He wrote Clinton, "I cannot help expressing my wishes that the Chesapeake may become the seat of war, even at the expense of abandoning New York." Clinton apparently assumed that Greene had fled north from Cornwallis's army. He responded, "It is my wish that you should continue to conduct operations as they advance Northerly; for except as a visitor, I shall probably not move to Chesapeake, unless Washington goes thither in great force. The success which has hitherto attended your Lordship excites the fullest assurance of its continuance." In Virginia, William Phillips was under a similar impression, writing Clinton, "the year 1781 may prove the glorious period of your command in America, by putting an end to the rebellion." Phillips himself believed that with Cornwallis's aid, he could drive north into Maryland, eventually retaking Philadelphia.[40]

As word of British losses at Guilford reached Clinton and Phillips, their moods changed. Clinton became enraged upon learning the actual situation of the British army in the South and that Greene still dominated the Carolinas. His indignation, and the heated correspondence that followed between him and Cornwallis, became known as the "Clinton-Cornwallis Controversy." Clinton attempted to have Cornwallis court-martialed, and one story, although likely apocryphal, claims Clinton challenged him to a duel. Phillips was equally outraged. In a letter to Clinton, Phillips stated that Cornwallis's supposed success was "that sort of victory which ruins an army and the Carolinas, like all America, are lost in rebellion." Phillips's anger may have been tempered by ill health. He died in Petersburg on 13 May of a contagious fever.[41]

On 25 April 1781, Cornwallis departed Wilmington for Virginia. Despite small skirmishes with North Carolina militia units at Rockfish Creek, Swift Creek, Peacock's Bridge, and Halifax, the British entered Virginia on 12 May. Upon their arrival in Petersburg, Capt. Lt. Samuel Graham, an English officer serving with Arnold's force, commented on the veterans of Cornwallis: "Words can ill describe the admiration in which this band of heroes was held . . . even by the light infantry—the elite of the army, who had fought and generally led in every action during the war." Fourteen days later Cornwallis wrote to Clinton, "if offensive war is intended, Virginia appears to me to be the only province in which it may be carried on." He united with Phillips's and Arnold's forces and advanced on the capital of Richmond, intent on destroying American supply depots and the small force under the Marquis de Lafayette. Lafayette abandoned the city on 27–28 May and moved his small army of Virginia Continentals and militia north. The Virginia legislature fled to Charlottesville and Staunton.[42]

Cornwallis pursued the retreating Americans and dispatched Tarleton on a raid to Charlottesville, intending to capture the Virginia General Assembly. Cornwallis told Clinton that Tarleton's men were hardened veterans, although "in distress for want of arms, clothing, boots, and indeed appointments of any kind." He ordered the 2nd Battalion, 71st Highlanders, to detach a contingent to serve as mounted infantry with the British Legion. The Highland officers protested against serving under the man they felt had sacrificed their 1st Battalion comrades at Cowpens. Instead, Tarleton received a company of the Royal Welch Fusiliers led by Capt. Forbes Champagne. The British arrived at Charlottesville on 4 June, but most legislators had already fled. Seven patriot politicians were taken, and Tarleton came literally within minutes of capturing Thomas Jefferson at Monticello. Jefferson and Edward Stevens, who was recovering from his Guilford wound in Charlottesville, both escaped as a result of the actions of Virginia militia officer Jack Jouett. Jouett spotted Tarleton's dragoons the night before, and perceiving their intentions, rode ahead to warn the general assembly and inhabitants of the town.[43]

After the Charlottesville raid, Cornwallis focused on destroying Lafayette's army but failed to intercept him before the Frenchman received reinforcements from Washington's Main Army led by Gen. "Mad" Anthony Wayne.

Some of Lafayette's light infantry penetrated behind Cornwallis, threatening his supply lines. In this precarious position, Cornwallis withdrew to Richmond and then Williamsburg. On 21 June Cornwallis received reinforcements and dispatches from the north. Clinton wrote asking that men be sent north because George Washington and the Comte de Rochambeau were threatening New York. In early July, Cornwallis abandoned Williamsburg, retreating southeast along the James River. On 6 July, a portion of Cornwallis's men defeated an American force at the battle of Green Spring near James City, but Cornwallis did not follow up the victory and instead fortified himself inside Portsmouth. Several weeks later, in what Clinton afterward described as a "mortifying" move, Cornwallis abandoned the strong position at Portsmouth for the village of Yorktown.[44]

Unbeknownst to Cornwallis, Washington and Rochambeau had given up plans to take New York and were instead focused on destroying the British in Virginia. On 19 July Washington wrote, "I am of Opinion, that under these Circumstances, we ought to throw a sufficient Garrison into W Point; leave some Continental Troops and Militia to cover the Country contiguous to New York, and transport the Remainder (both French and American) to Virginia, should the Enemy still keep a Force there." Washington received word on 14 August that the French fleet of the Marquis de Grasse was sailing for Chesapeake Bay and could provide a blockading force to help conquer Cornwallis. Washington and Rochambeau set out for the south, joining Wayne and Lafayette on 28 September. Shortly before they arrived, de Grasse's fleet defeated Sir Thomas Graves's fleet in the battle of the Chesapeake Capes, preventing the Royal Navy from resupplying or extracting Cornwallis's army. Washington and Rochambeau then laid siege to Cornwallis's army.[45]

Over the next three weeks, American and French siege lines came closer and closer to the British, and storming parties captured key British redoubts. A number of Guilford veterans died in the 14 October assaults on two redoubts. Despite casualties, the Fusilier Redoubt on the western end of the British line held until the surrender. Redoubts 9 and 10, on the eastern end of the line, were taken. First Lt. Stephen Guyon and 2nd Lt. Edward Place of the 23rd Foot died, as did Capt. John Kerr and Capt. Lt. Charles Curzon. The 2nd Battalion, 71st Foot, lost Lieutenants Angus Cameron and Thomas Fraser, as well as Ens. John Grant, and the Von Bose Regiment lost Capt. Herman Kristian Rall. Fully resigned to defeat and unaware that a potential relief force under Henry Clinton was en route, Cornwallis offered to surrender on 17 October.[46]

Two days later, the 7,000-man British army marched out of Yorktown, laid down their arms, and entered captivity. Cornwallis himself did not attend, claiming illness; and he may have indeed been sick, as was most of his army. He sent in his stead Gen. Charles O'Hara, who either by mistake or as an insult offered Cornwallis's sword to Rochambeau, but the Frenchman's deputy, Mathieu Dumas, reportedly responded, "Vous vous trompez, le général en chef de notre armée est à la droite (You are mistaken, the commander in chief of our army is to the right)." O'Hara then turned to Washington, who subsequently passed the honor on to his deputy, Benjamin Lincoln, who Cornwallis and Clinton had defeated at Charleston more than a year earlier.[47]

Although fighting continued for nearly two more years, the majority consisted of skirmishes and minor actions between expeditionary forces. Cornwallis's men went into prison camps, then were later paroled, exchanged, and many sent back to England with the evacuation of British forces following the Treaty of Paris in September 1783. Although Washington's and Rochambeau's troops could rightly claim that they had inflicted the final defeat on Cornwallis and thus sped along the war's end, Greene's Southern Army deserves no lesser laurels. What began on the back roads of the Carolina Piedmont in January 1781 ended on the banks of the York River that October. Until 15 March the campaign for the South was anyone's game, but Guilford Courthouse changed that. Cornwallis's losses that day led to his retreat to Wilmington. Depressed and demoralized with the failing prospect of conquering the Carolinas, his lordship then chose to invade Virginia, resulting in the eventual capitulation of his army and the collapse of British resolve to further prosecute the war. In those respects, the fighting at Guilford Courthouse formed an integral link in the chain of events that led to American independence.

*The event . . . had caused*
*him much unhappiness*
*from its occurrence to*
*the end of his life.*
—CAPT. THOMAS
WATKINS, *Virginia*
*Militia Dragoons*

CHAPTER TEN  THE GUILFORD
"CROSSROADS"

By the first decade of the nineteenth century, the Guilford Courthouse village had ceased to exist, being subsumed by the town of Greensboro. For those men who fought at Guilford and survived the war, the battle became nothing but a memory, perhaps an intentionally repressed memory, of one incredible event in their past. Many of those who lived through the fighting at Guilford and their descendants went on to play significant roles in the history of their respective nations in the decades following the conflict.

Paroled after Yorktown, Cornwallis returned to New York, where he met with Gen. Sir Henry Clinton in late November. He returned to Britain the following month, having been exchanged for South Carolina rice merchant and Continental Congress delegate Henry Laurens. Cornwallis's surrender affected him surprisingly little, politically or socially, after the war. Clinton engaged him publicly in print over who deserved blame for the loss of the American colonies, but Cornwallis appears to have come out on top. In 1785, King George III appointed him special envoy to the court of Frederick the Great of Prussia and the following year named him governor-general of India. From 1786 to 1793, Cornwallis reorganized British rule in India. The

"Cornwallis Reforms," as his alterations became known, attempted to eradicate corruption within the country's administration and rein in the East India Company's excessive power. He also reorganized the Indian civil services by requiring that Europeans hold all positions having an annual salary over £500. Cornwallis divided British India into twenty-three administrative districts and encouraged British tax rules on the local village heads.

In addition to being an administrator, Cornwallis also utilized his considerable military skills. In 1789, Tipu Sahib, ruler of Mysore, invaded the Indian state of Travancore, a British protectorate. Tipu allied himself with the French, hoping for their military aid. Three years later, Cornwallis defeated Tipu with a combined force from Britain, Hyderabad, and Maratha at the Siege of Seringapatam. The following year, Cornwallis returned to Britain, citing obstructive Bengal officers and a lack of parliamentary interest in further curbing the power of the East India Company. For his actions in India, Cornwallis received the title of marquis in 1794. The following year, he accepted appointment as the master of the ordnance, a position overseeing distribution of munitions throughout the military. In 1798, George III appointed Cornwallis lord-lieutenant of Ireland and sent him to put down the Irish Rebellion. His lordship crushed the rebels and a French expeditionary force sent to Ireland in September. He later oversaw the 1801 Act of Union but resigned his post when the king would not grant Catholic emancipation. Despite their differences over Ireland, George III appointed Cornwallis to meet with Napoleon Bonaparte as a peace negotiator in November 1801. Negotiations continued until March 1802, and Cornwallis eventually brokered a short-lived peace between Britain and France. Perhaps hoping to find peace and quiet, Cornwallis retired to his country home in Suffolk.

Three years later king and country called again, and the marquis became the governor-general of India a second time, replacing Lord Wellesley. His time in India lasted only a few short months. Cornwallis, the general who chased Nathanael Greene across North Carolina and whose men fought so courageously at Guilford Courthouse and Yorktown, died at the age of sixty-seven of a fever on 5 October 1805, near Ghazipur, a small village in Uttar Pradesh state. He is buried nearby in a mausoleum overlooking the Ganges River.[1]

Nathanael Greene, Cornwallis's American counterpart, returned home to Rhode Island at the war's conclusion beset by mounting debts resulting from his personal endorsement of loans defaulted on by contractor John Banks, loans that Greene had backed in an effort to supply the Southern Army.

Greene received some relief when South Carolina and Georgia both awarded him plantations and he sold the South Carolina property to pay off creditors. In 1785, he made his permanent home with his wife and five children at Mulberry Grove, the confiscated Savannah, Georgia, plantation of former loyalist lieutenant governor John Graham. In addition, he built a summer home, Dungeness, on Cumberland Island off the Georgia coast. Greene remained a close and affectionate friend of George Washington, naming a son after his former commander as well as christening his daughter Martha Washington Greene.

Greene spent much of his time traveling between Georgia and Rhode Island while finalizing his family's move south. In 1786, having finally settled down, he visited a friend's plantation to inspect crops. Touring his host's rice fields without a hat in the oppressive summer sun, Greene soon complained of a headache. Taken home, he became bedridden, and those present noted a swelling of the head and intense sweating. Doctors bled him and applied plasters, but to no avail. A few hours later, Greene fell into a coma. Anthony Wayne, former Continental general and close friend who had recently moved to Georgia, came to offer support for his ailing comrade. Greene's condition did not improve during the night, and at 6:00 A.M. the following morning, 19 June 1786, five years, three months, and four days after Guilford Courthouse, Washington's most trusted and reliable subordinate died at age forty-four from what was assumed to be a combination of sunstroke and fever.[2]

Banastre Tarleton and Henry Lee are perhaps the two individuals other than Cornwallis and Greene most representative of the Southern Campaign, not only for their actions, but also because they left detailed memoirs and suffered similar falls from grace after the war. After Guilford, Tarleton continued with the British army and surrendered at Yorktown with Cornwallis. He suffered humiliation when he was the only British officer not invited to dine with the American and French commanders after the capitulation. In November, he sailed for New York, where he befriended George III's youngest son, the Duke of Clarence. The following month, Tarleton embarked for Britain, but French privateers captured his vessel near the English Channel. His captors intended to land at Boulogne, France, but a storm blew them off course, and they instead harbored in Dungeness, England (ironically, the town Greene's summer home would be named after), where Tarleton paid £400 ransom and was released. He finally reached Liverpool in February 1782.

Haunted by his notoriety and the war, Tarleton became an inveterate gambler and alcoholic in addition to falling into a fifteen-year relationship with Mary Robinson, a famous London actress, whom he seduced on a bet. When Tarleton's creditors came calling, Robinson sought out several of Tarleton's former comrades for help. Many former officers shunned him, but Lord Cornwallis came to his aid financially. Shortly thereafter, Mary miscarried. The traumatized couple, still hounded by creditors, fled to France, where they received shelter from an old enemy, the Duke de Lauzun, formerly of Rochambeau's army.

While in France, Tarleton began writing his memoirs, *A History of the Campaigns of 1780 and 1781 in the Southern Provinces of North America*. He returned briefly to Britain in 1786 when Cornwallis was offered the governor-generalship of India. His former commander intended on giving Tarleton a position in his new administration, but the Tory-dominated Parliament refused to allow Tarleton, a Whig, to accept the post. Enraged, Tarleton erroneously blamed Cornwallis for the slight and turned to Henry Clinton for advice in publishing his work. What resulted was a memoir of the southern campaign that served as a scathing attack on the generalship and competence of Cornwallis. The book was not well received by the British public and prompted Roderick Mackenzie, a former officer in the 71st Highlanders who had been wounded and captured at Cowpens, to write a rebuttal titled *Strictures on Lt. Colonel Tarleton's Campaigns*. Furthering the controversy, Tarleton's second in command, George Hanger, replied with *An Address to the Army in Rebuttal to "Strictures," by Roderick Mackenzie* that supported Tarleton's account.

Tarleton returned to Britain and won a seat in Parliament in 1790 representing Liverpool, despite the controversy surrounding his book. He held the post for the next twenty-two years, although he angered many by his defense of the slave trade, and soon began gambling again. His relationship with Mary becoming strained, he left her in 1798 for Sallie Bertie, a wealthy young daughter of the Duke of Lancaster several years his junior. In December of that year, he took command of British forces in Portugal but was recalled in October 1799. He remained in the British army, rising to the rank of lieutenant general in 1811, but never saw further action. During the remainder of the Napoleonic Wars, he commanded the backwaters of western England. In 1816, he received a baronet and was later titled a knight of the Order of Bath. His last years were spent racked with gout and "unable to move from his chair" at his home in Shropshire. "Bloody Ban" died on 16 January 1833, one day short of the fifty-second anniversary of Cowpens.[3]

"Light Horse Harry" Lee served at Yorktown as well, resigning shortly after the siege, citing ill health. In April 1782, he married his cousin Matilda and took up farming at Stratford Hall, his wife's family home in eastern Virginia. He named his first son, who died in infancy, Nathanael Greene Lee, one of the few southern campaign veterans to so honor their commander. A complete failure as a farmer, Lee embarked on a political career. He served briefly in the Continental Congress, 1786–88, and as a member of the Virginia General Assembly, 1789–91. Elected Virginia's governor in 1791, Lee held the position until 1794, when he took command of the United States Army and joined Washington and Alexander Hamilton in putting down the Whiskey Rebellion in western Pennsylvania. From 1799 to 1801, Lee served in the United States House of Representatives, where he wrote the eulogy used by John Marshall describing George Washington as "first in war, first in peace, and first in the hearts of his countrymen."

Lee's life spiraled downward after his congressional service. Following the death of Matilda in 1790, Lee married Anne Skipwith Carter, the cousin of fellow Guilford veteran Henry Skipwith. With Anne, Lee fathered six children, in addition to the two surviving children he had with Matilda. Caring for such a large family, coupled with losses from ill-advised land speculations, destroyed the Lees' finances. In 1807, just as his fifth child, Robert Edward Lee, the future commander of the Army of Northern Virginia, was learning to walk, "Light Horse Harry" was marched off to debtor's prison. Much like Tarleton, Lee used this period as a time of reflection and writing. Confined in a twelve-by-fifteen-foot prison cell, he wrote his *Memoirs of the War in the Southern Department of the United States*. In 1810, he finished the work and was released from prison after selling nearly all of his possessions.

Lee moved to Alexandria and published his book to mixed reviews in 1812. Like Tarleton, Lee had used his memoirs to criticize his former commander. Many people were outraged by the apparent attack on Greene, who had been rightfully entered into the pantheon of American heroes. While in Baltimore on business, 27 July 1812, Lee attempted to help Alexander Contee Hanson, a close friend and editor of the *Baltimore Federal Republican*, escape from a Democratic-Republican mob angered by Hanson's opposition to the War of 1812. The ruffians beat Lee senseless, inflicting serious injuries to his internal organs and head. The wounds to his face severely limited his speech, and Lee, disfigured, discredited, and despondent, fled to the West Indies. While returning to the United States in 1818, he was shipwrecked off the Georgia coast. He appeared, physically demolished and thoroughly drunk, on the doorstep of Greene's summer home, Dungeness. He died there, age sixty-two, in the care of his former commander's daughter on 25 March, ten days after the thirty-seventh anniversary of Guilford Courthouse.[4]

Cornwallis's two senior subordinates, O'Hara and Leslie, led quite different lives after the war. Charles O'Hara took the surrender at Yorktown entirely in stride. The evening after he tendered Cornwallis's sword, O'Hara dined with Washington and Rochambeau and completely charmed his captors. One French officer expressed shock at O'Hara's "sangfroid and gaiety" on the evening. Paroled to New York, O'Hara received a promotion to major general and was exchanged in February 1782. Two months later, Clinton placed him in command of a detachment sent to reinforce Britain's Caribbean possessions. In the fall of 1782, he returned to England, where his gambling and drinking eventually put him thoroughly in debt. Like Tarleton, O'Hara absconded to the continent to avoid creditors.

While in Italy he met author Mary Berry, with whom he embarked on a fifteen-year courtship, although the two were never married. O'Hara returned to Britain in 1785 after Cornwallis offered to help pay his debts. Offered a post when the earl left for India, O'Hara declined and instead took command of the British garrison at Gibraltar, commencing in 1792. O'Hara was beloved by his men, who referred to him affectionately as the "Old Cock of the Rock." He was also known for his eccentricities and warped humor. A 1788 issue of the *Times* records an incident in which a young officer under O'Hara's command wished to marry his own aunt but was refused permission by local priests unless he could obtain dispensation from the pope. The man applied to O'Hara, who immediately wrote an order stating, "The bearer hereof has my permission to marry his aunt, or his grandmother, whoever he chuses [*sic*]." It was signed "Charles O'Hara, Major General and Pope."

In 1792, O'Hara was appointed lieutenant governor of Gibraltar, and with the outbreak of war with revolutionary France the following year, became military governor of Toulon. During the subsequent French siege of Toulon, O'Hara was wounded and taken prisoner yet again. His captor was a young French junior officer named Napoleon Bonaparte. Napoleon treated O'Hara with great kindness but could do nothing for him after he was handed over to the political machinations of Robespierre. Taken to Paris, O'Hara was labeled an insurrectionist and forced to watch mass guillotine executions, with the obvious implication that the same fate awaited him. Paraded through the city's streets and severely beaten by several mobs, he was incarcerated at Luxembourg prison. He was finally exchanged in August 1795. Upon his return to Britain, O'Hara was ordered to take the post of governor of Gibraltar, replacing his former superior, Sir Henry Clinton.

During the last years of his life, O'Hara was racked with pain from wounds he had received at Guilford Courthouse and Toulon. Adm. Sir William Hotham reported that O'Hara's congenial nature had left him. "He is not a good tempered man subject to fits of ill humour which he was at no pains to conceal. This was partly attributed to the sufferings and privations he had undergone while in the Luxembourg, which had permanently soured his disposition." O'Hara fathered four illegitimate children with two local women and managed to build an impressive fortune. At his death, 21 February 1802, he left nearly £80,000 to them as well as £7,000 for his black servant. In his obituary, he was remembered as "a brave and enterprising soldier, a strict disciplinarian, and a polite accomplished gentleman."[5]

Unlike most of his fellow Guilford veterans, Alexander Leslie did not suffer through the siege and surrender at Yorktown. The Carolinas campaign broke his health, and Cornwallis sent him to Charleston to recuperate. Shortly afterwards, Clinton ordered Leslie to New York City, where he arrived that summer. Clinton wrote Cornwallis on 27 August 1781, concerned "to find [Leslie] in so bad a state of health on his arrival, but it is now much altered for the better, he embarks tomorrow on his way to Charlestown." Having recovered from his ailments, Leslie returned to Charleston and took over command of the southern theater. His situation did not improve after returning to the south. In January 1782, Leslie wrote Clinton complaining of a fall from his horse that had severely injured him. Two months later, he began a series of tragic letters to his commander pleading to be allowed to return to Europe. "You know, Sir, that my constitution is much impaired from having served the whole war. . . . Independent of my public situation, and even state of ill health, I have an aged mother going into her grave, and only wishing to see me." Clinton responded that he hoped "to find shortly some general to succeed him." The replacement never came. Leslie remained, sullen and disparaged, in Charleston until the British evacuation in December 1782.

Little is known of Leslie's life after his return to Scotland. In December 1794, he helped put down a mutiny by a Scottish fencible regiment stationed in Glasgow. While marching the ringleaders to Edinburgh Castle for trial, Leslie and his party were "assailed . . . by a number of riotous people, who accused them of being active in sending away the prisoners." The mob began throwing rocks, one of which struck Leslie in the head. Carried to a nearby home, Leslie died from his injuries three days after Christmas.[6]

The postwar life of Cornwallis's third brigadier, John Howard, also remains something of a mystery. In 1782, Howard left the Guards and became colonel of the 97th Regiment, serving the next two years at sea and on station at Gibraltar. Descended from a long line of nobility, Howard became the fifteenth earl of Suffolk and the eighth earl of Berkshire in 1783. He subsequently withdrew from public life and the army, remaining on his estates, still nursing the foot wound received at Guilford. From 1806 to 1812, he served as governor of Londonderry and Culmore Fort in Ireland and died 23 January 1820 at age eighty.[7]

Many veterans of both armies later took part in further wars, as both Great Britain and the fledgling United States attempted to expand their holdings. Nowhere is this more apparent than looking at the Britons serving in India. Cornwallis's personal secretary, Maj. Alexander Ross, served as the marquis's adjutant general in India and in 1812 was promoted to general. Capt. Forbes Champagne of the 23rd spent several years with the regiment in India before returning to Europe and fighting against Napoleon. He became a lieutenant general in 1816. Lt. Henry Haldane, the mapmaker whose work appeared in Tarleton's memoir (see Map 4 in Chapter 4), became quartermaster general of the British army in India. He met his wife and mother of his seventeen children in Calcutta in 1793. Haldane achieved the rank of colonel in the Engineers before his death in 1825. Capt. Francis Skelly of Fraser's Highlanders later became lieutenant colonel of the 74th Foot and fought at Seringapatam. His journal remains one of the finest primary sources concerning that siege.[8]

Other British Guilford veterans fought against Napoleon. Lt. John McLeod, Cornwallis's artillery commander after Augustus O'Hara's death, eventually became a lieutenant general and was knighted by George III. McLeod served throughout the Napoleonic Wars. In 1809, he commanded the artillery contingent of the doomed British military expedition to Walcheren and three years later lost a son at the storming of Badajoz during the Peninsular War. He became director general of the Royal Artillery before his death in 1833. Cornwallis's other surviving artillery officer, Lt. John Smith, also went on to serve against Napoleon, seeing action in the West Indies and Holland, before taking command of the artillery at Gibraltar under Charles O'Hara. Smith followed McLeod as director general of the artillery, a post he held until his death in 1837. The Guards' Capt. Augustus Maitland recovered from his Guilford wound, became a lieutenant colonel in 1792, and was killed in action at Beverwyck, Holland, on 6 October 1799. Ens. Ralph Gore of the 33rd Foot recovered from injuries received at Guilford and remained in the regiment until the early 1800s. He lost a son at Waterloo. Second Lt. Henry Montressor of the Royal Welch also served against Napoleon and was commandant of Elba Island during the Frenchman's incarceration. He died shortly after his promotion to general in 1836.[9]

Guilford veterans also took part in the Egyptian campaign in 1800–1801. Two, John Stuart and Hildebrand Oakes, are represented in Thomas Stothard's painting *Death of Abercromby*, which memorializes the final moments of Gen. Sir Ralph Abercromby, who was killed at Alexandria. Stuart, a former ensign in the 3rd Guards, had only slightly recovered from his "dangerous wound in the groin, which was attended with such severe pain, and such lingering circumstances, that, although thirty years have since elapsed, [he] still occasionally suffers from its effects." Stuart remained in the British army after the war. He saw action against Napoleon in Holland, France, Egypt, and Portugal, before taking command of a British division in the defense of southern Italy. In 1810, Stuart received command of British forces in the entire Mediterranean. He died a lieutenant general in 1815, two months after being knighted in the Order of the Bath. Hildebrand Oakes, once a captain in the 33rd, served alongside Stuart in the Mediterranean. As a general, he briefly commanded the British fortress at Malta before his death in 1822.[10]

Still other veterans took charge of Britain's expanding empire. Capt. Francis Dundas rose through the ranks, becoming a general in 1812. He served as acting governor of the Cape Colony (South Africa) from 1798 to 1803. In 1804–5 he commanded the Kent division of the army posted along the southern coast of England during the invasion alarms. Dundas apparently never accepted the American victory in the Revolution. In 1799, he wrote John Elmslie, a young U.S. Navy officer appointed diplomatic consul to Cape Town, "Sir, remember you are a British Subject only, cloaked under an American certificate, and if you persist in such improper conduct towards the Government, or appear in public as you have done [in a U.S. Navy uniform], I will try you and punish you, Sir, as a subject under His Majesty's allegiance. Remember before whom you are, and that you are in a British Colony." Dundas retired from the military in the late 1810s and died 15 January 1824 in Dumbarton, Scotland. Lt. Harry Calvert remained with the army, fought in Holland in the 1790s, and became a lieutenant general in 1810. In the 1820s, he served as the administrator of Chelsea Hospital and the adjutant general of all British forces, in which capacity he wrote a number of training manuals for infantry and cavalry drill. Before his death in 1826 at age sixty-three, Calvert helped organize the military colleges at High Wycombe and Marlow, schools that provided the foundation for the Royal Military Academy at Sandhurst.[11]

Many British veterans chose to live in Canada after the war. Former members of Tarleton's British Legion went to Nova Scotia and Newfoundland, where they settled among loyalist refugees. Maj. Richard England, Cornwallis's quartermaster general, later served as commander of Detroit and evacuated the post when ordered to do so in 1795, leaving it to the Americans. He later became lieutenant governor of Plymouth and one of the first settlers in western Upper Canada. England died a full general in 1812. His son and namesake served throughout the Napoleonic Wars, the War of 1812, the Kaffir War in South Africa, and the first Afghan War, before rising to great acclaim commanding a division in the Crimean War. The commander of the Guards Grenadier Company at Guilford, Capt. Napier Christie, retired in 1806 as a lieutenant general. He married the daughter of Ralph Burton, the governor of Montreal. Napier took his wife's last name as his own. An inveterate gambler, Napier Burton sold £12,000 of his wife's estate to pay his debts. He served briefly in Parliament and in the Napoleonic Wars, before settling in Montreal. In 1822, the son of one of his former soldiers attempted to kill him in his home. Napier Christie Burton survived, and the attacker was hung for attempted murder. Afterwards Burton returned to London, where he died in 1835. Thomas Saumarez rose to the rank of major general and commanded the garrison of Halifax, Nova Scotia, during the War of 1812. Afterwards he returned to his home on the island of Guernsey and became head of the local militia. In 1838, at the coronation ceremony of Queen Victoria, Saumarez, the last Revolutionary War veteran actively serving in the British army, received a promotion to full general. He was the last surviving British officer who had fought at Guilford Courthouse when he died at his home in Guernsey on 4 March 1845 at age eighty-eight.[12]

Other British officers remained in Great Britain after the war, either too old or too tired of fighting to continue on active duty in the army. Lt. Col. Chapple Norton remained in the Guards, becoming a general in 1802 and receiving an appointment as governor of Charlemont in Ireland. Ironically, Norton served as parliamentarian for the Borough of Guildford in Surrey several times after 1784. He died at age seventy-two on 19 March 1818. Capt. Francis Richardson, a Pennsylvania loyalist turned Foot Guards officer, left the army in 1794. He never returned to America and spent the remainder of his life in Great Britain. Richardson lived in London until 1792 and served as a customs agent for the East India Company. He then settled in Suffolk with his wife, Letitia Moseley, the daughter of a prominent London haberdasher. Charles Stedman moved to England, where he was appointed to oversee the financial claims and settlements of former loyalists. In 1794 he published his work, *The History of the Origin, Progress, and Termination of the American War*. Three years later he was appointed the accountant general of stamp revenue for Great Britain. He died in 1812.[13]

Little is known of Guards officer Robert Lovelace's whereabouts after the conflict. After his humiliation at Guilford, Lovelace disappeared from the historical record. Several possibly apocryphal stories say he died a drunk, impoverished pariah in a London gutter; however, this is highly unlikely. Lovelace had at least six children, two of whom were married in Ontario in the early 1810s, suggesting that, after the war, Lovelace moved his family to Canada, something no gutter-dwelling alcoholic would have likely accomplished. His home, Quidenham Hall, in Norfolk passed into the hands of Sir George Keppel, third earl of Albemarle, and remained in the Keppel family until 1948, when it became a Carmelite nunnery. History does not record what happened to Lovelace's watch or whether William Washington ever returned it.[14]

The German officers who fought at Guilford Courthouse are particularly difficult to track after the war. Friedrich Wilhelm von Roeder, who commanded the jaegers, may be related to Friedrich Erhardt von Roeder, who fought with distinction in the Prussian army during the Napoleonic Wars and was awarded the Pour le Mérite. Major Du Buy of the Von Bose disappears after Yorktown. From John Eager Howard's notes to historian and fellow veteran John Marshall, it is apparent that Du Buy visited America after the war and spent some time as a guest at Howard's home. Du Buy's senior captain, Friedrich von Scheer, remained in the Hessian army after the war. He may be an ancestor of Reinhard Scheer, commander of the German navy during the World War I battle of Jutland.[15]

The few British and Hessian enlisted men whose journals and memoirs provide details to the story of Guilford Courthouse led varied lives after the war. Roger Lamb surrendered with his regiment at Yorktown but managed to escape (his second such action of the war, the first being after Saratoga) and made his way into British-occupied New York. After the war he left the army, married, and became master of a Methodist Free School in Dublin. He produced two monographs about his experiences in the war: *A Journal of the Occurrences during the Late American War*, published in 1809, and *Memoir of My Own Life*, in 1811. Lamb lived the remainder of his life in peace, applying for and receiving a shilling-per-day pension from Chelsea Hospital, before dying in 1830. Pvt. John Robert Shaw of the 33rd Foot, who had been captured just prior to Guilford, joined the American army and served with a Virginia militia regiment until Yorktown. After the war, he remained in the new United States and settled in Lexington, Kentucky, taking up the trade of a well digger. In 1807, he produced a wonderful autobiography of his adventures and misgivings titled *A Narrative of the Life and Travels of John Robert Shaw, the Well-Digger, Now Resident in Lexington, Kentucky*.[16]

Lamb's and Shaw's German counterpart, Berthold Koch, surrendered at Yorktown. His diary, discovered in the early twentieth-century, records that as the Von Bose prisoners were marched to captivity in Frederick, Maryland, they were accosted along the way by "men, women and children . . . [who] when they saw us . . . old and young called out, 'That is the regiment, the rascals, who killed our husbands, our fathers!'" Koch erroneously attributed this to the riflemen at Guilford having been Marylanders. What he actually witnessed were Virginians who were likely related to members of Campbell's riflemen. After returning to Germany in 1784, Koch remained in the army and took part in a war between the principalities of Hesse-Cassel and Bückeburg in 1786. At that conflict's end, he became a farmer, settling near Hofgeismar, where he died 14 May 1823 at age eighty-one.[17]

The muster rolls of the 33rd and Von Bose Regiments provide a representative picture of what occurred to those British and Hessian veterans of Guilford who survived the war. At the end of the conflict, 372 men of the 33rd Foot returned home to Great Britain. Of that number, 199 stayed in the army, while 173 were discharged and went on to civilian life. Many, namely those with ten or more years' experience or those who had been disabled in service, received pensions from Chelsea Hospital in later life for their services in America. Only about one-third of the Von Bose Regiment who arrived in America in 1775 returned home in 1784. Most probably returned to their prewar occupations, although some, such as Berthold Koch, obviously reenlisted in 1784 and took part in later wars within the German principalities. Several of the Von Bose veterans settled in among the German populations of the North Carolina Piedmont, evidenced by the fact that twenty-eight of them deserted during the Guilford campaign. There apparently was no pension system in place for the German veterans of the American Revolution.[18]

For Greene's men who survived the war, the world may have seemed, if only on the surface, full of opportunity. Some veterans returned home and entered public service as politicians and administrators. A few returned to military service, seeing combat against Native Americans and again facing their former enemies of the British empire in the War of 1812. Most men, however, simply returned to their home states or moved west, spending the rest of their lives in relative peace as farmers and merchants.

Greene's Continental brigade commanders, on the whole, had much better luck than Henry Lee in the postwar era. Otho Holland Williams continued in his dual capacity of adjutant general and Maryland brigade commander until after Eutaw Springs. At war's end, Williams returned to Maryland where, despite a complete lack of knowledge concerning maritime matters, he received an appointment from Maryland governor William Paca as the naval officer for the Port of Baltimore. In 1785, he married Mary, daughter of William Smith, one of the wealthiest merchants in Baltimore, and was also elected to the House of Representatives. By 1789, Williams's health began to deteriorate, in part because of his experiences as a prisoner of war and during the southern campaign. He suffered tremendously from severe coughing fits and repeated bouts of influenza. In the winter of 1792, he turned down an offer to become second in command of the United States Army and left for Barbados, thinking warmer weather would aid his health, returning in May 1793 after the death of his five-year-old daughter. He died in July 1794 while attempting to reach a health spa near Bath, Virginia.[19]

Williams's fellow brigade commander, Isaac Huger, remained with the Southern Army after Guilford, leading the Virginia brigade at Hobkirk's Hill. He left the army that summer and in January 1782 was elected to the South Carolina state legislature. In 1785, he became sheriff of the Charleston District and four years later was appointed the first federal marshal for South Carolina. He died in October 1797, leaving a wife and eight children. His son, Benjamin Huger, was a U.S. congressman, and his grandnephew was Maj. Gen. Benjamin Huger of the Confederate army.[20]

The Maryland regimental commanders who survived the war, John Eager Howard and John Gunby, both returned to their native state in 1783. Howard entered politics, serving briefly in the Continental Congress in 1788 before accepting the governorship of Maryland, a position he held until 1791. Service from 1791 to 1795 in the Maryland state senate followed, before he accepted the remainder of the term of U.S. Senator Richard Potts, who had resigned, from 1796 to 1797. Elected to his own Senate term in 1797, Howard remained in the U.S. Congress until 1803. In 1816, he ran as Rufus King's vice presidential candidate for the Federalist Party but lost to James Monroe and David Tompkins.

Howard's decisions after the Revolution hint that he had had enough of war. He declined an offer to be George Washington's secretary of war, as well as a commission as brigadier general during the Quasi-War with France. Howard died on 12 October 1827, in Baltimore. He left a wife, Peggy Chew, over whose family land he had fought at Germantown in 1777, and several children, including a future Maryland governor and U.S. congressman. The line "Remember Howard's Warlike Thrust," in the official Maryland state song, "Maryland, My Maryland," memorializes Howard. Portions of his plantation became downtown Baltimore, where streets are named after his battles at Monmouth, Camden, Eutaw Springs, and Guilford Courthouse.[21]

Unlike Howard, John Gunby chose not to enter politics. Having survived aspersions on his honor after Hobkirk's Hill, an already ill Gunby left the Southern Army and did not fight at Eutaw Springs. He returned to Maryland, where he lived the remainder of his life as a planter on his farm called Snow Hill. Although he remained active in the Society of Cincinnati, Gunby never held public office. He died on 17 May 1807.[22]

Two of the arguably most courageous members of the 1st Maryland, Captains John Smith and Richard Anderson, settled in South Carolina after the war. Smith, whose trials and tribulations during the southern campaign read almost like a novel, left Maryland for South Carolina in the late 1790s. He became a pine log forester and with business partner Samuel Mathis made a substantial living in the Darlington District. For the remainder of his life he was known as "Colonel" John Smith. He served briefly in the South Carolina state legislature before dying peacefully at his farm in 1811. Anderson settled in the Sumter District, where he owned a large plantation. He received a pension shortly before his death in 1835. His grandson, Lt. Gen. Richard Heron Anderson, commanded a division and a corps in the Confederate Army of Northern Virginia.[23]

The Delaware companies of Captains Robert Kirkwood and Peter Jacquett remained with the Maryland brigade for the remainder of the conflict. After the war, Kirkwood moved with his family to the Northwest Territory, having purchased 260 acres in what became Jefferson County, Ohio. Widowed in 1787, Kirkwood settled there with his two young children, serving as a justice of the peace in 1790. In 1791, tensions flared on the frontier, and shortly after Native Americans attacked Kirkwood's cabin near Bridgeport, he accepted a commission as a captain in the 2nd U.S. Infantry and joined Gen. Arthur St. Clair's frontier army. On 4 November 1791, near Fort Recovery, Ohio, a Native American force led by Little Turtle of the Miami and Blue Jacket of the Shawnee annihilated St. Clair's troops. The defeat was the worst ever suffered by an American army at the hands of Native Americans. Among the 623 American dead lay Capt. Robert Kirkwood. One of his companions later wrote, "There, resting beneath a tree, lay old Kirkwood scalped, his head smoking like a chimney." It was thirty-five-year-old Kirkwood's thirty-third and final battle.

Peter Jacquett returned home to Delaware, but unlike Kirkwood never took up arms again. He spent the rest of his life at Long Hook, his family farm near Wilmington, Delaware. Memories of the war may have affected Jacquett's personal life after the war, as in his elder years he became known as a "cross, morose, quarrelsome man" with whom "it was a hard matter for any one to keep on speaking terms." In 1828, Jacquett became one of the few Continental officers who applied for and received a pension. He died six years later and was buried at Old Swedes' Cemetery in Wilmington, Delaware.[24]

Virginia Continental regimental commanders John Green and Samuel Hawes both survived the conflict and returned to their native state. Green never returned to active duty after Guilford due to poor health. He lived out his life as a Virginia planter and was buried on his plantation at Liberty Hall in 1793. In his memoirs, Henry Lee recalled Green as "one of the bravest of the brave." In 1911, his and his wife's remains were moved to Arlington National Cemetery. Green's counterpart, Samuel Hawes, served with the Southern Army until the war's end. He then returned to his father's Caroline County farm, but the impact of nearly eight years of active campaigning had taken its toll on his body. Hawes died, unmarried, from an unknown ailment in 1788 at the age of thirty-eight.[25]

Most of the officers of Green's and Hawes's battalions survived the war. Maj. Thomas Ridley left the army in 1781 and returned to his plantation in Virginia. For his service in the war, Ridley received nearly 7,000 acres in the Ohio Territory. He died in Southampton County in 1815. His son's plantation, Bonnie Doon, served as a fortified refuge for whites fleeing Nat Turner's Rebellion in 1831. Maj. Smith Snead served at Hobkirk's Hill and Ninety Six. He led the 1st Virginia at Eutaw Springs while Richard Campbell commanded the Virginia brigade. In the winter of 1782, shortly before being wounded at the battle of Kedge's Straits, he killed the Marquis de Malmedy in a duel over an unrecorded slight. After the war he returned home to Northampton County, where he died in 1792. Lieutenants Ballard Smith and Matthew Clay both became U.S. congressmen after the war. Lt. Matthew Rhea, who commanded a platoon that served as the rear guard for Greene's withdrawing army, moved to Tennessee after the war, where he died in 1816. His son and namesake became a geologist and cartographer, producing one of the earliest maps of Tennessee in 1832. On 7 November 1861, his grandson, Capt. Matthew Rhea II of the 13th Tennessee Infantry, was killed in action at the battle of Belmont, Missouri. Union soldiers stripped his sword, described as a "grand old relic," from his body as a souvenir. On its blade they found the inscription, "Presented by Genl. Greene to Matthew Rhea, the last man to retreat from the Battle of Guilford Courthouse."[26]

North Carolina Continental officers Reading Blount, Henry "Hal" Dixon, and Edward Yarborough stayed with the army after Guilford. Blount and Dixon commanded regiments at Eutaw Springs, where their units were both cited for conspicuous gallantry. Suffering his third wound of the war at Eutaw, "Hal" Dixon attempted to stay on with the North Carolina brigade, but in the summer of 1782 his injuries, combined with a severe fever, finally killed him. Reading Blount survived the war, became a merchant, and died peacefully in 1807. Yarborough served with Pinkatham Eaton in Georgia and fought under Blount at Eutaw Springs. A prosperous merchant after the war, he hosted George Washington at his home in Salisbury during the president's southern tour in 1791. Yarborough died a wealthy man in 1805. Both he and Blount were original members of the Society of Cincinnati.[27]

The Continental artillery officers Edward Carrington, Anthony Singleton, and Ebenezer Finley who served at Guilford survived the war and returned home. Carrington, Greene's most trusted aide, returned to practicing law and the managing of his property. In 1785–86, he attended the Continental Congress as a Virginia delegate. In September 1789, George Washington appointed Carrington the first federal marshal of Virginia. Carrington served as marshal for just over two years, after which Washington appointed him supervisor of distilled spirits for Virginia. He held this office until 1794, when his private affairs compelled retirement from public office. Carrington remained closely tied to the United States Army and received a commission as brigadier general during the Quasi-War. He also served as mayor of Richmond for three years and was foreman of the jury during Aaron Burr's trial for treason. He died at age sixty-two in October 1810. Anthony Singleton remained an artillery officer with the Southern Army until Yorktown. After the war, he became George Washington's personal accountant and settled in

Richmond. He died while on business to Newport, Rhode Island, in 1795. Ebenezer Finley, Singleton's friend and fellow battery commander, suffered from severe ailments as a result of his wartime service. He died in Maryland in 1784. Finley's descendants included the geographer Jedediah Morse and Samuel Finley Breese Morse, inventor of the telegraph and Morse code.[28]

Like their Continental counterparts in the infantry and artillery, Greene's horsemen also went on to varied pursuits after the war. Until he was wounded and captured at Eutaw Springs, William Washington played a major role in redeeming the southern states from British control. He remained a prisoner in Charleston until he was exchanged in 1782. He married Jane Elliott, a South Carolina rice heiress, while on parole and eventually settled into the life of a planter outside Charleston after the war. He served in the South Carolina legislature from 1787 to 1804 but refused a nomination for governor, stating that he was "not born a Carolinian." He returned to duty briefly as a brigadier general commanding military forces in Georgia and South Carolina during the Quasi-War with France from 1798 to 1800. Washington died 6 March 1810 at the age of fifty-eight. The Washington Light Infantry of Charleston, one of the oldest militia units in the country, formed in 1807, was named for William and his more famous cousin. In 1827, William's wife donated her husband's regimental flag, which still remains in the Washington Light Infantry collection in Charleston.[29]

The officers of Lee's Legion who survived took up various pursuits after the war. Maj. Joseph Eggleston, Lee's second in command, served in the U.S. Congress, 1798–1801, and died in 1811. Captains James Armstrong and Ferdinand O'Neal both moved to Georgia after the war. Armstrong died at O'Neal's plantation while visiting his friend in 1800. O'Neal died sometime prior to 1820. Capt. Michael Rudolph returned to his native Maryland after the war and became a merchant. He was lost at sea in 1795 while transporting tobacco from Baltimore to Europe. Lt. James Heard, whose troopers had fired the first shots on the morning of 15 March, died in New Jersey in 1831. Lt. Laurence Manning of the Legion infantry moved to South Carolina after the war, where he died in 1804. His son, grandson, and great-grandson all became governors of South Carolina. Lt. Peter Johnston became a judge in Washington County, Virginia, after the war. Serving in this capacity nearly until his death in 1841, Johnston had the honor of overseeing several pension applications by his former men. His son, Gen. Joseph Eggleston Johnston, named in honor of his former company commander and major, surrendered the Confederate Army of Tennessee to Gen. William Tecumseh Sherman at Bennett Place, North Carolina, in 1865.[30]

Militia dragoon captain Marquis de Bretigny remained in North Carolina, taking command of units defending New Bern. He also served as the state's liaison to the French colony of Martinique. After the war, Bretigny settled in New Bern and served on the Governor's Council but died, impoverished, in 1793, having lost his landholdings and hereditary title in the French Revolution. His Virginia counterparts, Thomas Watkins and Philemon Holcombe, both survived the war and returned to Virginia to pursue farming. Watkins married his childhood sweetheart, but the memories of the war plagued him. Shortly before his untimely death at age thirty-six in 1797, Watkins admitted to a close confidant that, "in a cavalry charge at Guilford, in a personal encounter with a British officer, the latter asked for 'quarter,' but, in his impetuosity, the Colonel stated that he killed his adversary. The event, he added, had caused him much unhappiness from its occurrence to the end of his life." Holcombe moved to Fayette County, Tennessee, where in the early 1820s he was one of many veterans who wrote the general assembly supporting Peter Francisco's claim for a pension. According to Holcombe's grandson, "No persuasions could induce him, to the day of his death at the age of 77 to deviate from his old army custom of taking three small glasses of 'grog' every day, one just before each meal." Holcombe died in 1834 at age eighty-two.[31]

Like their Continental counterparts, several Virginia militia and rifle regimental officers led distinguished lives after Guilford. Virginia militia brigade commanders Robert Lawson and Edward Stevens both survived the war. Lawson commanded a brigade at Yorktown and after the war became a planter and Society of Cincinnati member. He moved briefly to Lexington, Kentucky, but died in Richmond in 1805. Edward Stevens recovered from his Guilford wound, commanded a brigade at Yorktown, and became a major general in the Virginia militia. After the war, he retired to his plantation at Culpepper, served eight years in the Virginia legislature, and died in 1820.[32]

Robert Lawson's regimental officers included plantation owners, a poet, and a future Virginia governor. Beverley Randolph was the first governor elected in Virginia after the ratification of the Constitution in 1788. He died in 1797 in Cumberland County on his farm, Green Creek. Robert Munford never recovered from the gout that afflicted him. After his death in 1783, his sons published a collection of his poems and plays. John Holcombe and Henry Skipwith returned to their plantations, living the remainder of their lives in quiet peace, Skipwith dying in 1815, followed by Holcombe three years later.[33]

St. George Tucker, whose letters to his wife provide such intriguing details concerning Guilford, led perhaps the most interesting postwar life of any of Lawson's officers. After commanding a regiment at Yorktown, Tucker practiced law in the Petersburg area until 1788 when his wife Fanny died, shortly after bearing their sixth child. That year he accepted appointments as a professor of law at the College of William and Mary and as judge of the Virginia General Court at Richmond. He succeeded George Wythe at the school and was described by one of his students, William Taylor Barry, as "a Man of genuine Cleverness and of the most exalted talents." During these years he also edited Blackstone's *Commentaries on the Laws of England*. Published in Philadelphia in 1803, the work earned Tucker an honorary title in the press as the "American Blackstone."

Tucker was also something of an inventor and is credited with the construction of Williamsburg's first bathroom, having converted his backyard dairy house and installed in it a copper bathtub with drain into which heated water was piped. An amateur astronomer and an avid gardener, he was a charter member and officer of a "Society for the Promotion of Useful Knowledge" in Williamsburg. In 1794, Tucker established a French "Telegraphe," a semi-mechanical semaphore signaling system, at the Capitol to signal him at the college on the other end of Duke of Gloucester Street. Tucker was a prolific writer. In 1796, he published his pamphlet, *A Dissertation on Slavery; with a Proposal for the Gradual Abolition of It in the State of Virginia*. Upon appointment to the Virginia Court of Appeals in Richmond, Tucker left William and Mary and in 1813 became the U.S. District Court judge at Richmond. He died on 10 November 1827 at the age of seventy-five.[34]

Edward Stevens's regimental officers all survived the war. Peter Perkins received £95 as compensation for the use of Berry Hill Plantation as a hospital during the Guilford campaign. After the war he moved to South Carolina, where he died in 1813. George Moffett returned to Virginia after the war. His daughter married Joseph "Pleasant Gardens" McDowell of King's Mountain fame. He became one of the first trustees of Washington College before his death in 1811. Nathaniel Cocke settled in Washington County, Georgia, where he died in 1807. His widow applied for a pension in 1830 but was denied on the grounds that Cocke had not served long enough as a Continental officer to receive pay.[35]

Samuel McDowell moved to Kentucky after the war, where he became the first federal judge for the district and served as president of the new state's constitutional convention in 1792. Alexander Stuart, who took command of McDowell's regiment during that officer's illness, returned home but his Guilford wound never healed. On 21 July 1861, the great-grandsons of the two commanders of the Augusta and Rockbridge county militias squared off against one another at the first battle of Manassas. James Ewell Brown (better known as J. E. B.) Stuart commanded a Virginia cavalry regiment. Across the field stood Irvine McDowell, the commander of the Union's Army of the Potomac.[36]

Rifle unit commanders Charles Lynch and William Campbell both briefly commanded brigades in the Yorktown campaign. Lynch left soon after accepting a position as sheriff of Bedford County. From 1784 to 1789, he served as a member of the Virginia legislature. His Quaker sensibilities appear to have returned in his final years. In 1793, three years before his death, he freed five of his slaves, stating in their manumission "that all men are by nature free, and agreeable to the command of our Savior Christ believe it our duty to do unto all men as we would they should do unto us." William Campbell returned to the army after Guilford and led a militia brigade during the early stages of the Yorktown campaign, but he never forgave Henry Lee for abandoning him and his men to Tarleton's dragoons at Guilford Courthouse. Had he survived the war, Campbell might well have challenged Lee's version of the events of 15 March, but he died on 22 August 1781, of "camp fever" contracted along the mosquito-infested banks of the James River.[37]

Both North Carolina militia brigadier generals, John Butler and Thomas Eaton, survived the war. Butler led North Carolina militia at Lindley's Mill and Elizabethtown in the fall of 1781. In 1782, he brokered a peace with David Fanning, the notorious loyalist leader who had captured North Carolina governor Thomas Burke in a brazen daylight raid. After the war, Butler served briefly in the North Carolina legislature before his death in 1786. Eaton never served on active duty again, instead retiring to his plantation and becoming one of North Carolina's largest owners of land and slaves. At a dinner party shortly before his death in 1809, Eaton sat across the table from John Hamilton, former leader of the Royal North Carolina Provincial Regiment, who had captured Eaton's boots during the rout of American forces at Briar Creek, Georgia, in 1779. Hamilton offered to return them, sarcastically mentioning that they were too small for his feet. Eaton responded by beating Hamilton senseless and throwing him out of the house.[38]

Nearly all of Greene's North Carolina militia regimental commanders survived the conflict. William Linton became commander of the prison at Halifax, North Carolina. In 1781 he ordered the execution of Michael Quinn, a former North Carolina Continental officer who switched sides and led an attack on Edenton. Convicted in 1783 of the murder of Quinn, Linton was pardoned the following year by Governor Alexander Martin. He died in late 1786 a pauper, having spent his fortune fighting the charges. William Moore, Thomas Farmer, and John and Joseph Taylor all returned to their farms in Caswell, Orange, and Granville counties. North Carolina Continental Robert Mebane, who may have led the Orange County regiment, did not survive the war, having been murdered in October 1781. James Martin, the brother of Governor Martin, went into the ironworks business with fellow Guilford veteran Peter Perkins after the war. In 1832, two years before his death, Martin applied for and received a pension, one of the highest-ranking veterans to have done so. Joseph Winston, commander of the North Carolina riflemen on the southern flank, served as both a state legislator and U.S. congressman after the war. He died on 21 April 1815 in Stokes County at age sixty-nine. Winston-Salem, North Carolina, carries his name.[39]

Three future North Carolina governors fought at Guilford Courthouse. William R. Davie, Greene's commissary general, became a leading Federalist and participated in the 1787 Constitutional Convention in Philadelphia. He introduced the bill to ratify the document in North Carolina in 1789. Davie remained politically active at the state level and in 1798 was appointed governor of North Carolina. He resigned the following year after President John Adams named him a peace commissioner to end the Quasi-War with France. As a member of the North Carolina General Assembly, Davie sponsored the bill that led to the formation of the University of North Carolina. In his later years, Davie moved to South Carolina, where he died in 1820. Benjamin Williams, who commanded the Warren and Franklin county militia with such distinction on the northern flank, became governor on Davie's resignation. He served until 1805 and then again in 1807–8 and died in 1814. The third future governor, Jesse Franklin, who barely escaped Tarleton's dragoons at Guilford, served as a U.S. congressman from 1807 to 1813 and as a peace commissioner to the Chickasaw Indians. At the age of sixty he served as governor, 1820–21, and died two years after leaving office.[40]

As for the American enlisted men among the Guilford veterans, they present a thin section of southern society during the Revolutionary War. Most were farmers and laborers, although the rankers included men from nearly every occupation in the social network. Upon returning home, these men took advantage of every possible benefit the new nation afforded them, whether bounty land for their services or money provided by the Pension Acts of 1818 and 1832. For those who went home already owning land or having a trade, they likely remained in their communities. Those who did not have property or employment, often did something they had become accustomed to during the war: they moved.

Of the 980 American servicemen whose pensions were used in this study, 562 could be tracked from their place of birth and enlistment to their final place of postwar settlement and eventual death. (See Appendix C, "Postwar Location of Pensioners by State of Service.") The data demonstrate quite clearly that Frederick Jackson Turner's hotly debated conception of the frontier as a sort of safety valve providing opportunities for Americans to expand spatially does have a ring of truth. Across the board, 36 percent of them remained in their home state after the conflict, while 64 percent left. Several studies have clearly shown the economic differences between those men who served in the Continental army and those in the militia. The results of this study do not necessarily run counter to that finding; however, it is worth noting that the overall percentages for Continentals who stayed or moved west (precisely 35 percent staying, 65 percent leaving) match almost exactly the data for militia (37 percent staying, 63 percent leaving). This may indicate that perhaps unlike in the north, southern militiamen (or at least those raised in 1781 Virginia and the North Carolina Piedmont) came from the same social classes, or had just as few ties to their local communities, as the Continentals. It is possible that southern militiamen were given sizable land warrants for their service during the 1780–81 crises, something that does not seem to have happened in the northern states. However, it may also simply reflect the fact that westward movement among southerners was attractive regardless of one's social origins or type of service rendered. More research is clearly necessary.[41]

For those who did move, the pension data quite clearly show patterns. The majority of Virginia veterans moved to Kentucky or Tennessee, although a number of those from the Shenandoah Valley settled in Indiana, Illinois, and Ohio. Marylanders and Delawares ended up most often in western Virginia or Ohio, while North Carolinians tended to migrate to Kentucky, Tennessee, and Georgia. Some men ultimately ended up in Missouri, Alabama, and Mississippi, often after moving several times. Ninety percent of the men moved south of the Ohio River, indicating that a large majority of Guilford veterans at least liked the prospect of owning slaves. Moves did not simply follow a direct route, however. Many men spent time in several areas before finally settling where they took their pensions.

The enlisted veterans whose accounts were used extensively in this study also provide a glimpse into the American experience. Samuel Houston, the rambunctious young Rockbridge County militiaman who left such a stirring journal of the campaign, returned home after Guilford and became a Presbyterian minister. He remained in Virginia, and in 1837, two years before his death, left a final anecdote illustrating the effects of military life on the common man. "As I said before profane language was very little used and continued to be so until the return of the soldiers and militia from the army of the revolution; after their return however it became very prevalent and I believe was much used for many years afterward." Houston died at age eighty-one in 1839 in Rockbridge County. His younger cousin, also named Samuel (Sam) Houston, became a hero of the Texas Revolution and served as president of the Texas Republic.[42]

Jorge Farragut, the soldier of fortune who served in Bretigny's command, moved to Tennessee in 1790 and became a planter. In 1807, he received an appointment as a U.S. Navy sailing master and was assigned to New Orleans. Farragut remained in the navy until 1814. In his later years, he became something of a noted daredevil, once piloting a small open boat from New Orleans to Havana. He died in 1817 at his plantation at Point Plaquet, Mississippi. His son, David Dixon Farragut, carried on his father's seafaring tradition and entered the navy as a midshipman at age nine in 1810. He retired as a full admiral and is perhaps best known for his possibly apocryphal statement, "Damn the torpedoes, full steam ahead!" at the battle of Mobile Bay in 1864.[43]

Virginia militia dragoon Peter Francisco survived his injuries and went home to Buckingham County to recuperate. While on his way home, Francisco met with a party of British dragoons at Benjamin Ward's tavern in Nottoway County. Although unarmed, Francisco, according to his own account, managed to kill one of the dragoons with his own sword and severely wound another before driving off the remaining troopers. Postwar authors mythologized this account as well, later claiming that Francisco either single-handedly killed or captured all of his attackers. Francisco survived the war, became a farmer, and married three times, fathering several children. Fellow veteran Alexander Garden remarked, "I scarcely ever met with a man in Virginia who had not some miraculous tale to tell of Peter Francisco." Francisco applied for a pension in 1818 but ironically was rejected, until several former officers came to his assistance. Partly in recompense, the Virginia legislature appointed him sergeant-at-arms of the assembly and in 1824 he acted as a bodyguard to the Marquis de Lafayette during his tour of the eastern portions of Virginia. Seven years later, Francisco died of appendicitis at the age of seventy-one. His comrade and fellow Guilford veteran Lt. William Evans left an unintentional but fitting eulogy in his supporting affidavit for Francisco's pension application, writing that the he was "one of the most meritorious soldiers I have ever been acquainted with."[44]

William Seymour of the Delaware Regiment, the sergeant major who chronicled the entire southern campaign in his journal, completely disappears from the historical record after the war. Since no 1790 Delaware census exists, it stands to reason that if Seymour had lived past 1800 his name would have appeared on that census, but it does not. Although he received bounty land, Seymour never applied for a pension. The courageous sergeant apparently returned home after the war and died before 1800.

By the late 1850s, only a handful of Revolutionary War veterans remained alive. The 8 October 1859 edition of the *San Andreas Independent*, a newspaper printed in Calaveras County, California, listed Peter Rife, age ninety-seven, and Henry Willoughby, age one hundred, among the eight last-known veterans of the conflict. Sergeant Rife, whose recollections provided intriguing glimpses into the role of the North Carolina militia on the first line, moved back to his native Virginia after the war, settling in Wythe County as a clockmaker and cabinetmaker. The Art Museum of Western Virginia exhibits a clock showing his handiwork.

Illustrating how slowly news traveled cross-country in 1859, the paper was actually outdated by nearly a year. Peter Rife had died on 21 December 1858 at his Virginia home, at age ninety-six. The paper entry however was correct concerning Henry Willoughby, a former private in Green's Virginia Regiment who fought at Guilford, Hobkirk's Hill, and Eutaw Springs. At war's end, he had returned to Spotsylvania County, where he spent the remainder of his life farming. Henry Willoughby died in August 1860 at the age of one hundred and one, the last surviving veteran of Guilford Courthouse. Had he and Rife lived just a little while longer, one wonders how they would have felt watching the country tear itself apart that they struggled so valiantly to help create one "long, obstinate, and bloody" afternoon in March 1781.[45]

*Marched to Guilford*
*Court House, a place*
*remarkable for ye action*
*between genl Greene and*
*Cornwallis, and encamped*
*on part of the battle field.*
—LT. JOHN TILDEN,
*December 1781*

# EPILOGUE

The epigraph is an entry from the journal of Lt. John Bell Tilden recorded on 8 December 1781, nearly nine months after the battle of Guilford Courthouse. Gen. Anthony Wayne's Pennsylvania Continental Line Brigade had encamped on the Guilford battleground en route to South Carolina and Georgia, where they were intended to participate in American offensives against Savannah and Charleston. Delayed on the field for the next three days due to incessant rains, the Pennsylvanians actually performed the first archaeology on the site. Camped among the detritus of the battle, Lt. William McDowell of the 1st Pennsylvania recorded in his journal digging up "a number of but[t]s of muskets lying on the ground which the enemy had broke."[1]

The authors of this book sincerely hope that our work successfully extends that which the Pennsylvanians so crudely began that cold, rainy December afternoon. Wayne's Continentals likely had questions about what actually had taken place at Guilford, and so did we. Our research into the battle derived from an examination of North Carolina's Continental officers as well as enlisted men who claimed service at Guilford. It had been generally assumed that no North Carolina Continentals were involved in the battle in a regular capacity; uncovering the truth proved quite intriguing. As we continued to pursue leads, the project expanded into a study of the engagement as a whole.

Further research raised a number of interesting questions. These revolved around the influence of the terrain, the flight and condemnation of the North Carolina militia, the accuracy of the casualty figures, and the actual events of the third line fighting. How did the American and British cavalry operate on grounds that were heavily forested? Terrain certainly played an important role in determining how different portions of the battle developed and influenced all the participants' understanding of the situation. A fresh examination was also needed that would depart from traditional Whig accounts that focused solely on Guilford as a "victory in defeat" for the Americans and instead honestly represented the courage and bravery demonstrated by the redcoat infantry. The most confusing portions of the battle to dissect were the flank fighting, events that were so bewildering to research one can only imagine how much more so they were to fight. Finally, who were the actual participants? By weeding through hundreds of pension files as well as other primary sources and records, we have been able to reconstruct a more accurate accounting of the numbers and types of units who participated. All of these questions and problems forced us to reevaluate documentary sources as well as material culture and ultimately led to this book.

When the British arrived west of Guilford in the late morning hours of 15 March they faced a three-line, European-style, defense in depth formation comprised of Continentals, militia, riflemen, cavalry and artillery. This formation does not explain, however, the fighting that Nathanael Greene intended. Inspired by Daniel Morgan's example at Cowpens the previous January, Greene had reversed the strength of his linear formations, creating progressively stronger defensive lines. This provided a mental as well as physical gauntlet for the British. As Cornwallis's men pushed each American line from the field, they anticipated victory only to face another, tougher force. Greene had also deployed flankers consisting of riflemen and light infantry to play on the British flanks and force them to deploy their reserves.

Although Greene's deployments were sound and based on Morgan's example, the terrain of Guilford differed considerably from Cowpens. Whereas the latter consisted of a fairly open field with a few small hills and swales, the Guilford battlefield was a mixture of open fields separated by thick forest and undulating ridgelines. Whereas Morgan positioned himself where he could physically see the battle unfold, Greene was positioned several hundred yards from the first and second line actions, unable to witness those fights firsthand. Therefore, while Morgan was able to react to the situation at hand, Greene had no tactical command over the first two lines and thus had to rely on the brigadiers, colonels, and captains to take charge of their men. On the opposite side of the field, Cornwallis at the very least attempted to follow directly behind his main line into battle. Although he obviously became disoriented and separated from the main force, his position on the field allowed him to see some of the fighting in the center of the first and second lines. The very fact that he had two horses shot from under him says something about his proximity to the fighting.

Greene's position on the field also calls into question his abject condemnation of the North Carolina militia and absolute approbation of the Virginians. Arguments over the role of the North Carolinians at Guilford have continued virtually from the end of the fighting to the present day. First, Greene's comments must be placed in context. His correspondence throughout the war repeatedly demonstrates his outright disregard for militia. His opinions were not wholly unwarranted, for he had on several occasions witnessed undisciplined militia fall apart in the face of the enemy, or simply fade away, as in the example shown by certain North Carolina and Virginia militiamen just prior to Guilford, when their tours of service were up, regardless of the Main Army's need for them. Yet how could Greene, posted so far to the rear, have any idea what actually happened on the first line? His initial notion of the collapse of the first line was likely based on previous experience with militiamen like Nathan Slade scurrying back toward the courthouse. If anything, Greene learned what took place there from secondhand sources. His letters after the battle are quite revealing, as he went from crediting the North Carolinians with three volleys, then two, then one, until finally commenting that many had never even fired. The last comments would have been a shock to the British soldiers deployed on line when the North Carolinians fired their first volley. British accounts quite clearly and almost unanimously state that the volley did considerable damage. So what happened after the initial volley? Documents show that Greene and Henry Lee were probably right: The vast majority of the North Carolinians did break and run. Those on the northern and southern flanks however, protected by woods and led by either experienced Continental veterans or local men literally defending their hearth and home, stood and fought.

Greene's praise of the Virginia militia is also perhaps not as justified as commonly viewed. After all, most of the Virginians north of the road stayed only a few minutes, if not seconds, longer than the North Carolinians had upon their first clash with the British, and that was likely due in part to terrain, not excessive courage or leadership. Nor did the Virginians south of the road fight harder simply because they had more Continental veterans in their ranks. Again, terrain played a major factor. In the woods they simply had more protection, but also less visibility. The North Carolinians saw a wall of bayonets coming at them, while the Virginians saw a disorganized mob. Greene's relationship with Virginia must also be taken into account. He relied heavily on the state for supplies and provisions, and insulting or condemning the militia from Virginia would not likely have been in his best interests.

The terrain at Guilford also dictated how the most confusing episodes of the battle would play out: the fighting on the flanks and the initial deployment of the American cavalry. North of the road, the jaegers and the Guards light infantry squared off against Kirkwood's Delawares, Huffman's Virginians, and Lynch's riflemen in a confusing maelstrom of fighting in the woods. Washington's dragoons, both the Continental light dragoons and the North Carolina and Virginia light horse, were probably unable to operate in the thick woods where even Kirkwood's Continental infantry was fighting behind trees. It is more likely that they were held as a reserve in the open space immediately north of the courthouse where the army had camped in February. This interpretation is supported by John Watkins, a North Carolina militiaman, who clearly stated that "Washington's horse were at the Court House at the commencement of the engagement, and formed and rode over the Branch to the opposite Hill where the battle was raging and charged the enemy."[2]

South of the Great Salisbury Road a side road played a central role in the development of the "battle within a battle." The dragoons of Lee's Legion faced the same daunting woods as Washington's men. Positioned behind Campbell's rifles, Lee's Legion infantry, and Wallace's Virginians, the cavalry had to utilize the road. That path courses off to the southeast, which explains in part how the southern flank fighting developed. As Lee withdrew from the first line toward the second, his cavalry likely used the road as a guide, and the light infantry simply followed. Exactly how Lee's dragoons later extracted themselves from the fighting and managed to retreat along the same road Greene's army took remains uncertain.

Another issue illuminated through research was the assumption that Greene's casualties were fairly light compared to Cornwallis's. At face value, this perception is correct. Utilizing both the American and British casualty returns and omitting the missing, as most authors have had a tendency to do, the casualties come to 5–7 percent for the Americans versus 27 percent for the British. If one includes the missing however, as they ought to be included, given that most of those men did not return to service until months later, and add them to the casualty statistics presented in this study, one finds that Greene's army was reduced by something more like 30–33 percent. In other words, whereas American historians have relished the fact that Greene lost substantially smaller numbers of men compared to Cornwallis, the men who made it to Speedwell Ironworks on the night of 15 March might have had something of a different view. Granted, many of the North Carolinians who ran from Guilford Courthouse later served under duress as Continentals, but the point remains that the story is much more complex than has previously been documented.

British intelligence reports at the time also had a problem with numbers. Cornwallis, as well as most of his men, was fully convinced that he faced a force of nearly 7,000 men. British intelligence of course was wrong; however, the Americans still outnumbered their enemy two to one. Facing such odds, having had little to eat in nearly twenty-four hours, and having marched roughly ten miles fighting numerous running skirmishes prior to engaging Greene's first line, it is a wonder that the British army didn't fully collapse at Guilford. Yet they didn't. Instead, Cornwallis's men persevered with the kind of courage and tenacity that did them great honor. Regardless of the eventual outcome of the overall campaign, the accomplishments of the British soldiers at Guilford cannot and should not be overlooked.

The authors hope that this study will generate further interest in the southern campaign. The courageous men and women of both armies deserve to have their individual stories told. There are many more accounts and narratives to be located, and further archaeological investigation is surely warranted. We hope that our work serves as something of a baseline for future research, so that the veterans of Guilford Courthouse will not be forgotten but long be remembered with the dignity and respect that they earned through their shared struggle and sacrifice.

British Army: Lt. Gen. Charles, 2nd Earl Cornwallis, 1,900–2,200 men

    The Brigade of Guards: Brig. Gen. Charles O'Hara, 481 men

        1st Battalion: Lt. Col. Chapple Norton, 160–80 men

        2nd Battalion: Lt. Col. James Stuart, 160–80 men

        Guards Light Infantry Company: Capt. John Goodricke, 70–90 men

        Guards Grenadier Company: Capt. William Home, 70–90 men

    Webster's Brigade: Lt. Col. James Webster, 472 men

        23rd Foot: Capt. Thomas Peter, 238 men

        33rd Foot: Capt. Frederick Cornwallis, 234 men

    Leslie's Brigade: Maj. Gen. Alexander Leslie, 565 men

        2nd Battalion, 71st Foot: Capt. Robert Hutcheson, 244 men

        Von Bose Regiment: Maj. Johann Du Buy, 321 men

    Auxiliary Troops, 356 men

        British Legion: Lt. Col. Banastre Tarleton, 272 men

        Jaeger Company: Capt. Wilhelm Friedrich von Roeder, 84 men

        Royal Artillery, 45–50 men

            1st Section: Lt. John McLeod, 18–20 men, 2 six-pounder cannon

            2nd Section: Lt. Augustus O'Hara, 18–20 men, 2 six-pounder cannon

3rd Section: Lt. John Smith, 10–12 men, 2 three-pounder cannon
Baggage Train Guard, 220–60 men
  Royal North Carolina Regiment: Lt. Col. John Hamilton, 100–140 men
  Detached from Guards Brigade: Capt. Charles Horneck, 40 men
  Detached from Webster's Brigade: Capt. Henry Broderick, 54 men
  Detached from Regiment Von Bose—Unknown lieutenant or ensign,
    23 men

American Army: Maj. Gen. Nathanael Greene, 4,000–4,400 men
  Maryland Continental Brigade: Col. Otho Holland Williams, 700–800 men
    1st Maryland: Col. John Gunby, 350–400 men
    2d Maryland: Lt. Col. Benjamin Ford, 350–400 men
  Virginia Continental Brigade: Brig. Gen. Isaac Huger, 800–900 men
    1st Virginia: Col. John Green, 400–450 men
    2nd Virginia: Lt. Col. Samuel Hawes, 400–450 men
  Lt. Col. Henry Lee's Partizan Legion, 190–240 men
    Legion Infantry: Capt. Michael Rudolph, 120–50 men
    Legion Dragoons: Maj. Joseph Eggleston, 70–90 men
  Brig. Gen. John Butler's North Carolina Militia, 500–600 men
    Caswell County Militia: Col. William Moore, 100–150 men
    Granville County Militia: Col. Joseph Taylor, 100–125 men
    Orange County Militia: Col. Thomas Farmer, 100–125 men
    Orange County Militia: Col. John Taylor, 100–125 men
    Rockingham, Randolph, and Chatham County Militias: unknown officer,
      50–75 men
    Rowan and Mecklenburg County Militias: Capt. James Billingsley,
      20–25 men
    Guilford County Militia: Col. James Martin, 60–70 men
  Brig. Gen. Thomas Eaton's North Carolina Militia, 500–600 men
    Warren County Militia: Col. Benjamin Williams, 150–200 men
    Franklin County Militia: Col. Pinkatham Eaton, 150–200 men
    Nash, Edgecombe, Halifax, Martin, and Northampton County Militias: Col.
      William Linton, 150–200 men
  Brig. Gen. Edward Stevens's Virginia Militia, 550–750 men
    Pittsylvania County Militia: Col. Peter Perkins, 150–200 men
    Halifax, Lunenburg, and Prince Edward County Militias: Col. Nathaniel
      Cocke, 150–200 men
    Augusta County Militia: Maj. John Pope, 100–150 men
    Augusta and Rockbridge County Militias: Maj. Alexander Stuart,
      150–200 men

Brig. Gen. Robert Lawson's Virginia Militia, 500–650 men
    Amelia, Cumberland, and Powhatan County Militias: Col. Beverley
        Randolph, 200–250 men
    Amelia, Charlotte, Powhatan, and Mecklenburg County Militias: Col. John
        Holcombe, 200–250 men
    Brunswick, Mecklenburg, and Powhatan County Militias: Maj. Henry
        Skipwith, 100–150 men
Auxiliary Troops
    Delaware Continental Light Infantry Company: Capt. Robert Kirkwood,
        50–60 men
    Virginia Continental Light Infantry Company: Capt. Phillip Huffman,
        50–60 men
    Virginia Continental Light Infantry Company: Capt. Andrew Wallace,
        50–60 men
    North Carolina Continental Company: Capt. Edward Yarborough,
        20–40 men
    Virginia Rifle Battalion: Col. Charles Lynch, 150 men
    Virginia Rifle Battalion: Col. William Campbell, 80–100 men
    North Carolina Rifle Battalion: Maj. Joseph Winston, 50–60 men
    Continental Light Dragoons: Lt. Col. William Washington, 84 men
    Virginia Militia Dragoons: Capt. Thomas Watkins, 30 men
    North Carolina Militia Dragoons: Marquis de Bretigny, 30–40 men
    Continental Artillery
        1st Section: Capt. Anthony Singleton, 18–20 men, 2 six-pounder cannon
        2nd Section: Capt. Lt. Ebenezer Finley, 18–20 men, 2 six-pounder cannon

# BATTLE CASUALTIES

The casualty figures given for the British side are from Charles Cornwallis's official report to Lord George Germain. The figures given for the American side are from Otho Holland Williams's after-action report to Congress. In some cases, the numbers have been broken down to the battalion or company level, while others are only available at the brigade level. The totals include officers and enlisted men, and the known casualties among the officers are identified using the following symbols: k = killed, m = missing, mw = mortally wounded, pow = captured, w = wounded. For our interpretation of those statistics, see Chapter 9, "The Aftermath."

British Army: 93 killed, 413 wounded, 26 missing
    Brigade of Guards: 37 killed, 157 wounded, 22 missing. Brig. Gen. Charles
        O'Hara (w), Brig. Gen. John Howard (w)
        1st Battalion: Capt. William Maynard (mw), Capt. Augustus Maitland (w),
            Ens. John Stuart (w), Adj. James Colquhoun (w)
        2nd Battalion: Lt. Col. James Stuart (k), Capt. William Schutz (mw), Capt.
            Thomas Swanton (w)
        Guards Light Infantry Company: Capt. John Goodricke (k)
        Guards Grenadier Company: Capt. William Home (mw)

Webster's Brigade: Lt. Col. James Webster (mw)
    23rd Foot: 13 killed, 55 wounded. 2nd Lt. William Robins (k)
    33rd Foot: 11 killed, 65 wounded. Ens. Talbot (k), Capt. Lt. Charles Curzon
        (w), Lt. Arthur Beaver (w), Lt. James Harvey (w), Lt. Anthony Slavin
        (w), Lt. George Wynard (w), Ens. John Fox (w), Ens. Ralph Gore (w),
        Ens. John Hughes (w), Ens. John Kelly (w)
Leslie's Brigade
    2nd Battalion, 71st Foot: 13 killed, 50 wounded. Ens. Malcolm Grant (k), Ens.
        Archibald McPherson (k), Ens. Donald McPherson (k)
    Von Bose Regiment: 15 killed, 47 wounded, 12 captured. Capt. Alexander
        Wilmousky (mw), Ens. Phillip Ernst Von Trott (mw), Capt. Johann
        Eichenbrodt (w), Lt. Johann Schweiner (w), Lt. Phillip Ernst Geise (w)
Auxiliary Troops
    British Legion: 3 killed, 14 wounded. Lt. Col. Banastre Tarleton (w)
    Jaeger Company: 4 killed, 3 wounded, 1 missing
    Royal Artillery: 2 killed, 4 wounded. Lt. Augustus O'Hara (k)

American Army: 79 killed, 184 wounded, 1,046 missing
    Greene's Staff: Capt. Alexander Ewing (w)
    Maryland Continental Brigade: 15 killed, 42 wounded, 97 missing (plus 3 killed,
        8 wounded, in Peter Jacquett's Delaware company in the 1st Maryland)
        1st Maryland: Capt. Samuel Hobbs (k), Capt. John Smith (w), Lt. Roger
        Nelson (w)
        2nd Maryland: Maj. Archibald Anderson (k)
    Virginia Continental Brigade (includes the casualties in the light infantry
        companies): 29 killed, 40 wounded, 39 missing. Brig. Gen. Isaac
        Huger (w)
        Huffman's Virginia Light Infantry Company: Capt. Phillip Huffman (k)
        Wallace's Virginia Light Infantry Company: Capt. Andrew Wallace (k),
        Ens. Alexander Brownlee (k)
    Lee's Partizan Legion: 3 killed, 9 wounded, 7 missing
        Legion Dragoons: Lt. Jonathan Snowden (w)
    North Carolina Militia Brigades: 6 killed, 5 wounded, 563 missing
        Martin's Regiment: Capt. Arthur Forbis (mw), Lt. William Wiley (w)
    Stevens's Brigade, Virginia Militia: 11 killed, 36 wounded, 141 missing. Brig. Gen.
        Edward Stevens (w), Maj. John Williams (m)
        Pope's Regiment: Capt. James Tate (k), Ens. Robert Dunlap (k)
        Stuart's Regiment: Capt. Alexander Tedford (k), Maj. Alexander Stuart
        (w, pow), Capt. John Paxton (w)
        Perkins's Regiment: Capt. William Fitzgerald (w)

Cocke's Regiment: Lt. Matthew Maury (w), Ens. James Speed (w)

Lawson's Brigade, Virginia Militia: 1 killed, 16 wounded, 87 missing

Skipwith's Regiment: Ens. Jack Smith Davenport (mw)

Kirkwood's Delaware Continental Light Infantry Company: 4 killed, 5 wounded, 15 missing. Lt. George Vaughan (w)

Rifle Battalions: 3 killed, 16 wounded, 94 missing (Williams lumped all the rifle units together)

Lynch's Virginia Rifle Battalion: Capt. William Jones (k), Capt. Thomas Helm (mw), Capt. James Moon (mw), Capt. David Beard (w)

Campbell's Virginia Rifle Battalion: Capt. John Thompson (k)

North Carolina Rifle Battalion: Lt. Robert Taliaferro (k)

Continental Light Dragoons: 3 killed, 8 wounded, 3 missing (whether this includes Watkins's Virginia Militia Dragoons Company is unknown). Capt. Griffin Fauntleroy (mw, pow), Capt. William Barrett (w, pow)

North Carolina Militia Dragoons: 1 killed, 1 wounded

| STATE OF SERVICE | TOTAL | POSTWAR RESIDENCE | | | | |
|---|---|---|---|---|---|---|
| | | AL | AR | GA | IL | IN |
| Virginia | | | | | | |
| Continentals | 128 | 1 | | | 4 | 4 |
| Militia/Riflemen | 211 | 6 | | | 6 | 8 |
| North Carolina | | | | | | |
| Continentals | 15 | 1 | | 1 | | |
| Militia/Riflemen | 186 | 6 | 1 | 15 | 8 | 10 |
| Maryland/Delaware | | | | | | |
| Continentals | 21 | | | | | |
| New Jersey/Pennsylvania | | | | | | |
| Continentals | 2 | | | | | |

# POSTWAR LOCATION OF PENSIONERS BY STATE OF SERVICE

| KY | LA | MD | MO | MS | NC | NJ | OH | PA | SC | TN | VA |
|----|----|----|----|----|----|----|----|----|----|----|----|
| 31 |    |    | 2  |    | 9  |    | 9  |    | 5  | 17 | **46** |
| 36 |    | 5  | 1  |    | 7  |    | 7  |    | 4  | 30 | **96** |
| 2  |    |    |    |    | 7  |    |    |    | 1  | 1  | 2  |
| 21 | 1  |    | 4  | 2  | 55 |    | 1  | 1  | 8  | 51 | 2  |
| 2  | **5** |  |    |    | 1  | 1  | 6  |    |    | 1  | 5  |
| 1  |    |    |    |    | 1  |    |    |    |    |    |    |

Note: Figures in boldface are the number of pensioners who remained in their home state.

GLOSSARY

**adjutant** The military title of an administrative officer of a regiment who issues orders on behalf of the commander, provides details about men assigned to detachments, and maintains muster rolls and other records.

**aide-de-camp** An officer who assists higher-ranked officers (usually generals), providing them a number of services, carrying their orders, and speaking with their authority. The aide received extra pay and was often considered a member of the general's "family."

**backcountry** The interior of the southern colonies adjacent to the frontier. This was a thinly settled zone of small farms and few towns.

**battalion** A unit of infantry composed of at least four companies. The term also came to be used interchangeably with "regiment," in part because most Revolutionary War regiments by the time of Guilford Courthouse were under strength. See **regiment**.

**bayonet** A triangular steel blade that attached to the muzzle of a musket. In effect, this made the musket a spear for close combat. The bayonet allowed men to attack the enemy and defend themselves when their muskets were unloaded.

**brevet** An unpaid rank awarded an officer to recognize achievement that gave him a higher command and served to establish seniority; for example, a brevet major, paid the same as a captain, would outrank a captain.

**brigade** A tactical and administrative formation that consisted of at least two regiments (or two battalions). Ideally, a brigade would consist of four regiments and be commanded by a brigadier general. During 1781, brigades usually had two regiments and might be commanded by a colonel, lieutenant colonel, or, in rare cases late in the war, a major.

**brigadier general** The lowest ranking general, who usually commanded a brigade.

**buck and ball** A musket cartridge that has one big lead ball (.69 to .75 caliber), plus three to seven smaller balls (.28 to .33 caliber) called buckshot. Designed to increase lethality, it was mandated by Gen. George Washington as early as 1777.

**captain** The military rank of an officer between major and first lieutenant who usually commands a company.

**captain lieutenant** A military rank usually found in an artillery regiment that signified greater responsibility for the lieutenant. In an infantry regiment, a captain lieutenant commanded the colonel's company.

**case shot** A close-range antipersonnel artillery projectile formed by putting a quantity of small iron or lead shot, equivalent in weight to the cannon's solid ammunition, into a tin container, or canister, that fit the cannon's bore. Also called canister shot.

**colonel** The military rank of an officer who leads a regiment, or occasionally, a brigade.

**commissary** The person responsible for obtaining, inspecting, and issuing the provisions and stores of an army. The commissary was usually a civilian appointment, but during 1781, officers filled this role.

**commission** The authority to hold a rank granted by the government.

**company** In the eighteenth century, a military unit generally consisting of 40–100 men and led by a captain. Four companies formed a battalion and eight a regiment. A company usually had two tactical sub-units called platoons. Under the system devised by Baron Friedrich Wilhelm von Steuben, two companies comprised a tactical combat unit called a division.

**Continental** Pertaining to the American regulars, men who usually were enlisted for three years or "during the war" in the permanent standing army of the United States. Many were well trained and fully equal to the British regulars on southern battlefields. Late in the war, due to a shortage of enlistments, some Continentals were enlisted for only nine, twelve, or eighteen months.

**cornet** The junior officer in a cavalry troop, equivalent to an ensign in the infantry.

**Crown** Referring to the British monarchy, or more generally, to Great Britain.

**division** A military unit within a regiment composed, ideally if at full strength, of two companies (four platoons) for marching or firing. Due to the shortage of men late in the war, a single company might occasionally serve as a division. Alternatively: A tactical and administrative unit composed of at least two brigades and led by a major general.

**dragoon** Originally, a mounted infantryman, but over time the term became generally interchangeable with "cavalryman."

**ensign** The lowest ranking infantry officer, so called because they traditionally carried the regimental colors.

**fusilier** Originally, an infantryman who carried a lightweight musket called a "fusil" and distinguished by special headgear when the Revolutionary War began, although this practice did not extend to the Southern campaigns.

**grape shot** A long-range antipersonnel artillery projectile composed of small shot, sized to fit the bore of the cannon, that was bagged and wrapped with cord. At sea, it was designed to cut rigging and limit damage to a potential prize.

**Guards** A composite British brigade composed of fifteen men from each company of three infantry regiments designated Foot Guards (1st, Coldstream, 3rd) that served in North America.

**jaeger** Member of a German unit that fought for the British comprised largely of hunters and woodsmen, who carried rifles and served as scouts, skirmishers, and flankers.

**legion** A combined arms force of dragoons and infantry, the best known of which were Henry Lee's Partizan, or Partisan, Legion and the British Legion under Banastre Tarleton.

**lieutenant** The military rank of a subaltern or junior officer. The first lieutenant in a company was second in command to the captain and often commanded a platoon. The second lieutenant was junior to the first.

**lieutenant colonel** The military rank of the assistant to a colonel. As the war went on, many lieutenant colonels were placed in command of regiments, with the title lieutenant colonel commandant.

**light horse** Another term for cavalry or dragoons.

**light infantry** Lightly equipped, highly mobile troops, used for scouting and covering flanks and rear, often regarded as elite soldiers.

**loyalist** One who was "loyal" to the king. Also called a "Tory" or a "royalist."

**major** The military rank of an officer between lieutenant colonel and captain who is second in command of a battalion and responsible for its training, equipment, and management.

**militia** Initially, the colonial self-defense force. During the Revolution, militias were called up (drafted) for service as needed, serving for short periods, such as six weeks or three months, or in emergencies, for only a few days. Generally, militiamen were not well trained and did not turn out in great numbers or in a timely fashion.

**musket**  Also called the firelock, this was the most common shoulder arm of the Revolutionary War. A flintlock, smoothbore, .65 to .75 caliber weapon, the musket could take a bayonet, was easier and faster to load than a rifle, but was accurate for only about 50 yards. The British used a .75 caliber musket called the "Brown Bess," while American regulars by the time of Guilford Courthouse were armed with French weaponry.

**parole**  The release of a prisoner of war who promises to return when ordered and not to take up arms again until exchanged.

**partisan, partizan**  An irregular soldier, or light trooper, used for scouting and raiding. The equivalent modern term would be "guerilla."

**patriot**  A person who served his country. Since the Whigs won and the American colonies became independent, the term has come to mean one who supported the Whig side in the Revolutionary War. In reality, both Whig and Tory saw their actions as patriotic.

**paymaster**  The officer charged with paying a regiment. This position did not require other service and was not always filled by a commissioned officer.

**pioneer**  In eighteenth-century military terminology, a skilled laborer responsible for building fortifications, repairing roads, and general construction.

**provincial**  Pertaining to Americans or American military units fighting on the British side on a full-time basis, such as Tarleton's British Legion.

**quartermaster**  An officer assigned to encamping a regiment, issuing equipment and supplies, and making returns of them.

**ranger**  A scout, or raider, usually mounted and generally operating on the frontier. When formed into companies or battalions, rangers served in advance of main force units. Their role in the South was primarily against Indians and Tories. Among the southern states, only South Carolina raised a Continental Ranger unit (the 3rd South Carolina).

**regiment**  A military formation composed of at least five, and as many as ten, companies commanded by a lieutenant colonel or colonel. "Regiment" and "battalion" were used interchangeably during the Revolutionary War. Technically speaking, a regiment was composed of two battalions; but a regiment with less than 350 men would be formed as a single battalion.

**regular**  A member of a permanent standing army. In the eighteenth century, this term referred to the British soldier enlisted for long service and generally well trained and disciplined.

**rifle**  A shoulder weapon with spiral grooves cut into the barrel's interior that cause the bullet to spin, thus giving great accuracy. Rifles of the eighteenth century were slow to load, could not use a bayonet, and thus were not as numerous as one might think, being used mainly by specialized units or experienced frontiersmen.

**royalist**  One who supported the king, or the king's side, during the American Revolution.

**state troops**  The "regulars" raised by some states who were restricted from serving outside their states and generally enlisted for 18 months, or half the term demanded of Continentals. Virginia, North Carolina, South Carolina, and Georgia raised several such groups including infantry and cavalry. Occasionally, the term was applied to those who enlisted for less than three years, although many of these units were called Continentals.

**surgeon**  The chief medical officer of a regiment or a hospital.

**Tidewater**  The low-lying coastal zone of the southern states.

**Tory**  An American who supported the British king and opposed American independence.

**Whig**  An American who supported the revolutionary movement against royal authority and for independence.

# A NOTE ON SOURCES

For a southern campaign battle, Guilford Courthouse is fairly well documented, even if the sources are scattered, often confusing, and in conflict with each other. For battle overviews, there are the reports of Nathanael Greene and Charles Cornwallis, plus the books written by Henry Lee, Charles Stedman, and Banastre Tarleton. For more specific battle episodes, there is the book written by Roger Lamb, the memoir by William Seymour, and the diary of Samuel Houston. There are also letters by Otho Holland Williams, St. George Tucker, Johann Christian Du Buy, William Campbell, and others that describe particular episodes. Taken as a group, this body of participant accounts creates a skeleton that can be fleshed out by the pension documents.

After the war, Congress allowed pensions in special cases; then in 1818, if the veteran was impoverished; and finally, in 1832, if he was still alive and could prove his service. The applications were sworn testimony, often stating that the recollections were to the best of the applicant's memory. Of the more than one thousand applications used in this study, only one was known to have been challenged by another person, although many were rejected for some administrative reason.

The pension applications, when looked at as a group, form patterns around commanders, units, and dates. These patterns further flesh out the battle and, when joined with the anecdotal references that many applications include, add much detail to the fighting at the private soldier's level. We used the same procedures that proved so successful in Lawrence E. Babits's *Devil of a Whipping: The Battle of Cowpens*, but did not achieve the same results in some particular ways. Guilford Courthouse was a bigger battle, fought in dense woods, and often by men who had served together for less than a month. Consequently, it was not possible to identify the precise alignment of companies in each regiment. It was, however, possible to identify regimental positions in each brigade. This problem was as true of Continentals as of militia. It was simply a larger engagement.

Among the participants who wrote about Guilford Courthouse, on the British side, it is clear that most of them did not see the whole battle. Cornwallis wrote of things he didn't see, and so did Tarleton. Lamb reported some battle sequences simply by quoting Cornwallis's commissary general, Charles Stedman, who obviously saw a lot of the Guilford battlefield. It is probable that Stedman was with the 1st Guards Battalion in the southern flank fighting. His map reflects details of the British right flank found nowhere else, and his account bears up under comparison with other contemporaries and modern analysis.

We could find no account of the events on the British left, where the Ansbach jaegers, the Guards light infantry, and 33rd Foot were engaged. The 33rd's John Robert Shaw was captured a few days before the battle. For details about the 23rd, we have excerpts from Roger Lamb's two books, as well as accounts from Forbes Champagne, Harry Calvert, and Thomas Saumarez. It is unfortunate that the full account by twenty-year-old Saumarez has not survived because the excerpts are particularly interesting. For the 2nd Guards Battalion, we have Charles O'Hara's letters. These are often more helpful for what they do not say, allowing us to challenge other accounts; however his description of the night after the battle is a classic. For the 71st Foot, Dugald Stewart's letters are helpful but only tantalizing. For the Von Bose Regiment, there are two accounts. The best known is the exaggerated tale by Sgt. Bernard Koch. Despite the exaggeration, it contains grains of truth that can be abstracted, such as his recalling that the regiment fought in two directions and that in one instance their firing set the woods ablaze. Major Du Buy's account (which may actually be that of Friedrich von Scheer) is the most lucid, clearly spelling out what the regiment did and why. We relied on it for reconstructing the sequence of the Hessian movements that helps explain what happened to the Guards and the American flanking parties. For the 1st Guards, we have little material, except for that provided by Stedman. His account, however, is truly valuable because it provides both an overview and the minutiae of events in a forthright and almost dispassionate manner.

For the Americans, there is more material available, albeit quite scattered. On the flank fighting, Lee's 1812 account is often confusing and misleading. Historians have for too long utilized it uncritically. On the northern flank, Sergeant Major Seymour provides details about such things as driving the British three times and where the 33rd, and presumably the jaegers and the Guards light infantry, took position after their repulse from the American third line. For the North Carolinians on the first line, there is no overall accounting, but the pension accounts generated a framework and filled in certain details that can be matched to British observations. On the second line, aside from the pension declarations, we have the words of St. George Tucker's letter home, revealing a remarkable level of detail about Lawson's brigade and clarifying what Roger Lamb saw on the other side of the line. For Stevens's brigade, there is little overall evidence aside from pension records except for Samuel Houston's diary, and that is largely concerned with the southern flank.

On the third line, it is clear Greene did not see much. He was involved in the repulse of the 33rd and probably nearly captured after the 2nd Guards Battalion broke the 2nd Maryland. His account, and his decision making, reflects what little he did see. Otho Holland Williams wrote about the battle and clarified many details about the third line as well as testifying to the ferocity of the second line fighting. John Eager Howard's letters to John Marshall and Henry Lee in which he responded to questions of fact and error are an indispensable source for the third line. William R. Davie's book about the war is important for his recollection of what happened to the 2nd Maryland and his inclusion of a Samuel Mathis letter about John Smith's duel with James Stuart.

Secondary sources contributed a great deal. For the chapter dealing with the American withdrawal from South Carolina and the British pursuit following Cowpens, we were immensely helped by John Buchanan's overview study, *The Road to Guilford Courthouse*, especially his chapter explaining what happened from Cowan's Ford to the Dan River crossing. Despite the numerous details, the book never gets bogged down in telling the story, and it provides an excellent outline. For even more details, there is a very useful pamphlet by Thomas Edmonds, *The Tactical Retreat of General Nathanael Greene*, in which Edmonds draws heavily on an earlier, unpublished paper by Kenneth Haynes called "Edge of the Sword," about what happened on February 9–14, 1781. These two authors reside in the "Race to the Dan" countryside, and with their extensive knowledge of the region they were able to provide exceptionally important information about road networks, time, and space involved in the armies marching through the central Piedmont.

Other sources included the work of Eli W. Caruthers, who collected information into the early nineteenth century and walked the battlefield with numerous veterans, recording their memories. These recollections, although not sworn testimony like the pension documents, still contribute to the local lore much in the way that Lyman Draper did for Kings Mountain. David Schenck, who saved the battlefield, wrote a book on the British invasion titled *North Carolina, 1780–1781*. It is replete with errors but does provide another starting point for examining the battle. His acquisition of the battlefield was crucial to its survival, even if he misrepresented some elements in the interest of telling a good story.

On the battlefield itself, there are several modern sources. Ranger John Lloyd Durham wrote a paper several years ago titled "Historical Marking of the 3rd Line of Battle at the Battle of Guilford Courthouse," in which he discussed the distance between battle lines and the modern landforms. This supplemented a 1983 cartographic study by Thomas W. Taylor, titled "The Landmarks of the Battle of Guilford Courthouse," that assembled most of the historical and regional maps to shed light on where things happened. (Both manuscripts are on file at the Guilford Courthouse National Military Park in Greensboro, N.C.) The sources of archaeological evidence are a series of reports by the National Park Service, Wake Forest University, and University of North Carolina archaeologists going back to the 1970s. We do not agree with most of their archaeological conclusions, in part because those authors did not utilize many original or historical accounts, nor did they have the chance to do so. We opted to use the archaeological data, not as the "handmaiden of history," but as an equal partner, using our own archaeological experience and knowledge of the documents. We were aided by information generated by local relic hunters, some of whom operated clandestinely yet shared their knowledge with Guilford Battlefield staff. If this information were grandfathered and the violations committed in gathering it were pardoned, so that these individuals could come forward and present a more precise accounting of their finds, some of the conclusions presented here might well be challenged. As it is, knowing where a 33rd Foot button and a Coldstream Guards buckle were found clarified interpretations already reached from the documents. There is a lot more yet to learn, both from earlier work and from a comprehensive, systematic study of the whole park area.

# NOTES

### ABBREVIATIONS

*Hetrina* Veröffentlichungen der
Archivschule Marburg,
Institut für Archivwissenschaft. *Hessische Truppen im
amerikanischen Unabhän-
gigkeitskrieg* (Publications
of the Institute at Marburg
for Archival Science. Hessian
Troops in the American War
for Independence). 6 vols.
Marburg, Ger.: Archivschule
Marburg, 1974.

MHS Maryland Historical Society,
Baltimore

NAE National Archives, Kew,
England

*ODNB* *Oxford Dictionary of
National Biography.* Edited
by H. C. G. Matthew and
Brian H. Harrison. 60 vols.
New York: Oxford University
Press, 2004.

RWP Revolutionary War Pension
Application Files, Microcopy
M805, National Archives,
Washington, D.C.

WLCL William L. Clements Library,
Ann Arbor, Mich.

INTRODUCTION

1  J. Howard, "'Things Here Wear a Melancholy Appearance.'"
2  James Simpson to Richard Pearis, 3 May 1780, Treasury Office Papers, TO 1/645, NAE.
3  James Craig to Nesbitt Balfour, 28 May 1781, Charles Cornwallis Papers, PRO 30/11/6, NAE.
4  Moultrie, *Memoirs of the Revolution*, 1:368.
5  Buchanan, *Road to Guilford Courthouse*, 119–21.
6  Henry Clinton to William Phillips, 25 May 1780, Sir Henry Clinton Papers, WLCL.
7  Wickwire and Wickwire, *Cornwallis: The American Adventure*, 182–84. Andrew Pickens of the Long Canes, South Carolina, settlement, was one of the back-country leaders who initially elected to stay on parole after Charleston surrendered. When his plantation was raided in late 1780, he sent a letter to the local commandant at Ninety Six saying his parole had been violated and he was no longer bound by its conditions. From Cowpens, 17 January 1781, until the end of the war, he was a key militia leader cooperating with Greene. Thomas Sumter never was paroled. He continued to resist and served as a beacon, drawing other militiamen to resistance. At Blackstock's, 20 November 1780, Sumter was badly wounded and knocked out of action for some time. After he returned, he was not the dominant figure he had been and was seen as a thorn in the side of the regular forces since he made constant demands for supplies but never effectively cooperated with the Continentals.
8  Babits and Howard, "Continentals in Tarleton's Legion."
9  Edgar, *Partisans and Redcoats*, is a modern, articulate exponent of their views.
10  The exact quote is "We must separate to live, but unite to fight." Quoted in Count Yorck von Wartenburg, *Napoleon as a General*, 40.
11  Selesky and Boatner, *Encyclopedia of the American Revolution*, 1076; Nathanael Greene to an Unidentified Person, unknown date, in Showman et al., *Papers of General Nathanael Greene*, 7:175.
12  Greene to Daniel Morgan, 16 Dec. 1780, in Showman et al., *Papers of General Nathanael Greene*, 7:589–90; Jones, *Journal of Alexander Chesney*, 21, 125–26.
13  Babits, *Devil of a Whipping*, 49. The original quote appeared in a letter from Cornwallis to Tarleton, 2 Jan. 1780, in Tarleton, *Campaigns*, 244.

CHAPTER ONE

1  The authors recognize that the accepted date for the beginning of the "race" is in February; however, we would argue that the entire campaign began just after Cowpens when Morgan marched north.

2 Charles Cornwallis to Francis Rawdon, 21 Jan. 1781, Charles Cornwallis Papers, PRO 30/11/84, NAE.

3 Cornwallis to Henry Clinton, 6 Jan. 1781, Sir Guy Carleton Papers, PRO 30/55, NAE; Cornwallis to George Germain, 17 Mar. 1781, Cornwallis Papers, PRO 30/11/76, NAE.

4 Cornwallis to Germain, 17 Mar. 1781.

5 Lossing, *Pictorial Fieldbook of the Revolution*, 2:395n.

6 Tarleton, *Campaigns*, 222–23; Cornwallis to Germain, 17 Mar. 1781.

7 Cornwallis to Germain, 17 Mar. 1781.

8 Charles O'Hara to Augustus Henry Fitzroy, the Duke of Grafton, 20 Apr. 1781, in Rogers, "Letters of Charles O'Hara," 174.

9 Cornwallis to Germain, 17 Mar. 1781; Newsome, "British Orderly Book," 287–88.

10 Daniel Morgan to Nathanael Greene, 28, 29 Jan. 1781, in Showman et al., *Papers of General Nathanael Greene*, 7:211, 215.

11 Greene to Isaac Huger, 29 Jan. 1781, in ibid., 7:220–22.

12 J. Graham, "Graham's Narrative," 257.

13 Ibid., 260–63. Webster had been promoted to full colonel on 17 Nov. 1780; however, the promotion may have only been "in America," or news may never have reached the army, as Cornwallis consistently referred to him in letters and field returns as a lieutenant colonel.

14 Henry, *Narrative of the Battle of Cowan's Ford*, 4–7.

15 Lamb, *Original and Authentic Journal*, 343; J. Graham, "Graham's Narrative," 259; Henry, *Narrative of the Battle of Cowan's Ford*, 6–14.

16 Lamb, *Original and Authentic Journal*, 343–45; Henry, *Narrative of the Battle of Cowan's Ford*, 11–14.

17 J. Graham, "Graham's Narrative," 258–59; Henry, *Narrative of the Battle of Cowan's Ford*, 11–14.

18 Cornwallis to Germain, 17 Mar. 1781; Lamb, *Original and Authentic Journal*, 344.

19 Henry, *Narrative of the Battle of Cowan's Ford*, 14; Davidson, *Piedmont Partisan*, 114; Nathanael Greene to Thomas Sumter, 3 Feb. 1781, in Showman et al., *Papers of General Nathanael Greene*, 7:245–47.

20 Cornwallis to Germain, 17 Mar. 1781; Henry, *Narrative of the Battle of Cowan's Ford*, 13–14; J. Graham, "Graham's Narrative," 263–64.

21 J. Graham, "Graham's Narrative," 262; Tarleton, *Campaigns*, 263–65.

22 Cornwallis to Germain, 17 Mar. 1781; J. Graham, "Graham's Narrative," 263–64.

23 J. Graham, "Graham's Narrative," 262–64; Tarleton, *Campaigns*, 264; Newsome, "British Orderly Book," 294.

24  J. Graham, "Graham's Narrative," 264–65; Tarleton, *Campaigns*, 264; pension applications of Elisha Evans, 8 Oct. 1832, Roll 308, Jonas Clark, 7 Aug. 1832, Roll 189, RWP.

25  Cornwallis to Germain, 17 Mar. 1781; Tarleton, *Campaigns*, 252–54; Newsome, "British Orderly Book," 293.

26  John Eager Howard to William Johnson, unknown date, 1822, Rocky Mount Collection, DuPont Library, Stratford Hall, Stratford, Virginia.

27  Powell, *North Carolina Gazetteer*, 450; Seymour, "Journal," 295–96; Howard to Johnson, 1822.

28  Howard to Johnson, 1822; Seymour, "Journal," 396.

29  Nathanael Greene to the Militia Officers Posted on the Catawba River and Marching to Camp, 1 Feb. 1781, Greene to Isaac Huger, 1 Feb. 1781, Ichabod Burnet to Henry Lee Jr., 2 Feb. 1781, in Showman et al., *Papers of General Nathanael Greene*, 7:231–35; Pleasants et al., *Archives of Maryland*, 88; Seymour, "Journal," 296.

30  Anderson, "Journal of Lieutenant Anderson," 209; Cullen et al., *Papers of Thomas Jefferson*, 4:495–96; Buchanan, *Road to Guilford Courthouse*, 349–50.

31  Charles Cornwallis to Nathanael Greene, 4 Feb. 1781, in Showman et al., *Papers of General Nathanael Greene*, 7:250–51.

32  J. Graham, "Graham's Narrative," 264–65.

33  Buchanan, *Road to Guilford Courthouse*, 350; Nathanael Greene to Isaac Huger, 5 Feb. 1781, in Showman et al., *Papers of General Nathanael Greene*, 7:251–52; Seymour, "Journal," 296.

34  Nathanael Greene to the Commanding Officer of the Guilford Militia, 5 Feb. 1781, Greene to the Officer Commanding the Militia in the Rear of the Enemy, 6 Feb. 1781, in Showman et al., *Papers of General Nathanael Greene*, 7:253–54.

35  Tarleton, *Campaigns*, 228; Fries, ed., *Records of the Moravians*, 4:1765.

36  Tarleton, *Campaigns*, 228; Residents of Salem, North Carolina, to Nathanael Greene, 8 Feb. 1781, in Showman et al., *Papers of General Nathanael Greene*, 7:260–61; Caruthers, *Revolutionary Sketches*, 115–16.

37  Fries, *Records of the Moravians*, 4:1741–42.

38  Ibid., 4:1675–76.

39  Seymour, "Journal," 296.

40  Orderly Book, Otho Holland Williams Papers, MHS.

41  Isaac Huger to Nathanael Greene, 8 Feb. 1781, Greene to Thomas Sumter, 9 Feb. 1781, Proceedings of a Council of War, 9 Feb. 1781, in Showman et al., *Papers of General Nathanael Greene*, 7:259–60, 261–62, 266.

42  Orderly Book, Williams Papers, MHS; Babits, *Devil of a Whipping*, 105.

43  Nathanael Greene to George Washington, 9 Feb. 1781, in Showman et al., *Papers of General Nathanael Greene*, 7:267–69.

44 Ibid., 7:271n; Buchanan, *Road to Guilford Courthouse*, 355.

45 Nathanael Greene to Henry Lee, 10 Feb. 1781, Greene to Baron Von Steuben, 10 Feb. 1781, Greene to Col. Francis Locke and Others in the Rear of the Enemy, 9 Feb. 1781, Greene to Abner Nash, 9 Feb. 1781, François Malmedy to Greene, 10 Feb. 1781, in Showman et al., *Papers of General Nathanael Greene*, 7:262–65, 270–72, 274–75.

46 Buchanan, *Road to Guilford Courthouse*, 351.

47 Newsome, "British Orderly Book," 366.

48 H. Lee, *Memoirs*, 1:277; Seymour, "Journal," 297.

49 Otho H. Williams to Nathanael Greene, 11 Feb. 1781, in Showman et al., *Papers of General Nathanael Greene*, 7:283; Seymour, "Journal," 296–97.

50 Edmonds, *Tactical Retreat*, 1–2; Williams to Greene, 11 Feb. 1781.

51 H. Lee, *Memoirs*, 1:280–83.

52 Ibid., 1:280–85; Heitman, *Historical Register*, 349–50.

53 H. Lee, *Memoirs*, 1:284–85.

54 Ibid., 1:285; Williams to Greene, 11 Feb. 1781.

55 H. Lee, *Memoirs*, 1:279–87; Edmonds, *Tactical Retreat*, 2–3; Caruthers, *Revolutionary Sketches*, 118–20, 138; Greene to John Butler, 12 Feb. 1781, in Showman et al., *Papers of General Nathanael Greene*, 7:283–84.

56 Greene to Williams, 13 Feb. 1781, Williams to Greene, 13 Feb. 1781, in Showman et al., *Papers of General Nathanael Greene*, 7:285–86.

57 Greene to Williams, 14 Feb. 1781, in ibid., 7:287; Gordon, *History of the United States*, 4:45.

58 Buchanan, *Road to Guilford Courthouse*, 356–58.

59 Newsome, "British Orderly Book," 367; Tarleton, *Campaigns*, 229.

60 Newsome, "British Orderly Book," 291, 378.

61 Ichabod Burnet to Benjamin Walker, 15 Feb. 1781, in Showman et al., *Papers of General Nathanael Greene*, 7:287; Charles Cornwallis to George Germain, 18 Apr. 1781, in Ross, *Correspondence of Cornwallis*, 1:90–91.

CHAPTER TWO

1 Nathanael Green to Andrew Pickens, 3 Feb. 1781, Greene to Francis Locke and others, 9 Feb. 1781, Pickens to Greene, 19 Feb. 1781, Greene to Pickens, 20 Feb. 1781, Pickens to Greene, 20 Feb. 1781, in Showman et al., *Papers of General Nathanael Greene*, 7:241, 262, 320, 322, 325. Perhaps the best reconstruction of the events that took place after recrossing the Dan is Buchanan's chapter "Patience and Finesse," in *Road to Guilford Courthouse*.

2 J. Graham, "Graham's Narrative," 212–311.

3 H. Lee, *Memoirs*, 1:304–6.

4  Ibid., 1:308–12; J. Graham, "Graham's Narrative," 319; Buchanan, *Road to Guilford Courthouse*, 362–65.

5  H. Lee, *Memoirs*, 1:310–12; Buchanan, *Road to Guilford Courthouse*, 364; pension application of Moses Hall, 9 Nov. 1835, Roll 390, RWP. Hall's pension application is provided in full in Dann, *Revolution Remembered*, 202–4.

6  "Forbes Champaign [*sic*] to Josiah C. Champaign, April 17, 1781," *Leeds Intelligencer*, 26 June 1781; Andrew Pickens to Nathanael Greene, 26 Feb. 1781, in Showman et al., *Papers of General Nathanael Greene*, 7:358.

7  Fries, *Records of the Moravians*, 4:1744; Pickens to Greene, 26 Feb. 1781, Hugh Crockett to Greene, 26 Feb. 1781, Otho H. Williams to Greene, 26 Feb. 1781, in Showman et al., *Papers of General Nathanael Greene*, 7: 354, 355–58, 360–61.

8  Pension application of John Ewing, 3 Apr. 1833, Roll 310, RWP; Tarleton, *Campaigns*, 233.

9  Thomas Jefferson to Nathanael Greene, 18, 19 Feb. 1781, Greene to William Washington, 16 Feb. 1781, in Showman et al., *Papers of General Nathanael Greene*, 7:298, 312–13.

10  Greene to John Butler, 21 Feb. 1781, Greene to Jefferson, 10 Mar. 1781, in ibid., 7:326–27, 419–20; Jefferson to Robert Lawson, 25 Feb. 1781, in Cullen et al., *Papers of Thomas Jefferson*, 7:7–8.

11  Charles Cornwallis to George Germain, 17 Mar. 1781, Charles Cornwallis Papers, PRO 30/11/76, NAE; Newsome, "British Orderly Book," 373; Wickwire and Wickwire, *Cornwallis*, 289.

12  Ward, *Delaware Continentals*, 404.

13  Pension application of William Eddings, 28 Sept. 1832, Roll 295, RWP; Buchanan, *Road to Guilford Courthouse*, 365–66; "Declaration of General Joseph Graham," in W. Clark, *State Records*, 19:960. The Fletcher's Mill skirmish is documented in Davies, *Documents of the American Revolution*, 20:89, and O'Kelley, *Nothing but Blood and Slaughter*, 3:106.

14  Dunkerly, "Prelude to Guilford Courthouse," 37–39; Steele, *Lost Battle*, 114–35; Tarleton, *Campaigns*, 234–36; H. Lee, *Memoirs*, 1:264; Turner, *Journal and Order Book*, 14; W. Clark, *State Records*, 19:960–63, 969–70; Newsome, "British Orderly Book," 378, 282. See also Otho Holland Williams to Nathanael Greene, in Showman et al., *Papers of General Nathanael Greene*, 7:381–82, for a description of the skirmish.

15  Dunkerly, "Prelude to Guilford Courthouse," 38–39; Steele, *Lost Battle*, 122–24; Tarleton, *Campaigns*, 235–36; W. Clark, *State Records*, 19:969–70.

16  Dunkerly, "Prelude to Guilford Courthouse," 39; W. Clark, *State Records*, 19:969–70; J. Graham, "Graham's Narrative," 284; Fries, *Records of the Moravians*, 4:1684, 1746.

17  Otho Holland Williams to Nathanael Greene, 26 Feb. 1781, Henry Lee to Greene,

4 Mar. 1781, in Showman et al., *Papers of General Nathanael Greene*, 7:360, 391–93.

18 Fries, *Records of the Moravians*, 4:1684, 1746.

19 Ibid., 4:1684.

20 Lamb, *Original and Authentic Journal*; Hagist, *British Soldier's Story*, 83; Dunkerly, "Prelude to Guilford Courthouse," 40–43; Williams to Greene, 6, 7 Mar. 1781, in Showman et al., *Papers of General Nathanael Greene*, 7:406–8. The skirmish is described in detail in H. Lee, *Memoirs*, 1:323–28.

21 Dunkerly, "Prelude to Guilford Courthouse," 40–43; J. Graham, "Graham's Narrative," 290–91.

22 H. Lee, *Memoirs*, 1:325.

23 Seymour, "Journal," 297–98.

24 Charles Magill to Thomas Jefferson, 10 Mar. 1781, in Palmer et al., *Calendar of Virginia State Papers*, 1:567; Fries, *Records of the Moravians*, 4:1685

25 Pension application of John Scott, 3 Dec. 1832, Roll 721, RWP; Nathanael Greene to Andrew Pickens, 8 Mar. 1781, Greene to Thomas Jefferson, 10 Mar. 1781, in Showman et al., *Papers of General Nathanael Greene*, 7:410–11, 419–20; Thomas Jefferson to His Excellency the President of Congress, 19 Mar. 1781, in Lipscomb et al., *Writings of Thomas Jefferson*, 4:168.

26 John Butler to Nathanael Greene, 8 Mar. 1781, Greene to Thomas Jefferson, 10 Mar. 1781, in Showman et al., *Papers of General Nathanael Greene*, 7:411, 419–21. Data taken from the Guilford Veterans Pension Database compiled by Lawrence E. Babits and Joshua Howard in 2004–7. The database consists of the pensions of 980 Americans who claimed to have served at Guilford Courthouse in their pension declarations. Hereafter cited as Babits and Howard, "Guilford Veterans Database."

27 Samuel Houston, "Houston's Journal," in Foote, *Sketches of Virginia*, 142–47; Babits and Howard, "Guilford Veterans Database."

28 Charles Magill to Thomas Jefferson, 10 Mar. 1781, in Palmer et al., *Calendar of Virginia State Papers*, 1:567; Houston, "Houston's Journal," 142–45.

29 Richard Campbell to Nathanael Greene, 8 Mar. 1781, Greene to Thomas Jefferson, 10 Mar. 1781, Greene to Baron Von Steuben, 11 Mar. 1781, in Showman et al., *Papers of General Nathanael Greene*, 7:411, 419–20, 427; Houston, "Houston's Journal," 144; Charles Magill to Thomas Jefferson, 13 Mar. 1781, in Cullen et al., *Papers of Thomas Jefferson*, 5:138.

30 Charles O'Hara to Augustus Henry Fitzroy, the Duke of Grafton, 20 Apr. 1781, in Rogers, "Letters of Charles O'Hara," 177–78; Shaw, *Narrative*, 60; Cornwallis to Germain, 17 Mar. 1781, Cornwallis Papers, NAE.

31 Shaw, *Narrative*, 61; Charles Magill to Thomas Jefferson, 13 Mar. 1781, in Cullen et al., *Papers of Thomas Jefferson*, 5:138.

32 Newsome, "British Orderly Book," 386–87; Seymour, "Journal," 298; Newlin, *Battle of New Garden*, 30–31.

33 Cornwallis to Germain, 17 Mar. 1781; St. George Tucker to Frances Tucker, 14 Mar. 1781, in Tucker, "Southern Campaign, 1781," 36–46; Johann Christian Du Buy to Wilhelm von Knyphausen, 18 Apr. 1781, in Bestand 4h, Nr. 3101, Hessisches Staatsarchiv Marburg, Lidgerwood Collection of Hessian Transcripts, Morristown Historical Park, Morristown, N.J.; S. Graham, "Account."

34 Newlin, *Battle of New Garden*, 31–32, 35–36.

35 H. Lee, *Memoirs*, 1:335–36.

36 Newlin, *Battle of New Garden*, 36–39.

37 Tarleton, quoted in Newlin, *Battle of New Garden*, 36.

CHAPTER THREE

1 Newlin, *Battle of New Garden*, 37–39; H. Lee, *Memoirs*, 1:336–38.

2 Caruthers, *Revolutionary Sketches*, 139, 145–48.

3 Newlin, *Battle of New Garden*, 38–45.

4 H. Lee, *Memoirs*, 1:338–39.

5 Coffin, "Letter from Addison Coffin."

6 Tarleton, *Campaigns*, 271.

7 Pension applications of John Wason, 3 Sept. 1832, Roll 841, Frederick Fender, 6 May 1833, Roll 316, Peter Rife, 14 July 1834, Roll 690, Isaac Sampson, 22 Nov. 1821, Roll 714, John Garner, 27 July 1834, Roll 349, RWP.

8 *Annual Register.*

9 Babits, *Devil of a Whipping.*

10 There are numerous excellent studies of the Continental Line. See Berg, *Encyclopedia of Continental Army Units*; Carp, *To Starve an Army at Pleasure*; Cox, *Proper Sense of Honor*; Holton, *Forced Founders*; Martin and Lender, *Respectable Army*; Montross, *Rag, Tag, and Bobtail*; Neimeyer, *America Goes to War*; Royster, *Revolutionary People at War*; Shy, *A People Numerous and Armed*; Urwin, *United States Infantry*; Wright, *Continental Army.*

11 Daniel Morgan to Nathanael Greene, 20 Feb. 1781, in Showman et al., *Papers of General Nathanael Greene*, 7:324.

12 Pension application of Jeremiah Gurley, 30 Oct. 1832, Roll 383, RWP; Babits and Howard, "Guilford Veterans Database"; Heitman, *Historical Register*. The five battalion commanders were Benjamin Williams, Pinkerton Eaton, William Linton, Henry Dixon, and James Martin. If Robert Mebane and Archibald Lytle were present, as some pension declarations indicate, then they would have made the sixth and seventh Continental veterans out of eleven total battalion commanders. The two majors were James Powers and William Brinkley, and the six

company grade officers included Elijah Moore, William Hicks, Hardee Bryan, William Williams, Matthew McCauley, and William Lytle.

13 Babits and Howard, "Guilford Veterans Database"; Heitman, *Historical Register*. The militia battalion commanders with Continental service were John Holcombe and Nathaniel Cocke. The majors included William Cunningham, Thomas Hubbard, and Henry Conway, and the company commanders were John Ogilby, John Holcombe Overstreet, and John Morton. The former regulars serving as rifle company officers included James Dillard, William Jones, Thomas Helm, Jacob Moon, John Daniel, and William Christian.

14 Babits and Howard, "Guilford Veterans Database."

15 Baker, *Another Such Victory*, 43–45; pension application of Wade Mosby, 19 Sept. 1832, Roll 602, RWP; W. Clark, *State Records*, 19:534; Nathanael Greene to Alexander Martin, 2 Sept. 1783, in Governor Alexander Martin Papers, North Carolina State Archives, Raleigh.

16 Powell, *Dictionary of North Carolina Biography*, 2:130–131; "Eaton Family" (typescript), in Southern Historical Collection, University of North Carolina, Chapel Hill; W. Clark, *State Records of North Carolina*, 15:428–29. The War of the Regulation was an insurrection of the North Carolina Backcountry against the Tidewater due to taxes, exorbitant land fees, lack of representation, and other matters. It culminated in the Battle of Alamance, 16 May 1771, when government forces, largely from the Tidewater, defeated the rebels.

17 Babits and Howard, *Fortitude and Forbearance*, 144–45, 179, 218; Babits and Howard, "Guilford Veterans Database." Information concerning unit position and placement was determined through a variety of primary sources including Showman et al., *Papers of General Nathanael Greene*, H. Lee, *Memoirs*, veterans' depositions given to Eli W. Caruthers, and pension accounts. Traditionally, secondary accounts have only placed the North Carolina militia brigades on the field as a whole without investigating where each regiment or battalion was located. By utilizing pension accounts that describe unit locations, we are able to give a more accurate account of battalion positions. However, we make no claim to complete accuracy, only that the positions described are the most likely, based on available evidence.

18 Powell, *Dictionary of North Carolina Biography*, 1:290–91.

19 Babits and Howard, *Fortitude and Forbearance*, 152. See Powell, *When the Past Refused to Die*; Owen and Vanaman, *History and Genealogies*; Blackwelder, *Age of Orange*; Babits and Howard, "Guilford Veterans Database." For mention of Henry Dixon, see pension applications of John Meadows, 28 Sept. 1832, Roll 578, Charles Allen, 3 Sept. 1832, Roll 12, Willoughby Blackard, 8 Oct. 1832, Roll 92, Gabriel Ferrell, 4 May 1833, Roll 318, RWP. For Rowan and Mecklenburg County

men, see pension applications of Jonas Clark, 7 Aug. 1832, Roll 189, John Billingsley, 23 Dec. 1832, Roll 87, RWP.

20  Pension applications of Chelsey Barnes, 29 Aug. 1832, Roll 51, Benjamin Bowen,
5 Mar. 1833, Roll 108, Eles Chaffin, 3 June 1833, Roll 172, John Findley, 20 Aug.
1832, Roll 320, Peter Lesley, 25 Oct. 1832, Roll 524, William Lesley, 3 Sept. 1832,
Roll 524, Robert Rankin, 7 Sept. 1832, Roll 675, Mattias Swing, 1 Nov. 1832, Roll
786; William Wiley, 12 Nov. 1832, Roll 868, RWP.

21  Pension application of James Martin, 7 Oct. 1832, Roll 555, RWP.

22  Nathaniel Pendleton to William Poythress, 5 Mar. 1781, in Showman et al., *Papers
of General Nathanael Greene*, 7:396; pension application of Edmund Brooke,
3 June 1828, Roll 124, RWP.

23  J. Howard, "North Carolina Continentals at Guilford Courthouse." The first indication of the possibility of a small North Carolina company at Guilford came
while researching *Fortitude and Forbearance*, when the authors discovered that
a number of North Carolina Continentals had enlisted in January 1781. Further
analysis showed that these men were in service in the spring, many of them in
Capt. Edward Yarbourgh's company. These men are shown on Otho Holland
Williams's February returns as having joined Greene's army. Furthermore, several men known to be January 1781 Continentals are on the "List of Prisoners
Taken by Cornwallis's Army in North Carolina, 1781," although they are simply
lumped with the remainder of the militia. The suggestion that these men operated as infantry support for Singleton's guns comes from two points. First, this
same company of Continentals performed the exact same service at Eutaw
Springs in September 1781, and second, it explains how Singleton's men, despite
having their horses killed, managed to extricate themselves and their guns from
the collapse of the first line. In addition, several North Carolina Continental
pension declarations have been located for the January 1781 enlistees (as well as
several enlisted in late 1780), who state that they participated at Guilford Courthouse. See Hay, *Roster of North Carolina Soldiers*; pension applications of James
Adkinson, 21 Apr. 1824, Roll 7, Gabriel Ferrell, 4 May 1833, Roll 318, Willoughby
Blackard, 8 Oct. 1832, Roll 92, Thomas Ralph, 17 July 1820, Roll 673, Jesse Gattin,
5 May 1818, Roll 351, Zachariah Elliott, 6 Jan. 1836, Roll 300, RWP. A military
laboratory at this time was where supplies were put together for the army. In this
case, along with shoes, clothing, and leather goods, some ammunition was also
made into cartridges from barrels of powder and lead melted into musket balls
and buckshot.

24  Baker, *Another Such Victory*, 44–45; Fralin, "Charles Lynch." The dragoons were
seen here by North Carolina militiaman John Watkins after he retreated from
the first line, but this was later in the battle, and they could have moved here just
before the third line fighting began.

25 Delaney, "Biographical Sketch of Robert Kirkwood"; Ward, *Delaware Continentals*, makes the claim that the Delawares were outfitted in hunting shirts and striped overalls or trousers made from bed ticking, stating that the material came from North Carolina. He cites no source for this oft-repeated claim, and there is no extant evidence that supports Ward's assertion. Alternatively, the Delawares likely received clothing shipments intended for the Maryland Line, but apparently reflected their autonomy by maintaining gold ribbon on their cocked hats.

26 See Haller, *William Washington*; Shaffer, *Peter Francisco*; Moon, *Peter Francisco*.

27 W. Clark, *State Records*, 14:592, 17:1038; Dill, "Eighteenth Century New Bern," 354.

28 See Haywood, *Major George Farragut*; S. Williams, "George Farragut."

29 See Abercrombie, *Rockbridge County*; Ruley, *Revolutionary Pension Applications*; Waddell, *Annals of Augusta County*; Summers, *Annals of Southwest Virginia*; pension application of Isaac Robinson, 3 Dec. 1832, Roll 697, RWP; Ross, *Correspondence of Cornwallis*, 1:514; Johann Christian Du Buy to Wilhelm von Knyphausen, 18 Apr. 1781, in Bestand 4h, Nr. 3101, Hessisches Staatsarchiv Marburg, Lidgerwood Collection of Hessian Transcripts, Morristown National Historical Park, Morristown, N.J. Although it has often been suggested that William Preston's Botetourt militia remained to fight, they did not fight as an organized body. See William Preston to Jefferson, 13 Apr. 1781, in Cullen et al., *Papers of Thomas Jefferson*, 7:436–38, in which he explicitly details his and Hugh Crockett's journey home after Weitzel's Mill.

30 Powell, *Dictionary of North Carolina Biography*, 6:247–48; pension applications of John Stonecypher, 3 Sept. 1832, Roll 778, Benjamin Jones, 12 Dec. 1832, Roll 478, Barnabas Fair, 6 Oct. 1832, Roll 311, Arthur Scott, 16 Aug. 1832, Roll 721, RWP; Caruthers, *Revolutionary Sketches*, 142–43.

31 Sherman, "Lee's Legion Remembered"; J. Graham, "Graham's Narrative," 272–73.

32 Heitman, *Historical Register*, 343; See Bradshaw, *History of Prince Edward County*; "Memoir of a Stay at the Iron Works, March 1781," Colonial Williamsburg, Inc., Williamsburg, Virginia.

33 Heitman, *Historical Register*, 181, 295, 305. See Hudgins, *History of Amelia County*; Couture, *Powhatan*; Neale et al., *Brunswick Story*; Cullen, *St. George Tucker*; Kneebone and Bearss, *Dictionary of Virginia Biography*.

34 Heitman, *Historical Register*, 519. See Green and Slaughter, *Genealogical and Historical Notes*.

35 Heitman, *Historical Register*, 162, 168. See Simpson-Poffenbarger, *Battle of Point*

*Pleasant*; Lewis, *History of the Battle of Point Pleasant*; May, *Wolfe's Army*; Clement, *History of Pittsylvania County*.

36  Heitman, *Historical Register*, 446. See Abercrombie, *Rockbridge County*; Ruley, *Revolutionary Pension Applications*; Waddell, *Annals of Augusta County*; Summers, *Annals of Southwest Virginia*; Clement, *History of Pittsylvania County*.

37  Samuel Houston to Sidney S. Baxter, unknown date, 1837, Mss2 H8184 a1, Collections of the Virginia Historical Society, Richmond.

38  Samuel Houston, "Houston's Journal," in Foote, *Sketches of Virginia*, 144–45.

39  Baker, *Another Such Victory*, 44–46.

40  Steuart, *Maryland Line*, 148–49

41  Babits, *Devil of a Whipping*, 24–27.

42  Gunby, *Colonel of the Maryland Line*, 27; William H. Wroten, "Colonel John Gunby Served under General George Washington in the Revolution," *Salisbury (Md.) Times*, 7 Sept. 1959.

43  Babits, *Devil of a Whipping*, 25–27; B. Howard, *Memorial*; C. Howard, "John Eager Howard"; Read, "John Eager Howard"; Greene to an unidentified person, 14 Nov. 1781, in Showman et al., *Papers of General Nathanael Greene*, 9:571–72.

44  Steuart, *Maryland Line*, 26–27; Babits, "Fifth Maryland."

45  Babits, "Fifth Maryland," 374–76; Batt, "Maryland Continentals."

46  Babits, "Fifth Maryland," 375–78; Steuart, *Maryland Line*. The key indicators of assignment to the 2nd Maryland are prior service in the 5th Maryland or a January 1781 transfer to the 5th Maryland. The officers listed are not all the transfers but those whose service in the south from February to June 1781 is not in question. The totals agree with Williams's 17 March 1781 recollection that the 2nd Maryland had nine officers. The ten officers named included Maj. Archibald Anderson, who was killed 15 March.

47  Griswold, *Washington and the Generals*, 2:282–90.

48  Nathanael Greene to Thomas Jefferson, 24 Feb. 1781, in Cullen et al., *Papers of Thomas Jefferson*, 5:22–23.

49  Heitman, *Historical Register*, 260; H. Lee, *Memoirs*, 1:350; G. Greene, *Life of Nathanael Greene*, 3:186–187.

50  Heitman, *Historical Register*, 142.

51  Babits and Howard, "Guilford Veterans Database"; Richard Campbell to Thomas Jefferson, 3 Apr. 1781, in Cullen et al., *Papers of Thomas Jefferson*, 5:325. "Osnabrigs" is the contemporary spelling of a coarse cotton cloth now called osnaburg.

52  Nelson, Goldeberg, and Fletcher, "Revolutionary Ranks"; Hening, *Statutes at Large*, 9:280; See also McDonnell, *Politics of War*; and Holton, *Forced Founders*.

53  Christian, *Muster Rolls*, 579; pension application of John Clark, 4 June 1818,

Roll 189, RWP. There has been considerable debate over whether Finley's first name was Samuel or Ebenezer. See *Southern Campaigns of the American Revolution*, vols. 3 and 4. The problem is that with the exception of Lossing's *Pictorial Fieldbook of the Revolution*, every subsequent source that indicates the name is Samuel is a secondary work. Tracing the citations back to their source, one finds that they have cited each other, continuing a circle of incorrect information. It appears that Lossing first made the mistake and then it was continued down the pedagogical chain of historical inquiry. Ebenezer Finley served as the second in command of William Brown's battery that was effectively annihilated at Camden. He is the only artillery officer named Finley located in any American unit during the war. The man who fought at Guilford was Ebenezer Finley, not Samuel. Samuel Finley, a Virginia Continental officer, did not serve with the Southern Army. He was in service in Virginia in 1781, as is shown in several Virginia pension accounts of those who took part in the operations on the James River in June 1781. Ebenezer's post as deputy judge advocate general in no way circumscribed him from participating in Greene's campaign nor from serving on the battlefield at Guilford.

54 Pension applications of John Harper, 21 Aug. 1832, Roll 399, John W. Huitt, 3 Apr. 1833, Roll 453, John Searcy, 1 Oct. 1832, Roll 723, Philemon Thomas, 6 Feb. 1833, Roll 798, Samuel Shepherd, 28 Aug. 1832, Roll 732, RWP.

55 Pension applications of William Cashwill, 17 Sept. 1832, Roll 169, Henry Cashwill, 17 Sept. 1832, Roll 169, Richard Bond, 8 May 1833, Roll 103, Richard Fretwell, 24 Dec. 1832, Roll 340, Jehu Simmons, 17 Sept. 1832, Roll 738, RWP.

56 Pension applications of Samuel Gann, 25 Aug. 1832, Roll 347, John Gibson, 16 July 1833, Roll 355, Solomon Mitchell, 12 Nov. 1832, Roll 591, RWP.

57 Caruthers, *Revolutionary Sketches*, 136, 146–48; pension application of Gideon Johnson, 2 Oct. 1832, Roll 473, RWP.

58 Richard Harrison to Anne Harrison, 15 Mar. 1781, in Browning, *American Historical and Monthly Gazette*, 1123–24; Buchanan, *Road to Guilford Courthouse*, 373.

59 Pension applications of William Lesley, 3 Sept. 1832, Roll 524, David Williams, 23 Aug. 1832, Roll 871, RWP.

60 Caruthers, *Revolutionary Sketches*, 134.

CHAPTER FOUR

1 Bass, *Green Dragoon*, 5–18; Raddall, "Tarleton's Legion." Perhaps the best, and certainly the most current, research on Tarleton is in Scotti, *Brutal Virtue*. Babits, *Devil of a Whipping* provides a thorough analysis of the Cowpens engagement.

2 Raddall, "Tarleton's Legion"; Babits, *Devil of a Whipping*, 46–47. See also Cannon, *Historical Record of the Seventeenth Light Dragoons*.

3 A few of the multitude of secondary sources available concerning the German mercenaries in the Revolution include Eelking, *German Allied Troops*; Atwood, *Hessians*; Lowell, *Hessians and Other German Auxiliaries*.

4 "Field Return of the Troops under the Command of Lieutenant-General Earl Cornwallis in the Action at Guilford, 15 March 1781," British Headquarters Papers, WLCL. "State of the Troops That Marched with the Army under the Command of Lieutenant-General Earl Cornwallis," Charles Cornwallis Papers, PRO 30/11/5, NAE, shows the jaegers as having 97 men; however, only 84 took part in the battle. This is because a sergeant and 12 privates were on detached duty prior to the engagement. Accounts differ whether these men were Ansbach or Hessian; however, they are not the Hessian company led by Johann Ewald at Yorktown, as they remained in Wilmington when Cornwallis marched to Virginia from that city in April 1781. A 17 July 1781 muster roll titled "Compagnie des Chasseurs du Capitaine de Roder, des Trouppers pour son Altesse Serenissime le Margrave de Brandenbourg Anspac pour 182 Jours de 25me Decbr. 1780 jusqu'au 24me Juin 1781," Treasury Office Papers, TO 38/812, NAE, clearly shows that only a portion of von Roeder's company was deployed with Cornwallis. The document lists 42 men as being on detached service in Virginia out of a total strength of 114, indicating the remainder of the unit came from another jaeger company. Further information on the jaegers comes from Burgoyne, *Ansbach-Bayreuth Diaries* and *Diaries of Two Ansbach Jägers*; Ewald, *Diary of the American War*.

5 Information on the Guards Brigade on American service can be gleaned from Thomas Glyn's journal, transcribed by Bass. See F. Hamilton, *Origin and History*; MacKinnon, *Origin and Services*; Burke and Bass, "Preparing a British Unit"; William Howe Orderly Book, 1776–78, WLCL; Orders, Returns, Morning Reports, and Accounts of British Troops 1776–81, and Field Return of the Troops . . . 15 Mar. 1781, British Headquarters Papers, WLCL. See also Burke and Bass, "Brigade of Guards"; and Bass, "Company and Battalion Organization" (unpublished manuscripts).

6 Chambers, *Traditions of Edinburgh*; Clinton, *American Rebellion*, 95, 131; Tarleton, *Campaigns*, 281.

7 See Glover, *That Astonishing Infantry*; McCance and Cary, *Regimental Records*; Urban, *Fusiliers*.

8 "Field Return of the Troops . . . 15 March 1781," British Headquarters Papers, WLCL; Urban, *Fusiliers*, 203, 212, 214. Urban's work is the best study of the 23rd Foot available; Webster's brigade detached 1 captain (Henry Broderick of the 33rd), 2 subalterns, 3 sergeants, 3 corporals, and 45 privates, but it is unclear how many of these men were from the 23rd Foot, or if the figure given in the 15

March field return included them. For an analysis of British regimental tactics that demonstrates the commonality of the use of wings, see Spring, *With Zeal and Bayonets Only*.

9  See Savory and Brereton, *History of Wellington's Regiment*; A. Lee, *History of the Thirty-Third Foot*; Lamb, *Memoir*, 90.

10  Field Return of the Troops . . . 15 March 1781, British Headquarters Papers, WLCL; Lamb, *Memoir*, 90; Nathanael Green to Edward Carrington, 11 Mar. 1781, in Showman et al., *Papers of General Nathanael Greene*, 7:342n, 425–26.

11  Muster rolls of the 33rd Foot, War Office Papers, WO 12/4803, part 1, NAE. Frey, *The British Soldier in America*, one of the finest studies available concerning the British redcoats of the American Revolution, makes a convincing argument that combat cohesiveness was directly related to the bonds of brotherhood established among British enlisted men through long service together in their respective regiments. However, Houlding, *Fit for Service*, and Spring, *With Zeal and Bayonets Only*, have demonstrated that the ranks of British regiments were often in great flux, with men coming and going, making it unlikely that such men were able to establish any long-standing sort of brotherhood. Spring makes the point that in some regiments nearly one-fifth of the unit was young and inexperienced soldiers with less than three years' service prior to the war. Yet, this still means that four-fifths of the regiment, the overwhelming majority, had substantial service. Furthermore, years in service do not automatically dictate the formation of bonds of comradeship. Men who served together for three years are theoretically just as likely to form such bonds as those with longer service periods. Some of the finest American infantry regiments to see action in World War II had less than two years' training together before they deployed and yet still became renowned for their fighting abilities. The evidence suggests that, although the average British soldiers may not have been the thirty-three-year-old veterans with ten years' service put forth by Frey, they were still men of experience who had become bonded by their shared experiences.

12  Selesky and Boatner, *Encyclopedia of the American Revolution*; Kay, *Series of Original Portraits*, 2, sketch 197; Peebles, *Diary of a Scottish Grenadier*, 340, 379, 390.

13  Conway, "British Mobilization"; Babits, "Shoe Life in the 71st Foot" and *Devil of a Whipping*, 44–45.

14  "Field Return of the Troops . . . 15 March 1781," British Headquarters Papers, WLCL; Troiani, Coates, and Kochan, *Soldiers in America*, 43. See the Application for Pension by Sarah Pearsall Campbell, in the Letters of Thomas Pearsall, Bayard-Pearsall-Campbell Papers, New York Public Library Rare Books and Manuscripts Room, New York, N.Y.; Robert Hutcheson to Cornwallis, 9 April 1781, Cornwallis Papers.

15  Atwood, *Hessians*, 138–39.

16  Field Return of the Troops . . . 15 March 1781, British Headquarters Papers, WLCL; Atwood, *Hessians*, 138–39; Simcoe, *Simcoe's Military Journal*, 140–42.

17  Johann Christian Du Buy to Wilhelm von Knyphausen, 24 Apr. 1781, in Bestand 4h, Nr. 3101, Hessisches Staatsarchiv Marburg, Lidgerwood Collection of Hessian Transcripts, Morristown National Historical Park, Morristown, N.J.

18  Burke and Bass, "Brigade of Guards"; Bass, "Company and Battalion Organization"; Howe Orderly Book, 1776–78, WLCL.

19  Burke and Bass, "Brigade of Guards"; Bass, "Company and Battalion Organization."

20  Howe Orderly Book, 1776–78, WLCL; "Orderly Book: British Regiment Foot Guards, New York and New Jersey" (covering Aug. 1776–Jan. 1777), reel 3, doc. 37, "Orderly Book: Second Brigade, British Foot Guards, New York" (covering Aug.–Dec. 1778), reel 6, doc. 65, "Orderly Book: First Battalion of Guards, British Army, New York" (covering all but a few days of 1779), reel 6, doc. 77, *Early American Orderly Books Series* (microfilm), Research Publications (Woodbridge, Conn., 1977); Almon, *Remembrancer*, 2:366. See Burke and Bass, "Preparing a British Unit"; Newsome, "British Orderly Book," 57–78, 163–86, 273–90 366–92; "Orderly Book: Brigade of Guards, Commencing 29th January 1778," George Washington Papers, Series 6B, vol. 4, reel 118, Presidential Papers Microfilm, Library of Congress.

21  Brydges, *Collins' Peerage of England*, 168.

22  Griffin, "General Charles O'Hara"; Walpole, *Correspondence*, 18:104.

23  Griffin, "General Charles O'Hara," 180–82.

24  Clinton, *American Rebellion*, 100n; Wickwire and Wickwire, *Cornwallis*, 171; Clinton, "Sir Henry Clinton's Review," 370.

25  Field Return of the Troops . . . 15 Mar. 1781, British Headquarters Papers, WLCL; Burke and Bass, "Guards in the Battle"; "Return of the Troops at Guilford Courthouse, Enclosed in a Letter to General Leslie," Government Papers, GD 26/9/523, Scottish National Archives, Edinburgh.

26  Gilbert and Baule, *British Army Officers*, 138, 164; Tarleton, *Campaigns*, 312; Duncan, *History of the Royal Artillery Regiment*, 1:367–68.

27  Newsome, "British Orderly Book," 387–88; Nathanael Greene to Edward Carrington, 11 Mar. 1781, in Showman et al., *Papers of General Nathanael Greene*, 7:324n, 425–26.

28  Charles Cornwallis to George Germain, 17 Mar. 1781, Cornwallis Papers, PRO 30/11/76, NAE; pension application of Jeremiah Gurley, 30 Oct. 1832, Roll 383, RWP; Hagist, "Unpublished Military Writings." For an excellent analysis of the tactics of the British Army in North America and a detailed examination of the

maneuvering of British regiments on the field, see Spring, *With Zeal and Bayonets Only*.

29 Cornwallis to Germain, 17 Mar. 1781; Tarleton, *Campaigns*, 271–73, 275; Newsome, "British Orderly Book," 377, 385–86. A careful analysis of the "British Orderly Book," British army field returns, and Cornwallis's correspondence indicates that the British had four six-pounders and two three-pounders. The company (battery) had three lieutenants, seven sergeants and forty rank and file present on the day of the battle.

30 Tarleton, *Campaigns*, 273; Caruthers, *Revolutionary Sketches*, 142.

31 Cornwallis to Germain, 17 Mar. 1781; Johann Christian Du Buy to Wilhelm Von Knyphausen, 18 Apr. 1781, transcript with English translation in the Lidgerwood Collection, Morristown National Historical Park, Morristown, N.J.

32 Cornwallis to Germain, 17 Mar. 1781.

33 Du Buy to Knyphausen, 18 Apr. 1781.

34 "Journal of Thomas Saumarez," quoted in McCance and Cary, *Regimental Records*, 1:180; Lamb, *Memoir*, 360–61; Cornwallis to Germain, 17 Mar. 1781.

CHAPTER FIVE

1 "Statement of Abram Forney," in Schenk, *North Carolina*, 304–5; Garden, *Anecdotes of the American Revolution*, 40.

2 Harvey, *Manual Exercise*, 13; Pickering, *Easy Plan of Discipline for a Militia*, 41; G. Smith, *Universal Military Dictionary*, 198. A table showing distance versus time is provided in Babits, *Devil of a Whipping*, 114. The best analysis of British marching steps in relation to tactics is provided in Spring, *With Zeal and Bayonets Only*.

3 "Journal of Thomas Saumarez," in McCance and Cary, *Regimental Records*, 1:180.

4 Koch, *Battle of Guilford Courthouse*, 7–8.

5 Babits, *Devil of a Whipping*, 15–20; journal of Lt. Harry Calvert, 23rd Foot, Claydon House, Buckinghamshire, England. Calvert's journal clearly states that the Americans fired their first volley at 50 yards.

6 William Campbell to Charles Cummings, 28 Mar. 1781, in *Bulletin of the New York Public Library*, 9:464–65.

7 Pension application of James Martin, 5 Oct. 1832, Roll 555, RWP; Samuel Houston, "Houston's Journal," in Foote, *Sketches of Virginia*, 144–45; Lamb, *Memoir*, 361; Dugald Stuart (Stewart) to Unknown, 25 Oct. 1832, quoted in Caruthers, *Revolutionary Sketches*, 140.

8 Tarleton, *Campaigns*, 271–72; Lamb, *Memoir*, 361.

9 Lamb, *Memoir*, 361; Calvert Journal, Claydon House, Buckinghamshire, England.

10 Lamb, *Memoir*, 361; McCance and Cary, *Regimental Records*, 1:180–81.

11 Howard, Brenckle, and Babits, "Rifle Shot."

12 Babits, *Devil of a Whipping*, 114; Caruthers, *Revolutionary Sketches*, 140–41; pension applications of John Watkins, 27 Aug. 1832, Roll 829, and William Montgomery, 11 Sept. 1832, Roll 593, RWP; Houston, "Houston's Journal," 146–47.

13 Koch, *Battle of Guilford Courthouse*, 7; pension application of Nathan Slade, 3 July 1845, Roll 742, RWP.

14 McCance and Cary, *Regimental Records*, 1:180–82; Calvert journal, Claydon House, Buckinghamshire, England; Babits and Howard, "Guilford Veterans Database"; pension applications of Jeremiah Gurley, 30 Oct. 1832, Roll 383, William Griffis, 6 June 1836, Roll 379, John Dowtin, 28 Aug. 1832, Roll 281, Peter Bailey, 24 Apr. 1834, Roll 39, Elijah Hooten, 16 Apr. 1834, Roll 440, Zachariah Jacobs, 13 Dec. 1832, Roll 466, RWP.

15 Babits and Howard, "Guilford Veterans Database"; pension applications of William Boyce, 5 Oct. 1847, Roll 110, Eles Chaffin, 3 June 1833, Roll 172, RWP; Johann Christian Du Buy to Lieutenant-General Wilhelm Von Knyphausen, 18 Apr. 1781, in Bestand 4h, Nr. 3101, Hessisches Staatsarchiv Marburg, Lidgerwood Collection, Morristown National Historical Park, Morristown, N.J.

16 Nathanael Greene to Samuel Huntington, 16 Mar. 1781, Greene to Joseph Reed, 18 Mar. 1781, Greene to Daniel Morgan, 20 Mar. 1781, in Showman et al., *Papers of General Nathanael Greene*, 7:433–36, 448–51, 455–56.

17 H. Lee, *Memoirs*, 1:344–45.

18 Tarleton, *Campaigns*, 273; Koch, *Battle of Guilford Courthouse*, 7–8; Du Buy to Knyphausen, 18 Apr. 1781.

19 Houston, "Houston's Journal," 146–47; Caruthers, *Revolutionary Sketches*, 136, 141–42; pension application of Nathan Slade, 3 July 1845, Roll 742, RWP.

20 Caruthers, *Revolutionary Sketches*, 139, 146–48; Koch, *Battle of Guilford Courthouse*, 7; Du Buy to Von Knyphausen, 18 Apr. 1781; Houston, "Houston's Journal," 145–47.

21 Pension application of Henry Connelly, 15 Aug. 1833, Roll 212, RWP. See Caruthers, *Revolutionary Sketches*, 141–43, 146–47, for the stories of Wiley, Paisley, and Sartain.

22 Pension applications of William Lesley, 3 Sept. 1832, Roll 524, Elihu Ayers, 16 Nov. 1832, Roll 34, John Amos, 8 Sept. 1818, Roll 18, Westwood Armistead, 27 Aug. 1844, Roll 25, RWP; McCance and Cary, *Regimental Records*, 1:180–81.

23 Greene to Samuel Huntington, 16 Mar. 1781, in Showman et al., *Papers of General Nathanael Greene*, 7:434–35; H. Lee, *Memoirs*, 1:344–46; Davie, *Revolutionary War Sketches*, 31–33; pension application of Nathan Slade, 3 July 1845, Roll 742,

RWP; Caruthers, *Revolutionary Sketches*, 141–42; McCance and Cary, *Regimental Records*, 1:180–82

24 S. Graham, "Account."

25 Seymour, "Journal," 378–79; Caruthers, *Revolutionary Sketches*, 146.

26 Charles Cornwallis to George Germain, 17 Mar. 1781, Cornwallis Papers, PRO 30/11/76, NAE.

27 H. Lee, *Memoirs*, 1:341–42; Cornwallis to Germain, 17 Mar. 1781; S. Graham, "Account," 270; Tarleton, *Campaigns*, 276.

28 Pension application of Andrew Wiley, 1 Oct. 1832, Roll 868, RWP.


CHAPTER SIX

1 Pension application of William Dix, 8 May 1851, Roll 272, RWP; St. George Tucker to Frances Tucker, 17 Mar. 1781, in Tucker, "Southern Campaign, 1781."

2 St. George Tucker to Frances Tucker, 17 Mar. 1781.

3 Pension application of John Chumbley, 15 May 1833, Roll 184, RWP.

4 St. George Tucker to Frances Tucker, 18 Mar. 1781, in Tucker, "Southern Campaign"; Chumbley pension application; pension applications of William Ligon, 17 Aug. 1832, Roll 328, John Campbell, 21 Sept. 1832, Roll 156, RWP.

5 St. George Tucker to Frances Tucker, 17 Mar. 1781.

6 Lamb, *Memoir*, 175.

7 Ibid.

8 McCance and Cary, *Regimental Records of the Royal Welch*, 1:180; Chumbley pension application; Lamb, *Original and Authentic Journal*, 362.

9 St. George Tucker to Frances Tucker, 17 Mar. 1781.

10 Pension applications of Thomas Berry, 3 Oct. 1832, Roll 82, Bartlett Cox, 8 Oct. 1835, Roll 225, Jeremiah Dupree, 22 Apr. 1833, Roll 288, RWP.

11 Groh and Cornelison, *Battle Lines and Courthouses*, 22–23; Tarleton, *Campaigns*, 275; H. Lee Jr., *Campaign of 1781*, 172–73; Lamb, *Original and Authentic Journal*, 362.

12 John Eager Howard to John Marshall, unknown date, 1804, Bayard Papers, MHS.

13 Pension applications of Henry Adams, 24 Sept. 1832, Roll 4, Henry Brown, 22 Oct. 1832, Roll 128, Hubbard Brown, 20 Mar. 1834, Roll 128, Thomas Brown, 30 Aug. 1832, Roll 132, RWP; Edward Burress obituary, *Vital Statistics of the National Intelligencer*, 25 Oct. 1830; pension applications of Thomas Cook, 7 Nov. 1839, Roll 216, Nathanael Harris, 5 May 1834, Roll 402, Samuel Davison, 11 Oct. 1826, Roll 256, RWP.

14 Henry Brown and Hubbard Brown pension applications; disability affidavits of

Moses Hendricks, Isaac Ready, and Robert Church, Virginia State Library, Richmond.

15 Pension applications of Abraham Hamman, 13 Nov. 1832, Roll 393, Chelsey Calloway, 6 May 1833, Roll 154, RWP.

16 Charles Cornwallis to George Germain, 17 Mar. 1781, in Cornwallis Papers, PRO 30/11/76, NAE.

17 Samuel Houston, "Houston's Journal," in Foote, *Sketches of Virginia*, 143–45; disability affidavits for Phillip Russell and Nathan Rowland, Virginia State Library; pension applications of James Atkinson, 26 Dec. 1833, Roll 30, John Atkinson, 26 Feb. 1834, Roll 30, Thomas George, 18 Sept. 1832, Roll 303, RWP.

18 Otho Holland Williams to Elie Williams, 16 Mar. 1781, Williams Papers, MHS.

19 Pension applications of Thomas Anderson, 23 Oct. 1832, Roll 20, John Blankenship, 5 Sept. 1832, Roll 97, John Arrington, 29 Nov. 1832, Roll 28, Daniel McKee, 25 Sept. 1833, Roll 572, RWP; disability affidavit of James Speed, Virginia State Library; pension application of Nathaniel Cocke, 6 May 1830, Roll 199, RWP; Houston, "Houston's Journal," 145–46.

20 Pension applications of Joseph Ligon, 8 Jan. 1837, Roll 528, Ned Tuck, 3 Jan. 1822, Roll 813, Reese Gullet, 7 May 1836, Roll 383, Joseph Forsyth, 31 Oct. 1832, Roll 330, George Anderson, 26 Dec. 1846, Roll 19, Frederick Burkett, 10 June 1833, Roll 142, William Gaulding, 6 Apr. 1832, Roll 351, William Harris, 14 May 1839, Roll 402, RWP.

21 Stedman, *History of the American War*, 2:341–43; Cornwallis to Germain, 17 Mar. 1781; Rogers, "Letters of Charles O'Hara," 177–78.

22 H. Lee, *Memoirs*, 1:344–45; pension applications of John Weatherford, 12 Aug. 1845, Roll, 844, William Cocke, 4 Aug. 1832, Roll 199, Christopher Hand, 31 Dec. 1832, Roll 394, RWP.

23 Pension application of Isham East, 15 Sept. 1832, Roll 293, RWP.

24 Houston, "Houston's Journal," 146–47.

25 William Campbell to Reverend Charles Cummings, 28 Mar. 1781, in *Bulletin of the New York Public Library*, 9:464–65; Charles Magill to Thomas Jefferson, 16 Mar. 1781, in Cullen et al., *Papers of Thomas Jefferson*, 7:162–63; Davie, *Revolutionary War Sketches*, 62–63; Otho Holland Williams to Elie Williams, 16 Mar. 1781, Williams Papers, MHS.

CHAPTER SEVEN

1 Tarleton, *Campaigns*, 275.

2 Ibid.

3 Samuel Houston, "Houston's Journal," in Foote, *Sketches of Virginia*; Stedman, *History of the American War*, 2:341.

4  Stedman, *History of the American War*, 2:342–44.

5  Ibid., 342–43, 345n–46n.

6  Stuart, "Memoir," 242–48; pension application of Samuel Kennerly, 11 Nov. 1834, Roll 492, RWP.

7  Johann Christian Du Buy to Wilhelm von Knyphausen, 18 Apr. 1781, in Bestand 4h, Nr. 3101, Hessisches Staatsarchiv Marburg, Lidgerwood Collection of Hessian Transcripts, Morristown National Historical Park, Morristown, N.J.; Journal of the Honourable Hessian Infantry Regiment Von Bose, ibid.

8  Stedman, *History of the American War*, 2:341–43.

9  Ibid., 341–42; Tarleton, *Campaigns*, 273; H. Lee, *Memoirs*, 1:345–46; Du Buy to Knyphausen, 18 Apr. 1781.

10  Koch, *Battle of Guilford Courthouse*, 7–9; Du Buy to Knyphausen, 18 Apr. 1781; Journal of the Hessian Infantry Regiment.

11  Koch, *Battle of Guilford Courthouse*, 8–10; Hessian casualties extracted from the Journal of the Hessian Infantry Regiment and the *Hetrina*, vol. 2.

12  Pension application of Andrew Wiley, 1 Oct. 1832, Roll 868, RWP; "Return of the Killed, Wounded, and Missing of the Troops under the Command of Lieut. Genl. Earl Cornwallis in the Action at Guilford 15th March 1781," Cornwallis Papers, PRO 30/11/103, NAE; *Hetrina*, vol. 2.

13  Caruthers, *Revolutionary Sketches*, 137; Houston, "Houston's Journal," 143–44.

14  Houston, "Houston's Journal," 147; Waddell, *Annals of Augusta County*, 282; pension application of James Braden, 13 Nov. 1837, Roll 113, RWP; disability affidavit of Samuel Kirkpatrick (1787), Virginia State Library, Richmond; pension applications of Matthew Amix, 15 Dec. 1826, Roll 18, Joshua Davidson, 22 Apr. 1833, Roll 249, Samuel Kennerly, 11 Nov. 1834, Roll 492, RWP.

15  Pension applications of Isaac Robinson, 3 Dec. 1832, Roll 697, James Fugate, 4 July 1842, Roll 342, RWP.

16  Stedman, *History of the American War*, 2:343; Tarleton, *Campaigns*, 275–76.

17  Tarleton, *Campaigns*, 275–76; Stedman, *History of the American War*, 2:343; Du Buy to Knyphausen, 18 Apr. 1781; John Eager Howard to John Marshall, unknown date, 1804, Bayard Papers, MHS.

18  H. Lee Jr., *Campaign of 1781*, 175–76.

19  Houston, "Houston's Journal"; Caruthers, *Revolutionary Sketches*, 142, 157–59; pension application of David Gamble, 10 Sept. 1832, Roll 347, RWP.

20  Chastellux, *Travels in North America*, 2:402–3; pension application of David Steele, 2 Dec. 1820, Roll 768, RWP.

21  Waddell, *Annals of Augusta County*, 282–83; pension application of Joseph Horton, 18 Sept. 1832, Roll 443, RWP.

22  H. Lee, *Memoirs*, 1:339; Du Buy to Knyphausen, 18 Apr. 1781.

CHAPTER EIGHT

1 Scheer and Rankin, *Rebels and Redcoats*, 449; J. Marshall, *Life of George Washington*, 1:413.

2 John Eager Howard to John Marshall, unknown date, 1804, Bayard Papers, MHS. The gap occasioned by the gully and the copse can still be seen in aerial images of the vale's eastern slope today. The gully is almost certainly the one Washington's cavalry leapt over later in the third line fighting. The woods were dense enough that activity on one side could not be seen from the other.

3 St. George Tucker to Frances Tucker, 17 Mar. 1781, in Tucker, "Southern Campaign, 1781."

4 The west-trending ridge is clearly shown on topographic maps generated before widespread housing development obscured the landscape. The topographic maps provide clarity to the Tarleton map.

5 H. Lee, *Memoirs*, 1:346.

6 Ibid.

7 Davie, *Revolutionary Sketches*, 56–58.

8 Seymour, "Journal," 378–79

9 Ibid.

10 Ibid., 378; Howard to Marshall, 1804.

11 Charles Cornwallis to George Germain, 17 Mar. 1781, Cornwallis Papers, PRO 30/11/76, NAE; H. Lee, *Memoirs*, 1:347.

12 The quote about distance is from Howard to Marshall, 1804. Information about the shifting of personnel can be found in widely scattered references in *Maryland Archives*, 18:389, where one 1st Maryland Company roll mentions two NCOs from the "State Regt, joined 12 Mch '81."

13 Howard to Marshall, 1804.

14 Davie, *Revolutionary Sketches*, 57–58.

15 H. Lee Jr., *Campaign of 1781*, 187.

16 S. L. A. Marshall, *Soldier's Load*, 46; Fletcher, *Rebel Private Front and Rear*, 23.

17 Otho Holland Williams to Josiah Carvell Hall, 17 Mar. 1781, Guilford Courthouse National Military Park Library Collection, Greensboro, N.C.; James Armstrong to Mordecai Gist, 18 Mar. 1781, Mordecai Gist Papers, MHS; Cornwallis to Germain, 17 Mar. 1781; Howard to Marshall, 1804.

18 Tarleton, *Campaigns*, 274.

19 Pension applications of Thomas Ralph, 17 July 1820, Roll 673, Zachariah Elliott, 6 Jan. 1836, Roll 300, Zachariah Jacobs, 13 Dec. 1832, Roll 466, RWP.

20 Howard to Marshall, 1804.

21 Ibid.; Cornwallis to Germain, 17 Mar. 1781.

22 Howard to Marshall, 1804; pension application of Daniel Slade, 3 July 1845, Roll 742, RWP; Caruthers, *Revolutionary Sketches*, 136, 141–42.

23  Tarleton, *Campaigns*, 274–76; Cornwallis to Germain, 17 Mar. 1781.

24  Howard to Marshall, 1804; pension application of John Watkins, 27 Aug. 1832, Roll 829, RWP.

25  Pension application of Philemon Holcombe, 14 Apr. 1834, Roll 434, RWP.

26  Howard to Marshall, 1804.

27  Grossman, *On Killing*, 120.

28  Ibid., 122. Bayonet wounds are mentioned in Maryland and Delaware pensions referencing injuries received at Camden, Cowpens, Guilford Courthouse, Hobkirk's Hill, Ninety Six, and Eutaw Springs.

29  Thomas Hardy, "The Man He Killed," in Monroe and Henderson, *New Poetry*, 132; Williams to Hall, 17 Mar. 1781; Nathanael Greene to Samuel Huntington, 16 Mar. 1781, in Showman et al., *Papers of General Nathanael Greene*, 7:433–34.

30  Samuel Mathis to William R. Davie, 26 June 1819, Ms. on file, Historic Camden, Camden, South Carolina.

31  Ibid.; pension application of Hezekiah Carr, 18 Apr. 1818, Roll 164, RWP.

32  Garden, *Anecdotes of the American Revolution*, 186–87.

33  Lossing, *Pictorial Fieldbook of the Revolution*, 2:404. See also Shaffer, *Peter Francisco*; Moon, *Peter Francisco*.

34  "Letter from Peter Francisco to the Virginia General Assembly, November 11, 1820," *William and Mary Quarterly* 13 (1905): 217–19.

35  Howard to Marshall, 1804; Cornwallis to Germain, 17 Mar. 1781; James F. Armstrong to Mordecai Gist, 17 Mar. 1781, Mordecai Gist Papers, MHS.

36  H. Lee, *Memoirs*, 1:348, 353.

37  Howard to Marshall, 1804.

38  Johnson, *Sketches*, 21; St. George Tucker, "To Col. Lovelace of the British Guards, Who Counterfeited Death at the Battle of Guilford, March 15, 1781," Historical Society of Pennsylvania, Philadelphia; Robert Lovelace to Charles Cornwallis, 17 Apr. 1781, cited in Burke and Bass, "Guards in the Battle" (unpublished manuscript).

39  Cornwallis to Germain, 17 Mar. 1781.

40  Tarleton, *Campaigns*, 274–75; Cornwallis to Germain, 17 Mar. 1781.

41  Nathanael Greene to Samuel Huntington, 16 Mar. 1781, Greene to Catherine Greene, 18 Mar. 1781, in Showman et al., *Papers of General Nathanael Greene*, 7:433–34, 446. H. Lee, *Memoirs*, 1:353, cites Nathaniel Pendleton as the aide who saved Greene, but Greene's own writing says that it was Lewis Morris.

42  H. Lee, *Memoirs*, 1:353–54.

43  Pension application of Lewis Griffin, 6 Aug. 1833, Roll 378, RWP; Charles Magill to Thomas Jefferson, 16 Mar. 1781, in Cullen et al., *Papers of Thomas Jefferson*, 5:162–63.

44  H. Lee, *Memoirs*, 1:353; Otho H. Williams to Josiah Carvell Hall, 17 Mar. 1781,

Guilford Courthouse National Military Park Library Collection, Greensboro, North Carolina.

45 McCance and Cary, *Regimental Records*, 1:180–81.

46 Morton, "Col. William Morton"; pension application of Lewis Griffin, 6 Aug. 1833, Roll 378, RWP.

47 Williams to Hall, 17 Mar. 1781; Charles Magill to Thomas Jefferson, 16 Mar. 1781, in Cullen et al., *Papers of Thomas Jefferson*, 5:162–63; St. George Tucker to Frances Tucker, 17 Mar. 1781.

48 McCance and Cary, *Regimental Records*, 1:180–81; S. Graham, "Account," 267–68.

49 St. George Tucker to Frances Tucker, 17 Mar. 1781.

50 Caruthers, *Revolutionary Sketches*, 148.

51 Pension application of Josiah Grigg, 19 Nov. 1832, Roll 379, RWP.

CHAPTER NINE

1 Pension application of John Chumbley, 15 May 1833, Roll 184, RWP; Otho H. Williams to Josiah Carvell Hall, 17 Mar. 1781, Guilford Courthouse National Military Park Library Collection, Greensboro, N.C.; Greene to Morgan, 20 Mar. 1781, Greene to Samuel Huntington, 23 Mar. 1781, in Showman et al., *Papers of General Nathanael Greene*, 7:455–56, 464–66.

2 Samuel Houston, "Houston's Journal," in Foote, *Sketches of Virginia*; William Campbell to Reverend Charles Cummings, 28 Mar. 1781, *Bulletin of the New York Public Library*, 9:464–65.

3 Stedman, *History of the American War*, 2:346; Charles O'Hara to Augustus Henry Fitzroy, the Duke of Grafton, 20 Apr. 1781, in Rogers, "Letters of Charles O'Hara," 177–78.

4 Charles Cornwallis to George Germain, 17 Mar. 1781, Cornwallis Papers, PRO 30/11/76, NEA.

5 Gilbert and Baule, *British Army Officers*, 36, 38, 90, 156. Information gleaned from the muster rolls of the Von Bose in the *Hetrina*, vol. 3; Heitman, *Historical Register*, 194, 247, 442, 566, 568; Pindell, "Militant Surgeon"; Nathanael Greene to Charles Cornwallis, 16 Mar. 1781, Dr. James Browne to Capt. William Pierce Jr., 2 Apr. 1781, in Showman et al., *Papers of General Nathanael Greene*, 7:26, 433.

6 "Return of the Killed, Wounded, and Missing of the Troops under the Command of Lieut. Genl. Earl Cornwallis in the Action at Guilford 15th March 1781," Cornwallis Papers, PRO 30/11/103, NAE. See "Return of the Wounded at New Garden Meeting House," in Cornwallis Papers, PRO 30/11/65, NAE.

7 Garden, *Anecdotes of the Revolutionary War*, 310–11; "Return of the Killed, Wounded, and Missing"; Stuart, "Memoir," 242–48.

8   "Return of the Killed, Wounded, and Missing."

9   Lamb, *American War*, 360n; Charles Cornwallis to Dr. Webster, 23 Apr. 1781, in
    Ross, *Correspondence of Cornwallis*, 1:93.

10  "Return of the Killed, Wounded, and Missing"; *Hetrina*, vol. 3.

11  "Return of the Killed, Wounded, and Missing."

12  Otho Holland Williams, "Field Return, March 17, 1781," *Papers of the Continen-
    tal Congress*, 2:9–11, item 155, National Archives, Washington, D.C.; Babits and
    Howard, "Guilford Veterans Database."

13  Babits and Howard, "Guilford Veterans Database"; Caruthers, *Revolutionary
    Sketches*, 135–43.

14  St. George Tucker to Frances Tucker, 18 Mar. 1781, in Tucker, "Southern Cam-
    paign, 1781"; O. H. Williams, "Field Return"; Babits and Howard, "Guilford Vet-
    erans Database."

15  O. H. Williams, "Field Return"; Caruthers, *Revolutionary Sketches*, 148.

16  Babits and Howard, "Guilford Veterans Database"; Houston, "Journal"; O. H.
    Williams, "Field Return."

17  O. H. Williams, "Field Return"; Babits and Howard, "Guilford Veterans Data-
    base."

18  O. H. Williams, "Field Return"; "Return of the Men Killed and Wounded in Capt.
    Kirkwood's Light Infantry in Ye Action at Guilford Court House, 15 March 1781,"
    in *Delaware Archives*, 1:225, 2:1343.

19  O. H. Williams, "Field Return"; Babits and Howard, "Guilford Veterans Data-
    base."

20  O. H. Williams, "Field Return"; Babits and Howard, "Guilford Veterans Data-
    base."

21  O. H. Williams, "Field Return"; Babits and Howard, "Guilford Veterans Data-
    base." See "Return of the Hospital at Guilford, from March 15 to April 2," and
    "Return of the Hospital at Prince Edward from February 20 to March 20, 1781,"
    Nathanael Greene Papers, WLCL.

22  "Account of Articles Received at New Garden Meetinghouse for the Use of the
    Wounded," in "Return of the Killed, Wounded, and Missing"; Charles Corn-
    wallis to Nathanael Greene, 16 Mar. 1781, Greene to Cornwallis, 16 Mar. 1781,
    in Showman et al., *Papers of General Nathanael Greene* 7:433, 443; Caruthers,
    *Revolutionary Sketches*, 140. See "Return of the Hospital at Guilford, from March
    15 to April 2" and "Return of the Hospital at Prince Edward from February 20 to
    March 20, 1781."

23  See "Account of the Prisoners Taken at Guilford Received from Henry Whittles,
    Provost Marshall," in Cornwallis Papers, PRO 30/11/65; pension application of
    Robert Fulton, 28 Oct. 1833, Roll 344, RWP; Cornwallis to Germain, 17 Mar. 1781;

Seymour, "Journal," 379; "General Greene's Orders," 1 Apr. 1781, in Showman et al., *Papers of General Nathanael Greene*, 8:19.

24  Charles Cornwallis to Sir Henry Clinton, 10 Apr. 1781, in Clinton, *American Rebellion*, 508.

25  Abner Nash to Nathanael Greene, 7 Apr. 1781, in Showman et al., *Papers of General Nathanael Greene*, 8:64; Cornwallis to Germain, 17 Mar. 1781; Cornwallis to William Phillips, 10 Apr. 1781, in Ross, *Correspondence of Cornwallis*, 1:88.

26  "General Greene's Orders," 6 Apr. 1781, Nathanael Greene to George Washington, 29 Mar. 1781, in Showman et al., *Papers of General Nathanael Greene*, 8:58, 7:481–82. For Lee's assertion that he gave Greene the idea, see H. Lee, *Memoirs*, 2:40.

27  Pancake, *Destructive War*, 191–93.

28  Ibid., 196–97.

29  Nathanael Greene to Samuel Huntington, 27 Apr. 1781, in Showman et al., *Papers of General Nathanael Greene*, 8:155–58; Francis Rawdon to Cornwallis, 26 Apr. 1781, Cornwallis Papers, PRO 30/11/6; John Eager Howard to Henry Lee Jr., 19 Jan. 1819, quoted in H. Lee Jr., *Campaign of 1781*, 262.

30  Otho Holland Williams, "List of the Officers Killed, Wounded, and Taken Prisoner in the Action before Camden, the 25th of April 1781," cited in Tarleton, *Campaigns*, 470.

31  Samuel Mathis to William R. Davie, June 26, 1819, in Davie, *Revolutionary Sketches*.

32  Ibid.; Nathanael Greene to Lord Rawdon, 28 Apr. 1781, Major John Doyle to Greene, 29 Apr. 1781, Captain John Smith to Greene, 30 Apr. 1781, Greene to Lord Rawdon, 3 May 1781, in Showman et al., *Papers of General Nathanael Greene*, 8:169, 174, 180–81, 95–96.

33  Pension application of Guilford Dudley, 12 Oct. 1832, Roll 284, RWP; John Smith to Otho Holland Williams, 21 May 1781, MHS; Johnson, *Sketches*, 2:97.

34  Pancake, *Destructive War*, 200–218; H. Lee, *Memoirs*, 2:74–85; Henry Lee to Nathanael Greene, 23 Apr. 1781, Francis Marion to Greene, 23 Apr. 1781, in Showman et al., *Papers of General Nathanael Greene*, 8:xi–xiii, 139–43.

35  Pancake, *Destructive War*, 200–218; Bass, *Ninety-Six*. Benson's rescue is documented in Calderhead, "Thomas Carney"; "General Greene's Orders," in Showman et al., *Papers of General Nathanael Greene*, 8:408–9.

36  Pancake, *Destructive War*, 216–21; Piecuch, "Battle of Eutaw Springs."

37  Piecuch, "Battle of Eutaw Springs," 30–37.

38  Nathanael Greene to Chevalier de La Luzerne, 28 Apr. 1781, in Showman et al., *Papers of Nathanael Greene*, 8:167–68. Greene used a similar phrase, "We get fight, get beat, and fight again," in a letter to George Washington on 1 May; see ibid, 8:185–86.

39 Cornwallis, *Answer*, viii.

40 Cornwallis to Henry Clinton, 10 Apr. 1781, in Ross, *Correspondence of Cornwallis*, 1:88; Cornwallis, *Answer*, 10–14; Clinton to Cornwallis, 13 Apr. 1781, in Cornwallis, *Answer*, 18–20; William Phillips to Henry Clinton, 19 Apr. 1781, in Clinton, *Observations*, 81–82

41 Phillips to Clinton, 19 Apr. 1781, in Clinton, *Observations*, 81–82.

42 S. Graham, "Account," 269; Cornwallis to Clinton, 26 May 1781, in Clinton, *Observations*, 104–8.

43 Cornwallis to Clinton, 20 May 1781, in Cornwallis, *Answer*, 64–66; Tarleton, *Campaigns*, 295–96; Maass, "To Disturb the Assembly."

44 Clinton to Cornwallis, 15 July 1781, in Cornwallis, *Answer*, 146–51.

45 "Conference at Dobb's Ferry." This document, originally in the possession of the Château de Rochambeau in France, contains a series of questions and answers between Washington and Rochambeau and is now in the possession of the Virginia State Library, Richmond. Davis, *Campaign That Won America*, and Ketchum, *Victory at Yorktown*, provide two of the best overviews of the action.

46 Gilbert and Baule, *British Army Officers*, 27, 46, 69, 79, 82, 101, 145.

47 Balch, *Les Français en Amérique*, 174–81. See also Ketchum, *Victory at Yorktown*.

CHAPTER TEN

1 Numerous biographies of Cornwallis exist; the best include: Wickwire and Wickwire, *Cornwallis: The American Adventure*; Wickwire and Wickwire, *Cornwallis: The Imperial Years*; Ross, *Correspondence of Charles, First Marquis Cornwallis*; Reese, *Cornwallis Papers*. See Buchanan, *Road to Guilford Courthouse*, 388–90, as well.

2 Greene's life has been chronicled a number of times: F. V. Greene, *General Greene*; Showman et al., *Papers of General Nathanael Greene*; G. W. Greene, *Life of Nathanael Greene*; Johnson, *Sketches*; Simms, *Life of Nathanael Greene*; Stegeman and Stegeman, *Caty*; Thane, *Fighting Quaker*; Thayer, *Nathanael Greene*. See Buchanan, *Road to Guilford Courthouse*, 397–99.

3 Tarleton biographies include: Bass, *Green Dragoon*; Scotti, *Brutal Virtue*; Tarleton, *Campaigns*. See also Buchanan, *Road to Guilford Courthouse*, 386–88. An excellent resource on Tarleton as well as the other senior British officers engaged at Guilford is Marg Baskin's website focused on Tarleton, "Oatmeal for the Foxhounds," located at http://www.golden.net/~marg/bansite/_entry.html.

4 Lee's biographers include: Boyd, *Light Horse Harry Lee*; Gerson, *Light Horse Harry Lee*; Royster, *Light Horse Harry Lee*; H. Lee Jr., *Campaign of 1781*; H. Lee, *Memoirs*. The observation concerning children being named in honor of the

father's commanding officer is based on reading more than a thousand pension applications that contain references to sons. Northern campaign veterans often named a son after Washington; so did some southern campaign veterans. But few named their progeny after Greene.

5 The only formal biography of O'Hara that exists is Griffin, "General Charles O'Hara." Further information on his life can be gleaned from the writings of O'Hara's close friend Horace Walpole, in *Memoirs of the Reign* and *Correspondence*. Other sources include *Gentleman's Magazine* 72 (1802): 278; Hotham, *Pages and Portraits*; Berry and Berry, *Berry Papers; and* Berry, *Extracts of the Journals*.

6 There is no published biography of General Leslie. Information on his life comes from a variety of sources including Kay, *Series of Original Portraits*, sketch 197; Peebles, *Diary of a Scottish Grenadier*; Historical Manuscripts Commission, *Report on American Manuscripts*.

7 Doyle, *Official Baronage of England*, 3:458.

8 For a biography of Ross, see *ODNB*, 47:797–98. For Champagne's biography, visit <http://www.queensroyalsurreys.org.uk/colonels/067.html>; his death is noted in *Gentleman's Magazine* 86 (1816):469. Haldane is documented in Philippart, *Royal Military Calendar*, 4:303–4; his death was reported in *Gentleman's Magazine*, n.s., 3 (1835): 106. Skelly's information can be found in Stewart, *Sketches*, 2:112, 171, 186; Skelly's journal is in the collections of NAE.

9 John McLeod's obituary can be found in *Annual Biography and Obituary*, 18:445–46. For Smith's biography see *ODNB*, 51:209, and Philippart, *Royal Military Calendar*, 4:420. Maitland's name is listed on the Guards Memorial, Royal Military Chapel, Wellington Barracks, London; he is also mentioned in Lodge, *Genealogy of the Existing British Peerage*, 237. Gore is listed in Philippart, *Royal Military Calendar*, 4:325–26; his son Arthur, a lieutenant in the 33rd Foot, died at Waterloo. Montressor's obituary is in *Gentleman's Magazine*, n.s., 8 (1836): 312–15.

10 Stuart, "Memoir"; Stuart's biography is located in *ODNB*, 53:183–84. Oakes's biography is found in *ODNB*, 41:318–19.

11 Dundas's biography is in *ODNB*, 17:273–74. The quote is from Elmslie's papers and was cited by Chargé d'Affaires Donald Teitelbaum in his Independence Day remarks as part of the United States diplomatic mission to South Africa in 2006. Calvert's biography can be found in *ODNB*, 9:589–90.

12 Material on England can be found in the biography of his son, Richard England Jr., in *ODNB*, 18:445–46. Burton's information is in the Napier Christie Burton Papers, University of Hull, England. Saumarez's biography is in *ODNB*, 49:24–25.

13 Norton's biography is in *ODNB*, 41:162–63. Richardson's information can be found in Ruvigny, *Plantagenet Roll*, 399–400; Richardson's 1792 location was

documented in Sheppherd, "Argyll Street Area," 284–307. Stedman's biography is in *ODNB*, 52:343–44.

14 Burke, *Genealogical and Heraldic History*, 2:2008. Genealogical information can be located at www.ancestry.com. The Carmelite Nunnery website is <http://www.carmelite.org.uk/Quidenham.html>.

15 Hammelmann, *History*; John Eager Howard to John Marshall, unknown date, 1804, Bayard Papers, MHS; Trotha, *Admiral Scheer*.

16 In addition to Lamb's original works, see Hagist, *British Soldier's Story*. Shaw's original work has also spawned an edited volume, Teagarden and Crabtree, *John Robert Shaw*.

17 Koch, *Battle of Guilford Courthouse*, 1, 26.

18 Muster Roll of the 33rd Foot, in War Office Papers, WO 12/4803, part 1, NAE, and Muster Roll of the Regiment Von Bose compiled from the *Hetrina*.

19 Tiffany, *Sketch of the Life*; Kalmanson, "Otho Holland Williams."

20 *National Cyclopedia*, 7:514.

21 Ibid., 9:292; B. Howard, *Memorial of the Late Colonel*.

22 Gunby, *Colonel John Gunby*.

23 D. T. Smith, *Smiths of Lynches Creek*; Elliott, *Lieutenant General Anderson*.

24 Whiteley, "Revolutionary Soldiers of Delaware."

25 H. Lee, *Memoirs*, 1:350; Green and Slaughter, *Genealogical and Historical Notes*; Ryland, *Hawes of Caroline County*.

26 Thomas Parramore, "Covenant in Jerusalem," in Greenburg, *Nat Turner*, 58–79; Whitelaw, *Virginia's Eastern Shore*; pension application of Jonah Hill, 23 Jan. 1833, Roll 427, RWP; *Biographical Directory of the United States Congress, 1774–1987*, 789, 1825; Morris, *Eastin Morris' Tennessee Gazetteer*; Hughes, *Battle of Belmont*, 249.

27 Powell, *Dictionary of North Carolina Biography*, 1:180–81; 2:75–76; Babits and Howard, *Fortitude and Forbearance*, 132, 152, 221; *Raleigh (N.C.) Minerva*, 13 Jan. 1806; pension application of Edward Yarborough, 21 Mar. 1840, Roll 894, RWP.

28 Harrison, *Princetonians*, 214–15; Meyernick, *Guide to Published Genealogical Records*, 413.

29 See Haller, *William Washington*.

30 Woodruff, "Capt. Ferdinand O'Neal"; Sherman, "Lee's Legion Remembered"; *Georgia Gazette*, 31 June 1800; Rudolph, "Michael Rudolph."

31 Dill, "New Bern at Century's End," 496–97; Watkins, *Catalogue of the Descendants*; William Henry Holcombe diary, Southern Historical Collection, University of North Carolina at Chapel Hill.

32 *National Cyclopedia of American Biography*, 1:52, 70.

33 Kneebone and Bearss, *Dictionary of Virginia Biography*, 2:45–46; Baine, *Robert Munford*; "Genealogical Notes"; *Columbian Centinel*, 7 Oct. 1815; Holcombe

Family genealogy log, North Carolina Office of Archives and History, Raleigh, N.C.

34  P. Hamilton, *Making and Unmaking*. See also the biography of St. George Tucker on the website of Colonial Williamsburg at <http://www.history.org/Almanack/people/bios/biotuck.cfm>.

35  Clement, *Turn of the Wheel*; Hurt, *Intimate History*; Green, *Historic Families of Kentucky*, 25–29; pension application of Nathaniel Cocke, 6 May 1830, Roll 199, RWP.

36  Green, *Historic Families of Kentucky*, 31–39; Waddell, *Annals of Augusta County*, 282–83, 328.

37  Kneebone and Bearss, *Dictionary of Virginia Biography*, 2:138, 173. See also the Avoca Museum in Altavista, Virginia, at <www.avocamuseum.org> for information concerning Charles Lynch.

38  Powell, *Dictionary of North Carolina Biography*, 1:290–91, 2:131.

39  Babits and Howard, *Fortitude and Forbearance*, 179, 188; Powell, *Dictionary of North Carolina Biography*, 4:225–26, 6:247–48.

40  Powell, *Dictionary of North Carolina Biography*, 2:28–29, 235–36, 6:203–4.

41  Babits and Howard, "Guilford Veterans Database."

42  Ibid; Samuel Houston to Sidney S. Baxter, unknown date, 1837, Mss2 H8184 a1, Collections of the Virginia Historical Society, Richmond.

43  Powell, *Dictionary of North Carolina Biography*, 2:184–85.

44  "Letter from Peter Francisco"; Garden, *Anecdotes of the American Revolution*, 209; pension application of Peter Francisco, 11 Mar. 1823, Roll 335, RWP; Shaffer, *Peter Francisco*; Moon, *Peter Francisco*.

45  *San Andreas Independent*, 8 Oct. 1859; *United States Census: Virginia*, 1850; *United States Census: Virginia*, 1860; pension applications of Peter Rife, 14 July 1834, Roll 690, Henry Willoughby, 7 Aug. 1832, Roll 876, RWP.


EPILOGUE

1  Tilden, "Extracts from the Journal"; McDowell, "Journal."

2  Pension application of John Watkins, 27 Aug. 1832, Roll 829, RWP.

# BIBLIOGRAPHY

MANUSCRIPT SOURCES

Ann Arbor, Michigan
    William L. Clements Library
        British Headquarters Papers (Sir Guy Carleton Papers)
        Sir Henry Clinton Papers
        Nathanael Greene Papers
        William Howe Orderly Book
Baltimore, Maryland
    Maryland Historical Society
        Bayard Papers
            John Eager Howard Papers
        Mordecai Gist Papers
        Otho Holland Williams Papers
Buckinghamshire, England
    Claydon House
        Harry Calvert Journal
Camden, South Carolina
        Historic Camden Manuscripts

Chapel Hill, North Carolina
    University of North Carolina at Chapel Hill
        Southern Historical Collection
            William R. Davie Papers
            "Eaton Family" [typescript]
            William Henry Holcombe Diary
            Revolutionary War Papers
            Jethro Sumner Papers
Edinburgh, Scotland
    Scottish National Archives
        Government Papers, GD 26/9/523
Greensboro, North Carolina
    Guilford Courthouse National Military Park
        Park Library Collection
Hull, England
    University of Hull
        Napier Christie Burton Papers
Kew, England
    National Archives
        Sir Guy Carleton Papers, PRO 30/55
        Charles Cornwallis Papers, PRO 30/11
        Colonial Office Papers, CO 5/138–44, CO 5/182–84
        Treasury Office Papers, TO 1/645, TO 38/812
        War Office Papers, WO 34, WO 36/1–4, WO 12/4803, WO 116/1–7
Morristown, New Jersey
    Morristown National Historical Park
        Lidgerwood Collection
            Hessian Transcripts
New York, New York
    New York Public Library Rare Books and Manuscripts Room
        Bayard-Campbell-Pearsall Papers
            Correspondence, 1743–1805
Philadelphia, Pennsylvania
    Historical Society of Pennsylvania
Princeton, New Jersey
    Princeton University Library
        Thomas Glyn Journal
Raleigh, North Carolina
    Office of Archives and History, Department of Cultural Resources
        John Collett, "An Accurate Map of North-Carolina from an Actual Survey"
            (London, 1770)

    Foreign Papers
        British Records
    Governors Papers
        Thomas Burke Papers
        Richard Caswell Papers
        Alexander Martin Papers
        Abner Nash Papers
    Holcombe Family Genealogy Log
    Henry Mouzon, "An Accurate Map of North and South Carolina"
        (London, 1770)
    Treasurer and Comptrollers Papers
        Military Papers
Richmond, Virginia
  Virginia Historical Society Manuscripts
  Virginia State Library
    Chesterfield Supplement Papers
    Personal Papers Collection
        James Burnet Letter
        Henry Lee Papers
    Virginia Revolutionary War Disability Affidavits
    Virginia Revolutionary War Pension Applications
    Virginia Revolutionary War Public Service Claims
Stratford, Virginia
  Stratford Hall Plantation
    Rocky Mount Collection, DuPont Library
Washington, D.C.
  Library of Congress
    Presidential Papers Microfilm
    George Washington Papers
  National Archives
    *Papers of the Continental Congress*, 1774–89
    Orders, Returns, Morning Reports, and Accounts of British Troops, 1776–81,
        Microcopy M922
    Revolutionary War Pension Application and Bounty-Land Warrant
        Application Files, RG 15, Microcopies M804 and M805
Williamsburg, Virginia
  Colonial Williamsburg, Inc.
    British Headquarters Papers (Sir Guy Carleton Papers), PRO 30/55
    "Memoir of a Stay at the Iron Works, March 1781" (typescript)

NEWSPAPERS

*Columbian Centinel* (Boston)
*Georgia Gazette* (Savannah)
*Leeds Intelligencer* (Leeds, England)
*Minerva* (Raleigh, N.C.)
*Royal Gazette* (London)
*Royal South Carolina Gazette* (Charleston)
*Salisbury Times* (Salisbury, Md.)
*San Andreas Independent* (San Andreas, Calif.)
*Virginia Gazette* (Richmond)


BOOKS AND ARTICLES

Abercrombie, Janice. *Rockbridge County*. Athens, Ga.: Iberian, 1991.
Almon, John. *The Remembrancer; or, Partial Repository of Public Events*. 2 vols.
    London, 1775, 1784.
Anderson, Thomas. "Journal of Lieutenant Thomas Anderson of the Delaware
    Regiment, 1780–1782." *Historical Magazine* 1 (1867): 207–11.
*The Annual Biography and Obituary*. Vol. 18. London: Longman, 1834.
*The Annual Register; or, A View of the History, Politics, and Literature for the Year
    1781*. London: J. Dodsley, 1782.
Atwood, Rodney. *The Hessians: Mercenaries from Hessen-Kassel in the American
    Revolution*. Cambridge, Eng.: Cambridge University Press, 1980.
Babits, Lawrence E. *A Devil of a Whipping: The Battle of Cowpens*. Chapel Hill:
    University of North Carolina Press, 1998.
———. "The Fifth Maryland at Guilford Courthouse: An Exercise in Historical
    Accuracy." *Maryland Historical Magazine* 84 (1989): 381–89.
———. "Shoe Life in the 71st Foot, 1776–1777." *Military Collector and Historian* 34
    (1982): 84–86.
Babits, Lawrence E., and Joshua B. Howard. *Fortitude and Forbearance: The North
    Carolina Continental Line in the Revolutionary War, 1775–1783*. Raleigh: North
    Carolina Office of Archives and History, 2004.
Baine, Rodney M. *Robert Munford: America's First Comic Dramatist*. Athens:
    University of Georgia Press, 1967.
Baker, Thomas A. *Another Such Victory: The Story of the American Defeat at
    Guilford Courthouse That Helped Win the War for Independence*. New York:
    Eastern Acorn, 1981.
Balch, Thomas. *Les Français en Amérique pendant la guerre de l'indépendance des
    États-Unis 1777–1783*. Paris: A. Sauton, 1872.

Bass, Robert D. *The Green Dragon: The Lives of Banastre Tarleton and Mary Robinson*. New York: Holt, 1957.

———. *Ninety-Six: The Struggle for the South Carolina Backcountry*. Lexington, S.C.: Sandlapper Store, 1978.

Berg, Fred A. *Encyclopedia of Continental Army Units*. Harrisburg, Pa.: Stackpole, 1972.

Berry, Mary. *Extracts of the Journals and Correspondence of Miss Berry from the Year 1783 to 1852*. Edited by Lady Theresa Lewis. London: Longmans & Green, 1865.

Berry, Mary, and Agnes Berry. *The Berry Papers, Being the Correspondence Hitherto Unpublished of Mary and Agnes Berry*. Edited by Lewis Melville. London: John Lane, 1914.

Blackwelder, Ruth. *The Age of Orange*. Charlotte, N.C.: W. Loftin, 1961.

Boyd, Thomas. *Light Horse Harry Lee*. New York: Charles Scribner & Sons, 1931.

Bradshaw, Herbert C. *History of Prince Edward County*. Richmond: Dietz, 1955.

Broughton-Mainwaring, Roland. *Historical Record of the Royal Welch*. London: Hatchards, 1889.

Browning, Charles H., ed. *The American Historical and Monthly Gazette of the Patriotic Hereditary Societies of the United States of America, March 1895–August 1895*. Philadelphia: Historical Record, 1895.

Brydges, Edgerton, ed. *Collins' Peerage of England: Genealogical, Biographical, and Historical*. London: F. C. and J. Rivington, Otridge & Son, 1812.

Buchanan, John. *The Road to Guilford Courthouse*. New York: John Wiley & Sons, 1997.

*Bulletin of the New York Public Library*. Vol. 9. New York: New York Public Library, 1905.

Burgoyne, Bruce, ed. *Ansbach-Bayreuth Diaries from the Revolutionary War*. Bowie, Md.: Heritage, 1999.

———. *Diaries of Two Ansbach Jägers*. Bowie, Md.: Heritage, 1997.

Burke, Bernard. *A Genealogical and Heraldic History of the Colonial Gentry*. London: Harrison, 1895.

Burke, William W., and Linnea M. Bass. "Preparing a British Unit for Service in America: the Brigade of Foot Guards, 1776." *Military Collector and Historian* 47 (1): 2–12.

Calderhead, William L. "Thomas Carney: Unsung Soldier of the American Revolution." *Maryland Historical Magazine* 84 (1989): 319–26.

Cannon, Richard. *Historical Record of the Seventeenth Regiment of Light Dragoons— Lancers: Containing an Account of the Formation of the Regiment in 1759, and Its Subsequent Services to 1841*. London: J. W. Parker, 1842.

Carp, E. Wayne. *To Starve an Army at Pleasure: Continental Army Administration and American Political Culture, 1775–1783*. Chapel Hill: University of North Carolina Press, 1984.

Caruana, Adrian B. *Grasshoppers and Butterflies: The Light 3-Pounders of Pattison and Townshend*. Bloomfield, Ontario: Museum Restoration Services, 1980.

———. *The Light 6-Pdr. Battalion Gun of 1776*. Bloomfield, Ontario: Museum Restoration Services, 1977.

Caruthers, Eli W. *Revolutionary Incidents and Sketches of Character Chiefly in the Old North State*. Edited by Ruth F. Thompson. 2 vols. Greensboro, N.C.: Guilford County Genealogical Society, 1994.

Chalkley, Lyman. *Chronicles of the Scotch-Irish Settlement in Virginia*. Baltimore: Genealogical Publishing, 1966.

Chambers, Robert. *Traditions of Edinburgh*. Edinburgh: Published privately, 1824.

Chastellux, François Jean. *Travels in North America in the Years 1780, 1781, and 1782*. Edited by Howard C. Rice Jr. 2 vols. Chapel Hill: University of North Carolina Press, 1965.

Christian, Bernard, ed. *Muster Rolls and Other Records of Service of Maryland Troops in the American Revolution, 1775–1783*. Baltimore: Genealogical Publishing, 1972.

Clark, Murtie J. *Loyalists in the Southern Campaign*. 3 vols. Baltimore: Genealogical Publishing, 1981.

Clark, Walter, ed. *State Records of North Carolina*. 26 vols. Raleigh, N.C.: Nash Brothers, 1886–1907.

Clement, Maude C. *The History of Pittsylvania County*. Baltimore: Regional Publishing, 1973.

———. *The Turn of the Wheel: Sketches of Life in Southwest Virginia, 1756–1956*. Danville, Va.: J. T. Townes, 1956.

Clinton, Sir Henry. *The American Rebellion: Sir Henry Clinton's Narrative of His Campaigns, 1775–1782*. Edited by William B. Willcox. New Haven, Conn.: Yale University Press, 1954.

———. *Observations on Some Parts of Earl Cornwallis' Answer to Sir Henry Clinton's Narrative*. London: J. Debrett, 1783–84.

———. "Sir Henry Clinton's Review of Simcoe's Journal." Edited by Howard M. Peckham. *William and Mary Quarterly*, 2nd ser., 21 (1941): 361–70.

Coffin, Addison. "A Letter from Addison Coffin." *Guilford Collegian* 1 (1889): 40–41.

Collins, James P. *Autobiography of a Revolutionary Soldier*. Clinton, La.: Feliciana Democrat, 1859.

Conway, Stephen. "British Mobilization in the War of American Independence." *Historical Research* 72 (1999): 58–76.

Cornwallis, Charles. *An Answer to That Part of the Narrative of Lt. General Sir Henry Clinton, K.B.* London: J. Debrett, 1783.

Couture, Richard T. *Powhatan: A Bicentennial History*. Richmond: Dietz, 1980.

Cox, Caroline. *A Proper Sense of Honor: Service and Sacrifice in George Washington's Army*. Chapel Hill: University of North Carolina Press, 2007.

Crow, Jeffrey J., and Larry E. Tise. *The Southern Experience in the American Revolution*. Chapel Hill: University of North Carolina Press, 1978.

Cullen, Charles T. *St. George Tucker and Law in Virginia, 1772-1804*. New York: Garland, 1987.

Cullen, Charles T., Julian P. Boyd, L. H. Butterfield, and John Catanzariti, eds. *The Papers of Thomas Jefferson*. 32 vols. Princeton, N.J.: Princeton University Press, 1950–2000.

Curtis, E. E. *The Organization of the British Army in the American Revolution*. New Haven, Conn.: Yale University Press, 1926.

Dann, John C. *The Revolution Remembered: Eyewitness Accounts of the War for Independence*. Chicago: University of Chicago Press, 1980.

Davidson, Chalmers. *Piedmont Partisan*. Davidson, N.C.: Davidson College Press, 1951.

Davie, William R. *The Revolutionary War Sketches of William R. Davie*. Edited by Blackwell P. Robinson. Raleigh: North Carolina Office of Archives and History, 1976.

Davies, K. G. *Documents of the American Revolution*. Colonial Office Series. 21 vols. Shannon, Ireland: Irish University Press, 1972–81.

Davis, Burke. *The Campaign That Won America: The Story of Yorktown*. New York: Dial, 1970.

Dederer, John M. *Making Bricks without Straw: Nathanael Greene's Southern Campaign and Mao Tse-Tung's Mobile War*. Manhattan, Kans.: Sunflower University Press, 1983.

Delaney, Perry Benson. "Biographical Sketch of Robert Kirkwood." *Graham's Magazine* 28 (1846): 104.

Delaware, State of. *Delaware Archives: Military*. 3 vols. Wilmington, Del.: Public Archives Commission, 1911–19.

Diehl, George W. "Rockbridge Men at War, 1760–1782." *Daughters of the American Revolution Magazine*, Mar. 1968, 261–65, 360.

Dill, Alonzo. "New Bern at Century's End." *North Carolina Historical Review* 23 (1946): 496–97.

Doyle, James E., ed. *The Official Baronage of England*. London: Longmans & Green, 1886.

Duncan, Francis. *History of the Royal Regiment of Artillery*. 2 vols. London: J. Murray, 1879.

Dunkerly, Robert M. "Prelude to Guilford Courthouse." *Southern Campaigns of the American Revolution* 3 (2006): 34–43.

Edgar, Walter. *Partisans and Redcoats: The Southern Conflict That Turned the Tide of the Revolution.* New York: Morrow, 2001.

Edmonds, Thomas J. *The Tactical Retreat of General Nathanael Greene.* Greensboro, N.C.: Published privately, 2006.

Eelking, Max von. *The German Allied Troops in the North American War of Independence, 1776–1783.* Baltimore: Genealogical Publishing, 1969.

Elliott, Joseph C. *Lieutenant General Richard Heron Anderson.* Dayton, Ohio: Morningside House, 1985.

Ewald, Johann. *Diary of the American War: A Hessian Journal.* Translated and edited by Joseph P. Trustin. New Haven, Conn.: Yale University Press, 1979.

Fletcher, W. A. *Rebel Private Front and Rear.* Beaumont, Tex.: Press of the Greer Print, 1908.

Foote, William H., ed. *Sketches of Virginia, Historical and Biographical.* Philadelphia: W. S. Martien, 1855.

Ford, Worthington C. *British Officers Serving in the American Revolution, 1774–1783.* Brooklyn, N.Y.: Historical Printing Club, 1897.

Fortescue, J. W. *A History of the Seventeenth Lancers.* London: Macmillan, 1895.

Fox, Richard A. *Archaeology, History, and Custer's Last Battle.* Norman: University of Oklahoma Press, 1993.

Frey, Sylvia. *The British Soldier in America.* Austin: University of Texas Press, 1981.

———. *Water from the Rock: Black Resistance in a Revolutionary Age.* Princeton, N.J.: Princeton University Press, 1991.

Fries, Adelaide L., ed. *Records of the Moravians in North Carolina.* 13 vols. Raleigh, N.C.: Edwards & Broughton, 1922–2000.

Garden, Alexander. *Anecdotes of the American Revolution.* Charleston, S.C.: A. E. Miller, 1828.

———. *Anecdotes of the Revolutionary War.* Charleston, S.C.: A. E. Miller, 1822.

"Genealogical Notes and Queries." *William and Mary Quarterly,* 2nd ser., 8 (1928): 312–18.

Gerson, Noel B. *Light Horse Harry Lee: A Biography of Washington's Greatest Cavalryman.* Garden City, N.Y.: Doubleday, 1966.

Gilbert, Stephen, and Steven M. Baule. *British Army Officers Who Served in the American Revolution, 1775–1783.* Westminster, Md.: Heritage, 2004.

Glover, Michael. *That Astonishing Infantry: Three Hundred Years of the History of the Royal Welch Fusiliers, 1689–1989.* London: L. Cooper, 1989.

Gooding, S. James. *An Introduction to British Artillery in North America.* Ottawa, Ontario: Museum Restoration Services, 1965.

Gordon, William. *A History of the Rise, Progress, and Establishment of the Independence of the United States of America.* 4 vols. New York: Hodge, Allen & Campbell, 1789.

Graham, Joseph. "General Joseph Graham's Narrative of the Revolutionary War in North Carolina in 1780 and 1781." In *The Papers of Archibald D. Murphey*, edited by William Hoyt, 2:212–311. Raleigh, N.C.: E. M. Uzzell, 1914.

Graham, Samuel "An English Officer's Account of His Services in America—1779–1781." *Historical Magazine* 9 (1865): 267–75.

Graydon, Alexander. *Memoirs of His Own Time with Reminiscences of the Men and Events of the Revolution.* Harrisburg, Pa.: J. Wyeth, 1811.

Green, Raleigh T., and Phillip Slaughter. *Genealogical and Historical Notes on Culpepper County, Virginia.* Baltimore: Regional Publication, 1971.

Green, Thomas M. *Historic Families of Kentucky.* Cincinnati: Clarke, 1889.

Greenburg, Kenneth S., ed. *Nat Turner: A Slave Rebellion in History and Memory.* New York: Oxford University Press, 2003.

Greene, Francis Vinton. *General Greene.* New York: D. Appleton, 1893.

Greene, George Washington. *The Life of Nathanael Greene, Major-General in the Army of the Revolution.* 3 vols. New York: G. P. Putnam and Sons, 1867–71.

Greene, Robert E. *Black Courage, 1775–1783: Documentation of African American Service in the American Revolution.* Washington, D.C.: Daughters of the American Revolution, 1984.

Griffin, William D. "General Charles O'Hara." *Irish Sword* 10 (1972): 179–87.

Griswold, Rufus W. *Washington and the Generals of the American Revolution.* 2 vols. Philadelphia: Carey & Hart, 1847, 1855.

Groh, Lou, and John E. Cornelison. *Battle Lines and Courthouses: Archaeological Survey and Testing at Guilford Courthouse National Military Park, Greensboro, North Carolina.* Tallahassee, Fla.: National Park Service, 2007.

Grossman, Dave. *On Killing: The Psychological Impact of Killing on War and Society.* Boston: Little, Brown, 1995.

Gunby, A. A. *Colonel John Gunby of the Maryland Line.* Cincinnati: Clarke, 1902.

Hagist, Don N. "Unpublished Military Writings of Roger Lamb, Soldier in the 1775–1783 American War." *Journal of the Society for Army Historical Research* (in press).

———, ed. *A British Soldier's Story: Roger Lamb's Narrative of the American Revolution.* Baraboo, Wisc.: Ballindalloch, 2004.

Haller, Stephen E. *William Washington: Cavalryman of the Revolution.* Bowie, Md.: Heritage Books, 2001.

Hamilton, Frederick W. *The Origin and History of the First or Grenadier Guards.* London: Murray Publishing, 1874.

Hamilton, Philip. *The Making and Unmaking of a Revolutionary Family: The Tuckers of Virginia, 1752–1830.* Charlottesville: University of Virginia Press, 2003.

Hammelmann, William. *The History of the Prussian Pour Le Merite Order.* Hamburg, Ger.: Verlag Sammlerfreund, 1982–86.

Hanger, George. *An Address to the Army in Reply to Strictures by Roderick McKenzie (Late Lieut. Of the 71st Regmt.) on Tarleton's History of the Campaigns of 1780 and 1781*. London: J. Ridgeway, 1789.

Harrison, Richard A. *Princetonians, 1769–1775*. Princeton, N.J.: Princeton University Press, 1980.

Harvey, Edward. *The Manual Exercise, as ordered by his Majesty the King, 1764: Together with the Plans and Explanations of the Method Generally Practiced at Reviews and Field Days*. London: Adjutant General's Office, 1764.

Hatch, Charles E., Jr. *The Battle of Guilford Courthouse*. Washington, D.C.: National Park Service, 1971.

Hay, Gertrude Sloan. *Roster of North Carolina Soldiers in the American Revolution*. Baltimore: Genealogical Publishing, 1932.

Haywood, Marshall D. *Major George Farragut*. Montgomery, Ala.: Published privately, 1903.

Heitman, Francis B. *Historical Register of the Officers of the Continental Army*. Baltimore: Genealogical Publishing, 1994.

Hening, William Walter, ed. *The Statutes at Large: Being a Collection of All the Laws of Virginia from the First Session of the Legislature, in the Year 1619*. New York: Bartow, 1809–23.

Henry, Robert. *Narrative of the Battle of Cowan's Ford, February 1, 1781*. Edited by David Schenk. Greensboro, N.C.: D. Schenk, Sr., 1891.

Higginbotham, Don. *Daniel Morgan, Revolutionary Rifleman*. Chapel Hill: University of North Carolina Press, 1961.

Historical Manuscripts Commission. *Report on American Manuscripts in the Royal Institute of Great Britain*. 4 vols. London: Printed for His Majesty's Stationery Office, 1901–9.

Hoffman, Ronald, et al., eds. *An Uncivil War: The Southern Backcountry during the American Revolution*. Charlottesville: University of Virginia Press, 1985.

Holton, Woody. *Forced Founders: Indians, Debtors, Slaves, and the Making of the American Revolution in Virginia*. Chapel Hill: University of North Carolina Press, 1999.

Hotham, Sir William. *Pages and Portraits from the Past, Being the Private Papers of Sir William Hotham*. 2 vols. Edited by A. M. W. Stirling. London: H. Jenkins, 1919.

Houlding, John. *Fit For Service: The Training of the British Army*. London: Oxford University Press, 1981.

Howard, Benjamin C. *Memorial of the Late John Eager Howard*. Baltimore: Published privately, 1863.

Howard, Cary. "John Eager Howard: Patriot and Public Servant." *Maryland Historical Magazine* 62 (1967): 300–317.

Howard, Joshua B. "'Things Here Wear a Melancholy Appearance': The Battle of Briar Creek, Georgia, March 3, 1781." *Georgia Historical Quarterly* 88 (2004): 477–98.

Hoyt, William H., ed. *The Papers of Archibald D. Murphey.* 2 vols. Raleigh, N.C.: E. M. Uzzell & Company, 1914.

Hudgins, A. R. *A History of Amelia County.* Amelia, Va.: Amelia Historical Society, 1965.

Hughes, Nathaniel C. *The Battle of Belmont: Grant Strikes South.* Chapel Hill: University of North Carolina Press, 1991.

Hurt, Frances H. *An Intimate History of the American Revolution in Pittsylvania County.* Danville, Va.: Womack Press, 1978.

Johnson, William. *Sketches of the Life and Correspondence of Nathanael Greene, Major General of the Armies of the United States, in the War of the Revolution, Compiled Chiefly from Original Materials.* 2 vols. Charleston: A. E. Miller, 1822.

Jones, E. Alfred, ed. *The Journal of Alexander Chesney, South Carolina Loyalist in the Revolution and After.* Columbus: Ohio State University Press, 1921.

Katcher, Phillip R. N. *Encyclopedia of British, Provincial and German Army Units, 1775–1783.* Harrisburg, Pa.: Stackpole Books, 1973.

Kay, John. *A Series of Original Portraits and Caricature Etchings, by the Late John Kay, Miniature Painter, Edinburgh: With Biographical Sketches and Illustrative Anecdotes.* Edinburgh: H. Paton, Carver and Gilder, 1838.

Keegan, John. *The Face of Battle.* New York: Viking Press, 1976.

Keltie, John S. *A History of the Scottish Highlands, Highland Clans, and Highland Regiments.* Edinburgh: A. Fullarton, 1875.

Ketchum, Richard. *Victory at Yorktown: The Campaign that Won the Revolution.* New York: Henry Holt, 2004.

Kneebone, John T., and Sara B. Bearss, eds. *Dictionary of Virginia Biography.* 3 vols. Richmond: Library of Virginia, 1998–.

Koch, Berthold. *The Battle of Guilford Courthouse and the Siege and Surrender of Yorktown.* Translated and edited by Bruce E. Burgoyne. Bowie, Md.: Heritage Books, 2002.

Lamb, Roger. *Memoir of His Own Life.* Dublin: J. Jones, 1811.

———. *An Original and Authentic Journal of Occurrences during the Late American War.* Dublin: Wilkinson & Courtney, 1809.

Lee, Albert. *A History of the Thirty-Third Foot, the Duke of Wellington's Regiment.* Norwich, Eng.: Empire, 1922.

Lee, Henry. *Memoirs of the War in the Southern Department of the United States.* 2 vols. Philadelphia: Bradford and Inskeep, 1812.

Lee, Henry, Jr. *The Campaign of 1781 in the Carolinas.* Philadelphia: E. Littell, 1824.

Lee, Robert E., ed. *The American Revolution in the South*. New York: University Publishing Company, 1869.

Lesser, Charles H. *The Sinews of Independence*. Chicago: University of Chicago Press, 1976.

"Letter from Peter Francisco to the General Assembly, November 11, 1820." *William and Mary Quarterly* 13 (1905): 217–19.

Lewis, Virgil A. *History of the Battle of Point Pleasant*. Harrisonburg, Va.: The Tribune Printing Company, 1974.

Lipscomb, Andrew A., et al., eds. *The Writings of Thomas Jefferson*. Washington, D.C.: Thomas Jefferson Memorial Association, 1903–4.

Lodge, Edmund. *The Genealogy of the Existing British Peerage*. London: Saunders & Otley, 1832.

Lossing, Benjamin. *Pictorial Fieldbook of the Revolution*. 2 vols. New York: Harper & Brothers, 1850.

Lowell, Edward J. *The Hessians and Other German Auxiliaries of Great Britain in the Revolutionary War*. New York: Harper & Brothers Publishers, 1885.

Lumpkin, Henry. *From Savannah to Yorktown*. Columbia: University of South Carolina Press, 1981.

Maass, John. "To Disturb the Assembly: Tarleton's Charlottesville Raid and the British Invasion of Virginia, 1781." *Virginia Cavalcade* 69 (2000): 149–57.

MacKinnon, Daniel. *Origin and Services of the Coldstream Guards*. London: R. Bentley Publishing, 1833.

Martin, George A. *Vital Statistics of the National Intelligencer, 1800–1823*. Washington, D.C.: National Genealogical Society, 1952.

Martin, James Kirby, and Mark Edward Lender. *A Respectable Army: The Military Origins of the Republic*. Arlington, Ill.: Harlan Davidson, 1982.

Marshall, John. *The Life of George Washington*. 2 vols. Philadelphia: C. P. Wayne, 1804, 1807.

Marshall, S. L. A. *Men Against Fire*. New York: William Morrow & Company, 1947.

———. *The Soldier's Load and the Mobility of a Nation*. Quantico, Va.: Marine Corps Association, 1980.

Matthew, H. C. G., and Brian H. Harrison. *Oxford Dictionary of National Biography*. 60 vols. New York: Oxford University Press, 2004.

May, Robin. *Wolfe's Army*. London: Osprey, 1998.

McCance, Stouppe, and A. D. L. Cary. *Regimental Records of the Royal Welch Fusiliers, 1689–1918*. 2 vols. London: F. Groom, 1921–29.

McConnell, David. *British Smooth-Bore Artillery: A Technological Study*. Ottawa, Ontario: Museum Restoration Services, 1988.

McDonnell, Michael. *The Politics of War: Race, Class, and Conflict in Revolutionary Virginia*. Chapel Hill: University of North Carolina Press, 2007.

McDowell, William. "Journal of Lieutenant William McDowell of the 1st Pennsylvania Regiment in the Southern Campaign, 1781–1782." *Pennsylvania Archives*, 2nd ser., 15 (1890): 297–340.

Meyernick, Kory. *A Guide to Published Genealogical Records*. Baltimore: Genealogical Publishing Company, 1998.

Monroe, Harriet, and Alice Corbet Henderson, eds. *The New Poetry: An Anthology*. New York: Macmillan, 1917.

Montross, Lynn. *Rag, Tag, and Bobtail: The Story of the Continental Army, 1775–1783*. New York: Harper, 1952.

Moon, William. *Peter Francisco: Portuguese Patriot*. Winston-Salem, N.C.: Bradford Print, 1980.

Morrill, Dan L. *Southern Campaigns of the American Revolution*. Baltimore: Nautical & Aviation Publishing Company, 1992.

Morris, Eastin. *Eastin Morris' Tennessee Gazetteer*. Nashville: W. H. Hunt, 1834.

Morton, W. S. "Col. William Morton." *William and Mary Quarterly*, 2nd ser., 1 (1921): 285–86.

Moultrie, William. *Memoirs of the Revolution, So Far as It Related to the States of North and South Carolina, and Georgia*. 2 vols. New York: D. Longworth, 1802.

*The National Cyclopedia of American Biography*. 63 vols. New York: J. T. White, 1926–1984.

Neale, Gay W., et al. *Brunswick Story: A History of Brunswick County*. Lawrenceville, Va.: Brunswick Times-Gazette, 1957.

Neimeyer, Charles Patrick. *America Goes to War: A Social History of the Continental Army*. New York: New York University Press, 1996.

Nelson, Eddie D., Joseph A. Goldeberg, and Rita Y. Fletcher. "Revolutionary Ranks: An Analysis of the Chesterfield Supplement." *Virginia Magazine of History and Biography* 87 (1979): 182–89.

Neumann, George C. *The History of Weapons of the American Revolution*. New York: Harper & Row, 1967.

———. *Swords and Blades of the Revolution*. Harrisburg, Pa.: Stackpole Books, 1973.

Newlin, Algie I. *The Battle of New Garden*. Greensboro: North Carolina Friends Historical Society, 1977.

Newsome, A. R. "British Orderly Book." *North Carolina Historical Review* 9 (1932): 57–78, 163–86, 273–98, 366–92.

O'Kelley, Patrick. *Nothing but Blood and Slaughter*. 4 vols. Lillington, N.C.: Blue House Tavern, 2004–5.

Owen, Thomas M., and H. Vanaman. *History and Genealogies of Old Granville County, 1746–1800*. Greenville, S.C.: Southern Historical Press, 1993.

Palmer, William P., et al., eds. *Calendar of Virginia State Papers and Other Manuscripts, 1652–1781.* 11 vols. Richmond: R. F. Walker, 1875–93.

Pancake, John S. *This Destructive War: The British Campaign in the Carolinas, 1780–1782.* Birmingham: University of Alabama Press, 1985.

Papenfuse, Edward C., and Gregory A. Stiverson. "General Smallwood's Recruits: The Peacetime Career of the Revolutionary War Private." *William and Mary Quarterly,* 3rd ser., 30 (1973): 117–32.

Peebles, John. *The Diary of a Scottish Grenadier.* Edited by Ira Gruber. Mechanicsburg, Pa.: Stackpole Books, 1998.

Philippart, John. *The Royal Military Calendar, or Army Service and Commission Book.* 5 vols. London: A. J. Valpy, 1820.

Pickering, Timothy. *Easy Plan of Discipline for a Militia.* Salem, Mass.: Samuel & Ebenezer Hall, 1775.

Piecuch, James. "'One of the Most Important and Bloodiest Battles Ever Fought in America': The Battle of Eutaw Springs." *Southern Campaigns of the American Revolution* 3 (2006): 25–37.

Pindell, Richard. "A Militant Surgeon of the Revolution: Some Letters of Richard Pindell." *Maryland Historical Magazine* 18 (1923): 309–23.

Pleasants, J. Hall, et al., eds. *Archives of Maryland.* Vol. 47. Baltimore: Maryland Historical Society, 1930.

Powell, William S. *The North Carolina Gazetteer.* Chapel Hill: University of North Carolina Press, 1968.

———. *When the Past Refused to Die: The History of Caswell County, 1777–1977.* Durham, N.C.: Moore, 1977.

———, ed. *Dictionary of North Carolina Biography.* 6 vols. Chapel Hill, N.C.: University of North Carolina Press, 1979–96.

Quarles, Benjamin. *The Negro in the American Revolution.* Chapel Hill: University of North Carolina Press, 1961.

Raddall, Thomas H. "Tarleton's Legion." *Collections of the Nova Scotia Historical Society* 28 (1949): 1–50.

Ramsay, David. *The History of the American Revolution.* Philadelphia: R. Aitken & Son, 1789.

Rankin, Hugh F. *The North Carolina Continentals.* Chapel Hill: University of North Carolina Press, 1971.

Read, Elizabeth. "John Eager Howard." *Magazine of American History* 7 (1881): 277–79.

Reese, George H., comp. *The Cornwallis Papers.* Charlottesville: University of Virginia Press, 1969.

Rogers, George C. "Letters of Charles O'Hara to the Duke of Grafton." *South Carolina Historical Magazine* LXV (1964).

Ross, Charles, ed. *Correspondence of Charles, First Marquis Cornwallis.* 3 vols. London: J. Murray, 1859.

Royster, Charles. *Light Horse Harry Lee and the Legacy of the American Revolution.* New York: Knopf, 1981.

———. *A Revolutionary People at War: The Continental Army and American Character.* Chapel Hill: University of North Carolina Press, 1979.

Rudolph, Marilou Alston. "Michael Rudolph, Lion of the Legion." *Georgia Historical Quarterly* 45 (1961): 201–22.

———. "The Legend of Michael Rudolph." *Georgia Historical Quarterly* 45 (1961): 309–28.

Ruley, Angela M. *Revolutionary Pension Applications, Rockbridge County, Virginia.* Natural Bridge, Va.: Published privately, 1998.

Rumple, Jethro. *A History of Rowan County, North Carolina.* Edited by Edith M. Clark. Baltimore: Genealogical Publishing Company, 1974.

Ruvigny, Marquis de, et al. *The Plantagenet Roll of the Blood Royal: Exeter Volume.* London: Melville, 1907–11.

Ryland, Elizabeth Hawes. *Hawes of Carolina County.* Richmond: Published privately, 1947.

Sanchez-Saavedra, E. M., comp. *A Guide to Virginia Military Organizations in the American Revolution.* Richmond: Virginia State Library, 1978.

Savory, A. C. S., and J. M. Brereton. *The History of the Duke of Wellington's Regiment, 1702–1992.* Wellesley Park-Halifax: The West Riding Regiment, 1993.

Scheer, George F., and Hugh Rankin. *Rebels and Redcoats.* New York: Da Capo, 1957.

Schenk, David. *North Carolina, 1780–1781.* Raleigh, N.C.: Edwards & Broughton, 1889.

Scott, Douglas D., and Richard A. Fox, Jr. *Archaeological Insights into the Custer Battle.* Norman: University of Oklahoma Press, 1987.

Scott, Douglas D., Richard A. Fox, Jr., Melissa A. Connor, and Dick Harmon. *Archaeological Perspectives on the Battle of the Little Bighorn.* Norman: University of Oklahoma Press, 1989.

Scotti, Anthony J. *Brutal Virtue: The Myth and Reality of Banastre Tarleton.* Bowie, Md.: Heritage Books, 2002.

Selesky, Harold E., and Mark Mayo Boatner, eds. *Encyclopedia of the American Revolution.* Detroit: Charles Scribner & Sons, 2006.

Seymour, William. "Journal of the Southern Expedition, 1780–83, by William Seymour, Sergeant-Major of the Delaware Regiment." *Pennsylvania Magazine of History and Biography* 7 (1883): 286–98, 377–94.

Shaffer, Janet. *Peter Francisco, Virginia Giant.* Durham, N.C.: Moore Publishing Company, 1976.

Shaw, John Robert. *A Narrative of the Life and Travels of John Robert Shaw the Well-Digger, Now Resident in Lexington, Kentucky*. Lexington, Ky.: G. Fowler, 1807.

Sheppherd, F. H. W., ed. "Argyll Street Area." *Survey of London: St. James Westminster*. Vols. 31 and 32, pt. 2. London: London County Council, 1963. 284–307.

Sherman, William Thomas. "Lee's Legion Remembered: Profiles of the 2d Partisan Corps as Taken from Alexander Garden's *Anecdotes*." <http://www.american revolution.org/archives.html>.

Showman, Richard K., Dennis R. Conrad, and Roger N. Parks, eds. *The Papers of General Nathanael Greene*. 14 vols. Chapel Hill: University of North Carolina Press, 1976–2005.

Shy, John W. *A People Numerous and Armed: Reflections on the Military Struggle for American Independence*. New York: Oxford University Press, 1976.

Simcoe, John Graves. *Simcoe's Military Journal*. London: Published privately, 1784.

Simms, William Gilmore. *The Life of Nathanael Greene, Major General in the Army of the Revolution*. New York: G. F. Cooledge, 1849.

Simpson-Poffenbarger, Livia Nye. *The Battle of Point Pleasant*. Point Pleasant, W.Va.: State Gazette, 1909.

Smith, Dorothy Tedder. *Smiths of Lynches Creek and Beyond*. Bishopville, S.C.: Bosmith Furniture Company, 2006.

Smith, George. *An Universal Military Dictionary: A Copious Explanation of the Technical Terms, etc., used in the Equipment, Machinery, Movements, and Military Operations of An Army*. London: J. Millan, 1779.

Smith, Samuel, and John R. Elting. "British Light Infantry, 1775–1800." *Military Collector and Historian* 27 (1975): 87–89.

Smoler, Fredric. "The Secret of the Soldiers Who Didn't Shoot." *American Heritage* 40 (1989): 37–45.

Spring, Matthew H. *With Zeal and Bayonets Only: The British Army on Campaign in North America*. Norman: University of Oklahoma Press, 2008.

Stedman, Charles. *The History of the Origin, Progress, and Termination of the American War*. 2 vols. London: P. Wogan, P. Byrne, J. Moore & W. Jones, 1794.

Steele, Rollin M. *The Lost Battle of the Alamance, also Known as the Battle of Clapp's Mill: A Turning Point in North Carolina's Struggle with Their British Invaders in the Very Unusual Year of 1781*. Burlington, N.C.: Privately published, 1999.

Stegeman, John F., and Janet A. Stegeman. *Caty: A Biography of Catharine Littlefield Greene*. Providence: Rhode Island Bicentennial Foundation, 1977.

Steuart, Rieman. *A History of the Maryland Line in the Revolutionary War, 1775-1783*. Baltimore: Society of the Cincinnati of Maryland, 1969.

Stewart, David. *Sketches of the Characters, Manners, and Present State of the Highlanders of Scotland*. Edinburgh: John Menzies, 1825.

Stuart, John. "Memoir of Sir John Stuart, KB." *European Magazine and London Review* (April 1811): 242–48.

Summers, Lewis P. *Annals of Southwest Virginia*. Abingdon, Va.: Published privately, 1929.

Tarleton, Banastre. *A History of the Campaigns of 1780 and 1781 in the Southern Provinces of North America*. London: T. Cadell, 1787.

Teagarden, Oressa M., and Jeanne L. Crabtree. *John Robert Shaw: An Autobiography of Thirty Years, 1777–1807*. Athens: Ohio University Press, 1992.

Thane, Elswyth. *The Fighting Quaker: Nathanael Greene*. New York: Hawthorn Books, 1972.

Thayer, Theodore. *Nathanael Greene: Strategist of the American Revolution*. New York: Twayne Publishers, 1960.

Tiffany, Osmond. *A Sketch of the Life and Services of Gen. Otho Holland Williams*. Baltimore: J. Murphy, 1851.

Tilden, John Bell. "Extracts from the Journal of Lieutenant John Bell Tilden, Second Pennsylvania Line, 1781–1782." *Pennsylvania Magazine of History and Biography* 19 (1895): 51–63.

Treacy, M. F. *Prelude to Yorktown*. Chapel Hill: University of North Carolina Press, 1963.

Troiani, Don, Earl J. Coates, and James L. Kochan, eds. *Soldiers in America, 1754–1865*. Mechanicsburg, Pa.: Stackpole Books, 1998.

Trotha, Adolf von. *Admiral Scheer: Der Sieger vom Skagerak*. Lübeck, Ger.: Coleman, 1933.

Tucker, St. George. "The Southern Campaign, 1781, from Guilford to Court House to the Siege of York." *Magazine of American History* 7 (1881): 36–46.

Turner, Frederick Jackson. "Western State-Making in the Revolutionary Era." *American Historical Review* 1 (October 1895–July 1896): 70–87, 251–69.

Turner, Joseph Brown, ed. *The Journal and Order Book of Captain Robert Kirkwood of the Delaware Line*. Wilmington, Del.: Historical Society of Delaware, 1910.

United States Bureau of the Census. *A Census of Pensioners for Revolutionary or Military Service*. Washington, D.C.: Census Office, 1841.

Urban, Mark. *Fusiliers: The Saga of a British Redcoat Regiment in the American Revolution*. New York: Walker & Company, 2007.

Urwin, Gregory J. W. *The United States Infantry*. New York: Blandford, 1988.

Veröffentlichungen der Archivschule Marburg, Institut für Archivwissenschaft. *Hessische Truppen im amerikanischen Unabhängigkeitskrieg*. 6 vols. Marburg, Ger.: Archivschule Marburg, 1974.

Waddell, Joseph A. *Annals of Augusta County, Virginia*. Staunton, Va.: C. R. Caldwell, 1902.

Walpole, Horace. *Correspondence*. 48 vols. Edited by W. S. Lewis et al. New Haven, Conn.: Yale University Press, 1937–83.

———. *Memoirs of the Reign of George the Third*. Edited by G. F. R. Barker. London: Lawrence and Bullen, 1894.

Ward, Christopher. *The Delaware Continentals*. Wilmington: Historical Society of Delaware, 1941.

Watkins, Frances N. *A Catalogue of the Descendants of Thomas Watkins of Chicahomony, Virginia, Who was the Common Ancestor of Many of the Families of the Name in Prince Edward, Charlotte, and Chesterfield Counties, Virginia*. New York: J. F. Trow, 1852.

Whitelaw, Ralph T. *Virginia's Eastern Shore: Nansemond and Accomack Counties*. Gloucester, Mass.: P. Smith, 1968.

Whiteley, William G. "The Revolutionary Soldiers of Delaware," paper 14 in Volume 2 of the *Papers of the Historical Society of Delaware* (1896): 50–62.

Wickwire, Franklin B., and Mary Wickwire. *Cornwallis: The American Adventure*. Boston: Houghton Mifflin 1970.

———. *Cornwallis: The Imperial Years*. Chapel Hill: University of North Carolina Press, 1980.

Williams, Otho H. "A Narrative of the Campaign of 1780." In *Sketches of the Life and Correspondence of Nathanael Greene*, edited by William Johnson, 485–510. Charleston: A. E. Miller, 1822.

Williams, Samuel Cole. "George Farragut." *East Tennessee Historical Society's Publications* 1 (1929): 77–94.

Woodruff, Caldwell. "Capt. Ferdinand O'Neal of Lee's Legion." *William and Mary Quarterly*, 2nd ser., 23 (1943): 328–30.

Wright, Robin K. *The Continental Army*. Washington, D.C.: Center for Military History, U.S. Army, 1983.

Yorck von Wartenburg, Hans David Ludwig. *Napoleon as a General*. London: K. Paul, Trench, Trubner & Company, 1902.

DISSERTATIONS, THESES, AND UNPUBLISHED PAPERS

Babits, Lawrence E. "Military Documents and Archaeological Sites: Methodological Contributions to Historical Archaeology." Ph.D. diss., Brown University, Providence, Rhode Island, 1981.

Babits, Lawrence E., and Joshua B. Howard. "Continentals in Tarleton's Legion." Paper presented at the Tarleton Symposium, Augusta, Georgia, 2002.

Bartholomees, James B. "Fight or Flee: The Combat Performance of the North Carolina Militia in the Cowpens-Guilford Courthouse Campaign, January to March 1781." Ph.D. diss., University of North Carolina, Chapel Hill, 1978.

Bass, Linnea M. "Company and Battalion Organization of the Brigade of Guards on American Service." Unpublished manuscript, 1998.

Batt, Richard J. "The Maryland Continentals, 1780–1781." Ph.D. diss., Tulane University.

Burke, William W., and Linnea M. Bass. "Brigade of Guards on the American Service: A History." Unpublished manuscript, 1999.

———. "The Guards in the Battle of Guilford Courthouse." Unpublished manuscript, 1998.

Catron, Lisa. "Go West, Young Veteran: Testing the Turner Hypothesis with the Patriots of Cowpens." Ms. on file, Department of History, Armstrong State College, Savannah, Ga., 1989.

Conrad, Dennis M. "Nathanael Greene and the Southern Campaigns, 1780–1783." Ph.D. diss., Duke University, Durham, N.C., 1960.

Fralin, Gordon Godfrey. "Charles Lynch: Originator of the Term Lynch Law." Master's thesis, University of Richmond, 1955.

Glyn, Thomas. "Ensign Glyn's Journal on the American Service with the Detachment of 1,000 Men of the Guards commanded by Brigadier General Mathew in 1776." Princeton University Library, transcribed by Linnea M. Bass.

Howard, Joshua B. "North Carolina Continentals at Guilford Courthouse, March 19, 1781." Paper presented as a part of the Guilford Courthouse Battleground Annual Symposium, 2004.

———. "Our Captain Quinn: The British Raid on Edenton, May 1781." Paper presented at the Conference of the North Carolina Maritime Council, 2007.

Howard, Joshua B., Matthew Brenckle, and Lawrence E. Babits. "Rifle Shot and Buck 'n' Ball in the 1781 Southern Campaign." Paper presented at the Nathanael Greene Symposium, Historic Camden, 2003.

Kalmanson, Arnold W. "Otho Holland Williams and the Southern Campaign of 1780–1782." M.A. thesis, Salisbury State University.

# INDEX